THEORY AND DECISION LIBRARY

General Editors: W. Leinfellner (*Vienna*) and G. Eberlein (*Munich*)

Series A: Philosophy and Methodology of the Social Sciences
Series B: Mathematical and Statistical Methods
Series C: Game Theory, Mathematical Programming and Operations Research
Series D: System Theory, Knowledge Engineering and Problem Solving

SERIES C: GAME THEORY, MATHEMATICAL PROGRAMMING AND OPERATIONS RESEARCH

VOLUME 43

Editor-in-Chief: H. Peters (Maastricht University, The Netherlands); Honorary Editor: S. H. Tijs (Tilburg University, The Netherlands)
Editorial Board: E.E.C van Damme (Tilburg University, The Netherlands); H. Keiding (University of Copenhagen, Denmark); J.-F. Mertens (Université catholique de Louvain, Belgium); H. Moulin (Rice University, Houston, USA); Shigeo Muto (Tokyo University, Japan); T. Parthasarathy (Indian Statistical Institute, New Delhi, India); B. Peleg (Hebrew University, Jerusalem, Israel); T.E.S. Raghavan (University of Illinois at Chicago, USA); J. Rosenmüller (University of Bielefeld, Germany); A. Roth (Harvard University, USA); D. Schmeidler (Tel-Aviv University, Israel); R. Selten (University of Bonn, Germany); W. Thomson (University of Rochester, USA)

Scope: Particular attention is paid in this series to game theory and operations research, their formal aspects and their applications to economic, political and social sciences as well as to sociobiology. It will encourage high standards in the application of game-theoretical methods to individual and social decision making.

For further volumes:
http://www.springer.com/series/6618

Adrian Van Deemen · Agnieszka Rusinowska
Editors

Collective Decision Making

Views from Social Choice and Game Theory

 Springer

Editors
Dr. Adrian Van Deemen
Radboud University
Institute for Management Research
Thomas van Aquinostraat 3
6525 GD Nijmegen
The Netherlands
a.vandeemen@fm.ru.nl

Dr. Agnieszka Rusinowska
GATE Groupe d'Analyse et de
Théorie Economique
CNRS UMR 5824
Université Lumière Lyon 2
93, Chemin de Mouilles, B.P. 167
69131 Ecully Cedex
France
rusinowska@gate.cnrs.fr

ISSN 0924-6126
ISBN 978-3-642-02864-9   e-ISBN 978-3-642-02865-6
DOI 10.1007/978-3-642-02865-6
Springer Heidelberg Dordrecht London New York

Library of Congress Control Number: 2010925110

Cover design: Integra Software Services Pvt. Ltd., Pondicherry

Printed on acid-free paper.

Springer is part of Springer Science+Business Media (www.springer.com)

Preface and Introduction

Harrie de Swart is a Dutch logician and mathematician with a great and open interest in applications of logic. After being confronted with Arrow's Theorem, Harrie became very interested in social choice theory. In 1986 he took the initiative to start up a group of Dutch scientists for the study of social choice theory. This initiative grew out to a research group and a series of colloquia, which were held approximately every month at the University of Tilburg in The Netherlands. The organization of the colloquia was in the hands of Harrie and under his guidance they became more and more internationally known. Many international scholars liked visiting the social choice colloquia in Tilburg and enjoyed giving one or more presentations about their work. They liked Harrie's kindness and hospitality, and the openness of the group for anything and everything in the field of social choice.

The Social Choice Theory Group started up by Harrie consisted, and still consists, of scholars from several disciplines; mostly economics, mathematics, and (mathematical) psychology. It was set up for the study of and discussion about anything that had to do with social choice theory including, and not in the least, the supervision of PhD students in the theory. Members of the group were, among others, Thom Bezembinder (psychologist), Hans Peters (mathematician), Pieter Ruys (economist), Stef Tijs (mathematician and game theorist) and, of course, Harrie de Swart (logician and mathematician). The group has always been very serious and has had a clear view on social choice. Logic and mathematics are important for the theory; hence both should form an important component in the study of it. However, social choice theory also belongs to the social sciences and, consequently, the social scientific part is equally important. This two-component approach of the group to social choice theory nicely converged in the first two PhD students trained by the group and supervised by Harrie. One student (Ton Storcken) was a mathematician and the other one (Ad Van Deemen) was a social scientist.

The group met regularly, approximately once a month, not only to prepare the students to go to any length, but also to discuss a wide range of topics in social choice theory; from variations of Arrow's theorem to coalition formation in simple games. The first two PhD students graduated in 1990 and 1991 respectively; both with honors. However, this was not that much of a surprise considering the scientific strength, the involvement and the commitment of the group.

In fact, the group did not have a clear name; it was simply called: the Social Choice Theory Group or: the Social Choice Group. In the beginning of the nineties, the group expanded and more Dutch universities became involved. As a result, more PhD students followed. However, the group kept its easy-access and open status. The organization of the meetings remained in Harrie's hands and with that its inviting and informal character continued.

Only in 1999, the group became something of an administrative unit. The participating universities represented in the group were asked to do their bit and to contribute an annual amount to meet the costs for the colloquia. Consequently, from then on an annual meeting had to be held to discuss and approve the invitation policy and a financial report. These annual meetings were chaired by Harrie and, typically, never took more than half an hour. The administration and policies were always found to be in order. It was a small detail, if not a small distraction, which unfortunately had to be dealt with. The main objective was, and still is, social choice theory. Curiosity, openness, and hospitality remained the key words.

In 2009, the Social Choice Theory Group officially and formally existed 10 years. It was celebrated with an international social choice conference at the end of May 2009. Moreover, something completely different but nevertheless very important occurred in that year: in September Harrie de Swart reached the pension age and, as is obliged in The Netherlands, had to retire. Fortunately, the continuation of the Social Choice Group will not be in jeopardy. The organization of the colloquia will be gradually transferred to other hands, accompanied and supported by Harrie's experience and insights. It is clear that Harrie leaves behind a precious and important institution, operating in an informal way and directed primarily at studying social choice.

This book is dedicated to Harrie de Swart. It is to honor his initiatives and activities for the Social Choice Theory Group and the monthly Social Choice Colloquia. It is to thank him for all his efforts and energy he spent on this group and its colloquia. We think that he fulfilled an enormous task. The social choice colloquia are internationally well-known by now. Moreover, social choice theory became an important and strong scientific field in the Netherlands because of this.

In the colloquia, almost any topic within the field of collective decision making has been discussed; from voting and power distribution in the European Council to cabinet formation in the Netherlands; from plurality voting and the Borda count to restricted domains for Arrovian social welfare functions; from freedom, rights and networks to stability of network formation; from committee decision making to coalition formation games. We wanted a book that represents the open view on collective decision making and also reflects the richness and diversity of the colloquia. We approached a number of authors who have all presented one or more lectures in the social choice colloquia. They all responded very enthusiastically. Without exception, they wanted to contribute to Harrie's book as it is called on the fly. Clearly, not all topics discussed in the course of all those years are covered. However, we think that the result is a divers and rich reflection indeed.

In chapter "From Black's Advice and Arrow's Theorem to the Gibbard–Satterthewaite Result", Donald Saari gives, as ever, a challenging interpretation of

Arrow's Theorem and relates it to problems of paired comparison and strategic voting. In his view, the cause of Arrow's result lies mainly in the inter-profile condition of IIA. This condition requires a rule to ignore important information about the voters' transitivity of preference. Since IIA forces a rule to compare the alternatives pairwise, better partwise, and independently, the connecting information for the parts to create a whole is missing. In other words, the macro-result of an aggregation process satisfying IIA – the social choice or the social preference – is not based on all the preference information available on micro-level. It is interesting to note that also Amartya Sen approached the ordinal non-comparability framework of Arrow from an informational point of view (see Sen's *Collective Choice and Social Welfare*, 1970, San Francisco, Holden-Day, Inc). However, there is an important difference between Saari and Sen. According to Sen, the cause of Arrow's result lies in the fact that only ordinal preference (utility) information is used. The cause is in the exclusion of non-preference information. In the view of Saari, however, the cause lies in the fact that not all available ordinal preference information is used. Connecting information at the micro level (transitivity of preferences) is neglected. So, Arrow's Theorem is not caused by a shortage of information as stated by Sen, but by a neglect of available information. Clearly, this is fascinating.

In chapter "The Impact of Forcing Preference Rankings When Indifference Exists", William Gehrlein brings in an important contribution to the probability approach to the Condorcet paradox. Instead of the traditional Impartial Culture Condition, he uses the (much more difficult to handle) Impartial Weak Ordered Culture Condition and shows that partially indifferent voter preferences have a serious impact on the probability of a Condorcet winner. Subsequently, he studies what will happen with the probabilities of a Condorcet winner when indifferent voters are forced to change their indifference part into a ranking. He ingeniously calculates the probabilities for different proportions of voters who are forced to produce complete rankings. He shows that the probabilities of a Condorcet winner for partially indifferent voters are remarkably different from the probabilities under forced complete rankings.

In chapter "Connections and Implications of the Ostrogorski Paradox for Spatial Voting Models", Hannu Nurmi and Donald Saari deal with the difficult Ostrogorski paradox and reveal some of its secrets. They establish a clear and beautiful connection with McKelvey's Chaos Theorem: if the Ostrogorski paradox (and the related Anscombe paradox) occurs, the core of a spatial voting game will be empty. Hence, according to McKelvey's Theorem, a global cycle will then exist. Furthermore, they resolve Kelly's conjecture about the relationship between the absence of a Condorcet winner and the Ostrogorski paradox. It is a beautiful paper that might induce a stream of new research on the Ostrogorski paradox.

Chapter "Maximal Domains for Maskin Monotone Pareto Optimal and Anonymous Choice Rules" written by Olivier Bochet and Ton Storcken typically belongs to the hard core of social choice. In this contribution, domain restrictions are studied, not only as is traditional for the specific majority rule, but more general for a class of social choice rules satisfying Pareto optimality, Maskin monotonicity and anonymity. They employ a positive approach, that is, they construct and proof the existence of a maximal, strategy-proof and non-dictatorial possibility domain both for the three- or- more agent case as for the special case of two agents. It is an accurate and technically excellent elaborated study. We have met this professional skillfulness quite frequently in the social choice colloquia. It is what makes social choice theory such an attractive and beautiful field of science.

Chapter "Extremal Restriction, Condorcet sets, and Majority Decision Making" by Adrian Van Deemen and Elena Saiz re-examines a specific domain restriction called Extremal Restriction (ER). This restriction is supposed to be necessary and sufficient for the existence of a Condorcet winner. Some counter-examples for this result are given in the case that zero-assignments, that is assignments of preferences to no voter at all, are not allowed. Moreover, all maximal sets of preferences satisfying ER are enumerated for the three alternative case. Finally, a study of Condorcet sets, or as Saari calls them Condorcet profiles (see chapter "From Black's Advice and Arrow's Theorem to the Gibbard–Satterthewaite Result"), and of their extensions over weak orderings is given.

Chapter "Rights Revisited, and Limited" written by Maurice Salles and Feng Zhang is in the style of the famous non-starred chapters of Sen's *Collective Choice and Social Welfare*. It is an easy accessible and intuitive account of some important results on limited rights. (Limited) rights, liberty and Sen's famous liberalism theorem are studied both in the aggregation framework and the choice framework and are compared to each other. It is argued that in neither case limited rights are an escape route for the Sen-type impossibility results. An important and challenging point in their chapter is that liberalism can be studied in terms of obligation (necessity) and possibility. They therefore propose to use modal and related logics in the formal analysis of rights and liberty in the future. They believe that the use of these logics may throw new light on the problems with respect to rights and liberty.

In chapter "Some General Results on Responsibility for Outcomes", Martin Van Hees investigates the problem of responsibility for outcomes in committee decision making. His account of responsibility consists of two components. A member of a committee can be held responsible first if she is causally effective for the realization of an outcome and secondly if she has had the "opportunity to do otherwise". Clearly, a formal approach to this kind of responsibility will be notoriously difficult. However, Van Hees gives a very elegant and beautiful formal analysis, which leads to a clear insight in the relation between different forms of transparency in collective decision making and responsibility. We find this a path-breaking chapter that may lead to a stream of new research.

In chapter "Existence of a Dictatorial Subgroup in Social Choice with Independent Subgroup Utility Scales, an Alternative Proof", Anna Khmelnitskaya works within a research program of social choice theory that tries to extend the ordinal non-comparable framework of Arrow. She constructs new proof for an existing theorem (see Khmelnitskaya & Weymark, 2000, *Social Choice & Welfare, 17*, 739–748) about the existence of a dictatorial group for different extended measurability-comparability frameworks (see Sen's *Collective Choice and Social Welfare*, Chap. 8). The proof provides insight into the "structure of possible interrelations between utilities of different individuals".

Chapter "Making (Non-standard) Choices" written by Wulf Gaertner is about making non-standard choices. Using the axiomatic method, he describes choice functions that violate contraction and expansion consistency conditions. He finds that non-standard choices do not have a uniform structure. However, choice functions that violate the standard rationality conditions do not imply that individuals are behaving irrationally.

In the next interesting chapter "Puzzles and Paradoxes Involving Averages: An Intuitive Approach", Feld and Grofman study seemingly paradoxical aggregation results. They present the insight that sometimes these paradoxical puzzles can be solved by reconstructing them from their constituent parts by appropriately weighting these parts and sequentially by using the notion of weighted average. In this way, they are able to answer curious questions like "how can it be that most households in the United States are headed by unmarried adults, yet most adults are married?" or "How can family income be going down even though per capita income is going up?"

In chapter "Voting Weights, Thresholds and Population Size: Member State Representation in the Council of the European Union", Madeleine Hosli analyzes the empirical distribution of votes in the Council of the European Union in a solid and thorough way. Her empirical investigations clearly show that voting rules in this committee indeed embody an important trade-off between the number of individuals required for making a collective decision on the one hand, and the expected costs of decision making on the other. With this nice empirical result, she strongly confirms the well-known trade-off model of Buchanan and Tullock from *The Calculus of Consent* (1962, Ann Arbor, The University of Michigan Press),

Chapter "Stabilizing Power Sharing" is a challenging chapter about stability of power sharing written by Steven Brams and D. Marc Kilgour. They model power sharing both as a duel in which the players fire sequentially and as a duel in which they interact simultaneously. In both modeling approaches, the players are allowed to choose to share prizes. Moreover, they study which prize ratio renders power sharing stable. They find and explain that the incentives to share power in the simultaneous interaction case are greater than in the sequential interaction case. It is interesting to see the differences between sequential interactive decision making and simultaneous interactive decision making so clearly.

Chapter "Different Approaches to Influence Based on Social Networks and Simple Games", written by Michel Grabisch and Agnieszka Rusinowska, is a concise and in-depth overview of different approaches to influence processes among agents in collective decision making situations. The inclination of an individual to make a decision may clearly differ from his or her actual decision making behavior. Many kinds of influences may transform the inclination into a different decision. Grabisch and Rusinowska describe and discuss different approaches to these influence processes in collective decision making processes. The models presented are thoroughly discussed and reviewed both formally and informally. The result is a distinctive and amiable work that presents the state-of-the-art in this exciting field of research in a clear way. In addition, it presents an agenda of open problems for future research.

Chapter "Networks, Information and Choice" is written by René Janssen and Herman Monsuur. In this chapter, the focus is on information sharing in collaboration networks. They discuss a network model with feedback for situational awareness (i.e. "knowing what is going on") in which exogenously given characteristics of the nodes are combined with the topology of the network. Subsequently, the authors discuss several (stochastic) variations of the model and a game-theoretical model to study the evolution of networks. It is a solid and fascinating study that gives insight in the role of information sharing and communication in complex (military) management operations.

Chapter "Characterizations of Bargaining Solutions by Properties of Their Status Quo Sets" contains an admirably written and interesting study of several bargaining solution concepts. It is written by Hans Peters. In the more traditional axiomatic approach to bargaining, a mapping that assigns a solution to a bargaining problem is specified. The mapping is supposed to satisfy certain properties as expressed by the axioms. Crucial in this approach is the notion of status quo or point of disagreement. It represents the payoff to the players if no deal is agreed upon. In this chapter, the set of outcomes of a bargaining game depending on a status quo point are fixed as much as possible. Instead, the status quo point is varied. If two status quo points give rise to the same solution, they are said to belong to the same status quo set. Subsequently, the traditional bargaining solutions like the Nash Bargaining Solution or the Kalai-Smorodinsky Solution are characterized in terms of properties of their status quo sets.

The final chapter "Monotonicity Properties of Interval Solutions and the Dutta–Ray Solution for Convex Interval Games" written by Elena Yanovskaya, Rodica Branzei and Stef Tijs deal with interval games. These are games in coalitional form with uncertain payoffs. Only the bounds for the payoffs of coalitions are known for certainty. The chapter examines different monotonicity properties of the more classic cooperative game solutions for interval games.

It is obvious that social choice theory and game theory are very close to each other and that they do have many overlapping themes. However, to explain the structure of the Harrie's book, we would say that it starts with specific social choice theoretical themes like Arrow's Theorem and the probability approach to the Condorcet paradox, and that it ends with more specific game theoretical topics, like interval games in coalitional form. In between we see a mixture of views on collective decision making in which social choice theory and game theory each play their role. Most important however, is the fact that the several views on collective decision making presented in this book are quite divers, and it is this diversity that so elegantly covers the content of the Social Choice Colloquia in Tilburg as initiated and organized by Harrie de Swart.

Ecully, France   Adrian Van Deemen
Nijmegen, The Netherlands   Agnieszka Rusinowska
October 2009

Contents

Contributors

Olivier Bochet Department of Economics, University of Bern, 3012 Bern, Switzerland, olivier.bochet@vwi.unibe.ch

Steven J. Brams Department of Politics, New York University, New York, NY 10012, USA, steven.brams@nyu.edu

Rodica Branzei Faculty of Computer Science, "Alexandru Ioan Cuza" University, Iaşi 700483, Romania, branzeir@info.uaic.ro

Scott L. Feld Department of Sociology, Purdue University, West Lafayette, IN 47907, USA, sfeld@purdue.edu

Wulf Gaertner Department of Economics, Institute of Cognitive Science, University of Osnabrück, 49069 Osnabrück, Germany; Department of Philosophy, Logic and Scientific Method, London School of Economics, London, UK, Wulf.Gaertner@uni-osnabrueck.de

William V. Gehrlein Department of Business Administration, University of Delaware, Newark, DE 19716, USA, gehrleiw@lerner.udel.edu

Michel Grabisch Centre d'Economie de la Sorbonne, Université Paris I Panthéon-Sorbonne, 75013 Paris, France, michel.grabisch@univ-paris1.fr

Bernard Grofman Department of Political Science, Institute for Mathematical Behavioral Sciences, University of California, Irvine CA 92697-5100, USA, bgrofman@uci.edu

Madeleine O. Hosli Department of Political Science, Leiden University, 2333 AK Leiden, The Netherlands, hosli@fsw.leidenuniv.nl

René Janssen Netherlands Defence Academy, 1780 CA Den Helder, The Netherlands, RHP.Janssen@NLDA.NL

Anna B. Khmelnitskaya St. Petersburg Institute for Economics and Mathematics, Russian Academy of Sciences, 191187 St. Petersburg, Russia, a.khmelnitskaya@math.utwente.nl

D. Marc Kilgour Department of Mathematics, Wilfrid Laurier University, Waterloo, ON N2L 3C5, Canada, mkilgour@wlu.ca

Herman Monsuur Netherlands Defence Academy, 1780 CA Den Helder, The Netherlands, H.Monsuur@NLDA.NL

Hannu Nurmi Department of Political Science, University of Turku, 20014 Turku, Finland, hnurmi@utu.fi

Hans Peters Department of Quantitative Economics, Maastricht University, 6200 MD Maastricht, The Netherlands, h.peters@maastrichtuniversity.nl

Agnieszka Rusinowska GATE, CNRS UMR 5824, Université Lumière Lyon 2, Ecole Normale Supérieure LSH, 69131 Ecully Cedex, France, rusinowska@gate.cnrs.fr

Donald G. Saari Institute for Mathematical Behavioral Science, University of California, Irvine, CA 92697-5100, USA, dsaari@uci.edu

M. Elena Saiz Institute for Management Research, Radboud University, 6500 HK Nijmegen, The Netherlands, e.saiz@fm.ru.nl

Maurice Salles CREM, Université de Caen, 14032 Caen Cedex, France; Institute for SCW, 14111 Louvigny, France; London School of Economics, CPNSS, London, UK, maurice.salles@unicaen.fr

Ton Storcken Department of Quantitative Economics, Maastricht University, 6200 MD Maastricht, The Netherlands, t.storcken@maastrichtuniversity.nl

Stef Tijs Department of Econometrics and Operations Research, Center for Economic Research, Tilburg University, 5000 LE Tilburg, The Netherlands, S.H.Tijs@uvt.nl

Adrian Van Deemen Institute for Management Research, Radboud University, 6500 HK Nijmegen, The Netherlands, a.vandeemen@fm.ru.nl

Martin van Hees Faculty of Philosophy, University of Groningen, 9712 GL Groningen, The Netherlands, Martin.van.Hees@rug.nl

Elena Yanovskaya St. Petersburg Institute for Economics and Mathematics, Russian Academy of Sciences, St. Petersburg, Russia, eyanov@emi.nw.ru

Feng Zhang CREM, Université de Caen, 14032 Caen Cedex, France, zfeng7@yahoo.fr

From Black's Advice and Arrow's Theorem to the Gibbard–Satterthewaite Result

Donald G. Saari

Sequential paired comparisons are commonly used in daily practice. During the annual academic hiring season, for instance, applicants arrive for interviews in a sequence often determined by travel schedules. With the usual dating scenario, imagine a popular woman expecting several men to call asking for a date; with each call her response of "Yes," "No," or "Maybe" is based on a comparison of the current caller with someone still being considered. To ensure an orderly departmental meeting, the chair assembles an agenda that identifies the order in which items will be considered. In engineering, it is not uncommon to make pairwise comparisons of the alternatives to reach a final decision. These are but only four of many possible examples of the common situation where a decision and choice is made by comparing alternatives in pairs in a specified order. One of several questions addressed here is whether the order matters.

Problems of paired comparisons motivated Arrow's (1951) development of his troubling result about voting rules. While there now exists a benign interpretation of Arrow's result showing that this result does not mean what we thought it did for the last 60 years (Saari, 2008), the Finnish philosopher Aki Lehtinen (2005) raised questions about my development; two of them are addressed here. Finally, although Satterthwaite connected Arrow's theorem with the seminal Gibbard–Satterthwaite theorem about strategic behavior, the continual flow of papers describing when different voting rules admit strategic behavior makes it reasonable to review the fundamental source of strategic choices. My emphasis, which differs from Satterthwaite's, is a third theme of this paper.

D.G. Saari (✉)
Institute for Mathematical Behavioral Science, University of California Irvine,
CA 92697-5100, USA
e-mail: dsaari@uci.edu

A. Van Deemen, A. Rusinowska (eds.), *Collective Decision Making,*
Theory and Decision Library C 43, DOI 10.1007/978-3-642-02865-6_1,
© Springer-Verlag Berlin Heidelberg 2010

1 Black's Advice

Returning to the hopes of the young men hoping to win our young lady's affections, or an applicant trying to secure an academic position, Niemi and Gretlein (1985) recalled Duncan Black's (1958) sage advice that "the later any motion enters the voting, the greater its chance of adoption." In other words, to win, try to be the last considered. By using examples, Niemi and Gretlein formulated and proved their version of Black's assertion; they showed how the ordering of the paired comparisons can favor an alternative that is placed later in the sequence. As a way to introduce certain notions that are needed in my discussion of Arrow's result in Sect. 2, I improve upon this result by identifying what causes the problem and outlining a proof of Black's likelihood assertion.

The complete source of the problem is identified by a coordinate system that I developed to analyze n-candidate elections (Saari, 2000, 2008). To motivate what follows, recall that a coordinate system is useful for a project if it provides insights and it helps to resolve difficulties. For instance, the traditional x-y-z cartesian coordinates are not useful for problems of satellite tracking because they create computational difficulties. Instead, spherical coordinates, which describe the radius and angular position of the object, are more natural and valuable. Similarly for voting, an objective should be to identify appropriate configurations of voter preferences that affect the outcomes of certain voting rules but not the outcomes of other rules; doing so is a step toward creating a coordinate system for the space of profiles. This project is partially completed (Saari, 2000, 2008); the description given here emphasizes those particular profile coordinates that identify everything that can happen with paired comparisons. As described, we now know which profile coordinate directions cause all possible paired comparison voting problems.

To describe the trouble-causing directions for the n alternatives $\{A_1, \ldots, A_n\}$, select any ranking, say $A_1 \succ A_2 \succ \ldots \succ A_n$, and use it to generate a set of n-rankings by moving a ranking's top-place candidate to the bottom in the next ranking. This approach defines the set

$$\{A_1 \succ A_2 \succ \ldots \succ A_n, \quad A_2 \succ \ldots \succ A_n \succ A_1, \ldots, A_n \succ A_1 \succ \ldots \succ A_{n-1}\}. \tag{1}$$

Any ranking in this set generates the same set of n rankings, so there are $\frac{n!}{n} = (n-1)!$ distinct sets of this form. For technical reasons, these rankings define $\frac{(n-1)(n-2)}{2}$ orthogonal coordinate directions in profile space, but for pragmatic purposes, one should use a set defined by $A_1 \succ A_2 \succ \ldots \succ A_n$ as combined in a particular way with the set defined by its reversal $A_n \succ A_{n-1} \succ \ldots A_2 \succ A_1$; I call them the *Condorcet directions* or *Condorcet profiles*.

These Condorcet profiles are totally responsible for all possible paired comparison problems that could ever occur in voting theory (Saari, 2000), nothing else causes difficulties; i.e., if a profile is orthogonal to all of the Condorcet profile directions, then nothing goes wrong with that profile's paired comparisons. By this I mean that the paired comparison rankings are so surprisingly transitive that their tallies satisfy an amazing consistency property. Namely, if $\tau(A_k, A_j)$ is the difference between the A_k and A_j tallies in a pairwise comparison, then

$$\tau(A_k, A_j) + \tau(A_j, A_s) = \tau(A_k, A_s) \text{ for all } j, k, s. \tag{2}$$

As the paired comparisons for such a profile define a transitive ranking, they also define a Condorcet winner. Here the order in which the motions or alternatives are considered does not matter – whether introduced early or late in the process, the likelihood of adoption remains the same because the Condorcet winner always is selected.

The choice of a sequencing never matters with a Condorcet winner because she will win, so for Black's advice to have any substance, it must reflect those settings where a profile's Condorcet profile components are sufficiently dominant to deny having a Condorcet winner. To analyze this effect, first determine the paired comparison outcomes for any such direction, such as the one in Eq. (1). A direct tally shows that for each j, A_j beats A_{j+1} by $(n-1) : 1$, where A_{j+sn} is identified with A_j. (Thus A_n beats A_{n+1}, which is A_1, with the $(n-1) : 1$ tally.) Of importance to my analysis is that there also can be secondary, ternary, etc. cycles; e.g., for positive integer $k < \frac{n}{2}$, A_j beats A_{j+k} by $(n-k) : k$. The important fact is that there cannot be a Condorcet winner if and only if a profile's Condorcet components create a top-cycle.

An explanation for Black's advice now is immediate. For A_1 to have a chance of being elected, A_1 must be in the top-cycle where she loses to some alternatives in this cycle, but beats others. Thus if A_1 is introduced early in the comparisons, she must be compared with alternatives from the cycle that can beat her, so she is guaranteed to lose. To win, she must be positioned late enough in the sequencing to be compared only with alternatives she can beat. With no prior information, the ideal position is to be compared last. (She could lose, but she has a better chance of victory.)

To outline an approach to convert these comments into a probability statement, start with the simple case of three candidates A, B, C, (or where the top cycle consists of three candidates). With a cycle, A can only be elected if and only if she is last listed among these three. (If the cycle is $A \succ B, B \succ C, C \succ A$, then B beats C in the first stage, only to lose to A in the final stage. With the reversed cycle, C is advanced to be defeated by A.) So a comparison of the likelihood of A being elected by being listed in any position other than last, with her being listed last (i.e., after B and C), is a comparison between the probability A is a Condorcet winner with the probability A is a Condorcet winner plus the probability of a three-candidate top cycle.

A similar approach holds for more alternatives, but finding which sequencings allow A_1 to win involves finding all secondary, ternary, etc. cycles. By knowing these cycles, we can determine all successful sequencings. For instance and without loss of generality, suppose that the top cycle is $A_1 \succ A_2, A_2 \succ A_3, \ldots, A_{s-1} \succ A_s, A_s \succ A_1$. To use this cycle to create a sequencing that ensures A_1's victory, compare alternatives in the reverse order of the cycle; i.e., start by comparing A_{s-1}

with A_{s-2}, advance the winner (which is A_{s-2}) to be compared with A_{s-3}, ..., the winner of the comparisons to date with A_2, and the winner of this comparison (which is A_2) with A_1; A_1 wins.

For a general approach that involves all possible cycles, let S_{A_j} be the set of all candidates in the top-cycle that A_j beats; as there is a cycle, each S_{A_j} is non-empty and each A_k is in at least one S_{A_j}. To construct all possible agendas where A_1 wins, start from the end of the agenda and work toward the beginning. All such agendas must conclude with A_1 being immediately compared with, and, if followed, only with alternatives in S_{A_1}. If $A_k \in S_{A_1}$ is the item in a sequence with which A_1 is initially compared, then the alternatives between A_k and A_1, and the alternative with whom A_k is initially compared, must come from S_{A_k}. This process continues until all candidates are listed in the sequencing. All possible agendas where A_1 wins can be created in this manner; the agenda in the preceding paragraph illustrates this construction, so this process always creates examples. (This construction involves all alternatives, not just those in the top-cycle.)

Ignoring the alternatives that are not in the top-cycle (as they merely add insignificant terms in the computations), each S_{A_j} has at most $s-2$ elements. This is because if S_{A_j} contained $s-1$ alternatives, A_j would beat all of them, so there could not be a top-cycle. If $|S_{A_1}| = k \le s-2$, then, because A_1 cannot be the first listed of these $k+1$ alternatives, the above construction permits $(k+1)! - k! = k(k!)$ ways to rank these alternatives. Thus (because $j!k!\ldots m! < (j+k+\ldots+m)!$) the number of sequences of the above type where A_1 wins is less than

$$(k+1)!(s-(k+1))! \le (s-1)! < \frac{s!}{2}. \tag{3}$$

The number of sequences where A_1 wins divided by $s!$ provides an estimate on the likelihood of A_1 winning; this value is less than $\frac{1}{2}$. A_1 loses with all remaining sequences – including where she is listed earlier in the ordering. As this set has the larger value of over $\frac{1}{2}$, this completes the outline.

2 New Interpretations of Arrow's Result

For almost 60 years, the mystery associated with Arrow's (1951) result has generated a large literature. Motivated by a delightful 2008 discussion about Arrow's theorem that I had with Harrie de Swart in Lyon, France, it is reasonable to review the ways I developed to interpret this result and resolve its mysteries. (Details are in Saari, 2008.)

To review, Arrow's theorem uses the conditions:

1. Voters have complete, transitive preferences of the alternatives; there are no restrictions.
2. The societal outcome is a complete, transitive ranking.

3. (Pareto) The rule satisfies the *Pareto condition* in that if for some pair of alternatives, all voters rank the pair in the same manner, then that is the societal ranking for the pair.
4. (IIA) The societal ranking of each pair is determined only by the voters' relative ranking of that pair. Namely, if $\mathbf{p}_1$ and $\mathbf{p}_2$ are two profiles where, for each voter, the way the voter ranks the pair in $\mathbf{p}_1$ is the same as how the voter ranks the pair in $\mathbf{p}_2$, then the societal ranking of that pair is the same for both profiles.

Arrow's conclusion is that with three or more alternatives and two or more voters, the only rule that always satisfies these conditions is a dictatorship; i.e., de facto, the rule identifies a particular voter in that, for all profiles, the societal outcome agrees with his ranking.

Arrow's result has much broader consequences; e.g., in decision problems, "criteria" replace "voters." Now, a natural way to analyze the complexities associated with many problems is to use a "divide-and-conquer" approach; but dividing problems into parts cause some of these decision rules to satisfy versions of #3, 4. Whenever this happens, the conclusion is that the decision rule must depend upon the information coming from a single criterion.

The power of Arrow's theorem is that, in practice, we normally do not use dictatorial voting rules nor decision rules based on a single criterion. As a consequence, Arrow's result requires circumstances to arise where the rule violates at least one of the above conditions. To use an illustration from statistics, a non-parametric paired comparison rule clearly satisfies #3, 4. But even if the data satisfies #1, Arrow's result asserts that there exist configurations of transitive data where the outcome is non-transitive.

2.1 What Causes Arrow's Result

To appreciate the source of Arrow's theorem, notice the crucial role played by #1; if the voters did not have to have transitive rankings, we could not expect transitive societal outcomes. If all voters, for instance, had the same cyclic ranking, the Pareto condition would impose a cyclic societal ranking. But before describing the importance of this observation, let me mention that among the artists {Rembrandt, van Gogh, Monet}, I prefer van Gogh over Rembrandt. Are my preferences transitive? It is impossible to tell because more information is needed; to answer the question, you need to know my rankings of {Monet, Rembrandt} and {Monet, van Gogh}.

But now consider what happens when determining the {van Gogh, Rembrandt} societal ranking; the IIA condition (#4) requires the rule to ignore all information about how voters rank {Monet, van Gogh} and {Monet, Rembrandt}. In other words, IIA requires the rule to ignore the available, crucial, and connecting information that the voters have transitive preferences! (This comment, along with examples demonstrating how IIA severs the transitivity condition and forces a rule to replace the actual transitive preferences with cyclic ones, is developed in detail in Saari (2008).) Even though condition #1 is imposed, in practice it cannot be used because IIA makes it ineffective. But if #1 is not being used, then, as described in the preceding paragraph, Arrow's conclusion becomes obvious.

This analysis (see Saari, 2008 for details) leads to a new and useful interpretation of Arrow's result. To explain, it is reasonable to expect that an appropriate, complete, transitive societal ranking does exist; the problem is to find it. Indeed, proponents of different voting rules may argue that "their approach," whether it be the plurality vote, approval voting, or the Borda Count, delivers the appropriate "societal outcome of the whole." But any rule based on Pareto and IIA must try to assemble the "societal whole" by determining an outcome for each pair independent of what may be appropriate outcomes for all other pairs. This leads to a new interpretation whereby

> Arrow's Theorem asserts that with three or more alternatives and two or more agents (or criteria), situations exist where the structure of the whole does not resemble what is obtained from a rule that is based on the IIA and Pareto conditions; i.e., the structure of the whole does not resemble what is obtained by analyzing each part independently. More generally, settings exist where trying to construct an outcome for the whole by trying to find independent answers for each part will fail.

A way of viewing this assertion, which identifies a severe limitation of the common divide-and-conquer methodologies, is with the story about a group of blind men trying to determine the structure of an elephant; no matter how carefully they examine each part, it is not clear whether they will be able to accurately describe the whole. What is missing is a way for them to connect information about the parts; as described below, the same holds for Arrow's theorem.

But first, because all paired comparison problems are caused by the Condorcet profile directions (Sect. 1), Arrow's negative conclusion must also be caused by these profile directions. Indeed, by restricting the space of profiles so that no profile has any component in a Condorcet direction (in a linear algebra sense), Arrow's dictatorial conclusion is replaced by the Borda Count (where, when tallying an n-candidate ballot, $n - j$ points are assigned to the jth ranked alternative).

2.2 Positive Assertions

Knowing what causes Arrow's conclusion allows us to find positive resolutions. Namely, IIA forces an associated rule to drop the connecting information that the parts satisfy transitivity, so a way to resolve the problem is to replace IIA with a modified condition *that allows a rule to use the connecting transitivity information.* As an example, a given transitive ranking permits us to determine both the relative ranking of a pair and the intensity of this ranking in terms of the number of alternatives that separate them. This defines my "Intensity of IIA," or "IIIA" condition (Saari, 1995, 2008). To illustrate with the $A \succ B \succ C \succ D$ ranking in a $\{A, D\}$ comparison, IIA uses only the $\{A \succ D\}$ information, while IIIA permits using the $\{A \succ D, 2\}$ information indicating that, in the transitive ranking, A and D are separated by two alternatives.

This IIIA information provides a new way to compute pairwise rankings; when determining the $\{X, Y\}$ ranking and tallying a ballot by using the $\{X \succ Y, k\}$ information, assign $k + 1$ points to X to reflect (one point) that X is ranked above Y and (the other k points) to reflect the intensity of this ranking. The majority vote, however, does not use the "k" information. To show how this added information avoids problems, because the Condorcet profile directions cause all paired comparison difficulties, it suffices to use these profile directions to compare the usual majority vote (which satisfies IIA) with this new pairwise voting approach based on IIIA information. The general case reflects what happens with

$$A \succ B \succ C, \quad B \succ C \succ A, \quad C \succ A \succ B \tag{4}$$

where this profile's IIIA information is

Ranking	$\{A, B\}$	$\{B, C\}$	$\{A, C\}$
$A \succ B \succ C$	$\{A \succ B, 0\}$	$\{B \succ C, 0\}$	$\{A \succ C, 1\}$
$B \succ C \succ A$	$\{B \succ A, 1\}$	$\{B \succ C, 0\}$	$\{C \succ A, 0\}$
$C \succ A \succ B$	$\{A \succ B, 0\}$	$\{C \succ B, 1\}$	$\{C \succ A, 0\}$
Majority vote outcome	$A \succ B, 2 : 1$	$B \succ C, 2 : 1$	$C \succ A, 2 : 1$
IIIA vote outcome	$A \sim B, 2 : 2$	$B \sim C, 2 : 2$	$A \sim C, 2 : 2$

(5)

As each candidate in Eq. (4) is in first, second, and third position precisely once, it is arguable that the outcome should be a complete tie. But by using the limited IIA information reflecting only who is ranked above whom, rather than the expected complete societal tie, the majority vote outcome (Eq. 5) is the $A \succ B, B \succ C$, $C \succ A$ cycle with each tally being 2:1. In contrast, by using the added information reflecting the transitivity of voter preferences, the above IIIA tally avoids the cycle by defining the expected $A \sim B \sim C$ complete tie.

For a positive result (Saari, 1995, 2008), by replacing IIA in #4 with IIIA, Arrow's dictator is replaced with rules based upon the Borda Count. (This is because the Borda Count is equivalent to the Eq. (5) IIIA way of computing pairwise outcomes.) The acceptable rule could be the full Borda Count, a rule where only certain voters can vote but with the Borda Count, or Black's rule where a majority vote is used over pairs unless there is a cycle, then use the Borda Count. (For subtle reasons the rule must be based on the Borda Count rather than, say, the plurality vote.)

This discussion leads to a comment made by Lehtinen (2005) who accepts my analysis of the flaws of IIA and how it dismisses the assumption of transitive preferences but questions whether my critique of IIA validates the adoption of the Borda Count. He may be reading too much into my theorem because my result only asserts that with the goal of preserving the essence of Arrow's structure while obtaining positive conclusions, an answer is IIIA and the resulting Borda Count. But to claim that the Borda Count should be selected over other voting rules demands more; it requires identifying and comparing *all properties* of the Borda Count with those of other voting rules. This separate argument is, in part, described in Saari (2008).

Lehtinen also raises questions about the majority vote over pairs. As the pairwise vote satisfies IIA and Pareto, a flaw of this voting rule is captured by the above new interpretation of Arrow's result. Namely, if an appropriate structure of the whole exists, it cannot always be accurately captured with majority vote outcomes over the pairs; this rule loses important information about the transitivity of voter preferences. Moreover, recall (Sect. 1) that the Condorcet profile directions cause all problems about majority votes; e.g., if a profile has no components in the Condorcet directions, the Borda and paired comparisons outcomes agree (Saari, 2008). A general profile, however, has Condorcet components – while the Borda Count ignores them, these components can alter the paired comparison rankings. So, an immediate consequence of the profile coordinates is that any support in favor of the majority vote must include an argument why, for instance, the societal outcome for Eq. (4) should not be a complete tie.

3 Strategic Voting

A continual thrust in the area of social choice is to understand how to preserve the integrity of group decision issues such as voting. But to prevent fraud and discourage strategic attempts to alter election outcomes, we must appreciate how this can be done. While I will explain what can happen and why, the basic ideas are captured by the familiar phrases

"Don't waste your vote! Instead, vote for —!"   "Vote early; vote often!"

Campaign aims are clear: increase your vote, reduce your opponents' votes. Strategic voting and fraud adopt the same objectives, but they use approaches that jeopardize the goal of "reflecting the views of the voters." All of us have engaged in strategic voting as manifested by the "Don't waste your vote!" cry: voters tactically misrepresent actual preferences to achieve personally more favorable election outcomes. Fraud, on the other hand, is reflected by the "Vote often!" appeal, where additions and subtractions to voting tallies are manufactured in non-acceptable forms.[1]

To illustrate with a two candidate election, as I prefer Anni over Barb, I have two ways to vote: a vote for Anni is productive, while a vote for Barb is counterproductive. As this example makes clear, the two candidate setting provides no strategic opportunities, but it can admit fraudulent ways to provide Anni added votes and/or Barb with fewer.

Everything becomes more subtle with three or more candidates; to see this, suppose my sincere preference ranking is $A \succ B \succ C$ if Connie joins the race. Of the $3! = 6$ ways to mark my ballot, the sincere $A \succ B \succ C$ choice often is, but *not*

---

[1] It is interesting how the social choice literature extensively examines the issue of strategic voting, but I am unaware of any careful analysis of the mechanics of fraud.

always, productive (e.g., Nader supporters in the 2000 Florida presidential election discovered negative consequences of sincere voting). The reversed $C \succ B \succ A$ choice often is (but not always) counterproductive. An important point is that there remain four options; if one of these choices is personally productive for a current setting, it becomes a strategic opportunity. What permits strategic voting, then, are the extra options that always accompany three or more candidates but never arise with just two alternatives.

To capture this sense, treat strategic voting as a "directional derivative" problem. To see the connection, recall that a typical $\frac{\partial f(\mathbf{p})}{\partial \mathbf{v}}$ directional derivative concern from, say, finance or engineering, seeks a direction $\mathbf{v}$ of change from the current location of $\mathbf{p}$ to achieve a preferred f value. Similarly, the goal of strategic voting is to determine the direction (the way to mark the ballot) to move the election outcome from the current situation to one with an improved personal benefit. Indeed, in voting a shrewdly selected "voting direction" can alter the election outcome by adding support to certain candidates and/or reducing support for others.

3.1 Can Strategic Voting Be Avoided?

While one might try to design a voting rule that is immune to strategic action, the important Gibbard (1973)–Satterthwaite (1975) Theorem proves this is impossible to do as soon as there are three or more alternatives. As they prove, all reasonable rules (e.g., not a dictatorship) admit settings where some voter can obtain a personally better outcome by voting stategically. To appreciate this fascinating result, I will develop intuition as to why it is true, who can be strategic, how to identify successful strategic actions for a specified voting rule, and how to reduce strategic actions.

Actually, the ideas behind strategic voting are simple. But as details can change with the voting rule, the challenge is to simultaneously handle *all* reasonable rules. Satterthwaite did so, in part, by establishing an interesting connection between Arrow's result and the Gibbard–Satterthwaite Theorem (e.g., through IIA); as indicated above, my sense is that a more productive approach is to understand how the added opportunities provided by three or more alternatives generate strategic opportunities.

First, some notation is introduced. Let the six preference rankings be designated as

$$
\begin{array}{llll}
\text{Type} & \text{Ranking} & \text{Type} & \text{Ranking} \\
\hline
1 & A \succ B \succ C & 4 & C \succ B \succ A \\
2 & A \succ C \succ B & 5 & B \succ C \succ A \\
3 & C \succ A \succ B & 6 & B \succ A \succ C
\end{array}
\tag{6}
$$

Thus $(3, 4, 0, 6, 2, 2)$ represents the profile with three type 1 voters, four type 2, etc.

3.2 Illustrating Examples

To illustrate the basics of the Gibbard–Satterthwaite Theorem, suppose the sincere election outcome would be $A \succ B \succ C$ with A and B nearly tied; the voting rule assigns 3, 2, 0 points, respectively, to a voter's first, second, and third ranked candidates. To determine who can be strategic and what they should do, notice that only voters preferring $B \succ A$ (i.e., types 4, 5, 6) have an incentive to strategically change the outcome.

To determine who can do what, the following table describes changes in the $A−B$ tally should these voters vote strategically. Each row represents a voter of the indicated type; each column identifies how this voter can mark the ballot. A matrix entry indicates the advantage gained for B in the $B−A$ tally if the voter votes as indicated. For instance, a sincere type 6 ballot assigns 3 points to B and 2 to A, so B enjoys a point differential. But if this voter strategically votes as though of type 4, it would offer 2 points for B and 0 for A giving B a two point advantage. Thus the advantage gained for B by voting strategically in this manner is $2 − 1$; this is the matrix entry for the appropriate row and column. The underlined positive entries identify all strategic options.

Type	1	2	3	4	5	6
4	$-1-2<0$	$-3-2<0$	$-2-2<0$	0	$\underline{3-2>0}$	$1-2<0$
5	$-1-3<0$	$-3-3<0$	$-2-3<0$	$2-3<0$	0	$1-3<0$
6	$-1-1<0$	$-3-1<0$	$-2-1<0$	$\underline{2-1>0}$	$\underline{3-1>0}$	0

$$(7)$$

The negative values in the first three columns underscore the expected; with *this election rule,* a strategic voter's vote should never rank A above B. Somewhat surprisingly, voters with the strongest incentive to reverse the electoral outcome (type 5 with $B > C > A$ preferences) have no strategic opportunities. Only type 4 and 6 voters can be strategic: a type 4 voter should vote as though type 5, of the two strategic options for a type 6 voter the impact is maximized by pretending to be of type 5.

Now consider a runoff election where the first stage ranking (using (3, 2, 0)) is $A \succ B \succ C$ and B and C are nearly tied; the winner is determined by a runoff where polls show that C will beat A but A will beat B. Who can be strategic, and what should they do? As a two-person election offers no strategic advantages, all tactical actions are to influence who is advanced to the runoff. Thus voters preferring $A \succ C$ (types 1, 2, 6) wish to advance B, those preferring $C \succ A$ (types 3, 4, 5) want to advance C. So, although the strategic objective is to influence the final choice of A or C, all strategic machinations emphasize candidates B and C. Following the lead of Eq. (7), Eq. (8) indicates for types 1, 2, and 6 the advantages gained by B over C by voting as specified. For types 3, 4, and 5 (marked by stars), the entries compute the strategic advantages for C over B.

Type	1	2	3	4	5	6
1	0	$-2-2<0$	$-3-2<0$	$-1-2<0$	$1-2<0$	$3-2>0$
2	$2+2>0$	0	$-3+2<0$	$-1+2>0^\dagger$	$1+2>0^\dagger$	$3+2>0^\dagger$
6	$2-3<0$	$-2-3<0$	$-3-3<0$	$-1-3<0$	$1-3<0$	0
3*	$-2-3<0$	$2-3<0$	0	$1-3<0$	$-1-3<0$	$-3-3<0$
4*	$-2-1<0$	$\underline{2-1>0^\dagger}$	$3-1>0$	0	$-1-1<0$	$-3-1<0$
5*	$-2+1<0$	$\underline{2+1>0^\dagger}$	$\underline{3+1>0^\dagger}$	$\underline{1+1>0}$	0	$-3+1<0$

$$(8)$$

The underlined, positive entries identify all strategic opportunities. Notice how type 2 voters with $A \succ C \succ B$ preferences gain a strong strategic advantage by voting as though they have the *opposite* $B \succ C \succ A$ preferences (type 5). In Eq. (7), voters with extreme views about the two top candidates have no strategic opportunities; in Eq. (8), voters with extreme views between A and C (types 1 and 4) have strategic options. In other words, a problem with crafting a general theorem is that the types of voters with strategic opportunities can change with the voting rule.

To further emphasize my point that the choice of the rule can change the strategic options, convert the Eq. (8) runoff into an *instant runoff* whereby the same ballots cast in the first stage are used in the runoff. To see how this simple change eliminates strategic options, notice that while a type 2 voter (who favors A) has the strongest impact of advancing B to the runoff by voting as though type 6, this vote is counterproductive in an instant runoff because, by advancing B, the voter's vote in the runoff supports B rather than his favorite A. The daggers identify which strategic options from a standard runoff are not applicable in an instant runoff. While an "instant runoff" drops options with the largest strategic impact, strategic choices remain.

3.3 Lessons Learned

A way to identify strategic opportunities for any rule mimics the above (Saari, 2003). Small numbers of voters can be successfully strategic with a specified rule only if the sincere outcome is nearly a tie. For such a setting, create a table similar to Eqs. (7) and (8) to catalogue the consequences of each voter voting in all possible manners. This "cataloguing approach" identifies who can benefit by being strategic along with the action. An election rule with several stages (e.g., a runoff or an agenda) has strategic opportunities in determining which candidates are advanced to the next stage.

This cataloguing also identifies other oddities of election rules. For instance, with some rules, a voter could be rewarded with a personally better election outcome *by not voting* (Fishburn & Brams, 1983)! To see how this can happen with the Eq. (8) runoff election, if a type 2 voter fails to vote, C's tally is reduced on the first stage, which could advance B to the runoff – where the negligent voter's favored candidate

A now will win. Indeed, all sorts of phenomena, such as where a previously winning candidate now loses because she received added support, can occur with any multi-stage election rule (Saari, 1995, 2003). The reason is that the extra stages introduce a sense of nonlinearity and nonconvexity into the election rule that can negate the intended "monotonicity" (where more votes help, not hurt) and permit all sorts of counterintuitive behavior to arise.

The cataloguing approach (e.g., Eqs. (7) and (8) captures the essence of the proof for the Gibbard–Satterthwaite Theorem. The first cataloguing step requires a nearly tied vote; similarly, the theorem requires proving that all rules have boundaries that separate those profiles where one or another candidate wins. It is easy to ensure that such boundaries exist; just require the rule to allow each candidate to win with some profile. To see the effect of this condition, suppose *A* and *B* win with, respectively, profiles $\mathbf{p}_1$ and $\mathbf{p}_2$. In some order, change each individual's preference ranking in $\mathbf{p}_1$ to what it is in $\mathbf{p}_2$. At some point in the process, changing a voter's preferences alters the outcome; this transition defines part of the boundary separating profiles that support one or another candidate.

The next cataloguing step computes the effects of each voter's strategic choices. For a more general description, replace the $(3, 2, 0)$ voting rule with the $(w_1, w_2, 0)$ weights where $w_1 > 0$ and $w_1 \geq w_2 \geq 0$. In tallying such a *positional ballot*, assign w_j points to the jth *positioned* (ranked) candidate. There are, in general, six different tallies – except for the plurality vote ($w_2 = 0$) and the "vote-for-two" rule ($w_1 = w_2$) where each has three.

All of this is captured in Fig. 1. Figure 1a triangle is the simplex of non-negative entries where $x + y + z = 1$; it captures normalized election tallies where, say, $(\frac{1}{2}, \frac{1}{6}, \frac{1}{3})$ means that *A*, *B*, and *C* received, respectively, a half, a sixth, and a third of the total vote. Thus the ranking assigned to a point is determined by its proximity to each vertex; e.g., as the three bisecting lines in the interior represent tied outcomes, the bullet near the vertical line represents a $A \succ B \succ C$ outcome with a close *A–B* tally. (Figure 1a numbers identify the region's Eq. (6) ranking.)

A voter's vote moves the outcome as suggested in Fig. 1b. A type 3 voter, for instance, adds w_1 and w_2 points respectively to *C*'s and *A*'s tally, so the positional election outcome moves in the $(w_2, 0, w_1)$ direction toward *C*; this is depicted with the Fig. 1b arrow labeled with a 3. The fact that type 1, 2, 3 voters prefer *A* over

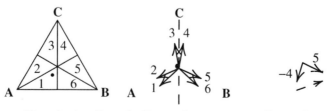

a. Near tie; $A \succ B$ **b.** Change in outcome   **c.** Computing "−4 plus 5"

Fig. 1 Geometry of strategic voting

B is reflected by the geometry where these arrows are on the A side of the dashed dividing line.

Strategic choices are captured by Fig. 1c. If, for example, a type 4 voter does not vote sincerely (or fails to vote), the sincere outcome moves *opposite* to the type 4 arrow in Fig. 1b to represent points lost in C's and B's tallies; in Fig. 2c, this arrow points downward to the left. Should this voter now vote as though type 5 (arrow pointing downward to the right), the dashed arrow (the vector sum of these two effects) captures the advantage gained; B is helped significantly and C somewhat. As an appropriately modified length of this dashed arrow moves Fig. 1a bullet to the right, it identifies a strategic option. (The dashed arrow's horizontal component is an Eq. (7) type entry.) Thus, if the sincere outcome is sufficiently close to the boundary (i.e., a tied vote), such a strategic nudge would successfully alter the outcome.

A point made by the above examples is that, in general, different rules have different kinds of boundaries allowing strategic behavior. Thus, to prove a general theorem such as the Gibbard–Saterthwaite result, we cannot specify in advance where the boundaries are located and how they should be crossed to provide a personal advantage. But this is not a problem because the directions admitted in Fig. 1b are such that wherever the boundary is positioned (i.e., whatever the rule), some combination of Fig. 1b vectors (as in Fig. 1c) can move the outcome toward and over the boundary to create a successful manipulative move. The essence of proof of the Gibbard–Saterthwaite theorem is similar. If a rule allows voters to vote in a way to help any specified candidate, a situation similar to Fig. 1b, c^2 emerges where differences can be combined to point roughly in any specified direction. Thus, if a sincere outcome is near a boundary, a strategic vote can be fashioned to cross the boundary and change the conclusion.

All sorts of embellishments are possible. Not all voters, for instance, need to have the same voting power, a voter's power can change with situations, and on and on. Whatever the specified conditions and while details differ, the basic idea of the proof remains the same. Namely, with a sufficiently rich space of outcomes (e.g., at least each of three candidates could be the winner), the admissible directions of change ensure there always exists a setting where some voter's change represents a strategic opportunity.

3.4 Minimizing Strategic Behavior

By understanding what causes the Gibbard–Satterthwaite Theorem, we obtain insight about how to minimize strategic action. For instance, the choice of a strategic vote is situation-specific; a strategy successful in one setting can hurt a voter's interest in other settings. Thus, a way to reduce strategic action is to make it difficult for a

---

[2] It is not necessary to require a vote *for* a candidate to help her; it may be that voting *against her* helps her. All that is needed is that some vote creates a change in the candidate's direction.

strategic voter to determine whether a strategic choice is personally productive or counterproductive.

A natural approach is to prevent voters from knowing, in advance, the likely sincere outcome. This suggests avoiding ways that convey the current election status, such as publishing polls, just prior to an election. As a personal illustration while serving on a committee to select one of five candidates, it became clear that everyone wanted either A or B to win, with C a possibility. But rather than a secret ballot, the chair erred by polling each person for his or her vote. Comments from the first voters made it clear that A would be the sincere winner; with the strategic voting of the remaining committee members, B won.

In this era of instant information, suppressing polling information is no longer realistic. A second approach is to follow the lead of the instant runoff by altering a rule so that it remains user friendly, but becomes too complicated to predict what can happen. As an illustration, suppose a n-candidate election is tallied with the Borda Count (assign $n - j$ points to a voter's jth ranked candidate). At the end of the first stage, drop all candidates who do not receive at least an average score; use the *same ballots* to rerank the remaining candidates with the Borda Count to determine the winner. With the complexity of determining who will survive the first stage, where it is not even clear how many candidates will advance, structuring a successful strategic option can be daunting.

As all voting rules admit strategic settings, a natural issue is to find which rule minimizes the *likelihood* of a small number of voters successfully manipulating the outcome. I solved this problem (Saari, 1990, 1995) for *positional rules*; e.g., the $(w_1, w_2, 0)$ rules. To suggest how this was done, the cataloguing shows that the answer depends on 1) how easily a strategic vote, with a specified rule, penetrates the boundary to change the election outcome and 2) how many opportunities (i.e., nearly tied outcomes) the rule provides for strategic action.

The first step uses the earlier directional derivative analogy where $\frac{\partial f}{\partial \mathbf{v}}$ is the scalar product of the gradient ∇f and the unit vector $\mathbf{v}$. My analysis replaced ∇f with a normal vector $\mathbf{N}$ of the boundary (e.g., the profiles with tie votes) that points in the desired direction of change. By normalizing to length one the voting direction defined by the $(w_1, w_2, 0)$ rules, the scalar product produced the answers needed for this step.

To handle the more complicated second step, notice that if a profile has the $A \succ B \succ C$ outcome, and if, for each voter, the A and B names are interchanged, the new profile's outcome is $B \succ A \succ C$. This symmetry (called "neutrality") means that, for each positional rule, each strict outcome is supported by the same portion of profiles in profile space. The goal is to determine how the boundary size changes with the rule. Notice how this problem resembles the calculus exercise of finding the rectangle of area one with the smallest perimeter, or the ellipse of area one with the smallest circumference. The answer is the most symmetrical object of, respectively, a square and a circle. Similarly, the voting rule with the smallest boundaries (i.e., offering the fewest strategic opportunities) is given by the symmetries of the $w_1 - w_2$ and $w_2 - 0$ values; it is where they agree so $w_1 = 2w_2$, which is the *Borda Count*.

To my surprise, the conclusion is that the Borda Count is the unique positional rule to minimize the likelihood of a successful strategic action. The likelihood increases as the rule differs from the Borda Count (i.e., as the symmetry between adjacent weights is lost) to reach its maximum value with the plurality and "vote-for-two" rules. This last conclusion is manifested by the familiar "Don't waste your vote" cries associated with the plurality vote.

4 Concluding Comments

While Satterthwaite (1975) nicely established a connection between Arrow's result and the Gibbard–Satterthwaite theorem, my sense is that the real connection between them is that both results require three or more alternatives and that Arrow's result depends on pairwise comparisons. After all, Arrow's theorem is based on the inability of those rules that emphasize the structure of parts (pairs) to handle the Condorcet profile directions, while the Gibbard–Satterthwaite theorem is a directional derivative result. A Condorcet profile direction requires at least three alternatives; to have enough directions to permit strategic voting options requires at least three alternatives. Thus, a real connection is the number of alternatives required to create the desired effects.

Satterthwaite showed that if a rule – in its definition *and the way in which voters use it* – satisfies Arrow's IIA, then the rule is not manipulable. To appreciate this condition, notice how it restricts the admissible directions of change to the lower dimensional "either-or" type associated with a pair where we know that strategic options do not exist. As indicated, strategic behavior requires enough effective directions so that combinations of not voting in one way but voting in another can force the conclusion to cross a boundary. Conversely, strategic behavior is not possible for settings that restrict the appropriate directions, thus results about where strategic behavior cannot occur tend to impose restrictions on possible directions of change.

Acknowledgments This research was supported, in part, by NSF DMS-0631362.

References

Arrow, K. (1951). *Social choice and individual values* (2nd ed., 1963). New York: Wiley.

Black, D. (1958). *The theory of committees and elections*. Cambridge: Cambridge University Press.

Fishburn, P., & Brams, S. (1983). Paradoxes of preferential voting. *Mathematics Magazine, 56*, 207–214.

Gibbard, A. (1973). Manipulation of voting schemes: A general result. *Econometrica, 41*, 587–601.

Lehtinen, A. (2005). *The role of interpersonal comparisons of utility in the theory of voting*. University of Helsinki, preprint.

Niemi, R., & Gretlein, R. (1985). A precise restatement and extension of Black's theorem on voting orders. *Public Choice, 47*, 371–376.

Saari, D. G. (1990). Susceptibility to manipulation. *Public Choice, 64*, 21–41.

Saari, D. G. (1995). *Basic geometry of voting*. New York: Springer-Verlag.

Saari, D. G. (2000). Mathematical structure of voting paradoxes 1: Pairwise vote. *Economic Theory, 15*, 1–53.

Saari, D. G. (2003). Disturbing aspects of voting theory. *Economic Theory, 22*, 529–556.

Saari, D. G. (2008). *Disposing dictators: Demystifying voting paradoxes*. New York: Cambridge University Press.

Satterthwaite, M. (1975). Strategy-proofness and Arrow's conditions. *Journal of Economic Theory, 10*, 187–217.

The Impact of Forcing Preference Rankings When Indifference Exists

William V. Gehrlein

1 Introduction

Consider an election involving n voters and three candidates $\{A, B, C\}$, with $A \succ B$ denoting the situation in which a voter prefers Candidate A to Candidate B. The preferences of individual voters are required to be transitive, which excludes the possibility of individual preference cycles on candidates, such as $A \succ B$, $B \succ C$ and $C \succ A$. The assumption of transitivity of individual preferences is a commonly held criterion of individual rationality for decision makers. There are then six possible complete preference rankings on the candidates that might represent the preferences of a voter when indifference between candidates is not allowed, as shown in Fig. 1.

Here, q_i denotes the probability that a voter who is randomly selected from the population of prospective voters will have the ith associated preference ranking on candidates in Fig. 1. For example, this voter will have the transitive preference ranking $B \succ A \succ C$ with probability q_3. The impartial culture condition (IC) was a commonly used assumption for voter preferences in early studies that considered the likelihood that various interesting election outcomes might be observed. With IC, it is assumed that $q_i = \frac{1}{6}$ for each $1 \leq i \leq 6$ and that all voters arrive at their preferences independently of the preferences of other voters.

The interesting election outcome that has received the most attention in the literature considers the probability that a Condorcet Winner exists. To describe this notion, we start by defining a voting situation as the specific outcomes of voters' preferences that are observed when each of n voter's preference rankings is determined by random selection from the possible rankings with the assumption of IC. Let n_i denote the number of voters in this voting situation that have the ith associated preference ranking on candidates in Fig. 1, with $\sum_{i=1}^{6} n_i = n$. Candidate A then defeats Candidate B by pairwise majority rule (PMR) if more voters have preference rankings with $A \succ B$ than have $B \succ A$. This situation is denoted as

W.V. Gehrlein (✉)
Department of Business Administration, University of Delaware, Newark, DE 19716, USA
e-mail: gehrleiw@lerner.udel.edu

A. Van Deemen, A. Rusinowska (eds.), *Collective Decision Making,*
Theory and Decision Library C 43, DOI 10.1007/978-3-642-02865-6_2,
© Springer-Verlag Berlin Heidelberg 2010

$$
\begin{array}{cccccc}
A & A & B & C & B & C \\
B & C & A & A & C & B \\
C & B & C & B & A & A \\
q_1 & q_2 & q_3 & q_4 & q_5 & q_6
\end{array}
$$

Fig. 1 The possible complete preference rankings on three candidates

AMB if $n_1 + n_2 + n_4 > n_3 + n_5 + n_6$ when no voter indifference is allowed. Candidate A is the pairwise majority rule winner (*PMRW*) if both AMB and AMC, and the PMRW is frequently referred to as the Condorcet Winner in the literature, since (Condorcet, 1785) observed that it was possible to have an intransitive PMR relationship, despite the fact that the individual voters all have transitive preferences. The possible existence of a PMR cycle is known as Condorcet's Paradox, such as with a voting situation in which AMB, BMC and CMA.

Condorcet was a strong supporter of the notion that the PMRW should be the winner of any election, whenever such a candidate exists. As a result, this standard for evaluating the effectiveness of election procedures has become known as the Condorcet Criterion, and it has received nearly universal acceptance. All of this has led to a significant interest in the probability that a PMRW exists, since the Condorcet Criterion has no meaning in the presence of a cyclic PMR relationship. The Condorcet Efficiency of a voting rule is defined as the conditional probability that the voting rule selects the PMRW as the election winner, given that a PMRW exists.

A landmark result in the extensive amount of study that has been conducted to develop representations for the probability that a PMRW exists is given in (Guilbaud, 1952). This result presents a representation for the probability $P_{PMRW}(3, \infty, IC)$ that a PMRW exists for a three candidate election in the limiting case for voters as $n \to \infty$ with the assumption of IC, with

$$
P_{PMRW}(3, \infty, IC) = \frac{3}{4} + \frac{3}{4\pi} \mathrm{Sin}^{-1}\left(\frac{1}{3}\right) \approx 0.91226. \tag{1}
$$

The condition of IC has become widely viewed as representing a scenario that exaggerates the probability that various paradoxical outcomes will be observed in voting situations, so the probability in (1) can be viewed as a lower bound on the probability that a PMRW exists. Therefore, there is a considerable resulting interest in the Condorcet Efficiency of voting rules, since it can then generally be anticipated that a PMRW will exist with a relatively high probability.

The Condorcet Efficiency of voting rules with the assumption of IC for large electorates as $n \to \infty$ was analyzed in (Gehrlein & Fishburn, 1978). The class of voting rules that were considered was the set of all weighted scoring rules (*WSR*'s). A WSR works in a three candidate election by having voters assign points to candidates, based on the positions of the candidates in the voters' preference rankings. With the WSR denoted as Rule λ, each voter gives one point to their most preferred candidate, λ points to their middle ranked candidate and zero points to their least preferred candidate, where $0 \leq \lambda \leq 1$. The winner is then determined as the candidate that obtains the greatest total number of points from all voters.

A representation is obtained for the Condorcet Efficiency, $CE\,(3, \infty, IC, \lambda)$, of Rule λ for three candidate elections in the limit of voters as $n \to \infty$ with IC, and

$$
CE(3, \infty, IC, \lambda) =
$$

$$
\frac{\left[\pi \left\{ \mathrm{Sin}^{-1}\left(\sqrt{\tfrac{2}{3z'}} \right) + \mathrm{Sin}^{-1}\left(\sqrt{\tfrac{1}{6z'}} \right) \right\} + \left\{ \left(\mathrm{Sin}^{-1}\left(\sqrt{\tfrac{2}{3z'}} \right) \right)^2 - \left(\mathrm{Sin}^{-1}\left(\sqrt{\tfrac{1}{6z'}} \right) \right)^2 \right\} \right.}{\pi^2 + 2\pi \mathrm{Sin}^{-1}\left(\tfrac{1}{3} \right)}
$$

$$
\left. + \frac{4\pi^2}{9} - \left\{ \int_0^1 \frac{\mathrm{Cos}^{-1}\left(\dfrac{6tz' - g'(t, z')}{2g'(t, z')} \right)}{\sqrt{36 - (3 - t)^2}} \right\} \right]
$$

(2)

where
$$
z' = 1 - \lambda(1 - \lambda) \text{ and } g'(t, z') = 4\left(3z' - 2\right)^2 - \left(3z' - 2 - tz'\right)^2 + 6\left(3z' - 2\right).
$$

The symmetry of the definition of z' leads directly to the observation that $CE\,(3, \infty, IC, \lambda) = CE\,(3, \infty, IC, 1 - \lambda)$, and it is also proved in (Gehrlein & Fishburn, 1978) that $CE\,(3, \infty, IC, \lambda)$ increases as λ increases for $0 \leq \lambda \leq 0.5$. Computed values of $CE\,(3, \infty, IC, \lambda)$ are listed in Table 1 for each value of $\lambda = 0.00\,(0.05)\,0.50$. The computed values in Table 1 clearly show that the selection of the λ that is used in a WSR can have a significant impact on the Condorcet Efficiency that results.

Table 1 Computed values of $CE\,(3, \infty, IC, \lambda)$

λ	$CE\,(\infty, \lambda, 0)$
0.00	0.7572
0.05	0.7749
0.10	0.7930
0.15	0.8113
0.20	0.8296
0.25	0.8473
0.30	0.8639
0.35	0.8786
0.40	0.8905
0.45	0.8984
0.50	0.9012

2 The Possible Existence of Voter Indifference

It is clearly possible that individual voters might be indifferent between some candidates, and indifference between Candidates A and B is denoted by $A \sim B$ for a voter's preference when neither $A \succ B$ nor $B \succ A$. The notion of IC is extended to apply it to the case that allows for voter indifference between candidates in (Fishburn & Gehrlein, 1980), where it is only required that voter preferences on candidates can be represented by weak orders. Voters with complete preference rankings, like those above in Fig. 1, represent a class of voters. A second class of voters have weak ordered preferences that reflect a partial degree of indifference on the candidates, in which there is voter indifference on one pair of candidates. The case of complete indifference in which a voter is completely indifferent between all three candidates is ignored, since there is no particular reason for such a voter to be involved in any associated election.

Partial indifference would be displayed by a voter who has $A \sim B$ but feels that both $A \succ C$ and that $B \succ C$. It is still required that voter's preferences must be transitive, so there are only six different weak ordered individual preference structures that represent partial indifference:

$A \sim B$	$A \sim C$	$B \sim C$	A	B	C
C	B	A	$B \sim C$	$A \sim C$	$A \sim B$
q_7	q_8	q_9	q_{10}	q_{11}	q_{12}

Fig. 2 The possible preference rankings with partial indifference on three candidates

Let k_1 denote the probability that a voter has preferences that are consistent with complete preferences in Fig. 1 and let k_2 denote the probability that a voter has preferences that are consistent with partial indifference in Fig. 2. Complete indifference is ignored, so $k_1 + k_2 = 1$ and $\sum_{i=1}^{12} q_i = 1$.

The Impartial Weak Ordered Culture Condition (*IWOC*) from (Fishburn & Gehrlein, 1980) defines the probability that a randomly selected voter has a specified preference ranking on the candidates when partial indifference is allowed. With IWOC, each of the six complete linear preference rankings in Fig. 1 is assumed to be equally likely to be observed as the preferences of a voter in this category, with probability $k_1/6$. Similarly, each voter in the class of voters with partial indifference has probability $k_2/6 = (1 - k_1)/6$ of having each of the six possible preference rankings with partial indifference in Fig. 2.

In order to determine if a PMRW exists when voter indifference is allowed, some modification must be made to our original definition of PMR. Let ANB denote the outcome that a majority of the voters who have some actual preference on Candidates A and B have $A \succ B$. For example, ANB in a specific voting situation if $n_1 + n_2 + n_4 + n_8 + n_{10} > n_3 + n_5 + n_6 + n_9 + n_{11}$. Note that the $n_7 + n_{12}$ voters with preferences containing $A \sim B$ are completely excluded in this definition of ANB. The probability $P_{PMRW}(3, \infty, IWOC)$ that a PMRW exists for a three-candidate election in the limit of voters with $n \to \infty$ under the IWOC assumption is given by the representation

$$P_{PMRW}(3, \infty, \text{IWOC}) = \frac{3}{4} + \frac{3}{2\pi} \text{Sin}^{-1}\left(\frac{1}{k_1 + 2}\right). \tag{3}$$

Table 2 Computed values of $P_{PMRW}(3, \infty, IWOC, k_1)$

k_1	k_2	$P_{PMRW}(3, \infty, IWOC, k_1)$
0.00	1.00	1.0000
0.10	0.90	0.9870
0.20	0.80	0.9753
0.30	0.70	0.9648
0.40	0.60	0.9552
0.50	0.50	0.9465
0.60	0.40	0.9385
0.70	0.30	0.9312
0.80	0.20	0.9244
0.90	0.10	0.9181
1.00	0.00	0.9123

The representation for $P_{PMRW}(3, \infty, IWOC)$ in (2) obviously reduces to the representation for $P_{PMRW}(3, \infty, IC)$ in (1) in the special case with $k_1 = 1$. Table 2 lists computed values of $P_{PMRW}(3, \infty, IWOC)$ for each $k_1 = 0.00\ (0.10)\ 1.00$ from (3). The proportion of voters that have partial indifference in their preferences, as measured by k_2, clearly has an impact on the probability that a PMRW exists, given the results in Table 2. Increasing levels of k_2 lead to increases in $P_{PMRW}(3, \infty, IWOC)$, with certainty that a PMRW exists in the extreme case of $k_2 = 1$. The requirement that a PMRW must exist in the case of such dichotomous preferences is well known from results that are presented in (Inada, 1964).

The assumption of IWOC is extended to consider the impact that voter indifference has on the Condorcet Efficiency of WSR's in (Gehrlein & Valognes, 2001), and this creates an additional complication. This complication arises because the combination of weights $(1, \lambda, 0)$ is not as easily distributed to candidates when partial indifference exists as it was with IC, when voter indifference between candidates was prohibited. There are two possible approaches to resolving this issue. First, the weights in the WSR can be modified to accommodate indifference in voters' preferences, when such indifferences exist. Second, the voters could be required to arbitrarily break indifference ties to produce a complete preference ranking on candidates, which would then allow a direct application of the WSR weights $(1, \lambda, 0)$. The objective of the current study is to consider what the difference in impact is for these two approaches to the problem of dealing with indifference ties.

The first of these approaches was taken in (Gehrlein & Valognes, 2001). For voting preference rankings with partial indifference, the $(1, \lambda, 0)$ weights were modified in different ways to keep fixed the total number of points that each voter has to distribute to candidates. For a situation in which a voter is indifferent between two top-ranked candidates that are both preferred to the third candidate, the two tied top-ranked candidates received $(1 + \lambda)/2$ points each, while the least preferred candidate receives zero points. For a situation in which a voter was indifferent between two tied bottom-ranked candidates that are both less preferred than the third candidate, the two tied bottom-ranked candidates each receive $\lambda/2$ points while the most preferred candidate receives one point. Each voter still assigns a total of $1 - \lambda$ points to candidates in both cases.

When this method is used to redistribute the points that voters allocate to the candidates in the presence of partial indifference, a limiting representation for the Condorcet Efficiency, CE $(3, \infty, \text{IWOC}, k_1, \lambda)$, of Rule λ as $n \to \infty$ is obtained as:

$$\text{CE}(3, \infty, \text{IWOC}, k_1, \lambda) =$$

$$\frac{\left[\begin{array}{c} \left[\text{Sin}^{-1}\left(\frac{k_1+3}{\sqrt{(k_1+2)z}}\right) + \text{Sin}^{-1}\left(\frac{k_1+3}{2\sqrt{(k_1+2)z}}\right)\right]\left[\text{Sin}^{-1}\left(\frac{k_1+3}{\sqrt{(k_1+2)z}}\right) - \text{Sin}^{-1}\left(\frac{k_1+3}{2\sqrt{(k_1+2)z}}\right) + \pi\right] \\ + \frac{4\pi^2}{9} - k_1 \int_0^1 \frac{\text{Cos}^{-1}\left(\frac{3k_1 t (k_1+3)^2 - g}{2g}\right)}{\sqrt{4(k_1+2)^2 - [2+k_1(1-t)]^2}} dt \end{array}\right]}{\pi^2 + 2\pi \text{Sin}^{-1}\left(\frac{1}{k_1+2}\right)}$$

$$\text{(4)}$$

where:

$$z = 4 + (3k_1 + 1)\left(1 - 2\lambda + 2\lambda^2\right),$$

and

$$g = 4(k_1 + 2)^2 z - (k_1 + 2 - k_1 t)^2 z - (3k_1 + 6 + 2k_1 t)(k_1 + 3)^2.$$

It is easily seen that CE $(3, \infty, \text{IWOC}, k_1, \lambda) = \text{CE}(3, \infty, \text{IWOC}, k_1, 1 - \lambda)$ from these definitions, and it is also proved in (Gehrlein & Valognes, 2001) that CE $(3, \infty, \text{IWOC}, k_1, \lambda)$ increases both as λ increases for $0 \leq \lambda \leq 0.5$ and as k_1 decreases (k_2 increases) for $0 \leq k_1 \leq 1$. Computed values of CE $(3, \infty, \text{IWOC}, k_1, \lambda)$ that are obtained by using numerical integration with the representation in (4) are listed in Table 3 for each combination of values with $\lambda = 0.00\,(0.05)\,0.50$ and $k_1 = 0.00\,(0.20)\,1.00$. These computed values clearly show that both the selection of the particular λ that is used by a WSR and the degree of partial indifference that is present in voters' preferences, as measured by k_2, can have a significant impact on the Condorcet Efficiency that results. It must be true from definitions that CE $(3, \infty, \text{IWOC}, 1, \lambda) = \text{CE}(3, \infty, \text{IC}, \lambda)$. Moreover, since CE $(3, \infty, \text{IWOC}, k_1, \lambda)$ decreases as k_1 increases, it follows that CE $(3, \infty, \text{IWOC}, k_1, \lambda)$ is minimized when $k_1 = 1$, which makes it equivalent to CE $(3, \infty, \text{IC}, \lambda)$ for any given λ.

Table 3 Computed values of CE $(3, \infty, \text{IWOC}, k_1, \lambda)$

$\lambda \backslash k_1$	0.00	0.20	0.40	0.60	0.80	1.00
0.00	0.8495	0.8156	0.7942	0.7787	0.7668	0.7572
0.10	0.8776	0.8456	0.8260	0.8121	0.8015	0.7930
0.20	0.9069	0.8756	0.8580	0.8459	0.8368	0.8296
0.30	0.9372	0.9038	0.8877	0.8773	0.8697	0.8639
0.40	0.9683	0.9261	0.9106	0.9014	0.8951	0.8905
0.50	1.0000	0.9354	0.9199	0.9111	0.9053	0.9012

3 The Impact of Requiring Forced Rankings

The existence of partial indifference in voters' preferences has been seen to have a significant impact on both the probability that a PMRW exists and on the Condorcet Efficiency of WSR's. So far, the existence of partial indifference has been dealt with by modifying the weights that are used in WSR's to accommodate this indifference. It has already been suggested that a second approach to this issue would be to require voters to arbitrarily break indifference ties in their preferences to report a complete preference ranking on the candidates. It would intuitively seem that the implementation of this forced ranking option should not produce dramatically different results in our observations. However, this is not actually the case, and some very bad outcomes can result from forcing voters to break ties in their preferences to produce complete rankings.

The results of (Gehrlein & Valognes, 2001) produce the first negative result from forcing rankings. It is shown that when voters are forced to produce rankings the net effect is that CE $(3, \infty, \text{IWOC}, k_1, \lambda)$ will be modified to be equivalent to CE $(3, \infty, \text{IC}, \lambda)$ for all values of k_1, which corresponds to the lowest level of Condorcet Efficiency that can be observed for any specified Rule λ. This provides compelling evidence to support the avoidance of forcing rankings in the context of applying WSR's to obtain an election winner, if the Condorcet Criterion is being considered as a measure of the effectiveness of voting rules.

The new result regarding the impact of forcing rankings that is considered here is the fact that the PMRW that would be observed in the forced complete rankings might be different than the PMRW that would be observed in the original voting situation that contains partial indifference. The probability that such a result might be observed turns out to be remarkably greater than intuition suggests. This observation is reached after we develop a limiting representation for the probability that the same PMRW exists under both cases as $n \to \infty$ under the assumption of IWOC.

The development of this representation begins with the definition of four discrete variables that describe the likelihood that various outcomes are observed as voters are randomly selected with preferences and associated probabilities as specified in Figs. 1 and 2. Let X_i^j denote the variable value for the jth voter for the ith measure of interest. The first two variables are defined by

$$
\begin{aligned}
X_1^j = +1 &: q_1 + q_2 + q_4 + q_8 + q_{10} \\
0 &: q_7 + q_{12} \\
-1 &: q_3 + q_5 + q_6 + q_9 + q_{11}
\end{aligned}
\tag{5}
$$

$$
\begin{aligned}
X_2^j = +1 &: q_1 + q_2 + q_3 + q_7 + q_{10} \\
0 &: q_8 + q_{11} \\
-1 &: q_4 + q_5 + q_6 + q_9 + q_{12}
\end{aligned}
\tag{6}
$$

The definition of X_1^j in (5) and the preference rankings in Figs. 1 and 2 indicate that $X_1^j = +1 \, (-1)$ if the preference ranking for the jth voter has $A \succ B \, (B \succ A)$, and $X_1^j = 0$ if $A \sim B$. Then, ANB for a given voting situation if $\sum_{j=1}^n X_1^j > 0$. If $\overline{X}_1$ denotes the average value of X_1^j, then ANB if $\overline{X}_1 > 0$ or $\overline{X}_1 \sqrt{n} > 0$. The same analysis with (6) leads to the conclusion that ANC in a voting situation if $\overline{X}_2 \sqrt{n} > 0$.

Variables X_3^j and X_4^j will be defined in the same fashion to determine if AMB and AMC in the voting situation that is obtained by having the jth voter arbitrarily break indifference ties if that voter has a preference ranking that contains partial indifference. These variables are formally defined by the q_i probabilities, with

$$
\begin{aligned}
X_3^j = &+1 : q_1 + q_2 + q_4 + q_8 + q_{10} + q_7^{ABC} + q_{12}^{CAB} \\
&-1 : q_3 + q_5 + q_6 + q_9 + q_{11} + q_7^{BAC} + q_{12}^{CBA}
\end{aligned}
\tag{7}
$$

$$
\begin{aligned}
X_4^j = &+1 : q_1 + q_2 + q_3 + q_7 + q_{10} + q_8^{ACB} + q_{11}^{BAC} \\
&-1 : q_4 + q_5 + q_6 + q_9 + q_{12} + q_8^{CAB} + q_{11}^{BCA}
\end{aligned}
\tag{8}
$$

Some additional discussion is needed to define the probabilities for these variables that result from having random tie breaking to force rankings on indifference pairs. Consider the event denoted by probability q_7 in which $A \sim B$ with $A \succ C$ and $B \succ C$. Let q_7^{ABC} denote the probability that a randomly selected voter has preferences with the partial indifference with $A \sim B$, and then randomly breaks the tie by ranking $A \succ B$ to lead to the transitive ranking $A \succ B \succ C$. Then, $q_7 = q_7^{ABC} + q_7^{BAC}$.

The definitions of the variables X_3^j and X_4^j lead to the conclusion that AMB if $\overline{X}_3 \sqrt{n} > 0$ and AMC if $\overline{X}_4 \sqrt{n} > 0$. It then follows that Candidate A will be the PMRW based both on the original voting situation and on the voting situation that results from forced ranking when $\overline{X}_i \sqrt{n} > 0$ for all $1 \le i \le 4$. In the limit as $n \to \infty$, the joint distribution between these four $\overline{X}_i \sqrt{n}$ variables becomes multivariate normal, and the correlations between these variables is the same as the correlation between the corresponding original X_i^j variables. The first step to obtaining these correlation terms is the determination of the expected values of the X_i^j variables, and these expected values are denoted by $E\left(X_i^j\right)$, with

$$
E\left(X_1^j\right) = (q_1 + q_2 + q_4 + q_8 + q_{10}) + 0\,(q_7 + q_{12}) - (q_3 + q_5 + q_6 + q_9 + q_{11})
$$

$$
E\left(X_2^j\right) = (q_1 + q_2 + q_3 + q_7 + q_{10}) + 0\,(q_8 + q_{11}) - (q_4 + q_5 + q_6 + q_9 + q_{12})
$$

$$
\begin{aligned}
E\left(X_3^j\right) = &\left(q_1 + q_2 + q_4 + q_8 + q_{10} + q_7^{ABC} + q_{12}^{CAB}\right) \\
&- \left(q_3 + q_5 + q_6 + q_9 + q_{11} + q_7^{BAC} + q_{12}^{CBA}\right)
\end{aligned}
$$

$$
\begin{aligned}
E\left(X_4^j\right) = &\left(q_1 + q_2 + q_3 + q_7 + q_{10} + q_8^{ACB} + q_{11}^{BAC}\right) \\
&- \left(q_4 + q_5 + q_6 + q_9 + q_{12} + q_8^{CAB} + q_{11}^{BCA}\right)
\end{aligned}
\tag{9}
$$

With the assumption of IWOC, $q_i = k_1/6$ for $1 \leq i \leq 6$ and $q_i = (1 - k_1)/6$ for $7 \leq i \leq 12$, and when the indifference ties are broken randomly $q_i^{XYZ} = (1 - k_1)/12$ for $7 \leq i \leq 12$.

All of this leads to the observation that $E\left(X_i^j\right) = 0$ for all $1 \leq i \leq 4$, so that $E\left(\overline{X}_i\sqrt{n}\right) = 0$ for all $1 \leq i \leq 4$. This allows for the definition of the probability that Candidate A will be the PMRW based both on the original voting situation and on the voting situation that results from forced ranking as being identical to the joint probability that $\overline{X}_i\sqrt{n} > E\left(\overline{X}_i\sqrt{n}\right)$ for all $1 \leq i \leq 4$. The probability that any variable takes on any specific value, including its expected value, in a continuous distribution is equal to zero, so this joint probability can be rewritten as the joint probability that $\overline{X}_i\sqrt{n} \geq E\left(\overline{X}_i\sqrt{n}\right)$ for all $1 \leq i \leq 4$. This describes a four-variate normal positive orthant probability, and much is known about the development of representations for these probabilities, once the correlation matrix has been obtained.

The definitions in (5) and (6) lead to $E\left(X_i^{j^2}\right) = \frac{2+k_1}{3}$ for $i = 1, 2$ and (7) and (8) lead to $E\left(X_i^{j^2}\right) = 1$ for $i = 3, 4$. The expected value of the cross-products of the original variables comes from:

$$E\left(X_1^j X_2^j\right) = q_1 + q_2 - q_3 - q_4 + q_5 + q_6 + q_9 + q_{10} = \frac{1}{3}$$

$$E\left(X_1^j X_3^j\right) = q_1 + q_2 + q_3 + q_4 + q_5 + q_6 + q_8 + q_9 + q_{10} + q_{11} = \frac{2+k_1}{3}$$

$$E\left(X_1^j X_4^j\right) = q_1 + q_2 - q_3 - q_4 + q_5 + q_6 + q_8^{ACB} - q_8^{CAB} + q_9 + q_{10} - q_{11}^{BAC}$$
$$+ q_{11}^{BCA} = \frac{1}{3}$$

$$E\left(X_2^j X_3^j\right) = q_1 + q_2 - q_3 - q_4 + q_5 + q_6 + q_7^{ABC} - q_7^{BAC} + q_9 + q_{10} - q_{12}^{CAB}$$
$$+ q_{12}^{CBA} = \frac{1}{3}$$

$$E\left(X_2^j X_4^j\right) = q_1 + q_2 + q_3 + q_4 + q_5 + q_6 + q_7 + q_9 + q_{10} + q_{12} = \frac{2+k_1}{3}$$

$$E\left(X_3^j X_4^j\right) = q_1 + q_2 - q_3 - q_4 + q_5 + q_6 + q_7^{ABC} - q_7^{BAC} + q_8^{ACB} - q_8^{CAB} + q_9$$
$$+ q_{10} - q_{11}^{BAC} + q_{11}^{BCA} - q_{12}^{CAB} + q_{12}^{CBA} = \frac{1}{3}$$

$$\tag{10}$$

Since $E\left(X_i^j\right) = 0$ for all $1 \leq i \leq 4$, the correlation terms are obtained from the general representation

$$\mathrm{Cor}\left(X_i^j, X_k^j\right) = \frac{E\left(X_i^j X_k^j\right)}{\sqrt{E\left(X_i^{j^2}\right)}\sqrt{E\left(X_k^{j^2}\right)}}. \tag{11}$$

The resulting correlation matrix is denoted by $\boldsymbol{R}$, with terms $r_{i,j}$, and all of the above leads to

$$
\boldsymbol{R} = \begin{bmatrix} 1 & \frac{1}{k_1+2} & \sqrt{\frac{k_1+2}{3}} & \sqrt{\frac{1}{3(k_1+2)}} \\ - & 1 & \sqrt{\frac{1}{3(k_1+2)}} & \sqrt{\frac{k_1+2}{3}} \\ - & - & 1 & \frac{1}{3} \\ - & - & - & 1 \end{bmatrix}. \tag{12}
$$

The correlation matrix $\boldsymbol{R}$ in (12) is similar to the general form of a correlation matrix for which an elegant closed form representation for the multivariate normal positive orthant probability is known. The correlation matrix $\boldsymbol{R}^*$, with terms $r_{i,j}^*$, has the general form

$$
\boldsymbol{R}^* = \begin{bmatrix} 1 & \alpha & \beta & \alpha\beta \\ - & 1 & \alpha\beta & \beta \\ - & - & 1 & \alpha \\ - & - & - & 1 \end{bmatrix}. \tag{13}
$$

The positive orthant probability for this joint distribution with correlation matrix $\boldsymbol{R}^*$ is $\Phi_4\left(\boldsymbol{R}^*\right)$, and (Cheng, 1969) proves that

$$
\begin{aligned}
\Phi_4\left(\boldsymbol{R}^*\right) = &\frac{1}{16} + \frac{1}{4\pi}\left\{\mathrm{Sin}^{-1}\left(\alpha\right) + \mathrm{Sin}^{-1}\left(\beta\right) + \mathrm{Sin}^{-1}\left(\alpha\beta\right)\right\} \\
&+ \frac{1}{4\pi^2}\left[\left\{\mathrm{Sin}^{-1}\left(\alpha\right)\right\}^2 + \left\{\mathrm{Sin}^{-1}\left(\beta\right)\right\}^2 - \left\{\mathrm{Sin}^{-1}\left(\alpha\beta\right)\right\}^2\right].
\end{aligned} \tag{14}
$$

Matrix $\boldsymbol{R}^*$ in (13) is the same as $\boldsymbol{R}$ in (12) with $\alpha = \frac{1}{k_1+2}$ and $\beta = \sqrt{\frac{k_1+2}{3}}$, except for $r_{3,4}$ and $r_{3,4}^*$.

A procedure that is described in (Plackett, 1954) is applicable in this situation to obtain a representation for $\Phi_4\left(\boldsymbol{R}\right)$ as

$$
\Phi_4\left(\boldsymbol{R}\right) = \Phi_4\left(\boldsymbol{R}^*\right) + I, \tag{15}
$$

where I is a bounded integral over a single variable, and the first step of this procedure is to obtain the matrix $\boldsymbol{C}(t)$, where

$$
\boldsymbol{C}(t) = t\boldsymbol{R} + (1-t)\,\boldsymbol{R}^*. \tag{16}
$$

Let c_{ij} denote the matrix entries for $C(t)$, and for this R and R^*, we obtain

$$
C(t) = \begin{bmatrix}
1 & \frac{1}{k_1+2} & \sqrt{\frac{k_1+2}{3}} & \sqrt{\frac{1}{3(k_1+2)}} \\
- & 1 & \sqrt{\frac{1}{3(k_1+2)}} & \sqrt{\frac{k_1+2}{3}} \\
- & - & 1 & \frac{3+t(k_1-1)}{3(k_1+2)} \\
- & - & - & 1
\end{bmatrix}.
\tag{17}
$$

The second step is to obtain the matrix inverse $H(t) = C(t)^{-1}$, with entries h_{ij}. Since R and R^* only differ for $r_{3,4}$ and $r_{3,4}^*$, Plackett's procedure obtains the integral I from the representation

$$
I = \frac{c'_{3,4}}{4\pi^2} \int_0^1 \left[\frac{1}{1 - c_{3,4}{}^2} \right]^{\frac{1}{2}} Cos^{-1} \left(\frac{h_{1,2}}{\sqrt{h_{1,1} h_{2,2}}} \right) dt.
\tag{18}
$$

Here, $c'_{3,4} = \frac{\partial c_{3,4}}{\partial t}$. The $H(t)$ matrix is very complex and is not reported here.

The objective is to develop a representation for the conditional probability, $P_{MA}(3, \infty, IWOC, k_1)$, that there is mutual agreement between the original PMRW in a voting situation that contains partial indifference between candidates and the PMRW that exists in the voting situation that results by forcing voters to report a complete ranking by arbitrarily breaking indifferences on pairs, given that a PMRW exists in the original voting situation. The symmetry of IWOC with respect to candidates and the assumption that $n \to \infty$ can be used to obtain a representation for $P_{MA}(3, \infty, IWOC, k_1)$ from the identity relationship

$$
P_{MA}(3, \infty, IWOC, k_1) = \frac{3\Phi_4(R)}{P_{PMRW}(3, \infty, IWOC, k_1)}.
\tag{19}
$$

By using Plackett's procedure with (19), substitution and significant algebraic reduction ultimately leads to:

$$
P_{MA}(3, \infty, IWOC, k_1) =
$$

$$
\frac{1}{16} + \frac{1}{4\pi} \left\{ Sin^{-1}\left(\frac{1}{k_1+2}\right) + Sin^{-1}\left(\sqrt{\frac{k_1+2}{3}}\right) + Sin^{-1}\left(\sqrt{\frac{1}{3(k_1+2)}}\right) \right\}
$$

$$
+ \frac{1}{4\pi^2} \left[\left\{ Sin^{-1}\left(\frac{1}{k_1+2}\right) \right\}^2 + \left\{ Sin^{-1}\left(\sqrt{\frac{k_1+2}{3}}\right) \right\}^2 - \left\{ Sin^{-1}\left(\sqrt{\frac{1}{3(k_1+2)}}\right) \right\}^2 \right]
$$

$$
- \frac{(1-k_1)}{4\pi^2} \int_0^1 \frac{Cos^{-1}\left(\dfrac{(k_1+3)\{(k_1-1)t - 3(k_1+1)(k_1+3-t)\} + g(k_1,t)}{g(k_1,t)} \right)}{\sqrt{\{(k_1-1)t + 3(k_1+3)\}\{3(k_1+1) - (k_1-1)t\}}} dt.
\tag{20}
$$

Table 4 Computed values of $P_{MA}(3, \infty, IWOC, k_1)$

k_1	k_2	$P_{MA}(3, \infty, IWOC, k_1)$
0.00	1.00	0.6908
0.10	0.90	0.7077
0.20	0.80	0.7253
0.30	0.70	0.7437
0.40	0.60	0.7634
0.50	0.50	0.7845
0.60	0.40	0.8076
0.70	0.30	0.8337
0.80	0.20	0.8645
0.90	0.10	0.9043
1.00	0.00	1.0000

Here, $g(k_1, t) = (k_1 + 2)\{3(k_1 + 3)(k_1 + 1) + (k_1 - 1)(t - 2)t\}$.

The bounded integral in (20) does not have a simple closed form solution, but it is easily evaluated with numerical integration for specific values of k_1, and computed values of $P_{MA}(3, \infty, IWOC, k_1)$ are listed in Table 4 for each value of $k_1 = .00(.10)1.00$.

One obvious result from Table 4 is that $P_{MA}(3, \infty, IWOC, 1) = 1.00$, along with the result that follows from intuition that $P_{MA}(3, \infty, IWOC, k_1)$ decreases as k_1 decreases. The very surprising result from Table 4 is the highly significant degree with which $P_{MA}(3, \infty, IWOC, k_1)$ decreases as k_1 decreases. At the extreme in which all voters have dichotomous preferences, with $k_1 = 0$, a PMRW must exist for each of the initial voting situations, but $P_{MA}(3, \infty, IWOC, 0)$ is only 0.6908.

4 Conclusion

Voters certainly could be indifferent between some pairs of candidates in three candidate elections, and such a response from voters creates complications for most voting rules, with approval voting being an exception. One option that could be used to avoid these complications is to force voters to arbitrarily break indifference ties and to report complete preference rankings. Previous research has shown that resorting to this tactic can have a significant negative impact on the Condorcet Efficiency of WSR's. We now find that this tactic can also have another dramatic negative impact, since it can result in a significant likelihood that a different PMRW will be observed in the resulting forced raking voting situation when compared to the PMRW that exists in the original voting situation. While it is generally acknowledged that assumptions like IWOC tend to exaggerate the probability of observing such paradoxical outcomes, the results that are observed here are so dramatic that this clearly signals that the option of forcing complete preference rankings can lead to real problems in election scenarios.

References

Cheng, M. C. (1969). The orthant probability of four Gaussian variables. *Annals of Mathematical Statistics, 40*, 152–161.

de Condorcet, M. (1785). An essay on the application of probability theory to plurality decision making: An election between three candidates. In F. Sommerlad & I. McLean (Eds.), *The political theory of Condorcet* (pp. 69–80). University of Oxford Working Paper.

Fishburn, P. C., & Gehrlein, W. V. (1980). The paradox of voting: Effects of individual indifference and intransitivity. *Journal of Public Economics, 14*, 83–94.

Gehrlein, W. V., & Fishburn, P. C. (1978). Coincidence probabilities for simple majority and positional voting rules. *Social Science Research, 7*, 272–283.

Gehrlein, W. V., & Valognes, F. (2001). Condorcet efficiency: A preference for indifference. *Social Choice and Welfare, 18*, 193–205.

Guilbaud, G. T. (1952). Les theories de l'intérêt general et le probleme logique de l'agregation. *Economie Appliquée, 5*, 501–584.

Inada, K. (1964). A note on simple majority decision rule. *Econometrica, 32*, 525–531.

Plackett, R. L. (1954). A reduction formula for normal multivariate integrals. *Biometrika, 41*, 351–360.

Sommerlad, F., & McLean, I. (1989). *The political theory of Condorcet*. University of Oxford Working Paper.

Connections and Implications of the Ostrogorski Paradox for Spatial Voting Models

Hannu Nurmi and Donald G. Saari

1 Introduction

Spatial models occupy an important position in modern social choice theory. From the early applications to party competition and electoral equilibrium they have spread to the study of inter-institutional power in the European Union (EU) and cabinet coalitions in multiparty systems (Downs, 1957; Napel & Widgrén, 2004; Napel & Widgrén, 1992; Laver & Shepsle, 1996). They have applications in expert systems by advising voters how to make choices in elections. These models use assumptions that allow modelers to assign voters or decision makers to points in a policy space, which often is a multi-dimensional Euclidean space. Similarly, the decision alternatives, or candidates, are typically positioned in the policy space as points or probability distributions over points. Work on spatial models has produced a variety of results ranging from the existence of stable outcomes (equilibria) of various various kinds (McKelvey & Schofield, 1987; Saari, 1997, Saari & Asay, 2009) to power distributions among voters (Steunenberg, Schmidtchen, & Koboldt, 1999) and suggestions for institutional design (Shepsle & Weingast, 1987).

An objective of this paper is to offer new connections by identifying the spatial models approach with well-known puzzles such as the Ostrogorski paradox. In this manner, new themes are introduced while several mysteries and conjectures are answered. We also question the standard condition whereby a voter prefers the candidate (or policy position) whose stance is closest to his. As we show, plausible variations in this basic assumption have implications suggesting reasonably stable outcomes in social choice, which may be more optimistic than suggested by the above mentioned results. After describing a variety of paradoxical settings, we explain why all of them occur.

H. Nurmi (✉)
Department of Political Science, University of Turku, 20014 Turku, Finland
e-mail: hnurmi@utu.fi

A. Van Deemen, A. Rusinowska (eds.), *Collective Decision Making,*
Theory and Decision Library C 43, DOI 10.1007/978-3-642-02865-6_3,
© Springer-Verlag Berlin Heidelberg 2010

The class of aggregation paradoxes that are emphasized here bears the name of Ostrogorski, a Russian diplomat and political theorist whose magnum opus (Ostrogorski, 1970) appeared in the opening years of the twentieth century (also see Rae & Daudt, 1976; Bezembinder & Van Acker, 1985). This paradox is introduced and analyzed in the next section, and its variant – the exam paradox (Nermuth, 1992) – is discussed in the section that follows it. We then answer some conjectures, connect these issues with the core and "chaos theorem" of spatial voting, and evaluate the implications that these paradoxes have for the spatial modeling of individual preferences. To indicate the generality of certain answers, Sect. 9 considers another aggregation paradox, viz. Simpson's (1951) paradox.

It is interesting how aggregation paradoxes have been the focus of scholarly attention for some time. As an illustration, the notion behind "Simpson's Paradox" was recognized by Cohen and Nagel back in 1934, which was nearly two decades before Simpson's important article. In 1940s and 1950s important contributions were made by May (1946, 1947). Of relevance to this current paper is his pioneering work (May, 1954) demonstrating how "cyclic preferences" make sense should an individual's preferences be determined by multiple criteria of performance. One of our points is related to May's: As we show, the basic tenet underlying many spatial models (that voter preferences have a particular spatial representation) is far from innocuous. Situations exist where rational individuals could choose between two alternatives the one that is further away from the individuals' optimum point.

2 Ostrogorski's Paradox

Consider an election involving 5 voters, 2 parties, and 3 issues where each voter views the issues to be of equal importance and no other considerations influence the voters' opinions about the parties. Consider two ways of determining the dominant party:

1. Each voter prefers the party that is closer to his/her (hereinafter his) opinion on more issues;
2. For each issue, the winner is the party that receives more votes than its competitor. Namely, the dominant party is the one winning on more issues than the other.

In a nutshell, Ostrogorski's paradox occurs when the outcome differs in these two cases.

Table 1 distribution of opinions about parties X and Y provides a strong version of the paradox because not only do the results differ under procedures (1) and (2), but the winner under (2) is unanimous. Replacing any one Y with an X creates a weaker version of the paradox where "just" a majority differs under (1) and (2).

It is reasonable to worry whether the qualitative nature of Table 1 is misleading; perhaps "closeness" of voters to parties should be captured in a more precise

Table 1 Ostrogorski's paradox

Issue	Issue 1	Issue 2	Issue 3	The voter votes for
Voter A	X	X	Y	X
Voter B	X	Y	X	X
Voter C	Y	X	X	X
Voter D	Y	Y	Y	Y
Voter E	Y	Y	Y	Y
Winner	Y	Y	Y	?

manner. To address this concern, represent each issue with a coordinate direction in a 3-dimensional Euclidean space $\mathbb{R}^3$ where $X = (4, 4, 4)$ and $Y = (3, 3, 3)$. Represent each voter's stance for the three issues with an ideal point in $\mathbb{R}^3$; let A's views be at $(4, 5, 3.2)$, B at $(5, 3.2, 4)$, C at $(3.2, 4, 5)$, D at $(2, 2, 2)$ and E at $(1, 1, 1)$. By comparing these component values with those of X and Y, the Table 1 conclusion of a majority support for Y for each issue follows. In contrast, each of A, B, and C is closer to X than to Y; the common distance from A, B, or C to X given by the sum of distances of each issue (called the l_1 distance) is $0.8 + 0 + 1 = 1.8$, which is smaller than the common l_1 distance of any of these three points to Y which is $0.2 + 1 + 2 = 3.2$. The conclusion holds with other distances; e.g., the common Euclidean distance to X is $\sqrt{(0.8)^2 + 0^2 + 1^2} = \sqrt{1.64}$ while that to Y is the larger $\sqrt{0.2^2 + 1^2 + 2^2} = \sqrt{5.04}$.

To introduce our concern about the appropriate way to represent a voter's preferences, in Table 1 replace "voter" with "criterion" and imagine an individual trying to determine whether to support candidate X or Y. The criteria may be relevant educational background, political experience, negotiation skills, political connections, etc. The issues might be education, economy, and foreign policy. Each row and column table entry indicates our voter's preference of a candidate for that criterion and issue. While there are at least two natural ways for our voter to make his choice, if all issues and criteria are deemed of equal importance, our voter's decision is ambiguous: emphasizing criteria (row-column aggregation) with the majority principle suggests supporting X; stressing issues (column-row aggregation) yields Y.

Geometrically, our voter's views can be represented with the above values for the locations of the criteria over issues; the l_1 distance of his opinions from Y is $3(3.2) + 3 + 6 = 18.6$ while that from X is $3(1.8) + 6 + 9 = 20.4$. Using the Euclidean metric, the distance from Y is $\sqrt{3(5.04) + 3 + 12} = \sqrt{30.04}$ while the distance from X is the larger $\sqrt{3(1.64) + 12 + 27} = \sqrt{43.92}$. With either metric, then, this individual's views are closer to that of candidate Y than of candidate X. While the standard spatial voting assumption has this individual selecting the closest candidate Y, is this the correct choice? In reality, it can not be inferred in a pairwise comparison between X and Y whether our voter would always accept Y. In fact, by resorting to the reasonable principle of basing his choice on the criterion-wise performance of candidates, he will vote for X because X outperforms Y on three criteria, while Y beats X on only two. This assertion corresponds to common usage where a voter justifies his support for a candidate in terms of her education, experience, skills, and so forth.

Because Y is closer to the individual's beliefs on each dimension, these problems cannot be resolved by assigning salience weights to issue dimensions. Strategic considerations – which may underly occasional votes against preferences – do not enter into the calculus dictating the choice of X rather than Y because there are only two alternatives and the other voters' ideal points are not known.

3 The Anscombe and Exam Paradoxes

Closely related to Ostrogorski's (1970) paradox is one described by Anscombe (1976). In a nutshell, it says that a majority of voters could be in a minority (i.e., on the losing side) on a majority of issues involving dichotomous choices. In Table 2, which illustrates this paradox, voters A, B and C are on the losing side on a majority of issues: A is on the losing side for issues 2 and 3, B on issues 1 and 3, and C on issues 1 and 2.

Because Table 2 is *not* an Ostrogorski's paradox, the example proves that these paradoxes are not equivalent. (Ostrogorski is a specialized Anscombe paradox.) Using this table to model our voter who is trying to determine which candidate to support, Anscombe's paradox captures the amusing but not uncommon situation where a voter's candidate of choice, as based on criteria, could disappoint the voter with her stance over issues.

But while an Anscombe paradox need not be an Ostrogorski paradox, it can always be converted into one with appropriately selected parties U and V (Nurmi & Meskanen, 2000).

Theorem 1 *For any Anscombe paradox based on specified positions of parties X and Y, there exist parties U and V (created by adopting various positions from parties X and Y) where the Anscombe paradox becomes an Ostrogorski paradox.*

Proof For an Anscombe paradox, let $\mathcal{M}$ be the set of voters in the majority where each is on the losing side for a majority of issues, and let $\mathcal{L}$ be the set of these issues. For each issue not in $\mathcal{L}$, let the stance of party U and V be, respectively, that of the winning and losing side. For each issue in $\mathcal{L}$, let the stance of the party U and V be, respectively, the stance of the losing and winning side.

Table 2 Anscombe's paradox

Issue	Issue 1	Issue 2	Issue 3
Voter A	X	X	Y
Voter B	Y	Y	Y
Voter C	Y	X	X
Voter D	X	Y	X
Voter E	X	Y	X
Winner	X	Y	X

By construction, each member of $\mathcal{M}$ agrees with party U over a majority of issues, so $\mathcal{M}$ constitutes the majority party. Also by construction, each member of $\mathcal{M}$ is on the losing side of a majority of issues. Thus an Ostrogorski paradox is created. If the original Anscombe paradox is a strong one (i.e., a majority of voters are on the losing side of all issues), then so is the corresponding Ostrogorski paradox. □

To illustrate this Anscombe and Ostrogorski connection, recall that Table 2 is not an Ostrogorski paradox because voters A and C support party X while voter B supports party Y. But with the U and V parties, these voters' preferences over issues become, respectively, (V, U, U), (U, V, U), (U, U, V), so all three of these voters support party U. (The other two voters unanimously support party V.) It is interesting how this change from X and Y to U and V is not dissimilar to how parties are formed and/or respond to changing circumstances.

The exam paradox introduced and analyzed by Nermuth (1992) generalizes Ostrogorski's paradox by positioning it in a domain where the proximity of alternatives to ideal points assumes degrees rather than dichotomous values. (This approach is similar to our example using points in $\mathbb{R}^3$ but where the l_1 and Euclidean distances are replaced with a related mathematical representation.) As an illustration of Nermuth's example, consider four issues and five criteria. One of two competitors, X, is located at the distances from the voter's ideal point in a multi-dimensional space given in Table 3. The score of X on each criterion is simply the arithmetic mean of its distances rounded to the nearest integer; with a tie, round down to the nearest integer. X's competitor Y, in turn, is located in the space as indicated in Table 4.

Table 3 X's distances from the voter's ideal point

Criteria	Issue 1	Issue 2	Issue 3	Issue 4	Average	Score
Criterion 1	1	1	2	2	1.5	1
Criterion 2	1	1	2	2	1.5	1
Criterion 3	1	1	2	2	1.5	1
Criterion 4	2	2	3	3	2.5	2
Criterion 5	2	2	3	3	2.5	2

Table 4 Y's distances from the voter's ideal point

Criteria	Issue 1	Issue 2	Issue 3	Issue 4	Average	Score
Criterion 1	1	1	1	1	1.0	1
Criterion 2	1	1	1	1	1.0	1
Criterion 3	1	1	2	3	1.75	2
Criterion 4	1	1	2	3	1.75	2
Criterion 5	1	2	1	2	1.75	2

4 Core Conditions and Aggregation Paradoxes

Perhaps the best-known results on spatial models pertain to the conditions under which a core outcome exists (Banks, 1995; McKelvey & Schofield, 1987; Saari, 1997). Recall: the core is the set of majority undominated outcomes:

$$x \in C \Leftrightarrow xMy, \forall y \in W$$

where M is the weak majority preference relation; i.e., xMy means either that x beats y with a majority of votes or that there is a tie between the two. These core results are based on the assumption that the ideal points, distance measures, and, more generally, utility functions of the individuals are well-defined in the policy space. The results characterize the number of issues for which a "stable core"[1] does, or does not, exist (Saari, 1997; see Saari, 2004 for an exposition) and explain how the majority rule performs when the core is empty (McKelvey, 1976, McKelvey & Schofield, 1987).

The definition of a core ensures that if the spatial representation of voter ideal points has a core and if, say, X is in the core, then the Ostrogorski paradox cannot occur. Even stronger:

Theorem 2 *If an Ostrogorski or Anscombe paradox occurs, then any spatial representation of the voters' ideal points has an empty majority vote core.*

Proof For **p** to be a majority vote core point over k issues, a majority of the voters' ideal points cannot be on either side of *any* hyperplane passing through **p**. (If a majority were on one side, there is a point on the normal to the plane at **p** that this majority prefers.) With an odd number of voters, this condition requires **p** to coincide with some voter's ideal point; with an even number of voters, either **p** coincides with some voter's ideal point, or each ideal point has a companion ideal point where their connecting line contains **p** forming a "Plott configuration" (Plott, 1967).[2] (For instance, four ideal points define a quadrilateral; the core point is the intersection of the two diagonals).

Because of Theorem 1, we can assume that $\mathbf{X} = (X_1, \ldots, X_k)$ and $\mathbf{Y} = (Y_1, \ldots, Y_k)$ are points selected to ensure that this is an Ostrogorski paradox where the ideal points for majority party members are closer to $\mathbf{X}$ than $\mathbf{Y}$ and each majority party voter is on the losing side of at least one issue. Suppose **p** coincides with some voter's ideal point. As a majority of the voters have their ideal points closer to $\mathbf{X}$ than to $\mathbf{Y}$, this voter cannot be in the minority; i.e., **p** coincides with the ideal point of a majority party voter. To be a member of the majority party, this voter must agree

---

[1] "Stable" means that if a core does exist, it continues to exist even with any very slight change in preferences. To illustrate instability, a core exists if three ideal points lie on a line in $\mathbb{R}^2$. But this core is unstable because it disappears by ever so slightly moving any point off the line.

[2] If **p** is not at an ideal point with an odd number of voters, any hyperplane passing through **p** and an ideal point must have less than half of the voter ideal points on either side. Slightly perturbing this plane moves the ideal point to one side and creates a plane with a majority on one side. If n is even and **p** is not an ideal point, select a plane passing through **p** than meets no ideal points; i.e., $\frac{n}{2}$ points are on either side. If moving the plane meets one ideal point, but not a companion, slightly change the plane to pass through this ideal point to create a setting with a majority on one side; thus each ideal point is accompanied by a companion on the line passing through **p**. As **p** must be in the convex hull defined by all majority settings of candidates, these companion points must be on opposite sides of **p**.

with **X** over a majority of the issues. The Ostrogorski paradox requires this party to lose a majority of the issues, so this voter is on the losing side of, say, the jth, issue. Pass a hyperplane through **p** that is orthogonal to the jth coordinate axis; i.e., the jth coordinate of this hyperplane agrees with that of the identified voter, so it is closer to X_j than to Y_j. As a majority of the jth coordinates of voter ideal points are closer to Y_j, a majority of the ideal points are on one side of this hyperplane, so **p** cannot be a core point.

The remaining case is where, with an even number of voters, **p** is not at an ideal point. The hyperplane argument shows that for the jth issue, $j = 1, \ldots, k$, a majority of the jth components of the ideal points cannot be larger than, or smaller than, the value of p_j; i.e., p_j is in the median of the jth component of all ideal points. Thus, if Y_j is the winning issue, all ideal points with their jth component on the Y_j side of p_j *and* at least one that is on the X_j side, are in the winning coalition. As **p** lies between each companion pair of ideal points p_j lies between their jth components for each j. Thus, at least one of these ideal points is on the winning side at least half of the time. (If k is odd, this is for a majority of the time.) As each ideal point is in a companion pair, at least half of the ideal points are on the winning side at least half of the time, so an Anscombe or Ostrogorski paradox cannot occur. This completes the proof.   □

So, with an Anscombe paradox, any spatial representation for the voters' ideal points has an empty core. But even if the core fails to exist, an Ostrogorski or Anscombe paradox need not arise. To see this, slightly modify the above numerical example by replacing each 3.2 value with 3.6; while these changes suffice to avoid the Ostrogorski paradox, the core remains empty. (Generically, the majority vote core is empty with three or more issues (Saari, 1997, 2004).) The reason the Ostrogorski paradox need not occur is that the more demanding core concept compares **X** with *all possible* **Y** locations, but Ostrogorski and Anscombe compare **X** only with a fixed **Y**.

Nevertheless, the core and Ostrogorski paradox remain closely intertwined in that whenever the voters' ideal points define an empty majority vote core, points **X** and **Y** can be selected to create an Ostrogorski paradox! To exhibit the ideas, which is a spatial voting extension of Theorem 1, this assertion is illustrated in the next theorem for five voters and two issues; the construction clearly extends to all settings.

Theorem 3 *Whenever five ideal points in $\mathbb{R}^2$ have an empty core, points **X** and **Y** can be selected to create an Ostrogorski paradox.*

Proof Let $\mathcal{P}_C$ be the convex hull (the triangle in Fig. 1) defined by any three ideal points forming a coalition C. This is the coalition's Pareto set because moving any point in $\mathcal{P}_C$ leads to a poorer outcome for at least one coalition member. Moreover, it follows from the triangle inequality that for any **q** not in the triangle, this coalition prefers the point $\tilde{\mathbf{q}}$ that is the closest point in the triangle to **q**. As such, if a core point exists, it must be in $\mathcal{P}_C$. But as the core is empty, the intersection of the 10 possible triangles is empty.

Fig. 1 Core vs. Ostrogorski

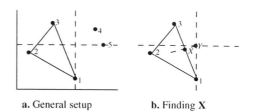

a. General setup   b. Finding **X**

For each issue (axis) find the median of the voters' ideal points; use these points to construct an axis in $\mathbb{R}^2$ (the dashed lines in Fig. 1a). Place **Y** at the center of this axis. Because the core is empty, we can select a triangle that does not include **Y**. Let **X** be the point in this triangle that is closest to **Y**. It follows from the triangle inequality that **X** is closer to each of these three ideal points than is **Y**; i.e., these three ideal points define the majority party.

To ensure that **Y** wins over each issue, it suffices to prove that **X** is in the interior of some quadrant (so that **X** is farther from each median line). If the leg of the selected triangle that is closest to **Y** is not parallel to any axis, then either **X** is an ideal point on the triangle or the point of the intersection of this leg and perpendicular line passing through **Y** (the slanted dashed line in Fig. 1b). In either case, the geometry forces **X** to be in the interior of a quadrant.

If this leg is on, or parallel to some axis, say the vertical one, and if this closest leg is parallel, but not on the axis, then all three points are strictly on the same side of **Y** for some issue, which violates the definition of **Y**. If all three ideal points are on the axis, and as **Y** is not in the triangle, all three ideal points are strictly on the same side of **Y** on this axis, which again violates the condition that **Y** is at the median of each issue. Thus, at least one ideal point is off this axis, and (again, to ensure **Y** is at the median) it must either be on, or on the other side of the remaining axis. Thus this leg is not parallel to any axis; this completes the proof.   □

The Ostrogorski paradox generated by the Fig. 1 example is in Table 5. This example reflects our concern whether a voter should be modeled as preferring a closest point, or in terms of his votes over issues. After all, the choice of **Y**, which is determined by the voters' votes over issues, is uniquely defined. In contrast, there are *five* three-voter coalitions in Fig. 1a satisfying the condition that their Pareto set misses **Y** (coalitions {1, 2, 3}, {2, 3, 4}, {3, 4, 5}, {1, 4, 5}, {1, 2, 5}); these different majorities create an ambiguity in the choice of the "closest point for a majority of the voters" as each coalition defines a different **X** choice ($\mathbf{X}_C$). Even more, it follows from the geometry that there is no Condorcet winner among these five $\mathbf{X}_C$ choices; e.g., all voters in {3, 4, 5} prefer their $\mathbf{X}_{3,4,5}$ choice over the $\mathbf{X}_{1,2,3}$ choice. Instead, these five $\mathbf{X}_C$ define the cycle

$$\mathbf{X}_{1,2,3} \succ \mathbf{X}_{1,4,5} \succ \mathbf{X}_{2,3,4} \succ \mathbf{X}_{3,4,5} \succ \mathbf{X}_{1,2,3} \qquad (1)$$

Table 5 Ostrogorski's
paradox with two issues

Issue	Issue 1	Issue 2	The voter votes for
Voter 1	Y	X	X
Voter 2	X	X	X
Voter 3	X	Y	X
Voter 4	Y	Y	Y
Voter 5	Y	Y	Y
Winner	Y	Y	?

5 Resolving Kelly's Conjecture

The conditions under which Ostrogorski's paradox occurs have been studied by several authors (e.g. Rae & Daudt, 1976; Deb & Kelsey, 1987; Kelly, 1989; Laffond & Lainé, 2000; Laffond & Lainé, 2009; Shelley, 1984). Rae and Daudt establish a connection between Ostrogorski's paradox and cyclic majorities.

To explain, in the Table 1 Ostrogorski setting, X beats Y with a majority vote. Could a third candidate Z enter the race where Z would beat X? Using a nice argument that improves upon the Rae and Daudt observation, Kelly (1989) shows that, yes, such a Z can be found, But, as Kelly also shows, Y would beat Z to create a cycle! Even stronger, Kelly proved for three issues that "every occurrence of the Ostrogorski paradox implies that among the 8 possible candidates there can be no Condorcet winners." In other words, no matter how another candidate Z is selected, she cannot be a Condorcet winner. Kelly conjectured that this "no Condorcet winner" relationship holds for an odd number of issues. This conjecture is captured by the Eq. (1) cycle where each $\mathbf{X}_C$ represents a candidate.

For our purposes, if Kelly's conjecture is true, it would cast doubt on the standard approach where voters select a candidate based on criteria rather than issues. This is because none of the many possible candidates dominates.

Insights about Kelly's conjecture follow from Theorem 2, which asserts that *any* spatial representation of the voters' ideal points with an Ostrogorski or Anscombe paradox must have an empty majority vote core. With an empty core, McKelvey's 1976 chaos theorem applies; namely, for *any* starting and intermediate points, $\mathbf{x}^s$ and $\mathbf{x}^i$, a majority vote agenda $\{\mathbf{x}_i\}$ can be crafted where the first and last terms are $\mathbf{x}^s$ and an intermediate term agrees with $\mathbf{x}^i$. With this agenda, $\mathbf{x}_{i+1}$ beats $\mathbf{x}_i$ for all i; i.e., if the core does not exist, expect to find cycles among candidates and proposals. Thus

> McKelvey's spatial voting result verifies Kelly's conjecture for any number of votes and issues; i.e., in a spatial context, an Ostrogorski or Anscombe paradox ensures that there is no Condorcet winner.

While this observation fully answers Kelly's conjecture in a spatial setting, it does not for the discrete setting. The problem is illustrated with Table 5 where, without having the advantage of using distances, it is not clear whether voters 1 and 3 are indifferent (which is the usual assumption with dichotomous choices), or whether they prefer X or Y. But as the next theorem shows, even with this complication,

Kelly's conjecture is true for *any number* of issues greater than two, not just for odd numbers of them.

Theorem 4 *For any number of issues greater than two, the occurrence of an Ostrogorski or Anscombe paradox means that there cannot be a Condorcet winner.*

Proof To convert preferences over k issues into vertices of a k-dimensional cube $[-1, 1]^k$, for each issue, designate the losing choice by a -1 and the winning choice by a 1; e.g., in Table 1, voter A's preferences become $(-1, -1, 1)$. Thus, for each j, the sum of the jth entries over all voter vectors is positive and the winning portfolio is the cube vertex $\mathbf{y} = (1, 1, \ldots, 1)$. As a candidate's platform is represented by a cube vertex, there are 2^k possible candidates. To compare voter preferences between two candidates, take the difference between the vectors; e.g., if $\mathbf{x} = (-1, -1, \ldots, -1)$ (representing the losing side on each issue), then $\frac{1}{2}(\mathbf{x} - \mathbf{y}) = (-1, -1, \ldots, -1)$. Thus $\frac{1}{2}(\mathbf{x} - \mathbf{y})$ is a normal vector for a plane passing through the cube's center; all voters with vectors (vertices) above this plane prefer $\mathbf{x}$, those below prefer $\mathbf{y}$, and those on the plane are indifferent; i.e., a voter's choice is determined by whether the dot product of $\frac{1}{2}(\mathbf{x} - \mathbf{y})$ with the voter's vector is, respectively, positive, negative, or zero. As each $\frac{1}{2}(\mathbf{x} - \mathbf{y})$ entry is a-1, the dot product with a voter's vector equals the difference between the number of issues for which this voter is on the losing and winning sides; e.g., a voter on the losing side of most issues has a positive value. An Anscombe paradox requires a majority of the voters to be on the losing side a majority of the time, so a majority of the voters prefers $\mathbf{x}$ to $\mathbf{y}$.

We now know that $\mathbf{x}$ is preferred to $\mathbf{y}$; we must show that for any other vertex, say $\mathbf{c}$, a vertex can be found that is preferred to $\mathbf{c}$. Other than $\mathbf{y}$, all vertices (candidate's positions) have at least one "-1" in its vector representation. Select any such candidate, say $\mathbf{c}$, where "-1" is in the jth position. Let $\mathbf{d}$ be the vector that agrees with $\mathbf{c}$ in all components except the jth where it has a $+1$. Thus $\frac{1}{2}(\mathbf{d} - \mathbf{c})$ is the vector with 1 in the jth component and zeros elsewhere; its scalar product with a voter's vector has a positive value (supporting $\mathbf{d}$ over $\mathbf{c}$) for a voter who is on the winning side of the jth issue. Thus the sum of jth components over all voter vectors is the difference between the number of voters preferring $\mathbf{d}$ to $\mathbf{c}$. This sum is positive, so $\mathbf{d}$ is preferred to $\mathbf{c}$. As this holds for any $\mathbf{c}$, the theorem is proved.   □

This argument can be used to fashion all sorts of cycles. The natural idea is that a candidate can improve her standing by assuming the winning side of an issue. What creates the cycle is the peculiar choice of preferences allowing an Anscombe paradox, as reflected by $\mathbf{x} \succ \mathbf{y}$, where a majority of the voters are on the losing side a majority of the times; e.g., for five issues,

$$(-1, -1, -1, -1, -1) \succ (1, 1, 1, 1, 1). \tag{2}$$

A five issue cycle is $(1, 1, 1, 1, 1) \succ (1, 1, 1, 1, -1) \succ (1, 1, 1, -1, -1) \succ 1, 1, -1, -1, -1) \succ (1, -1, -1, -1, -1) \succ (-1, -1, -1, -1, -1) \succ (1, 1, 1, 1, 1)$. To create a cycle involving all 32 candidates, vary the number of voters of different types.

6 Differences Between Dichotomous and Spatial Models

Deb & Kelsey (1987) derive the following necessary and sufficient condition for an Ostrogorski's paradox to occur:

$$kn - 2ny - 2kx - 12xy \geq 0. \tag{3}$$

Here $x = 1$ when n (the number of voters or criteria) is even, and $x = \frac{1}{2}$ when n is odd. Similarly, $y = 1$ when the number k of issues is even and $y = \frac{1}{2}$ when k is odd.

To illustrate, the Table 1 example has $n = 5$ and $k = 3$, so $x = y = \frac{1}{2}$. Substituting into Eq. (3) yields $(3)(5) - 2(5)\frac{1}{2} - 2(3)\frac{1}{2} - 12(\frac{1}{2})(\frac{1}{2}) = 15 - 5 - 3 - 3 = 4 > 0$, which means that an Ostrogorski example can be constructed. Now try to modify this example to create an Ostrogorski example that uses only two issues. Here, $n = 5, k = 2, x = \frac{1}{2}, y = 1$, so Eq. (3), has the negative $(2)(5) - 2(5) - 2(2)\frac{1}{2} - 12(\frac{1}{2})(1) = -2$ value. Thus, the Deb and Kelsey condition ensures that no such two-issue example exists.

But, in seeming contraction with the Deb and Kelsey condition, such two-issue examples do exist! One was constructed in Fig. 1 and Table 5. This conflict between whether such an example does, or does not, exist reflects the difference between dichotomous and spatial voting settings; the former is incapable of handling votes that could be interpreted as being a tie, such as with voters 1 and 3 in Table 5. In a spatial voting context, the more refined distances resolve these difficulties. The purpose of the Deb and Kelsey condition, then, is to identify all settings that suffer this ambiguity.

The following statement converts the Deb and Kelsey condition into a format that is easier to understand. As Corollary 1 shows, the main complexities arise with small number of even issues; this is precisely where problems occur about whether or not a voter's preferences indicate a tie vote.

Corollary 1 *An Ostrogorski paradox can be created in the following situations:*
Suppose both n and k are odd. If $k \geq 3$, then $n \geq 3$.
Suppose n is odd and k is even. If $k = 4$, then $n \geq 5$. Otherwise, $n \geq 3$.
Suppose both n and k are even. If $k = 4$, then $n \geq 10$; if $k = 6$ or 8 then $n \geq 6$; if $k \geq 10$, then $n \geq 4$.

Proof For odd values of k (so $y = \frac{1}{2}$), Eq. (3) assumes the $n \geq 2x + \frac{8x}{k-1}$ form. Thus, for $x = \frac{1}{2}$ (or n odd valed), $n \geq 3$; for $x = 1$ (or n even valued), $n \geq 2 + \frac{8}{k-1}$ and the assertion follows. Similarly, for even values of k (so $y = 1$), Eq. (3) assumes the $n \geq 2x + \frac{16x}{k-2}$ form; the remaining conclusions follow.   □

Notice, *ten voters* are required to create a four-issue Ostrogorski paradox! (see Table 6). But if distances could be used, voters in the majority could use (X, X, Y, Y) preferences that would be closer to X than Y. Without the aid of distances, however, such a preference must be judged as a tie. In turn, this ambiguity requires using preferences of the (X, X, X, Y) type. This change is what increases the number of

Table 6 Ostrogorski's
paradox with four issues

Issue	Issue 1	Issue 2	Issue 3	Issue 4
Voters 1 and 2	Y	X	X	X
Voters 3 and 4	X	Y	X	X
Voters 5 and 6	X	X	Y	X
Voters 7–10	Y	Y	Y	Y
Winner	Y	Y	Y	X

necessary voters from three to ten. Namely, the mysterious nature of Eq. (3) captures those kinds of situations involving ties that arise with small, even numbers of issues. In contrast, the general spatial voting theorem (using the obvious extension of Theorem 3 and Saari (1997) is that

> a spatial voting Ostrogorski paradox always can be created with any generic[3] placement of any odd number (greater or equal to three) of voters' ideal points with two or more issues, and any generic placement of any even number (greater or equal to four) of voter's ideal points with three or more issues.

Because the role of Eq. (3) is to identify which small numbers of voters and issues cause problems about who a voter prefers, there is no reason to believe that larger values of this inequality have any other meaning. Nevertheless, one might wonder whether larger values of this inequality might indicate a larger likelihood of the paradox. Although Kelly's (1989) computer simulations (using an impartial culture assumption) suggest that the paradox's probability increases with voters (or criteria), but decreases with an increase in issues, it is doubtful that Eq. (3) plays a role other than coincidental; likelihood issues must reflect those profile structures that allow the paradox. Our explanation of all such paradoxes sheds light on this and other questions.

7 Relating and Explaining the Paradoxes

Surprisingly, all of the "Yes–No," "X–Y" voting issues described in this article are consequences of the same kinds of profile configurations of voter preferences. As these configurations also explain all paired comparison votes, explanations for paradoxical problems in one setting can be transferred to explain puzzles in others. For instance, as we show next, the structure causing an Ostrogorski paradox is essentially that required to create a Condorcet cycle.

An important source of these problems (Saari & Sieberg, 2001, 2004) is that a voting rule's issue-by-issue outcomes are *not* determined by the actual profile, but rather by a *set of associated profiles*. In a real sense, then, problems arise because the voting rule cannot identify what is the actual profile; instead, the selected conclusion is an appropriate one for the largest subset of profiles in the associated set!

---

[3] Namely, either the ideal points, or an arbitrarily small change in them, will create an example.

To illustrate, the Table 1 outcomes occur because, for the first three voters, each issue has the $X \succ Y$ outcome with a 2:1 vote. Now suppose it is known only that the rule respects anonymity and, for each issue, there is the $X \succ Y$ outcome with a 2:1 vote. Armed with this information and by permuting the names of the voters, the following five profiles constitute all supporting choices; they are indistinguishable to the rule[4]:

1. $(X, X, X), (X, X, X), (Y, Y, Y)$ 2. $(X, X, X), (X, X, Y), (Y, Y, X)$
3. $(X, X, X), (Y, X, X,), (X, Y, Y)$ 4. $(X, X, X), (Y, X, X,), (X, Y, Y)$ (4)
5. $(X, X, Y), (X, Y, X), (Y, X, X)$

For each of the first four choices, the last voter's preferences are closer to Y than to X; only with the fifth – the actual choice – are all three of the voters positioned closer to X than to Y. By adding the remaining two Table 1 voters (who support Y on all issues), it follows from Eq. (4) that for 80% of the possibilities (i.e., where the two Y voters join with each of the first four choices), there is no paradox; Y wins with a majority vote over each issue and Y is the closest point for three of the five voters. Only one choice from this set – the actual profile – creates a conflict.

This example makes it reasonable to believe (as made mathematically precise in Saari (2001)) that the majority vote rule handles the ambiguity about the actual profile by selecting an outcome that is appropriate for *most profiles* within its associated set. Thus this approach provides an appropriate, non-paradoxical answer for a majority of the cases; e.g., for the first four cases, Y *is the winner* with either way of computing. This approach can create a paradoxical conflict only for a minority of settings, such as the Table 1 profile. This explanation – where a rule emphasizes the associated set of profiles rather than the actual one – holds for all of the above paradoxes.

As an illustration of this associated set, the Table 7 profile belongs to the associated set of profiles defined by the Table 2 profile. As Table 7 illustrates the Ostrogorski paradox, it follows that the Table 2 profile, which reflects just the Anscombe paradox, has an Ostrogorski paradox in its associated set.[5] The next question is to identify the configurations of profiles for which the associated set includes the foundation for an Ostrogorski and Anscombe paradox.

The kinds of profiles that cause these paradoxical concerns are identified with a coordinate system developed to analyze n-alternative voting problems (Saari, 2000, 2008). Certain profile coordinate directions are responsible for all possible problems

---

[4] The set associated with a given profile is the set of profiles that is obtained permuting each column in all possible ways.

[5] An Anscombe paradox need not include an Ostrogorski paradox in its associated set. To create an illustrating example, take a strong Ostrogorski paradox with an even number of issues where Y always wins. For the odd numbered issues, exchange the X and Y names to create a strong Anscombe example. The same majority loses over each issue, but as X and Y each win half the issues, no permutation of preferences can create an Ostrogorski paradox. We leave it as an exercise for the reader to determine necessary and sufficient conditions for an Ostrogorski paradox to be in an Anscombe associated set.

Table 7 Connecting
Anscombe and Ostrogorski

Issue	Issue 1	Issue 2	Issue 3
Voter A	X	Y	Y
Voter B	Y	X	Y
Voter C	Y	Y	X
Voter D	X	Y	X
Voter E	X	X	X
Winner	X	Y	X

Fig. 2 Ranking wheel

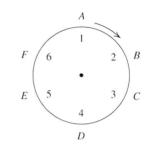

that affect paired comparisons. To construct these profile directions, use the Fig. 2 ranking wheel (Saari, 2000, 2008). Uniformly near the edge of the wheel place the numbers 1 to n; these are the ranks. On the wall, place the names of the alternatives in any specified order. Read off the ranking; in Fig. 2 it is $A \succ B \succ C \succ D \succ E \succ F$. Rotate the wheel so that the ranking number 1 is by the next name and read off the new ranking. Repeat until each candidate has been in first place precisely once. Figure 2 configuration is

$$A \succ B \succ C \succ D \succ E \succ F, \ B \succ C \succ D \succ E \succ F \succ A, \ C \succ D \succ E \succ F \succ A \succ B, \tag{5}$$
$$D \succ E \succ F \succ A \succ B \succ C, \ E \succ F \succ A \succ B \succ C \succ D, \ F \succ A \succ B \succ C \succ D \succ E.$$

Each ranking defines a unique set and each ranking in a set defines the same set, so there are $\frac{n!}{n} = (n-1)!$ distinct sets. These sets are the building blocks for the *Condorcet profile directions*; each Condorcet coordinate combines, in a particular manner, the set defined by a ranking and the set defined by reversal of this ranking. As such, there are $\frac{(n-1)!}{2}$ orthogonal Condorcet profile directions. (Orthogonality follows because each ranking is in one, and only one, Condorcet direction. But, because of a subtle feature caused by profiles that do not affect the outcomes of any voting rules, there are only $\frac{(n-1)(n-2)}{2}$ directions). The theorem (Saari, 2000) is that all paired comparisons problems are due to a profile's components in the Condorcet directions; e.g., if a profile is orthogonal to all Condorcet directions, then no paired comparison difficulties occur.

To see how the Condorcet directions cause non-transitivity problems, notice that the Eq. (5) profile defines the $A \succ B, B \succ C, C \succ D, D \succ E, E \succ F, F \succ A$ cycle where the tally for each pair is 5:1. An important point is that, for any number of alternatives, all non-transitive outcomes and other paired comparison problems are caused by the Condorcet profile directions – including the paradoxes of our interest.

To illustrate, Corollary 1 asserts that a six-issue Ostrogorski paradox can be created with three voters, so the majority has two voters. To create an example, select two alternatives from Eq. (5), say A and B, and relabel them with a Y; denote all other alternatives by X. Now, the first and third Eq. (5) choices become (Y, Y, X, X, X, X), (X, X, X, X, Y, Y). By letting the third voter have all Y's, the majority loses over the first, second, fifth, and sixth issues. An examination of all examples in this article shows that the preferences for the majority always have this structure; e.g., Table 1 has three issues, so the majority party's preferences can be constructed from the $A \succ B \succ C$, $B \succ C \succ A$, $C \succ A \succ B$ Condorcet direction. By replacing C with Y and replacing the names of the other two alternatives with X, the majority party's preferences are (X, X, Y), (X, Y, X), (Y, X, X) of the table.

This connection is not a coincidence. The next theorem asserts that this "renaming" process captures all Ostrogorski and Anscombe paradoxes.

Theorem 5 *For any Ostrogorski or Anscombe paradox, let $\mathcal{L}$ be the set of k issues over which a majority of the voters lose, but where each voter is on the winning side of at least one issue. The preferences of these voters over $\mathcal{L}$ can be identified with components in the Condorcet profile directions for k alternatives.*

The condition that each voter is on the winning side of at least one issue in $\mathcal{L}$ is for convenience. With the Ostrogorski paradox, for instance, each voter must support X on a majority of issues, so he must be on the winning side of at least one issue in $\mathcal{L}$.

Proof The proof reverses the renaming manner used to create the above three-voter, six-issue example. List the k issues in the standard column format with X's and Y's. For the jth column, $j = 1, \ldots, k$, rename the winning and losing issue, respectively, with $A_j \succ A_{j+1}$ and $A_{j+1} \succ A_j$, where A_{k+1} is identified with A_1. The winner for each issue (column) represents the pairwise tally for the particular pair of alternatives, which, by construction, is a cycle.

We must show that each row (voter's preferences) can be identified with a transitive ranking; what provides flexibility is that the renaming construction specifies only paired comparisons of the $\{A_j, A_{j+1}\}$ type. If these rankings of adjacently listed alternatives do not create a cycle, then the remaining pairs can be ranked to create a transitive ranking. The only way a cycle can be created by these k pairs is if this voter is on the winning side of each issue (which is impossible by being from an Anscombe paradox), or on the losing side of each of the k issues, which again is excluded by assumption.

The renaming process creates a set of transitive preferences that causes a cycle, so it follows from Saari (2000, 2008) that the cycle is caused by Condorcet direction components in the profile.   □

Theorem 5 finally establishes what probably has been long suspected; the Ostrogorski and Anscombe paradoxes must be intimately connected with non-transitive paired comparison behavior. An added benefit is how this connection explains our quandary about whether voters' preferences should be described by the closest point, or by issues. Namely, it is shown in Chap. 2 of Saari (2008) how, with the Condorcet profile directions, the pairwise vote drops the assumption that voters have transitive preferences (which then explains phenomena such as Arrow's Impossibility Theorem).

In the context of the Ostrogorski paradox, it means that voting over issues divorces the connection of how a voter relates the issues to a particular party. So, if issues are separate from one another, if they are not connected or related by a voter to determine his support for a party, then the issue-by-issue approach provides the better connection. But if the issues are related, e.g., if they are related in terms of, say, compromises to create a coherent platform, then the selection of the closest point is the appropriate choice. A similar description holds for the voter trying to select a candidate; if individual issues matter more than how their combination characterizes a criterion for a candidate, select the candidate according to issues. But if the combined stance over issues characterize how a candidate should be viewed with respect to specified criteria, then select the candidate whose position is the closest point in issue space.

8 Supermajority Voting

Theorem 5 proves that there is an intimate connection between the profiles that are derived from the ranking wheel construction and the profiles that cause the Ostrogorski paradox. We now use this observation to obtain new results where, rather than being based on the majority vote, the Ostrogorski paradox occurs with a more severe voting rule. To illustrate with the situation where our voter is trying to select between two candidates, he might use a more demanding decision rule whereby he continues to support a status quo favorite candidate (or party) unless its competitor is closer to his position on, say, more than two-thirds of the issues.

Indeed, as reflected by the super majority requirements that many countries impose on certain kinds of legislation to ensure some political stability, the status quo may be preferred unless more than, say, $\frac{3}{5}$ of the electorate prefers its competitor. This behavior is illustrated in Table 8 with 3 issues and 5 voters where the status quo party 1's position is 1 on every issue and the competing party 0's position is 0 on every issue. If each voter votes for 0 unless 1 is closer to his position and if it takes a $\frac{4}{5}$ vote to win on each of the issues, no Ostrogorski's paradox emerges. The lower $\frac{3}{5}$ requirement, however, does admit the paradox. (Comparing this example with the core, if the voting rule requires a winning position to have 3 out of 5 voters, the core is generically empty with three or more issues. The stronger rule requiring 4 of the 5 voters to pass a proposal can have a non-empty core (Saari, 1997)).

Table 8 Ostrogorski's paradox: 0-1 version

Issue	Issue 1	Issue 2	Issue 3
Voter A	1	1	0
Voter B	1	0	1
Voter C	0	1	1
Voter D	0	0	0
Voter E	0	0	0

Wagner (1983, pp. 305–306) shows that an Anscombe's paradox cannot arise if, on average, there is a sufficiently strong support over all winning issues:

> If N individuals cast yes-or-no votes on K proposals then, whatever the decision method employed to determine the outcomes of these proposals, if the average fraction of voters, across all proposals, comprising the prevailing coalitions is at least three-fourths, then the set of voters who disagree with a majority of outcomes cannot comprise a majority.

This assertion is about an *average "yea" vote over all issues*; it does *not* mean (as interpreted by some authors) that an Anscombe paradox can be avoided by using a three-fourths rule. Indeed, by using Theorem 5, we prove (Theorem 6) that such an interpretation is wrong because an Anscombe paradox can occur even with a rule that is just one vote shy of requiring unanimity support.

Definition 1 For integer $n > 2$, let q be an integer satisfying $\frac{n}{2} < q < n$. A "q rule with n voters" is where the winner of a paired comparison must receive q or more votes.

Theorem 6 *Suppose the majority party wants to pass all issues and each party member agrees with most of these issues. For any q rule, even a q rule that is one vote away from unanimity, the majority party can lose over a majority of the issues. Indeed, the majority party may never win a single issue.*

To indicate why this extreme result does not contradict Wagner's assertion, the example developed below has $2m - 1$ voters and issues. As the maximum number of "Yes" votes is $m + (m - 1)(2m - 1)$, the average of "Yes" votes is bounded by $\frac{m+(m-1)(2m-1)}{(2m-1)^2}$, which is slightly over a half and far from Wagner's three-fourths threshold.

Proof For $n = 2m - 1$, let the majority party have m voters, a minority party have $m - 1$ voters, and $q = n - 1 = 2m - 2$. For the first m of the $2m - 1$ issues, use the ranking wheel from Theorem 5 to create the set of m rankings

$$A_1 \succ A_2 \succ \cdots \succ A_m, \ldots \quad \ldots, A_m \succ A_1 \succ \ldots A_{m-1}. \tag{6}$$

To assign voters' choices in the majority party, create an $m \times m$ array as in Eq. (7). The kth row represents Eq. (6)'s kth ranking; the jth column represents A_j. The jth column, kth row entry is the ranking wheel position of A_j in the kth ranking. Thus, the first row's entries are $1, 2, \ldots, m$. For the second row, because A_2 is top ranked and A_1 bottom ranked, the entries are $m, 1, 2, 3, \ldots, m - 1$.

$$
\begin{array}{cccc}
A_1 & A_2 & \ldots & A_m \\
\hline
1 & 2 & \ldots & m \\
m & 1 & \ldots & m-1 \\
\ldots & \ldots & \ldots & \ldots \\
2 & 3 & \ldots & 1
\end{array}
\tag{7}
$$

The ranking wheel places each alternative in each position precisely once, so a specified integer in Eq. (7) is in precisely one row for each column and one column for each row.

To create an example that proves the theorem, treat each A_j as an issue to be decided by a "Yes–No" vote. Select an integer between 1 and m, perhaps 1. Everywhere this integer appears, replace it with a "Yes." Replace all other integers with a "No." For each of these m issues, have each of the $m - 1$ minority party members vote "No." Over each of these m issues, the "No" side wins with a $q = (m - 1) + (m - 1) = 2m - 2 = n - 1$ vote, which is one vote shy of unanimity.

For the remaining $m - 1$ issues, have each majority party member vote 'Yes." (As required, each majority party member agrees with the party a majority of the time.) Over these issues, assign either a "Yes" or "No" to each minority member. If "No" is assigned to each minority party member for each issue, the outcome is not decided (as neither side obtains the quota). Thus the majority party cannot win anything.

To create an illustrating example where the majority party barely loses on a $q = n - s$ rule, select s different integers from Eq. (7), and, in each column, rename each of these integers with "Yes"; rename the other integers in this column with "No." The rest of the construction is the same. However, to ensure that each voter of the majority party supports a majority of the party's issues, notice that over the m issues, he supports s of them, and disagrees on $m - s$. So, instead of adding $m - 1$ additional issues, it suffices to add l issues, where $l + s > m - s$, or to add only $m - 2s$ new issues. $\square$

As Theorem 5 asserts, all illustrating examples must be of this kind. To see why with a different argument, suppose a different example can be created for the $q = n - 1$ case. Each column has precisely one "Yes," and, as the same voter cannot vote "Yes" on more than one of the first m issues (to be a member of the majority party), each row has precisely one "Yes." In the first row, a sole "Yes" appears in some column; name that column A_1. In general, in the jth row, the number 1 appears in only one column; call that column A_j. The result, then, is a permutation of the columns of the original example. In other words, all examples are permutations of the columns and/or rows for Eq. (7).

As Theorem 6 makes no mention about the number of issues, it is reasonable to question whether this kind of super-majority voting result requires a certain number of issues. While we have not explored the answer for "Yea–Nay" voting, the answer is known for spatial voting. According to results in Saari (1997, 2004) about the existence of a core,

expect that a spatial voting q-rule Ostrogorski paradox can be created with at least $2q - n + 1$ issues.

So, it is possible to create a spatial voting example with a $q = 5, n = 7$ rule with at least $2(5) - 7 + 1 = 4$ issues where the ideal points do not define a three-dimensional subspace. The qualifying "expect" is added only because the existence of a core for $\frac{q}{n} > \frac{3}{4}$ has a complicated structure; for precise values, consult (Saari, 1997, 2004).

The Ostrogorski paradox requires each member of the majority party to support the party over a majority of the issues. To introduce a new, related class of paradoxes, we impose stronger conditions on what issues the majority party can adopt. Namely, it is reasonable to require a certain percentage of majority party members to support a specific proposal before it can be put forth by the party.

Definition 2 For α satisfying $0 < \alpha < 1$, a party provides α-support for an issue if at least the fraction α of party voters are in favor of it.

The choice of α may require αn to be just one vote, at least 25% support, a majority vote, or maybe even a particular supermajority. To simplify the arithmetic, replace the q rule with a $\beta > \frac{1}{2}$ rule requiring, for passage, that a rule has at least the fraction β support. (With n voters, the associated q-rule is $q = \beta n$). The new issue is to determine when Ostrogorski problems can plague the majority party if it has α-support over all issues and the passage of a measure requires a β rule.

Theorem 7 *Suppose a majority party has α-support over all issues. The party can lose in a majority of the issues if the β rule satisfies*

$$\frac{2 - \alpha}{2} \geq \beta. \tag{8}$$

If the majority party has a sufficient number of members, then Eq. (8) is a necessary and sufficient condition for this kind of Ostrogorski paradox.

So if α represents the majority (i.e., $\alpha > \frac{1}{2}$), then the specified problem occurs only for $\beta < \frac{3}{4}$ rules, which captures the spirit of Warner's result and strengthens it by imposing a particular rule (i.e., *both* $\alpha > \frac{1}{2}, \beta \geq \frac{3}{4}$). If a β rule determines outcomes *and* a majority party's support for an issue (so $\alpha = \beta$), the problem can exist for any $\beta < \frac{2}{3}$; a way to avoid the problem is to require $\alpha = \beta = \frac{2}{3}$.

Proof Again let $n = 2m - 1$; the most extreme case is with m voters in the majority party and $m - 1$ in the minority. As αm of voters from the majority party must vote "Yes," the number of possible "No" votes is $(1 - \alpha)m$ from the majority party and $m - 1$ from the minority for a total of $2m - 1 - \alpha m$ votes. This negative vote is victorious if and only if the β rule satisfies $2m - 1 - \alpha m \geq \beta(2m - 1)$, or

$$\beta \leq \frac{2m - 1 - \alpha m}{2m - 1} = \frac{2 - \alpha - \frac{1}{m}}{2 - \frac{1}{m}}.$$

As the derivative of $\frac{2-\alpha-x}{2-x}$ is positive, the function has its minimum value at $x = 0$, so $\frac{2-\alpha-\frac{1}{m}}{2-\frac{1}{m}} > \frac{2-\alpha}{2}$. So, the "No" side is assured victory if $\frac{2-\alpha}{2} \geq \beta$; i.e., examples exist where the majority party loses over each of these issues. For $\beta > \frac{2-\alpha}{2}$, there exist m values where $\beta > \frac{2m-1-\alpha n}{2m-1} = \frac{2-\alpha-\frac{1}{m}}{2-\frac{1}{m}}$, so the "Nea" side will not win.

Now add $m - 1$ other issues where each majority member votes "Yes." (This allows each member to support the majority party on a majority of the issues. But as each majority party voter already supports the party on αm issues, just add k new issues where the k value ensures that each majority party voter supports the party a majority of the time; i.e., a k value where $\frac{\alpha m + k}{m + k} > \frac{1}{2}$, or any k satisfying $k \geq m - 2\alpha m + 1$). To illustrate with the $q = n - 1$ rule of Theorem 6, $\alpha m = 1$, so the smallest $k = m - 2 + 1 = m - 1$). The majority party loses over each of the first m issues – a majority of the outcomes.

To prove that such scenarios exist, select a positive integer value for m so that αm is an integer; e.g., m is a multiple of the denominator of α. In the $m \times m$ array given by Eq. (7) select αm integers; replace each with a "Yes." Rename all other integers with a "No." Each issue (each column) has $(1 - \alpha)m$ "No" votes and each of these voters (each row) has "Yes" on αm of the issues. The rest of the construction follows the above.   □

9 Simpson's Paradox: A Shadow Over the Sure-Thing Principle

A basic theme of the last two sections is how the troubling paradoxes arise because, rather than the actual profile, the decision rule uses information from an associated set of profiles; the selected outcome is a "reasonable one" for most profiles in this set. The idea appears to extend to other paradoxical settings. For instance, Ostrogorski's paradox is only one of several compound majority paradoxes (e.g., see Nurmi, 1999); e.g., Simpson's paradox can arise when dealing with standard problems such as rates of improvement, recovery, growth etc. To quote Blyth (1972); for two general methods to generate these paradoxes (see Saari, 1990, 2001):

> ... Savage's sure-thing principle ("if you would definitely prefer g to f, either knowing that event C obtained, or knowing that C did not obtain, then you definitely prefer g to f.") is not applicable to alternatives f and g that involve sequential operations.

Consider the following example where f and g may represent incentive schemes or experimental treatments where the fractions indicate success, efficiency, or quality (e.g. frequencies of exceeding some performance threshold):

	g	f
Event C	1/3	1/4
Event non-C	2/3	1/2

While this example suggests that g is, indeed, preferable to f, the following table, which raises doubt about this assertion, is consistent with the above data:

	g	f
Event C	40 out of 120	10 out of 40
Event non-C	10 out of 15	45 out of 90
Total	50 out of 135	55 out of 130

The "total" row now makes it natural to accept the opposite conclusion that f, with its higher aggregate success rate, is preferred to g.

Formally, this paradox can be expressed as follows (Blyth, 1972): Let A, B and C denote three distinct properties or predicates, such as being a victorious candidate, being a big campaign spender, supporting certain legislation, living in a given neighborhood etc. Let A', B' and C' denote the absence of A, B and C, respectively, and let

$$P(A|B) < P(A|B');\qquad (9)$$

i.e., A is more likely to occur if B does not. Simpson's paradox occurs whenever inequalities 10 and 11 also hold.

$$P(A|B \cap C) \geq P(A|B' \cap C)\qquad (10)$$
$$P(A|B \cap C') \geq P(A|B' \cap C')\qquad (11)$$

More dramatic examples are where these inequalities (Eqs. 9, 10, and 11) involve larger margins. Blyth gives the conditions for extreme forms of Simpson's paradox. To outline of his conditions consider the comparing the effectiveness of using an innovative, rather than the standard approach to combat racial prejudice.

A = property of creating a more positive attitude about racial issues,
B = property of using the innovative educational approach,
B' = property of using the standard approach
C = educational program in district 1
C' = educational program in district 2.

The paradox associated with Eqs. (9), (10), and (11), then, is that, in general, the standard approach provides better results than the innovative approach (Eq. 9), but in both districts the innovative approach is more successful (Eqs. 10 and 11)! An extreme case of the paradox (which resembles the q-rules of the last section) is where Eqs. (10) and (11) are replaced with Eqs. (12) and (13) for a choice of $\gamma \geq 1$.

$$P(A|B \cap C) \geq \gamma P(A|B' \cap C)\qquad (12)$$
$$P(A|B \cap C') \geq \gamma P(A|B' \cap C')\qquad (13)$$

As shown below, we could have $P(A|B) \approx 0$ and $P(A|B') \approx \frac{1}{\gamma}$, so with $\gamma = 1$, we have $P(A|B) \approx 0$ and $P(A|B') \approx 1$, which suggests an extremely strong level of success with the standard approach, yet this association is reversed in each district!

To understand Simpson's paradox, consider the decomposition of the conditional probabilities $P(A|B)$ and $P(A|B')$ in terms of C and C':

$$P(A|B) = [P(C|B)]P(A|B \cap C) + [P(C'|B)]P(A|B \cap C') \qquad (14)$$

and

$$P(A|B') = [P(C|B')]P(A|B' \cap C) + [P(C'|B')]P(A|B' \cap C') \qquad (15)$$

As Eqs. (14) and (15) prove, $P(A|B)$ is a weighted average of $P(A|B \cap C)$ and $P(A|B \cap C')$; $P(A|B')$ is a weighted average of $P(A|B' \cap C)$ and $P(A|B' \cap C')$. The $P(C|B)$ and $P(C'|B)$ weights, then, represent the proportions of people from the two districts who are exposed to a particular educational approach. By varying these weights; all sorts of paradoxical examples follow. Some conditions, of course, avoid the problem; e.g., if B, B', C and C' are independent, no paradox could ensue.

If the ease with which instances of Simpson's paradox can be constructed is an indicator of how often they may occur, then Saari's (1990) procedure suggests that they may be very common. To illustrate with the above example, let x and y represent, respectively, the likelihood of the innovative and standard approach having success. As both values range over [0, 1], the (x, y) outcome lies in the square $S = [0, 1] \times [0, 1] \subset \mathbb{R}^2$. For instance, $(0, 0) \in S$ represents where both approaches have a zero success rate, while $(\frac{1}{2}, \frac{1}{3}) \in S$ is where the innovative approach enjoys a 50% success rate, but the standard one has only a 33.3% chance of success.

To create a Simpson's paradox choose two points, $X = (X_x, X_y) \in S$ and $Y = (Y_x, Y_y) \in S$, each of which is located below the $x = y$ line connecting (0,0) and (1,1); i.e., these points indicate that the innovative approach had a greater likelihood of success. These points represent what happens in each district; i.e., expressions (10) and (11).

Form a rectangle by drawing lines parallel to the coordinate axes through X and Y as in Fig. 3. A portion, denoted by A, of the area of the rectangle spanned by X and Y is located above the $x = y$ line; for these points, the standard approach is more likely to succeed. To create a paradox, select any $z = (z_x, z_y) \in A$ to represent the Eq. (9) outcome of what happens in general.

Fig. 3 Generating Simpson's
paradoxes

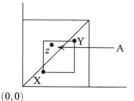

(0,0)

We now must select appropriate weights for the weighted averages of Eqs. (14) and (15). This is immediate; let

$$s = \frac{(z_x - X_x)}{(Y_x - X_x)}, \quad t = \frac{(z_y - X_y)}{(Y_y - X_y)}.$$

To explain these values by using the s term, notice that $X_x \leq z_x \leq Y_x$, so s merely determines the z_x location from X_x with the $X_x - Y_x$ scale. In other words,

$$z_x = sX_x + (1 - s)Y_x, \quad z_y = tX_y + (1 - t)Y_y. \tag{16}$$

Thus the s, $1-s$, t, $1-t$ values determine the appropriate Eqs. (10) and (11) weights.

This construction holds for any $z \in A$, so, in spirit, Simpson's paradox is related to the Ostrogorski paradox. This is because A is in the associated set of Eq. (9) outcomes defined by specific Eqs. (10) and (11) values. Again, notice that most outcomes (i.e., those *not* in A) are consistent.

By selecting different z values, we can explore the extremes of Simpson's paradox. For instance, choosing X near $(0, 0)$ and Y near $(1, 1)$, both below the $x = y$ line, represents nearly zero success for either approach in one district, but near certainty in the other. The z value now can be selected almost anywhere in S, meaning that anything can happen in general. Selecting z near the $(0, 1)$ vertex, for instance, corresponds to the earlier $P(A|B) \approx 0$ and $P(A|B') \approx 1$ assertion.

These are the basic outlines of Saari's procedure. It is based on geometrical properties of cones and, in particular, on the fact that cones can be used to represent a wide class of decision situations (for details, see Saari, 1990, 2001). Saari's paradox machine[6] begins with two sub-population distributions located on the same side of the $x = y$ line. The closer the points representing those sub-populations are to $(0, 0)$ and $(1, 1)$, respectively, the more freedom one has in generating instances of Simpson's paradox. Comparing this procedure with what was said above in the context of Blyth's analysis of Simpson's paradox, we see that moving the selected point z is tantamount to manipulating the weights $P(C|B)$, $P(C|B')$, $P(C'|B)$ and $P(C'|B')$ weights.

10 Conclusion

By establishing a connection between standard concerns in spatial voting, such as the existence of a core and the McKelvey "chaos theorem," new insights are obtained about long standing issues coming from the Ostrogorski and Anscombe paradoxes. We learn, for instance, that these paradoxes are discrete versions of the chaos theorem, that Kelly's conjecture about no Condorcet winner not only is true, but it is a version of the spatial chaos theorem, that while the Ostrogorski paradox is a special case of an Anscombe paradox, with the same ideal points a change in

---

[6] Nurmi coined this term in a previous paper.

the parties converts an Anscombe paradox into an Ostrogorski one, and that the reason a standard Ostrogorski paradox cannot arise with certain number of issues is primarily a matter of asserting whether a (X, Y) outcome represents a tie or support for a particular party.

Many distinguished researchers in this area have noted connections between Condorcet's voting problems and Ostrogorski's paradoxes (a partial list includes Bezembinder & Van Acker, 1985; Kelly, 1989; Laffond & Lainé 2006; Laffond & Lainé, 2009); we create a stronger connection by proving that they are essentially equivalent; with a renaming of the alternatives, one setting can be converted into the other. Then, by establishing that both the Condorcet cycles and Ostrogorski's problems arise with precisely the same kind of profile configurations, it becomes possible to relate q-rule voting problems to supermajority Ostrogorski voting paradoxes showing, for instance, that the Ostrogorski difficulty can occur even with a rule that is one vote shy of unanimity.

A reason the identified profiles cause these problems is that with issue-by-issue voting, or paired comparisons, the outcomes are not determined by a particular profile, but rather by an associated set of profiles. The actual outcome is one that proves to be reasonable for a wide selection of profiles in this associated set, but it can be paradoxical for the actual profile. This problem is not restricted to paired comparisons and Ostrogorski; as shown, it also identifies the cause of the statistical Simpson paradox.

What makes the Ostrogorski problem intriguing is its path dependency characteristic where reaching a decision in one manner differs from the conclusion that can occur when making the decision in a different manner. Which is correct? By understanding the kinds of profiles totally responsible for the Ostrogorski paradox, we now know that the pairwise vote strips away any connections – intended or otherwise – among the issues! (See Chap. 2 of Saari (2008) for a more complete discussion.) If the issues are, indeed, divorced from one another, the issue by issue approach probably is better. But should the issues be related, such as where the issue of health care may be modified to adjust the concerns from the issue of governmental deficits, then issue-by-issue voting defeats the purpose. In other words, pragmatics dictates that in the real world, Ostrogorski's paradox most surely will be with us for a long time.

Acknowledgments The authors are listed in alphabetical order. We are grateful to Marlies Ahlert and John Roemer for suggestions on an earlier draft. Saari's research was supported by NSF grant DMS-0631362 and Nurmi's by the Academy of Finland.

References

Anscombe, G. E. M. (1976). On frustration of the majority by fulfillment of the majority's will. *Analysis, 36,* 161–168.

Banks, J. (1995). Singularity theory and core existence in the spatial model. *Journal of Mathematical Economics, 24,* 523–536.

Bezembinder, Th., & Van Acker, P. (1985). The Ostrogorski paradox and its relation to nontransitive choice. *Journal of Mathematical Sociology, 11,* 131–158.

Blyth, C. (1972). On Simpson's paradox and the sure-thing principle. *Journal of the American Statistical Association, 67,* 364–366.

Deb, R., & Kelsey, D. (1987). On constructing a generalized Ostrogorski paradox: Necessary and sufficient conditions. *Mathematical Social Sciences, 14,* 161–174.

Downs, A. (1957). *An economic theory of democracy.* New York: Harper and Row.

Kelly, J. (1989). The Ostrogorski paradox. *Social Choice and Welfare, 6,* 71–76.

Laffond, G., & Lainé, J. (2000). Representation in majority tournaments. *Mathematical Social Sciences, 39,* 35–53.

Laffond, G., & Lainé, J. (2006). Single-switch preferences and the Ostrogorski paradox. *Mathematical Social Sciences, 52,* 49–66.

Laffond, G., & Lainé, J. (2009). Condorcet choice and the Ostrogorski paradox. *Social Choice and Welfare, 32*: 317–333.

Laver, M., & Shepsle, K. (1996). *Making and breaking of governments.* New York: Cambridge University Press.

May, K. (1946). The aggregation problem for a one-industry model. *Econometrica, 14,* 285–298.

May, K. (1947). Technological change and aggregation. *Econometrica, 15,* 51–63.

May, K. (1954). Intransitivity, utility, and the aggregation of preference patterns. *Econometrica, 22,* 1–13.

McKelvey, R. (1976). Intransitivities in multidimensional voting models and some implications for agenda control. *Journal of Economic Theory, 12,* 472–482.

McKelvey, R., & Schofield, N. (1987). Generalized symmetry conditions at a core point. *Econometrica, 55,* 923–933.

Napel, S., & Widgrén, M. (2004). Power measurement as sensitivity analysis: A unified approach. *Journal of Theoretical Politics, 16,* 517–538.

Napel, S., & Widgrén, M. (2006). The inter-institutional distribution of power in EU codecision. *Social Choice and Welfare, 27,* 129–154.

Nermuth, M. (1992). Two-stage discrete aggregation: The Ostrogorski paradox and related phenomena. *Social Choice and Welfare, 9,* 99–116.

Nurmi, H. (1999). *Voting paradoxes and how to deal with them.* Berlin-Heidelberg-New York: Springer.

Nurmi, H., & Meskanen, T. (2000). Voting paradoxes and MCDM. *Group Decision and Negotiation, 9,* 293–313.

Ostrogorski, M. (1970). *Democracy and the organization of political parties* (Vols. I and II). New York: Haskell House Publishers. (Original: Ostrogorski, M. (1902). *La démocratie et l'organisation des partis politiques.* Paris: Calmann-Levy.)

Plott, C. (1967). A notion of equilibrium and its possibility under majority rule. *American Economic Review, 9,* 787–806.

Rae, D., & Daudt, H. (1976). The Ostrogorski paradox: A peculiarity of compound majority decision. *European Journal of Political Research, 4,* 391–398.

Saari, D. (1990). Consistency of decision processes. *Annals of Operations Research, 23,* 103–137.

Saari, D. (1997). The generic existence of a core for q-rules. *Economic Theory, 9,* 219–260.

Saari, D. (2000). Mathematical structure of voting paradoxes 1: Pairwise vote. *Economic Theory, 15,* 1–53.

Saari, D. (2001). *Decisions and elections.* New York: Cambridge University Press.

Saari, D. (2004). Geometry of stable and chaotic discussion. *American Mathematical Monthly, 111,* 377–393.

Saari, D. (2008). *Disposing dictators, demystifying voting paradoxes.* New York, Cambridge University Press.

Saari, D., & Asay, G. (2010). Finessing a point: Augmenting the core. *Social Choice and Welfare, 34,* 121–143.

Saari, D., & Sieberg, K. (2001). The sum of the parts can violate the whole. *American Political Science Review, 95,* 415–433.

Saari, D., & Sieberg, K. (2004). Are partwise comparisons reliable? *Research in Engineering Design, 15,* 62–71.

Shelley, F. (1984). Notes on Ostrogorski's paradox. *Theory and Decision, 17,* 267–273.

Shepsle, K., & Weingast, B. (1987). Why are congressional committees powerful? *American Political Science Review, 81,* 935–945.

Simpson, E. (1951). The interpretation of interaction in contingency tables. *Journal of Royal Statistical Society B, 13,* 238–241.

Steunenberg, B., Schmidtchen, D., & Koboldt, Ch. (1999). Strategic power in the European Union. *Journal of Theoretical Politics, 11,* 339–366.

Wagner, C. (1983). Anscombe's Paradox and the rule of three-fourths. *Theory and Decision, 15,* 303–308.

Maximal Domains for Maskin Monotone Pareto Optimal and Anonymous Choice Rules

Olivier Bochet and Ton Storcken

1 Introduction

In reaction to the well-known impossibility results of Arrow, Gibbard and Satterthwaite domain restrictions were studied in the seventies and eighties of last century. Also the strategy-proofness condition was questioned to be too strong. The slightly weaker Maskin monotonicity property essential for implementation of choice rules in Nash equilibria appears, however, to reveal the same kind of impossibilities (see Muller and Satterthwaite, 1977). Here we will study domain restrictions which allow for Pareto optimal, Maskin monotone and anonymous choice rules.

In the work of Kalai and Muller (1977), Kalai and Ritz (1980), Ritz (1983, 1985) so called domain restrictions are studied. Each agent has a domain of admissible preferences. As this domain does not need to be the set of all possible preferences it is called a restricted domain. In this type of work restrictions for two types of collective decision rules are considered. (1) Pareto optimal, non-dictatorial or anonymous and independent of irrelevant alternatives welfare functions assigning to every combination of admissible preferences a collective preference and (2) Pareto optimal, non-dictatorial or anonymous and strategy-proof choice rules assigning to every combination of admissible preferences a collective choice. In characterizing and looking for admissible domains which are inclusion maximal it is possible to reveal the impact of the well-known impossibility results of Arrow (1978), Gibbard (1973) and Satterthwaite (1975). It is important to note that here we do not focus on a specific collective decision rule, but rather on collective decision rules satisfying some minimal requirements. Also it is assumed that agents may choose their preferences independently and in such this type of study differs from that of for instant Sen and Pattanaik (1969), where combinations of individual preferences arerestricted such that pairwise majority is acyclic or from Puppe and Tasnádi (2007)

O. Bochet (✉)
Department of Economics, University of Bern, 3012 Bern, Switzerland
e-mail: olivier.bochet@vwi.unibe.ch

A. Van Deemen, A. Rusinowska (eds.), *Collective Decision Making,*
Theory and Decision Library C 43, DOI 10.1007/978-3-642-02865-6_4,
© Springer-Verlag Berlin Heidelberg 2010

where domain restrictions are considered such that the Borda score rule is well-behaved. For a general discussion on restricted domains we would like to refer to Gaertner (2002).

A dual approach in revealing the impact of these impossibility theorems is by restricting as much as possible the set of admissible preferences such that the remaining domains prevail the impossibility, that is on such domain Pareto optimal and for instance strategy-proof choice rules are dictatorial. Aswal, Chatterji, and Sen (2003) and Storcken (1984) belong to this strand of literature.

The work presented here belongs to the former mentioned literature on the "positive" approach. Here we avoid the Muller and Satterthwaite (1977) impossibility, stating that on an unrestricted domain Pareto optimal and Maskin monotone choice rules are dictatorial, instead of those of Arrow (1978), Gibbard (1973) and Satterthwaite (1975). So, the domain of admissible preferences is restricted such that it allows for Pareto optimal, Maskin monotone and non-dictatorial choice rules. On the one hand to simplify the study and on the other hand to investigate what type of restriction is needed if these restrictions were independently imposed on agents, we restrict precisely the set of one agent, say agent i. In that way this work adds to the line started with Bochet and Storcken (2005). As in their work the collective choice rule admissible by such the domains is strongly hierarchical and therefore almost dictatorial. Here we replace non-dictatorship by anonymity to guarantee for more equal decisiveness power among the agents. In case of at least three agents it appears that the domain of admissible preferences of agent i is as follows. There is an alternative, say x, such that in all the admissible preferences of agent i this alternative x is either ordered best or second best. So, at most one alternative different from x can be ordered better than x by that agent i. This yields that at all combinations of individual preferences there is at most one alternative which is unanimously preferred to x. Consequently the *imputation* rule with status quo x is single valued and therefore a choice rule. On unrestricted domains the imputation rule is a choice correspondence, i.e. it assigns non-empty sets of alternatives to combinations of individual preferences. It chooses all alternatives which are Pareto optimal and at least as good as x for all agents. It is Maskin monotone, see also Moulin (1980). Moreover, on these restricted domains it appears to be the only type of rule that is simultaneously Pareto optimal, anonymous and Maskin monotone.

The two agents case is more technical than the three or more agents case. It appears that agent i may order alternative x strictly worse than second best and rules different from the imputation rule are possible on domains which allow for Pareto optimal, Maskin monotone and anonymous choice rules. We therefore treat this case separately.

The paper is structured as follows. In Sect. 2 the model and basic notions are defined, Sect. 3 deals with the three or more agents case and Sect. 4 with the two agents case. Section 5 tries to shed some light on the robustness of the results presented here.

2 Maskin Monotonic Choice Rules

Consider choice rules for a set N of $n \geqslant 2$ agents over a set of m alternatives say A. Although in general we assume that there are at least three alternatives sometimes also cases with one or two alternatives are considered. Only linear orderings, i.e. (strongly) complete, anti-symmetric and transitive relations on A are admissible as individual preferences. Let $L(A)$ denote the set of all linear orderings on A. Let R be a linear ordering on A and let x and y be two different alternatives in A. Then $x... = R$ denotes that x is the best alternative at R, $...x...y... = R$ denotes that x is strictly preferred to y at R, $...xy... = R$ denotes that x is strictly preferred to y at R and there is no alternative in between this preference and $x...y = R$ denotes that x is best alternative and y is worst alternative at R. So, $xy... = R$ means that alternative x is best and y is second best at R. Furthermore, the upper and lower contour of alternative x at R is defined as $up(x, R) = \{a \in A : a = x$ or $...a...x... = R\}$ and $low(x, R) = \{a \in A : a = x$ or $...x...a... = R\}$ respectively. As the set of individual preferences might be restricted let $\emptyset \neq L^{\{i\}} \subseteq L(A)$ be the domain of individual preferences of agent $i \in N$ and $L^N = \{p : p$ is a function from N to $L(A)$ such that $p(i) \in L^{\{i\}}$ for all $i \in N\}$ be the set of profiles. A choice rule K is a function from L^N to A. For coalitions M, a non-empty subset of agents, profile p is said to be a M-deviation of profile q if $p|_{N-M} = q|_{N-M}$. For an alternative x in A and agent i in N let $L_x^{\{i\}} = \{R \in L^{\{i\}} : x... = R\}$ be the set of preferences of agent i with best alternative x. Furthermore, for alternatives y let $L_x^M \times L_y^{N-M}$ denote the set of profiles p in $L(A)^N$ such that $p(i) \in L_x^{\{i\}}$ for all $i \in M$ and $p(j) \in L_y^{\{j\}}$ for all $j \in N - M$. In case $M = N$, we consider $L_x^M \times L_y^{N-M} = L_x^N$.

Next we rephrase some well-known conditions for choice rules in the notation at hand. Choice rule K is *anonymous* if in view of the domain restriction it is symmetrical in every possible argument change. That is for all profiles p in L^N and all permutations σ on N such that $p \circ \sigma$ is in L^N we have that $K(p) = K(p \circ \sigma)$. It is *Pareto-optimal* if for all alternatives x and y, with $x \neq y$, and all profiles p, such that for all agents i in N $...x...y... = p(i)$, $K(p) \neq y$. In that case we say that x *Pareto-dominates* y *at profile* p. Furthermore, let $Par(p)$ denote the set of all alternatives that are not Pareto-dominated at profile p. The choice rule K is *unanimous* if $K(p) = a$ for all alternatives a and profiles $p \in L_a^N$. It is *strategy-proof* if for all agents i and all profiles p and q, such that q is a $\{i\}$-deviation of p, we have $K(q) \in low(K(p), p(i))$. The choice rule K is *intermediate strategy-proof* if for all coalitions M of N and for all profiles p in L^N, such that there is a preference R in $L(A)$ with $p(i) = R$ for all $i \in M$, and all M-deviations q of p in L^N it holds that $K(q) \in low(K(p), R)$. Choice rule K is *Maskin-monotone* if $K(p) = K(q)$ for all profiles p and q such that $low(K(p), p(i)) \subseteq low(K(p), q(i))$ for all agents i.

A set of profiles L^N is called a *Maskin possibility domain* if there exist choice rules K from L^N to A which are simultaneous anonymous, Maskin-monotone and Pareto-optimal. Such a domain is called a *maximal Maskin possibility domain* if in addition there is no possibility domain say $\widehat{L}^N$ such that $L^N \subsetneq \widehat{L}^N$. Similarly we define a *strategy-proof possibility domains* and *maximal strategy-proof possibility domains*.

The following results logically link several of the conditions defined above and is well-known.

Theorem 1 *Let $K : L^N \to A$ be a choice rule. If choice rule K is strategy-proof, then it is Maskin-monotone.*

3 Three or More Agents

In this section we study maximal domains for Pareto-optimal, Maskin-monotone and anonymous choice rules where only the set of preferences of agent 1 is restricted. So, let $L^{\{i\}} = L(A)$ for all agents $i \geqslant 2$ and let K be such a choice rule from maximal Maskin possibility domain L^N to A. The domain of agent 1 is supposed to be *rich*: for all $x \in R$ there are $R \in L^1 \cap L_x$. It means that all alternatives can be ordered best by agent 1. Although for this section the same results hold without this condition it simplifies the case of two agents and it simplifies the proofs in this section. The main results are derived through the following notion of decisiveness. Let M be a coalition and (x, y) an ordered pair of alternatives, possibly $x = y$. We say that M is decisive on (x, y) at K, notation $(x, y) \in D_K(M)$, if $K(p) = x$ for all profiles $p \in L_x^M \times L_y^{N-M}$.

Lemma 1 *Let $n \geqslant 2$. Let M be a coalition, $p \in L^N$ and $x, y \in A$, with $x \neq y$. Let $K(p) = x$, $xy... = p(i)$ for all $i \in M$ and $y... = p(i)$ for all $i \in N - M$. Then $(x, y) \in D_K(M)$.*

Proof Let $q \in L_x^M \times L_y^{N-M}$. It is sufficient to prove that $K(q) = x$. Let $r \in L^N$ be an $(N - M)$-deviation of p and an M-deviation of q. Now Pareto optimality implies that $K(r) \in \{x, y\}$. If $K(r) = y$, then Maskin-monotonicity would imply the contradiction $K(p) = y$. So, $K(r) = x$. But then Maskin-monotonicity implies $K(q) = x$.

Lemma 2 *Let $n \geqslant 2$. Let M be a coalition such that $1 \notin M$, $x, y \in A$, with $x \neq y$. Let $K(p) = x$. Then $(x, y) \in D_K(M)$.*

Proof Consider M-deviation q of p such that $xy... = q(i)$ for all i in M. Then Maskin-monotonicity implies that $K(q) = K(p) = x$. So, the result follows from Lemma 1.

Lemma 3 *Let $n \geqslant 2$. Let $x, y \in A$, with $x \neq y$, and $(x, y) \in D_K(\{1\})$. Then $\{x\} \times A \subseteq D_K(\{1\})$.*

Proof There exist $p \in L^N$ such that $x... = p(1)$ and $y...x = p(i)$ for $i \in N - \{1\}$. As $(x, y) \in D_K(\{1\})$ we have by Maskin-monotonicity that $K(q) = x$ for all alternatives a and all profiles q such that $x... = q(1)$ and $a... = q(i)$ for all agents $i \geqslant 2$. But this means that $\{x\} \times A \subseteq D_K(\{1\})$.

Lemma 4 *Let $n \geqslant 2$. Let $x \in A$ such that $\{x\} \times A \subseteq D_K(\{1\})$. Then for all agents $i \in N - \{1\}$ we have $\{x\} \times A \subseteq D_K(\{i\})$.*

Proof Let $y \in A$ with $x \neq y$ and let $i \geqslant 2$. It is sufficient to prove that $(x, y) \in D_K(\{i\})$. Consider profile p such that $p \in L_x^{\{1\}} \times L_y^{N-\{1\}}$. Because of $(x, y) \in D_K(\{1\})$ it follows that $K(p) = x$. Now by anonymity it follows that $K(p) = K(p \circ \sigma)$ where σ is the permutation on N such that $\sigma(1) = i$, $\sigma(i) = 1$ and $\sigma(k) = k$ for all $k \in N - \{1, i\}$. But as $p \circ \sigma \in L_x^{\{i\}} \times L_y^{N-\{i\}}$ it follows by Lemma 2 that $(x, y) \in D_K(\{i\})$.

Let a be an alternative. Domain L^N is said to be an *a-at least second best* domain whenever $L^{\{1\}} = \{R \in L(A) :$ There are alternatives $b \in A - \{a\}$ such that $a... = R$ or $ba... = R\}$. So, at such domains at each preference of agent 1 alternative a is either best or second best. Clearly in case of a two alternatives set with $L^{\{1\}} = L(A)$ the domain L^N is an a-at least second best domain. Note that at every profile p in an a-at least second best domain $a \in \text{Par}(p)$ or $\text{Par}(p)$ is a singleton. So, we can define the following imputative choice rule K_a which is defined for an arbitrary profile p as follows: $K_a(p) = a$ if $a \in \text{Par}(p)$ else $K_a(p)$ is the alternative that Pareto-dominates a at p. Clearly K_a is well-defined Pareto-optimal and anonymous. It is straightforward and therefore left to the reader to proof that it is strategy-proof. The following Lemma shows that whenever L^N is a maximal possibility domain for $n \geqslant 3$ and $L_a^M \times L_b^{N-M} \neq \emptyset$, with $(a, b) \in D_K(\{1\})$ for some alternatives $a \neq b$, then L^N is an a-at least second best domain and $K = K_a$.

Lemma 5 *Let $n \geqslant 2$. Let $(a, b) \in D_K(\{1\})$ for some alternatives $a \neq b$.*

1. *Let profile p be such that $p(i) \in L_a^{\{i\}}$ for some agent i. Then $K(p) = a$.*
2. *Let q be a profile. Then $K(q) \in \cap\{up(a, q(i)) : i \geqslant 2\}$.*

Proof By Lemma's 3 and 4 it follows that $\{a\} \times A \subseteq D_K(\{1\})$ and $\{a\} \times A \subseteq D_K(\{i\})$ for all agents $i \in N - \{1\}$.

(Proof of statement 1) Suppose $i = 1$. Consider $b \in A - \{a\}$ and a $N - \{1\}$-deviation q of p such that $q(j) = b...a$ for $j \geqslant 2$. Now because of $\{a\} \times A \subseteq D_K(\{1\})$ it follows that $K(q) = a$. So, by Maskin-monotonicity it follows that $K(p) = a$.

Suppose $i \geqslant 2$ and $p(1) \in L_b^{\{1\}}$ for some $b \in A$. Consider $N - \{1, i\}$-deviation q of p such that $q(j) = b...a$ for $j \geqslant 2$ and $j \neq i$. Now because of $\{a\} \times A \subseteq D_K(\{i\})$ it follows that $K(q) = a$. So, by Maskin-monotonicity it follows that $K(p) = a$. This proves 1.

(Proof of statement 2) To the contrary suppose that $...a...K(p)... = p(i)$ for some agent $i \geqslant 2$. Then Maskin-monotonicity implies $K(q) = K(p)$ where q is an $\{i\}$-deviation of p such that $aK(p)... = q(i)$. But as $K(p) \neq a$. we have a contradiction with statement 1 which concludes the proof of this statement.

Lemma 6 *Let $n \geqslant 3$. Let $L_a^{\{1\}} \times L_b^{N-\{1\}} \neq \emptyset$, with $(a, b) \in D_K(\{1\})$ for some alternatives $a \neq b$. Then L^N is an a-at least second best domain and $K = K_a$.*

Proof Suppose that there are alternatives $b, c \in A - \{a\}$ with $b \neq c$ such that for some $R \in L^{\{1\}}$ we have $b...c...a... = R$. Consider profile q such that $q(1) = R$, $bca... = q(2)$ and $cba... = q(j)$ for all $j \geqslant 3$. Next consider $\{2\}$-deviation r of q defined by $r(2) = bac...$ and $\{3\}$-deviation v of q defined by $v(3) = cab...$. By statement 2 of Lemma 5 and Pareto optimality it follows that $K(r) = b$ and $K(v) = c$. But Maskin-monotonicity then implies from $K(r) = b$ that $K(q) = b$ and from $K(v) = c$ that $K(q) = c$. This contradiction proofs that L^N is a subset of an a-at least second best domain. Maximality of L^N now implies that it is an a-at least second best domain.

In order to prove that $K = K_a$ consider p a profile. In view of Pareto-optimality it is sufficient to prove that $K(p) \in \cap\{up(a, p(i)) : i \in N\}$. To the contrary suppose that $...a...K(p)... = p(1)$. By Lemma 5 we have that $...K(p)...a... = p(i)$ for all $i \geqslant 2$. Consider now profile q such that $aK(p)... = q(1)$ and $K(p)a... = q(i)$ for all $i \geqslant 2$. Then Maskin-monotonicity implies that $K(p) = K(q)$. This however contradicts $\{a\} \times A \subseteq D_K(\{1\})$. So, $K(p) \in \cap\{up(a, p(i)) : i \in N\}$ and $K = K_a$.

Remark 1 The following Theorem is based on the result of Gibbard (1973) and Satterthwaite (1975) which states that a strategy-proof choice rule F from a unrestricted domain L^N, with $n \geq 2$, to a set of alternatives A such that $F(L^N)$ contains at least three alternatives is dictatorial on these, which means that F is not anonymous.

Theorem 2 *Let $n \geqslant 3$ and $m \geqslant 3$. Let $L^{\{i\}} = L(A)$ for $i \geqslant 2$. Then L^N is a maximal Maskin possibility domain if and only if there are alternatives a such that L^N is an a-at least second best domain. Furthermore, if K is an anonymous, Pareto-optimal and strategy-proof choice rule on a maximal possibility domain, then there is an alternative a such that $K = K_a$.*

Proof (Only-if-part and Furthermore part) Let K be an anonymous, Pareto-optimal and Maskin monotone choice rule on a maximal possibility domain L^N. By Lemma 6 we are done if for some alternative $a \in A$ and $b \in A$ with $(a, b) \in D_K(\{1\})$ and $a \neq b$. So, suppose that for all $(a, b) \in A \times (A - \{a\})$ we have that $(a, b) \notin D_K(\{1\})$. We will prove the following. There is a $y \in A$ such that for all $x \in A$ we have that $L_x^{\{1\}} \subseteq \{R \in L(A) : xy... = R\}$. This of course contradicts the maximality of domain L^N and completes the proof of this part. Let $x_1, x_2 \in A$ with $x_1 \neq x_2$. It is sufficient to prove that there is a $y \in A$ such that $L_{x_i}^{\{1\}} \subseteq \{R \in L(A) : x_i y... = R\}$ for $i \in \{1, 2\}$. For $i \in \{1, 2\}$ let $R_i \in L_{x_i}^{\{1\}}$ and consider $K_i = K|_{\{R_i\} \times L^{N-\{1\}}}$. Clearly for $i \in \{1, 2\}$ we have that K_i is Maskin-monotone. Because the domain of K_i is actually unrestricted it follows that K_i is anonymous and strategy-proof. So by the result of Gibbard Satterthwaite implies that $\#K_i(L^{N-\{1\}}) \leqslant 2$. Note that because of unanimity for $i \in \{1, 2\}$ we have that $x_i \in K_i(L^{N-\{1\}})$. Furthermore, Maskin-monotonicity and the assumption on $D_K(\{1\})$ imply that $\#K_i(L^{N-\{1\}}) = 2$. Say $K_i(L^{N-\{1\}}) = \{x_i, y_i\}$, with $x_i \neq y_i$ for $i \in \{1, 2\}$.

Next we prove for $i \in \{1, 2\}$ that $x_i y_i... = R_i$. Without loss of generalization let $i = 1$. To the contrary let $x_1 z...y_1... = R_1$. Consider $p \in L^N$ such that $p(1) = R_1$ and $z...x_1 = p(i)$ for all agents $i \geqslant 2$. Because of Pareto-optimality of K it follows that $K(p) \in \{x_1, z\}$. Because of $K_1(L^{N-\{1\}}) = \{x_1, y_1\}$ it follows that $K(p) = x_1$ but then by Lemma 1 we have the contradiction $(x_1, z) \in B \times (A - \{x_1\})$ and $(x_1, z) \in D_K(\{1\})$.

Now we prove that $y_1 = y_2$. Consider $q \in L^N$ such that $q(1) = R_1$ and $q(2) = R_2$. Because of $K_1(L^{N-\{1\}}) = \{x_1, y_1\}$ it follows that $K(q) \in \{x_1, y_1\}$. By anonymity and $K_2(L^{N-\{1\}}) = \{x_2, y_2\}$ it follows that $K(q) \in \{x_2, y_2\}$. As $x_1 \neq x_2$ it follows that $y_2 = x_1$, $y_1 = x_2$ or $y_1 = y_2$. First we show that $y_2 \neq x_1$. To the contrary suppose that $y_2 = x_1$. Consider the profiles v and w defined such that $v(1) = R_1$, $w(1) = R_2$ and $v(i) = w(i) = y_1...x_2$ for $i \in N - \{1\}$. Then by Lemma 1 and the assumptions on $D_K(\{1\})$ it follows that $K(v) = y_1$. Because of the assumptions on $D_K(\{1\})$ it follows with Maskin-monotonicity that $K(w) \neq x_2$. So, as $K_2(L^{N-\{1\}}) = \{x_2, y_2\}$ it follows that $K(w) = y_2 = x_1$. But then K is not Maskin-monotone going from profile w to v. This contradiction implies that $y_2 \neq x_1$. Similarly we have that $y_1 \neq x_2$. Hence, $y_1 = y_2$ which is the desired result.

(If-part) Follows easily.

Corollary 1 *Let* $n \geqslant 3$ *and* $m \geqslant 3$. *Let* $L^{\{i\}} = L(A)$ *for* $i \geqslant 2$. *Then* L^N *is a maximal strategy-proof possibility domain if and only if there are alternatives a such that* L^N *is an a-at least second best domain. Furthermore, if K is an anonymous, Pareto-optimal and strategy-proof choice rule on a maximal possibility domain, then there is an alternative a such that* $K = K_a$.

4 Two Agents and Maskin Monotonicity

In this section we study the special case of two agents. It appears that other domains than at least second best domains allow for possibility results as well. In the three agent case it appears that agent 1 has some decisive power over an alternative which later appears to be the status quo x of the three or more agents case. Anonymity implies that this decisiveness is also present for every other agent i. It is straightforward to deduce that at any combination of individual preferences the outcome is in the intersection of the upper contours of x at these preferences. In case of three agents consider profile p such that $yzx... = p(2)$ and $zyx... = p(3)$. We have that the outcome is among y and z if both are in the upper contour set of agent's 1 preference. At a profile q where agent's 2 preference has changed to $yx... = q(2)$ and all the other agents have kept their same preference as at p, however, the outcome would be y. This because it is the only alternative in the upper contours of x at the preferences of profile q. Maskin monotonicity implies then that y is the outcome at the former combination. But similarly we may deduce that this outcome is z by changing the role of z and y and agent 2 and 3. This contradiction shows that x is never ordered less than second best by agent 1. In the deduction of this contradiction the presence of three agents is essential. Therefore in the two agents case alternative x is not necessarily ordered at least second best.

Let K be a Pareto-optimal, Maskin monotone and anonymous choice rules on domain L^N, where $N = \{1, 2\}$. First we prove that the set of decisive pairs of agent 2 is transitive and antisymmetric on B.

Lemma 7 $D_K(\{2\})$ *is transitive and antisymmetric, i.e. for* $x, y \in A$ *with* $x \neq y$*, if* $(x, y) \in D_K(\{2\})$*, then* $(y, x) \notin D_K(\{2\})$*.*

Proof (Proof of transitivity) Let $(x, y), (y, z) \in D_K(\{2\})$. It is sufficient to prove $(x, z) \in D_K(\{2\})$. Without loss of generality suppose x, y and z are three different alternatives. Consider profiles p, q and r such that $p(1) = r(1) \in L_c^{\{1\}}$, $xyz... = p(2) = q(2)$, $r(2) = yz...$ and $q(1) \in L_y^{\{1\}}$. In view of Lemma 2 it is sufficient to prove that $K(p) = x$. Now by Pareto-optimality we have $K(p) \in \{x, y, z\}$. Because of $(y, z) \in D_K(\{2\})$ it follows that $K(r) = y$. So, by Maskin-monotonicity we have that $K(p) \neq z$. Because of $(x, y) \in D_K(\{2\})$ it follows that $K(q) = x$. So, by Maskin-monotonicity we have that $K(p) \neq y$. Hence, we have the desired result $K(p) = x$.

(Proof of antisymmetry) This follows immediately because K is anonymous.

The following Lemma shows that decisiveness spreads over upper contours.

Lemma 8 *Let* x, y *and* z *be different alternatives and* R *a preference in* $L^{\{1\}}$ *such that* $y...z.....x... = R$*. Let* $(x, y) \in D_K(\{2\})$*. Then* $(z, y) \in D_K(\{2\})$*.*

Proof Let $q \in L^N$ such that $q(1) = R$ and $zy... = q(i)$ for all $i \in N - \{1\}$. By Lemma 2 it is sufficient to prove that $K(q) = z$. Consider p and r two $(N - \{1\})$-deviations of q such that $xzy... = p(i)$ and $zxy... = r(i)$ for all $i \in N - \{1\}$. Because of $(x, y) \in D(N - \{1\})$ it follows that $K(p) = x$. Pareto-optimality implies that $K(r) \in \{y, z\}$. If $K(r) = y$, then Maskin-monotonicity would yield the contradiction $K(p) = y$. So, $K(r) = z$ and Maskin-monotonicity implies $K(q) = z$.

The following Theorem characterizes maximal Maskin possibility domains.

Theorem 3 *Let* $N = \{1, 2\}$*. Then* L^N *is a maximal Maskin possibility domain if and only if there is an alternative* a *and for all* x, $y \in A$ *there exist subsets* Y_x *and* Y_y *of* A *and alternatives* $m_{\{x,y\}} \in Y_x \cap Y_y$ *such that*

1. $Y_a = \{a\}$, $x, a \in Y_x$ *and if* $y \in Y_x - \{x\}$*, then* $Y_y \subseteq Y_x - \{x\}$*;*
2. $L^{\{1\}} = V$ *where* $V = \{R \in L(A) : \text{if } R \in L_x^{\{1\}} \text{ then } up(a, R) = Y_x \text{ and } Y_x \cap Y_y \subseteq low(m_{\{x,y\}}, R) \text{ for all alternatives } y\}$*.*

Proof (Proof of the only-if-part) Let L^N be a maximal Maskin possibility domain and K a Pareto-optimal Maskin monotone and anonymous choice rule from L^N to A. For alternatives x in A and $R_x \in L_x^1$ define $Y_{R_x} = \{b \in A : b = K(p) \text{ where } p(1) = R_x\}$. Now if $b \in Y_{R_x}$, then Maskin monotonicity and Lemma 2 imply that $(b, x) \in D_K(\{2\})$. By the definition of decisiveness we have the reverse that if $(b, x) \in D_K(\{2\})$, then $b \in Y_{R_x}$. So, $Y_{R_x} = \{b \in A : (b, x) \in D_K(\{2\})\}$. As the left hand side of the equation is independent of the actual $R_x \in L_x^1$ we may conclude that $Y_{R_x} = Y_{R'_x}$ for all $R_x, R'_x \in L_x^1$. Therefore we may define $Y_x = Y_{R_x}$ for some $R_x \in L_x^1$.

Next we prove that $K(p) = \text{best}(p(2)|_{Y_{\text{best}(p(1))}})$. To the contrary let $p(1) \in L_x^1$, $y \in Y_x$ and $...y...K(p)... = p(2)$. Consider $\{2\}$-deviation q of p such that $yK(p)... = q(2)$. Maskin monotonicity implies $K(p) = K(q)$, but the findings on Y_x yields the contradiction that $K(q) = y$.

Considering $p \in L^N$ such that $p(1) = R_x \in L_x^1$ and $p(2) \in L_y^1$ and anonymity yields $\text{best}(p(2)|_{Y_x}) = \text{best}(p(1)|_{Y_y})$. So, there are $m_{\{x,y\}} \in Y_x \cap Y_y$ such that for all $R_x \in L_x^1$ and all $z \in Y_x \cap Y_y$ we have that $(m_{\{x,y\}}, z) \in R_x$. For $y \in Y_x - \{x\}$ Lemma 7 implies that $Y_y \subseteq Y_x - \{x\}$. In view of Lemma 8 we may assume for all $R_x \in L_x^1$ that $Y_x \times (A - Y_x) \subseteq R_x$.

Next we prove the existence of such an alternative a. Let $b \in A$ and $R_b \in L_b^{\{1\}}$. As $Y_x \times (A - Y_x) \subseteq R_x$, there is an alternative a such that $up(a, R_b) = Y_b$. As $a \in Y_b$ it follows that $Y_a \subseteq Y_b$. Hence $Y_a = Y_a \cap Y_b$. Because of $a \in Y_a = Y_a \cap Y_b \subseteq \text{low}(m_{\{a,b\}}, R_a)$ for some $R_a \in L_a^{\{1\}}$ it follows that $m_{\{a,b\}} = a$. Now by $Y_a \cap Y_b \subseteq \text{low}(m_{\{a,b\}}, R_b)$ and the definition of a it follows that $Y_a = \{a\}$. So, for all $R_x \in L_x^{\{1\}}$ for some $x \in A$ there are a_{R_x} with $up(a_{R_x}, R_x) = Y_x$ and $Y_{a_{R_x}} = \{a_{R_x}\}$. However, as for all x and y in A we have $m_{\{x,y\}} \in Y_x \cap Y_y \neq \emptyset$. It follows that for all x and y in A we have that $a_{R_x} = a_{R_y}$. So, there is an alternative a such that $Y_a = \{a\}$, for all $x \in A$ and all $R \in L_x^{\{1\}}$ we have $a \in Y_x$ and $up(a, R) = Y_x$.

All in all we have now that $L^1 \subseteq V$. Maximality of the domain and the if-part imply that $L^1 = V$.

(Proof of the if-part) Define choice rule K for an arbitrary profiles p as follows

$$K(p) = \text{best}(p(2)|_{Y_{\text{best}(p(1))}}).$$

First we prove that K is Pareto optimal, anonymous and Maskin monotone.

To prove Pareto optimality let $...x...y... = p(1)$ and $...x...y... = p(2)$. To prove $y \neq K(p)$. This is the case if $y \notin Y_{\text{best}(p(1))}$. Therefore suppose that $y \in Y_{\text{best}(p(1))}$. Because of $...x...y... = p(1)$ and $L^{\{1\}} = V$ it follows that $x \in Y_{\text{best}(p(1))}$. So, $y \neq K(p)$ because of $y \neq \text{best}(p(2)|_{Y_{\text{best}(p(1))}})$.

Anonymity follows straightforwardly because of $L^{\{1\}} = V$.

In order to prove Maskin monotonicity let p and q be two profiles such that $\text{low}(K(p), p(i)) \subseteq \text{low}(K(p), q(i))$ for all $i \in N$. To prove that $K(p) = K(q)$. As $\text{low}(K(p), p(1)) \subseteq \text{low}(K(p), q(1))$ it follows that $a \in \text{low}(K(p), p(1)) \cap \text{low}(K(p), q(1))$. Therewith, $K(p) \in Y_{\text{best}(q(1))} \subseteq Y_{\text{best}(p(1))}$ which yields that $K(p) = \text{best}(p(2)|_{Y_{\text{best}(p(1))}})$ implies that $K(p) = \text{best}(p(2)|_{Y_{\text{best}(q(1))}})$. Now because of $\text{low}(K(p), p(2)) \subseteq \text{low}(K(p), q(2))$ we may conclude that $K(p) = \text{best}(q(2)|_{Y_{\text{best}(q(1))}})$.

Next we prove that the domain is maximal. Let $\widehat{L}^N$ be a Maskin possibility domain such that $L^N \subseteq \widehat{L}^N$. It is sufficient to prove that $L^N = \widehat{L}^N$. Because of the finite setting we may assume that $\widehat{L}^N$ is a maximal Maskin possibility domain. So for the only-if-part it follows that there is an alternative $\widehat{a}$ and for all $x, y \in A$ there exist subsets $\widehat{Y}_x$ and $\widehat{Y}_y$ of A and alternatives $\widehat{m}_{\{x,y\}} \in \widehat{Y}_x \cap \widehat{Y}_y$ such that

1. $\widehat{Y}_{\widehat{a}} = \{\widehat{a}\}$, $x, \widehat{a} \in \widehat{Y}_x$ and if $y \in \widehat{Y}_x - \{x\}$, then $\widehat{Y}_y \subseteq \widehat{Y}_x - \{x\}$;

2. $\widehat{L}^{\{1\}} = \widehat{V}$ where $\widehat{V} = \{R \in L(A) : \text{if } R \in L_x^{\{1\}} \text{ then } up(\widehat{a}, R) = \widehat{Y}_x$ and $\widehat{Y}_x \cap \widehat{Y}_y \subseteq low(\widehat{m}_{\{x,y\}}, R)$ for all alternatives $y\}$.

Now by the assumption $L^{\{1\}} = V$ we have that $L_a^{\{1\}} = L_a$. This and $L^{\{1\}} \subseteq \widehat{L}^{\{1\}}$ implies subsequently $a = \widehat{a}$, $Y_x = \widehat{Y}_x$ for all x in A, $V = \widehat{V}$, and $m_{\{x,y\}} = \widehat{m}_{\{x,y\}}$ for all x and y. So, $L^N = \widehat{L}^N$.

Example 1 Taking $Y_x = \{x, a\}$ and $m_{\{x,a\}} = a$ for all alternatives x yields an a-at least second best domain. Clearly $K_a(p) = best(p(2)|_{Y_{best(p(1))}})$.

Next we show that in the two agents case (maximal) Maskin possibility domains can be different from at least second best domains.

Example 2 Let $A = \{a, b_1, b_2, b_3, b_4, c\}$ and take $L^{\{1\}} = \{R \in L :$

$$R = a... \text{ or}$$
$$R = ca... \text{ or}$$
$$R = b_i ca... \text{for some } i \in \{1, 2, 3, 4\}\}.$$

Think of a as the status quo, b_1 up to b_4 as four mutely exclusive changes of the status quo and c as a compromise of all these b_i's. Now the domain restriction reflexes the situation that agent 1 is a strong supporter of either the status quo, the compromise or one of these changes b_i. Taking $Y_{b_i} = \{b_i, c, a\}$ for $i \in \{1, 2, 3, 4\}$, $Y_c = \{c, a\}$, $Y_a = \{a\}$, $m_{\{b_i, b_j\}} = m_{\{b_i, c\}} = c$ and $m_{\{b_i, a\}} = a$ for $i, j \in \{1, 2, 3, 4\}$ with $i \neq j$, and $m_{\{a, c\}} = a$ yields by Theorem 3 that L^N is a maximal Maskin possibility domain. Clearly it is not an at least second best domain.

5 Conclusion

Theorem 2 and Corollary 1 characterize the maximal Maskin and strategy-proof possibility domain respectively in case there are at least three agents of which precisely for one agent's set of preferences is restricted. The maximal domain is an a-at least second best domain. Theorem 3 covers the case for maximal Maskin possibility domains in case there are two agents only of which precisely one agent's set of preferences is restricted. The admissible choice rules can loosely speaking be interpreted as follows. Agent 1 offers a set of alternatives which are at least as good as the status quo a. Now $N - \{1\}$ unanimously decides on this set. In order to have this unanimous decision unambiguously in case of more than two agents the set offered by agent 1 can contain at most one alternative different from the status quo a. This yields an a-at least second best domain. As now agent 1 offers at most two alternative overall this type of rule is an imputation rule with status quo. The case of two agents allows for a little more freedom. Now agent 1 may offer more than two alternatives as can be seen in Example 2. To guarantee Maskin monotonicity he can only offer subsets of these which coincide with the worst among what is offered and to guarantee anonymity there is always a unique best in the intersection of two sets that can be offered. This clarifies the conditions in Theorem 3. We further like to point out that the at least second best condition and those in Theorem 3 prevent in these domains two alternatives different from alternative a are connected in the sense of Aswal et al. (2003). This shows that their impossibility result is not applicable to the domains discussed here.

Although contrary to the result of Bochet and Storcken (2005) the rules that are admissible on these domains ad hand are by definition anonymous they lack neutrality. At the end of this section we want to point out that trading off a part of anonymity with neutrality may yield an impossibility. We show that there do not exist domains at which the set of admissible preferences of precisely one agent is restricted which allow for Maskin monotone, Pareto- optimal choice rules that have the absolute majority property. This property incorporates both a principle of anonymity and neutrality yet it demands for that only at special situation. Therefore it does not guarantee neither of the two conditions in full strength. Let choice rule K from L^N to A *respects absolute majority* if $K(p) = a$ for all profiles p such that $\#\{i \in N : \text{best}(p(i)) = a\} > \frac{n}{2}$. Or as a matter of speech in the setting at hand anonymity cannot be substituted by absolute majority.

Theorem 4 *Let* $n \geqslant 3$. *Let* $L^{\{i\}} = L(A)$ *for* $i \geqslant 2$. *Then there do not exist choice rules* K *from* L^N *to* A *which are simultaneously Pareto-optimal, Maskin monotone and respects absolute majorities.*

Proof Let K be a Pareto-optimal and Maskin monotone choice rule from L^N to A which in addition satisfies absolute majorities. For $R \in L^{\{1\}}$ consider choice rule K_R from $L^{N-\{1\}}$ to A defined for all $p \in L^{N-\{1\}}$ by $K_R(p) = K(q)$ where $q|_{N-\{1\}} = p$ and $q(1) = R$. Clearly because $n \geqslant 3$ and K respects absolute majorities it follows that K_R is unanimous. Also because K is Maskin monotone K_R is so. So, it follows by Muller Satterthwaite that K_R is dictatorial with dictator say $i_R > 1$. Now consider profile $r \in L^N$ such that $r(i) = R$ for $i \in N - \{i_R\}$ and $r(i_R) = R'$ where best $(R) \neq \text{best}(R')$. Because K respects absolute majority $K(r) = \text{best}(R)$ and because K_R is dictatorial with dictator i_R it follows that $K(r) = \text{best}(R')$ a clear contradiction.

References

Arrow, K. J. (1978). *Social choice and individual values* (19th ed.). New Haven, CT: Yale University Press.

Aswal, N., Chatterji, S., & Sen, A. (2003). Dictatorial domains. *Economic Theory, 22*, 45–62.

Bochet, O., & Storcken, T. (2005). *Maximal domains for strategy-proof or Maskin monotonic choice rules*. Meteor Working Paper, Maastricht University.

Gaertner, W. (2002). Restricted domains. In: K. J. Arrow, A. K. Sen, & K. Suzumura (Eds.), *Handbook of social choice and welfare* (Vol. 1, Chap. 3, pp. 131–170). Amsterdam: Elsevier.

Gibbard, A. (1973). Manipulation of voting schemes: A general result. *Econometrica, 41*, 587–601.

Kalai, E., & Muller, E. (1977). Characterization of domains admitting nondictatorial social welfare functions and nonmanipulable voting procedures. *Journal of Economic Theory, 16*, 457–469.

Kalai, E., & Ritz, Z. (1980). Characterization of the private alternatives domains admitting Arrow social welfare functions. *Journal of Economic Theory, 22*, 23–36.

Moulin, H. (1980). *The strategy of social choice*. Amsterdam: North Holland.

Muller, E., & Satterthwaite, M. A. (1977). The equivalence of strong positive association and strategy-proofness. *Journal of Economic Theory, 14*, 412–418.

Puppe, C., & Tasnádi, A. (2007). Nash implementable domains for the Borda count. *Social Choice and Welfare, 31*, 367–392.

Ritz, Z. (1983). Restricted domains, Arrow social welfare functions an noncorruptable and nonmanipulable social choice correspondences: The case of private alternatives. *Mathematical Social Sciences, 4*, 155–179.

Ritz, Z. (1985). Restricted domains, arrow social welfare functions an noncorruptable and nonmanipulable social choice correspondences: The case of private and public alternatives. *Journal of Economic Theory, 35*, 1–18.

Satterthwaite, M. A. (1975). Strategy-proofness and Arrow's conditions: Existence and correspondence theorem for voting procedures and social welfare functions. *Journal of Economic Theory, 10*, 187–217.

Sen, A. K., & Pattanaik, P. K. (1969). Necessary and sufficient conditions for rational choice under majority decision. *Journal of Economic Theory, 1*, 178–202.

Storcken, T. (1984). Arrow's impossibility theorem on restricted domains. *Methods of Operations Research, 50*, 83–98.

Extremal Restriction, Condorcet Sets, and Majority Decision Making

Adrian Van Deemen and M. Elena Saiz

1 Introduction

The domain condition of extremal restriction (ER) plays an important role in the theory of majority decision making. In its precise form, the condition states that if someone strictly prefers alternative x to alternative y and alternative y to alternative z, then anyone who strictly prefers z to x must strictly prefer z to y and y to x (Sen & Pattanaik, 1969, also cf. Sen, 1970, 1986). Sen & Pattanaik (1969, Theorem XI) prove ER to be both sufficient and necessary for transitivity of majority decision making and thus for the existence of a majority winner. The absence of a majority winner for a set of individual preferences is usually called a Condorcet paradox. ER belongs to the class of domain restrictions that forbid the occurrence of this paradox. However, ER guarantees more, namely the transitivity of the majority relation. For solid and concise studies of the Condorcet paradox, see (Gehrlein, 1983, 2006) and (Nurmi, 1999).

ER is a *qualitative* domain restriction. Such restrictions exclude configurations of individual preference orderings from the domain of majority rule in order to avoid cyclical majority preferences and with that the absence of majority decisions. The research after these domain restrictions has been initiated by Black (1958) and Arrow (1963). Black uses a point representation of alternatives, that is, he presents alternatives as points on the real line. Black shows that if individual preferences satisfy the domain restriction of single-peakedness and if the number of voters is odd, then majority decision will be transitive. One step further is to conceive alternatives as points in a (Euclidian) n-space. This step has lead to several interesting results about the existence of majority equilibrium. The first condition in this respect is pairwise symmetry (Plott, 1967), (i.e., Matthews, 1980). Others are the existence of a median in all directions (Davis, De Groot, Hinich, 1972), and the condition of intermediate preferences (Grandmont, 1979). All these results show the peculiarity of the existence of majority equilibrium in a multi-dimensional space.

A. Van Deemen (✉)

Institute for Management Research, Radboud University, 6500 HK Nijmegen, The Netherlands

e-mail: a.vandeemen@fm.ru.nl

A. Van Deemen, A. Rusinowska (eds.), *Collective Decision Making,*
Theory and Decision Library C 43, DOI 10.1007/978-3-642-02865-6_5,
© Springer-Verlag Berlin Heidelberg 2010

McKelvey (1976) shows the existence of global cycles when a majority equilibrium does not exist. This research line has led to the fascinating field of spatial voting theory (Enelow & Hinich, 1984) and the related theory of spatial voting games (Owen & Shapley, 1989).

Arrow (1963) uses the notion of single-peaked preferences in a different way. He formulates it within a finite combinatorial framework as a condition on triples of alternatives. Within this framework, Arrow formulates a possibility theorem which states that single-peakedness is a sufficient condition for the majority rule to be a social welfare function. Hence, imposing single-peakedness on the domain of the majority rule circumvents the problem of cyclic majority relations and with that the occurrence of the Condorcet paradox. The labeling "qualitative" stems from the fact that the exclusion of preference configurations takes place without referring to numbers or frequencies of voters having a non-excluded preference. In this respect, qualitative domain conditions also differ from the distributional or number-specific conditions (see Sen, 1986) like the condition of cyclically mixed preference profiles (Gaertner, 1979) and the condition of positive net preferences formulated by Feld & Grofman (1986). Also see Regenwetter, Marley, & Grofman (2003), Regenwetter, Grofman, Marley, & Tsetlin (2006).

Since the seminal work of Arrow, several alternative qualitative domain conditions have been formulated, among which single-caved preferences (Inada, 1969), limited agreement (Sen & Pattanaik, 1969) and Sen's value-restricted preferences (Sen, 1966). Extremal restriction was first formulated and studied in Sen & Pattanaik (1969). For review studies of qualitative domain conditions, consider Gaertner (2001), or Sen (1970, 1986). A probabilistic extension of value-restriction is given in Regenwetter et al. (2003, 2006). Qualitative domain conditions also play an important role in multiple criteria decision analysis. A study in this field is Arrow & Raynaud (1986).

ER has a unique place among these conditions since it is, as far as we know, the only combinatorial one which is both sufficient and necessary for transitivity of majority decision making. The Sen-Pattanaik Theorem therefore is not only a remarkable result but also an important marker in the history of the study of combinatorial domain conditions. It announced more or less the end of this research field (Kramer, 1973). However, there are at least two reasons to re-examine ER.

The first and most important reason is that ER is rather intractable. Consequently, and in contrast to e.g. single-peakedness and value restriction, it is difficult to give a clear interpretation of the condition. By showing which parts from the domain of majority decision making are exactly excluded and which parts are included by ER, we make the condition more tractable so that it is easier to find an interpretation. In our view, the question of what ER exactly means is difficult to answer without knowledge of this exclusion-inclusion pattern. The first aim of this paper therefore is to construct this pattern in order to make the condition more tractable and to find an interpretation of ER.

For this pattern construction a combinatorial method is presented and used. This method also can be used to study exclusion-inclusion patterns of other domain restrictions. The origin of this method is Kemeny & Snell (1962). Also see van

Deemen (1997) and Regenwetter et al. (2003, 2006). The method consists in the construction of a planar graph in which the vertices are weak preference orderings. An edge between two vertices is drawn if and only if the set symmetric difference of the two orderings represented by the vertices contains exactly one element. In this paper we zoom in on ER by means of this method. As used here, the method will result in a detailed exclusion-inclusion pattern of ER that exactly shows when a set of voter preference satisfies or violates the restriction.

The second reason to study ER concerns the necessity part of the Sen-Pattanaik Theorem. According to the necessity definition used by Sen and Pattanaik, if a set of rankings or preference orderings violates ER, then there must be assignments of these preference orderings to numbers of criteria such that majority rule yields an intransitive relation. The main point hereby is that zero-assignments – i.e. assignments of some preference ordering to no individual or criterion at all (cf. Sen & Pattanaik, 1969, especially footnote 5) – are allowed. However, bringing in preferences into the analysis which no individual or criterion bears, seems to be in contradiction with the essence of social choice theory and also of multiple criteria decision analysis in which only criteria will be selected by the decision maker which are "pertinent ones for the decision (Arrow & Raynaud, 1986, p. 8)". The aim of this paper is to find out what happens with the Sen-Pattanaik claim when zero-assignments are not allowed. It turns out that the theorem cannot endure this slight adaptation. In addition, we show that lists of preferences that violate ER but yield transitive majority relations can easily be constructed (also cf. Regenwetter et al., 2003). In our view, this implies that the search for a pure combinatorial domain condition which is both sufficient and necessary for transitivity of the majority relation is still open. To enable the search for such a condition, we enumerate all sets of weak orderings on a triple that lead to a Condorcet paradox. These sets will be called Condorcet sets. Furthermore we show that every list of weak preference orderings which is not a Condorcet set will yield transitive majority decisions.

2 Notation, Definitions, and the Sen-Pattanaik Theorem

We start with a few standard definitions and results. Let X be a finite set consisting of at least three alternatives. A preference R over X is a binary relation over X. As usual, we write xRy instead of $(x, y) \in R$. Define $xPy := (xRy \ \& \ \text{not} \ yRx)$ and $xIy := (xRy \ \& \ yRx)$. R is said to be

- *reflexive* if for all $x \in X : xRx$;
- *complete* if for all $x, y \in X : xRy$ or yRx;
- *symmetric* if for all $x, y \in X : xRy \Rightarrow yRx$;
- *anti-symmetric* if for all $x, y \in X : xRy \ \& \ yRx \Rightarrow x = y$;
- *transitive* if for all $x, y, z \in X : xRy \ \& \ yRz \Rightarrow xRz$; and
- *acyclic* if there is no cycle, i.e. if there are no $x_1, x_2, \ldots, x_m$ such that $x_1 P x_2 \ \& \ x_2 P x_3 \ \& \ \ldots \ \& \ x_{m-1} P x_m \ \& \ x_m P x_1$.

A preference over X is a *weak ordering* if it is complete and transitive (and hence reflexive). It is a *linear ordering* if it is complete, anti-symmetric and transitive. A weak ordering which is not linear is called a *nonlinear weak ordering*. The set of linear orderings is denoted by $L(X)$, the set of weak orderings over X by $O(X)$, the set of reflexive, complete and acyclic relations by $A(X)$, and the set of reflexive and complete relations by $B(X)$. Clearly,

$$L(X) \subseteq O(X) \subseteq A(X) \subseteq B(X).$$

Let $N = \{1, 2, \ldots, n\}$ denote the set of individuals (or criteria) where $n \geq 2$. A *preference profile* π is a mapping from N into $O(X)$. A weak ordering assigned to an individual is called an *individual preference*. The set of all profiles is denoted by Π.

A *collective choice rule* is a mapping from Π into $B(X)$. A *social decision function* is a collective choice rule the range of which is restricted to $A(X)$. A *social welfare function* is a collective choice rule the range of which is restricted to $O(X)$. Clearly, a social welfare function is a social decision function, but not conversely.

Let $N_\pi(x, y)$ denote the number of individuals who prefer x to y in profile π. The majority rule M is a collective choice rule such that for every profile $\pi \in \Pi$ and for every x, y:

$$x M(\pi) y \text{ if } N_\pi(x, y) \geq N_\pi(y, x).$$

$M(\pi)$ is called the *majority relation* for profile π. The asymmetric part of $M(\pi)$ is called the *strict majority relation* and is denoted by $S(\pi)$. Thus, $x S(\pi) y$ if $x M(\pi) y$ and not $y M(\pi) x$, i.e. if $N_\pi(x, y) > N_\pi(y, x)$. The symmetric part is denoted by $I(\pi)$. Thus, $x I(\pi) y$ if $N_\pi(x, y) = N_\pi(y, x)$. Note that $M(\pi)$ is complete. An alternative $x \in X$ is a *majority winner* if it has a majority over every other alternative. As is well known, there are profiles $\pi \in \Pi$ such that $M(\pi)$ is cyclic. In this case no majority winner exists. The standard example is the following profile:

$$1 \text{ voter} : xyz$$
$$1 \text{ voter} : zxy$$
$$1 \text{ voter} : yzx$$

Applying the majority rule yields the cyclic majority relation xSy, ySz and zSx. Hence there is no majority winner. A profile, for which there are no majority winners, is called a *Condorcet paradox*. Assigning preferences to criteria instead of voters leads to Condorcet paradoxes in the field of multiple criteria decision analysis (Arrow & Raynaud, 1986). We note that Condorcet paradoxes in this field cannot be avoided by weighting the criteria.

A set of individual preferences over X satisfies extremal restriction (ER) if and only if for every triple $\{x, y, z\} \subseteq X$,

$$(\exists i : x P_i y \ \& \ y P_i z) \Rightarrow (\forall j : z P_j x \Rightarrow z P_j y \ \& \ y P_j x).$$

See Sen & Pattanaik (1969). Also see Sen (1970, 1986). By implication, if $x P_i y$ & $y P_i z$, then $x P_i z$, since R_i is complete and transitive. Hence, according to ER, if $x P_i y$, $y P_i z$ and $x P_i z$ for some i, then $z P_j y$ and $y P_j x$ for any j with $z P_j x$. Thus, to satisfy the condition, P_j restricted to $\{x, y, z\}$ needs to be the converse of P_i restricted to $\{x, y, z\}$. Extremal restriction is a conjunction of Inada's conditions echoic preferences, antagonistic preferences and dichotomous preferences (Inada, 1969).

The Sen-Pattanaik Theorem states that ER is both sufficient and necessary for transitivity of majority decisions and hence for the preclusion of instances of the Condorcet paradox.

Theorem 1 (Sen-Pattanaik) *Extremal Restriction is a sufficient and necessary condition for the majority rule to be a social welfare function.*

For a proof, consider Sen & Pattanaik (1969), Sen (1970) or Mueller (2003).

The notion of necessity in this theorem deserves attention. Sen (1986, p. 1139) describes it in the following way:

"A domain restriction for some property of the range (e.g. that social preferences be all transitive) is *necessary*, in this sense, if every violation of the restriction leads to a list of preference orderings such that some assignment of these orderings over some number of individuals would lead to the violation of that property of the range (e.g. would lead to intransitive social preference)." Also see Sen & Pattanaik (1969).

To illustrate the meaning of this definition with respect to ER, consider the list $\{xyz, yzx\}$. Clearly, this set does not satisfy ER. Hence, according to the Sen-Pattanaik Theorem, there must be assignments of xyz and yzx to numbers of voters such that the majority relation is not transitive for the resulting profiles. To discover the assignments, consider:

$$n_1 : xyz$$

$$n_2 : yzx$$

If $n_1 > n_2$ or $n_1 < n_2$, then the majority relation is transitive. Remains $n_1 = n_2$ which leads to xIy, ySz and xIz. This violates transitivity of M. Clearly, $n = n_1 + n_2$ is even when $n_1 = n_2$. Hence, in this case we cannot find an intransitivity for odd numbers of voters.

3 Extremal Restriction: What It Excludes

In this section the exclusion pattern of ER is analyzed. Since ER is a triple condition, it suffices to restrict the analysis to triples (3-element sets) only. Consider a triple, say, $\{x, y, z\}$. There are thirteen weak orderings on this set. We leave out complete indifference $x/y/z$. The remaining twelve orderings are:

$$
\begin{array}{ccc}
xyz & zxy & yzx \\
x(yz) & z(xy) & y(zx) \\
xzy & zyx & yxz \\
(zx)y & (yz) & (xy)z
\end{array}
$$

Here, (uv) means u/v, and uv stands for uPv where $u, v \in \{x, y, z\}$.

We need some additional concepts. Two weak orderings R_i and R_j are said to be *adjacent* if their set-symmetric difference $(R_i \cup R_j) - (R_i \cap R_j)$ contains exactly one ordered pair. For instance, xyz and $x(yz)$ are adjacent since, writing (x, y) for xRy, we have,

$$
(\{(x, y), (x, z), (y, z)\} \cup \{(x, y), (x, z), (y, z), (z, y)\}) - (\{(x, y), (x, z), (y, z)\}
$$
$$
\cap \{(x, y), (x, z), (y, z), (z, y)\}) = \{(z, y)\}.
$$

Because of the fact that the set-symmetric difference of two linear orderings cannot contain exactly one ordered pair, the notion of adjacency cannot meaningfully be applied to two linear orderings. Therefore, we introduce the supplementary notion of nearest-neighbour. Two linear orderings are said to be *nearest-neighbours* if and only if their set-symmetric difference contains exactly two ordered pairs. For example, xyz and xzy are nearest-neighbours because their set-symmetric difference contains just two ordered pairs; to wit, yz and zy. Note that a linear ordering can be a nearest-neighbour to another linear ordering and be adjacent to a weak ordering (which cannot be a linear ordering). Thus, if we have xyz, $x(yz)$ and xzy, then xyz and xzy are adjacent to $x(yz)$ and, moreover, are nearest-neighbours of each other.

Now, represent the weak orderings over $\{x, y, z\}$ as points in the plane and draw a line between each pair of adjacent points. Leaving out complete indifference, we then obtain the following planar graph (see Fig. 1).

The numbers in the graph are for future references to the respective orderings. The adjacencies and nearest-neighbours of an ordering can be read off directly from this figure. For instance, zxy and zyx are nearest-neighbours while zxy and $z(xy)$ are adjacent. The linear orderings at the endpoints of the dashed lines in Fig. 1 are converses of each other. These orderings have no ordered pairs of elements in common.

We use the following procedure: Pick a linear ordering in the figure and investigate what is excluded by ER for that ordering. Then, pick one of the nearest-neighbours of the first selected linear ordering and analyze what is excluded for this one. Go on in this way until all linear orderings have been investigated. This will suffice because the antecedent in the formula $(\exists i: xP_iy \ \& \ yP_iz) \Rightarrow (\forall j : zP_jx \Rightarrow zP_jy \ \& \ yP_jx)$ precludes nonlinear weak orderings from having any exclusion potential. Implementing this procedure, we obtain:

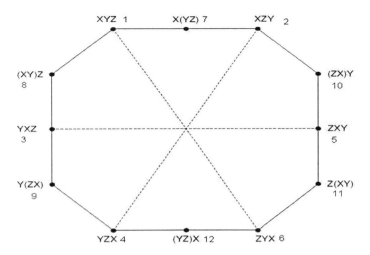

Fig. 1 Planar graph of adjacent weak orderings

1. Take *xyz*. If for some *i*: *xyz*, then for every *j* with *zx*: *zyx*. However, then for no *j*: *zxy*, *z*(*xy*), (*yz*)*x* or *yzx*.

2. Take *xzy*. If for some *i*: *xzy*, then for every *j* with *yx*: *yzx*. However, then for no *j*: *yxz*, *y*(*zx*), (*yz*)*x* or *zyx*.

3. Take *zxy*. If for some *i*: *zxy*, then for every *j* with *yz*: *yxz*. However, then for no *j*: *yzx*, *y*(*zx*), (*xy*)*z* or *xyz*.

4. Take *zyx*. If for some *i*: *zyx*, then for every *j* with *xz*: *xyz*. However, then for no *j*: *yxz*, (*xy*)*z*, *x*(*yz*) or *xzy*.

5. Take *yzx*. If for some *i*: *yzx*, then for every *j* with *xy*: *xzy*. However, then for no *j*: *xyz*, *x*(*yz*), (*zx*)*y* or *zyx*.

6. Take *yxz*. If for some *i*: *yxz*, then for every *j* with *zy*: *zxy*. However, then for no *j*: *xzy*, (*zx*)*y*, *z*(*xy*) or *zyx*.

The algorithm for finding an exclusion pattern ought to be clear by now: pick a linear ordering, look up its converse in Fig. 1 at the opposite of the dashed line, and then seek the adjacencies and nearest-neighbours of this converse. The orderings found around the opposite are precisely the ones which are excluded. They form the segment of exclusion. In this segment the opposite must be left out of course. For example, in (3) *zxy* is combined with its converse *yxz*. The adjacencies of *yxz* are (*xy*)*z* and *y*(*zx*), and its nearest-neighbours are *xyz* and *yzx*. Thus, the segment of exclusion runs from *xyz* through *yzx* with *yxz* left out. Further, the segments of exclusion rotate in the counter-direction with the next choice. For instance, take the linear ordering to the left of *zxy* and the segment of exclusion swings to the right; take the linear ordering to the right and it swings to the left. Considering this all, we arrive at the following proposition:

Proposition 1 *For each linear ordering over a triple, extremal restriction excludes the adjacencies and the nearest-neighbours of its converse.*

This proposition leads to a useful interpretation of ER: if someone has a strict preference then only the diametrically opposed strict preference is allowed in order to guarantee transitivity of majority decision making. Divergences of this diametrically opposed preference are not allowed. In terms of multiple criteria decision analysis it requires that if the decision maker has a strict preference on one criterion, then on any other criterion, he has to use the adjacent and nearest-neighbor preferences of this strict preference, or he has to use the diametrically opposed strict preference. Divergences from this diametrically opposed preference or from the adjacent and nearest-neighborhood preferences are not allowed. The allowance of diametrically opposed preferences for different individuals or criteria and the prohibition of slight deviations from these opposed preferences are remarkable. Full conflicting preferences are allowed but partially conflicting ones are excluded. There is either much consensus or much conflict; something in-between is forbidden. In other words: if there is a conflict, it rather should be a good one.

There is a similarity here with Plott's third symmetry condition in the spatial analysis of majority equilibrium (Plott, 1967). This condition requires that "all individuals for which the point [of equilibrium] is not a maximum can be divided into pairs whose interests are diametrically opposed (Plott, 1967 p. 790)." Apparently, ER is the combinatorial counterpart of Plott's symmetry condition.

4 Extremal Restriction: What It Includes

As usual, a set is called *maximal* with respect to some property if it cannot properly be included in another set with the same property. What are the maximal sets of weak orderings (over a triple) satisfying extremal restriction?

To construct a maximal set, pick a linear ordering, say xyz. Then, according to Proposition 1, the adjacencies and nearest-neighbours of zyx – to wit, zxy, $z(xy)$, $(yz)x$ and yzx – are forbidden (see Fig. 1). Hence, xyz can only be combined with the remaining weak and linear orderings. Take one of the remaining linear orderings, say, xzy. But xzy forbids zyx, $(yz)x$, $y(zx)$ and yxz (see Fig. 1). Together, xyz and xzy forbid zxy, $z(xy)$, zyx, $(yz)x$, yzx, $y(zx)$, and yxz. There remains $(xy)z$, $x(yz)$ and $(zx)y$. Thus, a maximal set satisfying ER is $\{(xy)z, xyz, x(yz), xzy, (zx)y\}$. Observe that the two linear orderings xyz and xzy together forbid all the remaining linear orderings from being in this set.

Now combine xyz with yxz. Since, according to Fig. 1, yxz forbids the segment from xzy through zyx with exclusion of zxy, and xyz forbids the segment from zxy through yzx with exclusion of zyx, we arrive at the maximal set $\{y(zx), yxz, (xy)z, xyz, x(yz)\}$. After this, combine xyz with its converse zyx. Since zyx excludes the segment from yxz through xzy with exclusion of xyz, this yields the maximal set $\{xyz, zyx, (zx)y, y(zx)\}$. Finally, combine xyz with the weak orderings which are not forbidden by ER. This yields the maximal set $\{xyz, x(yz), (zx)y, (xy)z, y(zx)\}$.

Proceeding in the same way for every linear ordering in Fig. 1, we obtain a list of 15 maximal sets satisfying ER. However, the list is not complete. The set of all *nonlinear* weak orderings over a triple also satisfies ER and therefore should be added to the list. So we arrive at:

(1) $\{(xy)z, xyz, x(yz), xzy, (zx)y\}$
(2) $\{x(yz), xzy, (zx)y, zxy, z(xy)\}$
(3) $\{(zx)y, zxy, z(xy), zyx, (yz)x\}$
(4) $\{z(xy), zyx, (yz)x, yzx, y(zx)\}$
(5) $\{(yz)x, yzx, y(zx), yxz, (xy)z\}$
(6) $\{y(zx), yxz, (xy)z, xyz, x(yz)\}$
(7) $\{xyz, zyx, (zx)y, y(zx)\}$
(8) $\{xzy, yzx, (xy)z, z(xy)\}$
(9) $\{zxy, yxz, x(yz), (yz)x\}$
(10) $\{xyz, x(yz), (zx)y, (xy)z, y(zx)\}$
(11) $\{(xy)z, x(yz), xzy, (zx)y, z(xy)\}$
(12) $\{x(yz), (zx)y, zxy, z(xy), (yz)x\}$
(13) $\{(zx)y, z(xy), zyx, (yz)x, y(zx)\}$
(14) $\{z(xy), (yz)x, yzx, y(zx), (xy)z\}$
(15) $\{(yz)x, y(zx), yxz, (xy)z, x(yz)\}$
(16) $\{x(yz), (zx)y, z(xy), (yz)x, y(zx), (xy)z\}$

Any subset of each of these 16 maximal sets satisfies ER. Moreover, there are no other sets satisfying it. As we already observed, any linear ordering over a triple together with another linear ordering over that triple which is not forbidden by the first both exclude all the remaining linear orderings over that triple. Inspecting the maximal sets, we indeed see that no set of weak orderings over a triple satisfying ER can contain more than two distinct linear orderings over that triple.

Proposition 2 *Any set of weak orderings over a triple with three or more distinct linear orderings violates extremal restriction.*

Generalized to preferences over an m-set with $m > 3$, this proposition implies that only one triple together with only three individual preference orderings whose restriction with respect to this triple are linear and distinct, are sufficient to let ER break down. In Kelly (1991) and Fishburn (1992), Craven's conjecture is studied that says that 2^{m-1} is the maximum number of linear orderings on m alternatives satisfying some constraints on triples. This conjecture is correct for $m = 3$, but is false for $m \geq 4$ (Fishburn, 1992). It clearly does not hold for ER According to Proposition 2: the maximum number is 2 for this constraint. To illustrate, consider $\{x, y, z, u\}$. There are 24 linear orderings on this set. For example, $\{zxyu, zxuy\}$ satisfies ER. Adding any linear ordering will violate this constraint.

Clearly, Craven's conjecture is about linear orderings. As Kelly (1991, p. 274) noticed, the combinatorics for weak orderings will probably be very difficult. However, as a first step, the complete list of sets maximal with respect to ER enables us to calculate the proportion of preference sets that satisfy ER. Remember that we left aside complete indifference in our analysis. Taking the set of nonempty subsets of each maximal set from the list above and avoiding double counts, we arrive at twelve 1-sets, forty eight 2-sets, eighty 3-sets (triples), sixty 4-sets, eighteen 5-sets, and one

6-set of weak orderings over a triple that satisfy ER. So, we count 219 nonempty sets satisfy it. Since there are $2^{12} - 1 = 4095$ nonempty subsets of weak orderings over a triple, we arrive at a proportion of $219/4095 = 0.053$ nonempty subsets of weak orderings over a triple that satisfy ER. Generalizing to $\#X \geq 3$, the number of triples is

$$C(m, 3) = m!/[(m - 3)!3!].$$

Obviously, the proportion of nonempty subsets of weak orderings over an m-set that satisfy ER will rapidly shrink when m increases.

5 Zero Assignments and Counter-Examples for the Sen-Pattanaik Theorem

In the Sen-Pattanaik Theorem, it is allowed that preferences are assigned to zero voters. In this section, it will be investigated what happens with the SP-Theorem when we impose the requirement that preferences cannot be assigned to nobody (i.e. to zero voters). We provide counter-examples for the theorem by using the maximal lists of preferences satisfying ER.

To start the analysis, consider the following profile:

$$n_1 : xyz$$
$$n_2 : xzy$$
$$n_3 : zxy.$$

Obviously, (xyz, xzy, zxy) does not satisfy ER (cf. Proposition 2). So, let us discover for which n_1, n_2 and n_3 the majority relation is intransitive. Since $x P_i y$ for every i: xSy. There are four cases to investigate:

Case 1: Suppose yMz. Thus ySz or yIz. First, suppose ySz. Now, ySz if $n_1 > n_2 + n_3$. But then xyz is the majority relation which is transitive. So, suppose yIz, i.e. $n_1 = n_2 + n_3$. Since xSy, we only have intransitivity if xIz or zSx. First, suppose xIz, i.e. $n_1 + n_2 = n_3$. Substituting this equation in $n_1 = n_2 + n_3$ yields $n_1 = 2n_2 + n_1$, which is true if and only if $n_2 = 0$. But then $n_1 = n_3$. Hence, if $n_2 = 0$ and $n_1 = n_3$, then the majority relation for this profile is intransitive. Now suppose zSx. Given the profile, zSx if $n_3 > n_1 + n_2$. Noting that $n_1 = n_2 + n_3$, this is possible only when $n_2 < 0$, which is not true. But then zxy is the majority relation which is transitive.

Case 2: Suppose zSy, i.e. $n_3 + n_2 > n_1$. Since xSy, we have transitivity for both xMz and zMx. Hence, for this case, we cannot find intransitivity.

Case 3: Suppose zMx, i.e. zSx or zIx. Both zSx and zIx are treated under Case 1.

Case 4: Suppose xSz, i.e. $n_1 + n_2 > n_3$. Since xSy, we have transitivity for both zMy and yMz.

This shows that if the list of preferences as presented above yields an intransitive majority relation, then $n_2 = 0$ and $n_1 = n_3$. Clearly, if $n_2 = 0$ and $n_1 = n_3$, then M is intransitive. Hence, M is intransitive for the above profile if and only if $n_2 = 0$ and $n_1 = n_3$. Thus if the assignment of xzy to $n_2 = 0$ is forbidden, the Sen-Pattanaik Theorem no longer holds.

To sum up, using every preference in the set $\{xyz, xzy, zxy\}$, that is, working with preference profiles which are onto with respect to this set, we only can find preference profiles for which the majority relation is transitive. To find an intransitivity, we need a zero-assignment which is precluded by the definition of a preference profile. Intuitively, the set $\{xyz, xzy, zxy\}$ must satisfy some unknown condition that is necessary for majority decision making to be transitive.

The above analysis implies that there are preference profiles that violate ER but that generate transitive majority relations. To see this, consider the maximal sets of preferences over a triple set satisfying ER as constructed in Sect. 4 of this paper. For example, consider Set 7: $\{xyz, zyx, y(zx), (zx)y\}$ and add the strict preference yzx. This gives, e.g., $(xyz, zyx, y(zx), (zx)y, yzx)$, which clearly violates ER. However, the majority relation is ySx, ySz, and zSx, which is transitive. Clearly, this it is a violation of necessity.

To give another example, consider the first maximal set satisfying ER given in Sect. 4: $\{(xy)z, xyz, x(yz), xzy, (zx)y\}$. Adding yzx to this set yields a set that violates ER. However, the profile $((xy)z, xyz, x(yz), xzy, (zx)y, yzx)$ yields xSy, xSz and ySz as the majority relation. Again, this is a violation of necessity of ER.

Now look at the complement of each maximal set. For example the complement of 1) is $\{yxz, y(zx), yzx, (yz)x, zyx, z(xy), zxy\}$. Investigating this list, it is clear that it violates ER. However, it leads to a weakly ordered (and hence transitive) majority relation. In this case, we have $(yz)x$. Call the complement of any maximal ER-set an *Anti-ER set*. Checking now for any Anti-ER list, we see that all of them yield weakly ordered majority relations. The complements of Sets 1 through 6 lead to weak orders with one indifferent pair, the complements of Sets 7 through 9 and Set 16 lead to complete indifference and the complements of Sets 10 through 15 lead to linear orderings. So we have the following proposition:

Proposition 3 *Any Anti-ER list leads to a weakly ordered majority relation.*

In order to satisfy this proposition, all elements in each Anti-ER set are needed. That is, they may contain proper subsets which lead to quasi-transitive or even cyclic majority relations. For example, the Anti-ER for the maximal ER set $\{xyz, x(yz), (zx)y, (xy)z, y(zx)\}$ is $\{xzy, yxz, yzx, zxy, zyx, z(xy), (yz)x\}$, which contains the subset $\{xzy, yxz, zyx\}$ that leads to acyclic majority relations.

6 Condorcet Sets

From now on we label the orderings by their numbers as given in Fig. 1. A *Condorcet set* is a set of preferences that lead to a Condorcet paradox. For example the set $\{1, 4, 5\}$ in Fig. 1 is a Condorcet set. It yields the typical (xyz, yzx, zxy)

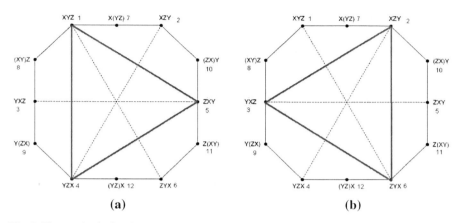

Fig. 2 The two basic Condorcet sets

as a Condorcet profile. Clearly any permutation of this set leads to a Condorcet paradox. The set {1, 4, 5} forms a triangle when connecting the points representing the preferences. See Fig. 2. Another basic set leading to a Condorcet paradox is {2, 3, 6}. It forms the other triangle in Fig. 2.

Any other Condorcet set than {1, 4, 5} and {2, 3, 6} must contain one of these sets and are therefore called *extended* Condorcet sets. For clear reasons, we call {1, 4, 5} and {2, 3, 6} the *basic* Condorcet sets.

The Condorcet sets are exhaustively enumerated in the following table (see Table 1). Consider Fig. 1 or 2 for the numbers. In the first column of Table 1 we find the extensions of the basic Condorcet set {1, 4, 5}; in the second one the extensions of {2, 3, 6}. Note that for any set in the first column, its complement is stated in the second one and vice versa. This immediately leads to the following proposition:

Proposition 4 *The complement of any Condorcet set is a Condorcet set.*

To illustrate the proposition, consider Fig. 3. In Fig. 3a the basic Condorcet set {1, 4, 5} and its complement {10, 2, 7, 8, 3, 9, 12, 6, 11} are given. The complement is an extension of the basic Condorcet set {2, 3, 6}. Figure 3b shows the extended

Table 1 Enumeration of Condorcet sets

1, 4, 5	2, 3, 6, 7, 8, 9, 10, 11, 12
1, 4, 5, 7, 12	2, 3, 6, 8, 9, 10, 11
1, 4, 5, 8, 11	2, 3, 6, 7, 9, 10, 12
1, 4, 5, 9, 10	2, 3, 6, 7, 8, 11, 12
1, 4, 5, 7, 9, 11	2, 3, 6, 8, 10, 12
1, 4, 5, 8, 10, 12	2, 3, 6, 7, 9, 11
1, 4, 5, 7, 8, 11, 12	2, 3, 6, 9, 10
1, 4, 5, 7, 9, 10, 12	2, 3, 6, 8, 11
1, 4, 5, 8, 9, 10, 11	2, 3, 6, 7, 12
1, 4, 5, 7, 8, 9, 10, 11, 12	2, 3, 6

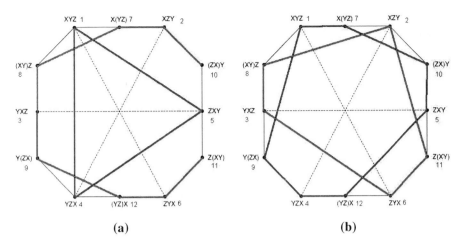

Fig. 3 Two Condorcet sets and their complement Condorcet sets

Condorcet set $\{1, 9, 4, 12, 5, 10, 7\}$ and its complement $\{2, 8, 3, 6, 11\}$, which is an extension of the basic Condorcet set $\{2, 3, 6\}$.

It can be observed that all extended Condorcet sets minus their basic part yield complete majority indifference relations. This indifference relation of an additional set joined with a basic Condorcet set operates, so to say, as an algebraic group identity element preserving the paradox of the basic list.

A proper subset of a Condorcet set is not necessarily a Condorcet set. Any set which is not a Condorcet set will be called a *majority set*. All these sets lead by construction to a majority decision. However, not all majority sets lead to a transitive majority relation. As we already saw, the list of transitive majority sets contains in any case the maximal ER sets, any proper subset of any maximal ER set, and the Anti-ER sets. Furthermore we notice that it is not an easy task to give a clear interpretation of the set of all majority sets, e.g. in terms of "super" symmetry. The only thing we can say is that being a member of the list of majority sets is a necessary and sufficient condition to avoid the Condorcet paradox.

7 Conclusion

The exclusion-inclusion pattern constructed by means of the Kemeny-Snell method shows that ER is a condition that allows full conflict between individual preferences or between preferences on criteria in the case of multiple criteria decision analysis. It includes diametrically opposed preferences and excludes the slightest deviation from these diametrically opposed preferences. Hence, partial conflicts are excluded. There is either much consensus or much conflict; something in-between is forbidden.

The inclusion analysis given in this paper shows that the meeting of ER in reality is remote. First, according to Proposition 2, any set with more than two different linear preference orderings cannot satisfy it. This is a discouraging proposition. It implies that if at least three individuals have distinct linearly ordered preferences or if a decision maker linearly orders the alternatives differently on at least three criteria, the condition will be violated. Secondly, the proportion of nonempty subsets of the set of weak orderings over a triple meeting the condition is small, namely 0.053. This proportion rapidly decreases when the number of alternatives increases. However, ER is not the only domain condition that prevents the occurrence of Condorcet paradoxes. Many other conditions among which value restriction, single-peakedness and limited agreement may be operational.

Checking whether the preferences in a profile belong to a majority set is both sufficient and necessity to find out whether the profile leads to a majority decision. However, as we already noted, it is difficult to find a suitable underlying interpretation of all these majority sets e.g. in terms of symmetry or conflict. Moreover, majority sets do not necessarily lead to transitive majority relations. In this respect, the search for a generalized and tractable sufficient and necessary condition for the transitivity of majority decision is still open.

References

Arrow, K. J. (1963). *Social choice and individual values*. New York: Wiley.
Arrow, K. J., & Raynaud, H. (1986). *Social choice and multicriterion decision-making*. Cambridge: The MIT Press.
Black, D. (1958). *The theory of committees and elections*. Cambridge: Cambridge University Press.
Davis, O. A., De Groot, M. H., & Hinich, M. (1972). Social preference orderings and majority rule. *Econometrica, 40*, 147–157.
Enelow, J. M., & Hinich, M. J. (1984). *The spatial theory of voting*. Cambridge: Cambridge University Press.
Feld, S. L., & Grofman, B. (1986). Partial single-peakedness: An extension and clarification. *Public Choice, 51*, 71–80.
Fishburn, P. (1992). Notes on Craven's conjecture. *Social Choice & Welfare, 9*, 259–262.
Gaertner, W. (1979). An analysis and comparison of several necessary and sufficient conditions for transitivity under the majority decision rule. In J. J. Laffont (Ed.), *Aggregation and revelation of preferences* (pp. 91–113). Amsterdam: North-Holland.
Gaertner, W. (2001). *Domain conditions in social choice theory*. Cambridge: Cambridge University Press.
Gehrlein, W. V. (1983). Condorcet's paradox. *Theory and Decision, 15*, 161–197.
Gehrlein, W. V. (2006). *Condorcet's paradox*. Berlin: Springer-Verlag.
Grandmont, J. M. (1979). Intermediate preferences and the majority rule. In J. J. Laffont (Ed.), *Aggregation and revelation of preferences* (pp. 115–129). Amsterdam: North-Holland.
Inada, K. (1969). The simple majority decision rule, *Econometrica, 37*, 490–506.
Kelly, J. S. (1991). Craven's conjecture. *Social Choice & Welfare, 8*, 269–274.
Kemeny, J. G., & Snell, J. L. (1962). *Mathematical models in the social sciences*. Cambridge, MA: The MIT Press.
Kramer, G. H. (1973). On a class of equilibrium conditions for majority rule. *Econometrica, 41*, 285–297.

Matthews, S. A. (1980). Pairwise symmetry conditions for voting equilibria. *International Journal of Game Theory, 9*, 141–156.

McKelvey, R. D. (1976). Intransitivities in multidimensional voting models and some implications for agenda control. *Journal of Economic Theory, 12*, 472–482.

Mueller, D. C. (2003). *Public Choice*. Cambridge: Cambridge University Press.

Nurmi, H. (1999). *Voting paradoxes and how to deal with them*. Berlin: Springer-Verlag.

Owen, G., & Shapley, L. S. (1989). Optimal location of candidates in ideological space. *International Journal of Game Theory, 18*, 339–356.

Plott, C. (1967). A notion of equilibrium and its possibility under majority rule. *American Economic Review, 57*, 787–806.

Regenwetter, M., Marley, A., & Grofman, B. (2003). General concepts of value restriction and preference majority. *Social Choice & Welfare, 21*, 149–173.

Regenwetter, M., Grofman, B., Marley, A., & Tsetlin, I. (2006). *Behavioral social choice. Probabilistic models, statistical inference, and applications*. Cambridge: Cambridge University Press.

Sen, A. K. (1966). A possibility theorem on majority decisions. *Econometrica, 34*, 491–499.

Sen, A. K. (1970). *Collective choice and social welfare*. San Francisco: Holden Day Inc.

Sen, A. K. (1986). Social choice theory. In K. J. Arrow & M. D. Intriligator (Eds.), *Handbook of mathematical economics III* (pp. 1073–1182). North-Holland: Elsevier.

Sen, A. K., & Pattanaik, P. K. (1969). Necessary and sufficient conditions for rational choice under majority decision. *Journal of Economic Theory, 1*, 178–202.

van Deemen, A. (1997). *Coalition formation and social choice*. Boston: Kluwer Academic Publishers.

Rights Revisited, and Limited

Maurice Salles and Feng Zhang

1 Introduction

In two recent papers, Salles (2008, 2009) introduced a notion of limited rights[1] first in an aggregation function framework (2008), then in the framework of social choice rules. Our purpose in this paper, is to provide a general exposition of these results from an intuitive viewpoint in a way that imitates in some sense the famous non-starred chapters in Sen (1970b).[2] The studies of rights, freedom, liberalism within social choice theory originated in Sen's magisterial paper (1970a). In this short contribution, Sen demonstrates that there is an incompatibility between some weak form of collective rationality of social preference, a Pareto unanimity condition and some specific form of what Sen called at that time liberalism. This latter condition can also be interpreted as an unequal distribution of power or as a violation of the so-called neutrality condition. Since 1970, rights etc. have been considered within other paradigms. For instance, rights have been introduced in game forms by Gärdenfors (1981, 2005), Gaertner, Pattanaik, and Suzumura (1992), Peleg (1998), and Suzumura (2006). Freedom (liberty) has been mainly analyzed in the context of opportunity sets following the pioneering paper of Pattanaik and Xu (1990).[3] Saari and Pétron (2006) and Li and Saari (2008) have recently revisited the foundational framework of Sen and of Gibbard (1974) by examining the informational structure of the aggregation procedures.[4]

In Sect. 2, we will present the necessary concepts for individuals and for society emphasizing the aggregation function approach compared to the social choice approach. In Sect. 3 we will describe Sen's theorem in both frameworks and give examples. We will allude to the Cartesian product structure to show how it can help

M. Salles (✉)
CREM, Université de Caen, 14032 Caen Cedex, France
e-mail: maurice.salles@unicaen.fr

---

[1] The first to have presented this notion in an unfortunately unpublished paper is Edi Karni (1974).

[2] In Sen's book the starred chapters are the formal chapters and non-starred chapters are informal.

[3] The ranking of sets is excellently surveyed in Barberá, Bossert, and Pattanaik (2004).

[4] See also Saari (2008).

A. Van Deemen, A. Rusinowska (eds.), *Collective Decision Making,*
Theory and Decision Library C 43, DOI 10.1007/978-3-642-02865-6_6,
© Springer-Verlag Berlin Heidelberg 2010

to formalize the notion of personal sphere. Section 4 will deal with limited rights as introduced by Salles in his recent papers. The two final sections will be devoted to a general discussion about welfarism and possible extensions of the analysis of rights within social choice using modal logic.

2 Necessary Concepts

We consider a group of people who have preferences over options that will be identified with social states. To simplify, we may consider a finite group of individuals who rank (with possible ties) a finite set of social states according to their preferences. Each individual having a ranking, the social choice question is to find either a *social* preference or some way to choose from any part of the set of social states. Procedures to obtain a social preference from a list of individual preferences will be called *aggregation functions* and procedures to obtain a choice for any set of options will be called *social choice functions*.[5]

The social preference can be a ranking or some other type of relations with less demanding rationality properties. For instance, with a ranking if someone prefers a to b and is indifferent between b and c she prefers a to c. If she is indifferent between a and b and between b and c, she is indifferent between a and c (this property is the transitivity of indifference–ties). For social preferences, we can consider also the case in which only strict preferences are transitive (when a is preferred to b and b to c, a is preferred to c), or in which the indifference relation is not transitive anymore (this has been called quasi-transitivity by Sen). One can also imagine that indifference can be in some sense *partly* transitive as in the case of semi-orders or interval orders. The strict social preference can be acyclic which means that there is no cycles of the type a preferred to b, b preferred to c, c preferred to d and d preferred to a.[6] In formal developments in choice theory, the acyclicity condition is strongly related to the existence of a choice within any finite subset of the set of options.

The other framework is to have, given the rankings of individuals, a rule to choose from any set of social states with the obligation that some social state must be chosen in *this* set. In decision theory and standard microeconomics, the choice of elements from a set can be defined by reference to a binary relation meaning "at least as good as" in which case the chosen elements are the best according to this relation (provided that they exist). But the chosen elements can be given and then one can infer a binary relation on the basis of choice. This is the central topic of revealed preference theory (the choice made by some individual reveals her preference).

---

[5] We use the word "function" even if the word 'correspondence' is more common. Here our function is accordingly a set-valued function.

[6] Here the cycle involves four options, but acyclicity excludes all cycles whatever the number of options.

3 Sen's Theorem

In the social preference framework, Sen considers the case where the collective rationality condition is rather weak, that is where strict social preferences are supposed to be acyclic. In particular, this means that indifference is not supposed to be transitive and even that strict preference is not supposed to be transitive – it is possible that a be preferred to b and b to c with an indifference between a and c). The so-called *Pareto condition* states that a is socially preferred to b whenever all individuals prefer a to b. In general people think that the Pareto condition is not questionable. It has however an important consequence. Given that individual preferences are sufficiently diverse, it excludes constant functions. It is sufficient that there exist two options a and b for which individuals can possibly prefer a to b or b to a, since in such cases it is possible that all individuals prefer a to b or all individuals prefer b to a and, in the aggregation functions setting, a is socially preferred to b or b is socially preferred to a. If the aggregation function is a constant function, the outcome is a fixed social preference whatever the individual preferences. This would be the case when the fixed preference has been determined by a moral or religious code. The *liberalism condition* attributes to each individual i some specific power over two social states, say a_i and b_i, viz. a_i is socially preferred to b_i whenever individual i prefers a_i to b_i and b_i is socially preferred to a_i whenever i prefers b_i to a_i. Sen's result can be obtained for a weaker form of liberalism, called *minimal liberalism*, where there are only two individuals who are endowed with the just described specific power.[7] Sen's Theorem shows that there is an incompatibility between the acyclicity of the social preference, the Pareto condition and the condition of minimal liberalism provided that there is a sufficient diversity of the individual rankings.

In the choice-theoretic framework, the Pareto condition takes the following form. In a subset of social states to which a and b belong, b is not chosen whenever all individuals prefer a to b. The condition of minimal liberalism regarding, say, individual i and social states a and b, amounts to say that b is not chosen in a set to which a belongs whenever individual i prefers a to b, and that a is not chosen in a set to which b belongs whenever individual i prefers b to a. It can then be shown that there is an incompatibility between the existence of a choice procedure, the Pareto condition and minimal liberalism provided that there is a sufficient diversity of the individual rankings.

Let us consider a famous example introduced by Sen about the reading of *Lady Chatterley's Lover*. This example involves two individuals, let us call them Mr. Prude and Mr. Lascivious, and three social states, namely, a, b and c. The social state a is the social state in which Mr. Prude reads *Lady Chatterley's Lover*, b is the same social state except that Mr. Lascivious reads the book and c, again, is the same

---

[7] We will only consider this minimal version of liberalism, even in its weak form, in the next section, since all impossibilities obtained for minimal liberalism have implicit corollaries for liberalism. Accordingly, we will not used systematically the term "minimal", "liberalism" meaning also, from now on, "minimal liberalism".

social state except that no one reads the book. One can find reasons for Mr. Prude ranking the options with c being top-ranked, a being ranked in second position and b in the third. It seems obvious that option c which amounts to censorship has his preference. However, ranking a before b means that he does not want that Mr. Lascivious can benefit in any way from reading the book and he is ready to sacrifice himself in this matter. In contrast, one can imagine that Mr. Lascivious will rank c at the bottom of his ranking. Being not only lascivious but also slightly sadistic, he has pleasure to imagine Mr. Prude having to read the book, and, accordingly, he top-ranks option a. Now, the liberalism condition can be applied as far as Mr. Prude is concerned to options a and c. This implies that in the social preference c will be ranked before a. The same condition regarding Mr. Lascivious is applicable to options b and c. This implies that in the social preference b will be ranked before c. But both individuals have ranked a before b, and as a consequence of the Pareto condition, a will be ranked before b in the social preference. One can see then that a is ranked before b which is ranked before c which is ranked before a, which is a cycle.

We believe that there is some ambiguity in this example; because it is rather unclear that if Mr. Prude reads the book, then Mr. Lascivious will be prevented to read the book. One way to deal with this difficulty is to introduce a Cartesian product structure for the options so that each option is in fact an ordered pair. In this framework option a where Mr. Prude reads the book is either Mr. Prude reads the book *and* Mr. Lascivious does not read the book or both Mr. Prude *and* Mr. Lascivious read the book. If for an ordered pair (x, y), the first coordinate, x, refers to Mr. Prude and the second, y, to Mr. Lascivious, one can write (r, n) for Mr. Prude reads the book and Mr. Lascivious does not read it, (r, r) for both read the book, (n, r) for Mr. Prude does not read the book and Mr. Lascivious reads the book, and (n, n) for no one reads the book. We now have four rather than three options and it seems that Sen's a is (r, n), b is (n, r) and c is (n, n). Suppose now that Mr. Prude ranks the four options as, from the most preferred to the least preferred, $(n, n), (r, n), (n, r), (r, r)$ and that Mr. Lascivious as $(r, r), (r, n), (n, r), (n, n)$. With this structure it seems natural that Mr. Prude has the "power" conferred by the liberalism condition over options (r, n) and (n, n) since in both cases Mr. Lascivious's situation is the same (he does not read the book), but also over options (n, r) and (r, r) since in both cases Mr. Lascivious reads the book. Similarly Mr. Lascivious should have the "power" over (n, n) and (n, r) since in both cases Mr. Prude does not read the book and also over (r, n) and (r, r) since in both cases Mr. Prude reads the book. Given this and the Pareto condition ((r, n) is ranked before (n, r) by both individuals), one obtains two cycles rather than one cycle, viz. a cycle $(n, n), (r, n), (n, r), (n, n)$ and a cycle $(r, r), (r, n), (n, r), (r, r)$.[8]

Let us return to Sen's original example but now in the choice-theoretic framework. Since a is preferred to b by both individuals, the Pareto condition requests

---

[8] This variation on Sen's example was presented in Salles (1996). It is also in Hausman and McPherson (2006). The first edition of Hausman and McPherson appeared in 1996.

that b be not chosen in the set made of a, b and c. But a is not chosen either, since given the power of Mr. Prude over a and c and the fact that Mr. Prude ranks c before a, a cannot be chosen in a set to which c belongs. Similarly, with Mr. Lascivious and options b and c, c cannot be chosen in a set to which b belongs. In conclusion, there is no option that can be chosen among the three options a, b and c.

In the modified Sen's example, if we consider a set of options made of (n, n), (r, n), (n, r), since (r, n) is ranked before (n, r) by both individuals, the Pareto condition excludes (n, r) as a possible choice. Since Mr. Prude prefers (n, n) to (r, n), (r, n) is excluded and since Mr. Lascivious prefers (n, r) to (n, n), (n, n) is also excluded so that there is no choice in this three-option set. Similarly, if we consider a set of options made of (r, r), (r, n), (n, r), the Pareto condition excludes (n, r), and the liberalism condition as applied to Mr. Lascivious and options (r, r) and (r, n) excludes option (r, n) and applied to Mr. Prude and options (n, r) and (r, r) excludes option (r, r) so that we are left with nothing as a possible choice in this set.

It should be noted that with the Cartesian product structure and liberalism being defined as a power conferred to individuals when other individuals' situation is unmodified it is possible to construct examples where cycles are obtained without using the Pareto condition (see, for instance, Salles (2000)). Furthermore, this Cartesian product structure seems to be an interesting formalization of the idea of *personal sphere* often associated to Mill's major work (1859).

In his book (1970b), Sen suggests other examples. For instance, he proposes options involving sleeping positions (on the back or on the belly) or involving the color of kitchen walls. He also develops his analysis and give further examples in a number of papers which are collected in his book of 2002.[9] Incidentally, we will use sleeping positions examples in the sequel.

4 Limited Rights

Salles's purpose in his two papers (2008, 2009) was to study a weakening of the conditions associated with the notion of individual liberty in a formal way. Even when restricted to two individuals, we consider this condition to be rather strong in the mathematical framework. In our view, only its interpretation makes it both acceptable and obvious. In his comments to a paper of Brunel (now Pétron) and Salles (1998), and Hammond (1998) writes:

> In the social choice rule approach …, local dictatorship become a desideratum, provided that the 'localities' are appropriate. Our feelings of revulsion should be reserved for non-local dictatorships, or local dictatorships affecting issues that should not be treated as personal.

Of course, we share this opinion, but there is nothing in the basic mathematical framework that guarantees this personal aspect (in contrast with a suitable Cartesian

---

[9] See also Sen (1976, 1982).

product structure). In this basic framework it is however possible to weaken dictatorships. What Salles demonstrates in his two papers is that this weakening does not offer a very interesting escape route from Sen's negative results. In particular, this is true in the framework of social choice rules as compared with the aggregation function framework.

In this section, we will first present the technical results as simply as possible. Then we will provide examples. Let us explain first why we think that it is important to consider a weakening of the liberalism conditions. In the social choice theoretic framework, there is some ambiguity in the treatment of liberalism regarding either the *ability* to throw out an option or the *obligation* to throw out an option, or, in the aggregation function framework regarding the fact that the individual endowed with a right over two options either necessarily imposes his strict preference over these two options to society or not. It seems that the liberalism as stated is about *obligation* or *necessity*.[10] A possible remedy to this slight defection is to require that the social preference is not the reverse preference of the individual endowed with mentioned right. In the choice framework, this means that the less preferred option of the concerned individual is either thrown out or is chosen along with the preferred option.

4.1 The Social Preference Framework

The Pareto condition remains identical: whenever all individuals prefer option x to option y, then x is ranked before y in the social preference. Let us now explain how the liberalism condition, as applied to only two individuals, is weakened. Let us suppose that the weak liberalism condition pertains to individual i regarding options a and b. Whenever i prefers one option, say, a, to the other option, b, then b cannot be ranked before a in the social preference. Given that social preference is supposed to be complete, this is equivalent to saying that either a is ranked before b or there is a tie at the social preference level between a and b. In such a situation we will say that a is socially *at least as good as b*. To have the weak liberalism condition, one, of course, needs to have something similar for another individual, say, j, and options c and d. Now consider a rule called the Pareto extension rule. According to this unanimity-based rule, option x is socially preferred to option y if all individuals prefer x to y. Otherwise, y is socially at least as good as x. Clearly, in this case each individual is endowed with the kind of power attributed by the weak liberalism condition not only over two options but over all options. It is very easy to see that the social strict preference (*preferred to* or *better than*) is transitive so that the kind of possible cycles obtained in Sen's analysis are not obtainable any more. However, if we ask for a stronger form of collective rationality, we get again an impossibility. In Salles (2008), three forms of stronger rationality conditions were considered.

---

[10] See, for clarifying comments, Pattanaik (1996).

The standard rationality condition is the transitivity of the social preference, viz. of the relation "at least as good as" which implies as already mentioned that both the strict preference, "better than," and indifference are transitive. The aggregation rule is then a *social welfare function* in the terminology of Arrow (1950, 1951, 1963). What Salles (2008) demonstrates is that there is no social welfare function satisfying the Pareto condition and the weak liberalism condition provided that the two options over which the two individuals have some power are not identical (this means, of course, that there are at least three options). To see how this is possible, we reconsider Sen's example about *Lady Chatterley's Lover*. Mr. Prude ranks the options in the order c, a, b (c, first, a second and b third) and Mr. Lascivious in the order a, b, c. Because of the weak liberalism condition as applied to Mr. Prude, c is socially as good as a, and as applied to Mr. Lascivious b is socially at least as good as c. Then by transitivity of the relation "at least as good as," b is socially as good as a. But the Pareto condition tells us exactly the opposite: a is socially better than b. When a Cartesian structure is introduced in this example we obtain two violations of transitivity. First, since (n, r) is socially at least as good as (n, n) by weak liberalism applied to Mr. Lascivious, (n, n) is socially at least as good as (r, n) by weak liberalism applied to Mr. Prude, we must have that (n, r) is socially as least as good as (r, n) by transitivity. This is contradicted by the fact that according to Pareto condition (r, n) is socially better than (n, r). Secondly, since (n, r) is socially at least as good as (r, r) by weak liberalism applied to Mr. Prude, and (r, r) is socially at least as good as (r, n) by weak liberalism applied to Mr. Lascivious, (n, r) is socially at least as good as (r, n) by transitivity. This is contradicted by the fact that (r, n) socially better than (n, r) by the Pareto condition.

Between transitivity of the relation "at least as good as" and transitivity of the relation "better than" (where the relation of indifference is not supposed to be transitive), two kinds of relations have been introduced: semi-orders and interval orders (Luce, 1959, 2000; Suppes, Krantz, Luce, & Tversky, 1989; Fishburn, 1985). Semi-orders and interval orders consider the possibility of, loosely speaking, partial transitivity of indifference. We will give an example for interval orders which is the relation that has the weakest form of rationality for which we obtain an impossibility. The kind of transitivity assumption for interval orders states that the relation "better than" is (implicitly) transitive and that if for four elements a, b, c and d, we have that a is better than b, b and c are indifferent, and c is better than d, then a must be better than d.[11] We will assume that a is a social state in which individual i sleeps on the back and that b is the same social state as a, except that individual i sleeps on the right side. Furthermore, c is a social state in which individual j takes a bath in any given morning and d is the same social state as c except that individual j takes a shower in the same given morning. The weak liberalism condition attributes power to individual i as far as social states a and b are concerned, and to individual j as far as social states c and d are concerned. Let us assume that individual i ranks

---

[11] Given completeness of the relation "at least as good as," this implication is equivalent to another implication which is generally used in measurement theory.

the four social states in the order d, b, a, c and individual j in the order a, c, d, b. Since both individuals rank a before c, and d before b, a is socially better than c and d is socially better than b by the Pareto condition. Since j has a power over c and d and since she prefers c to d, c is socially as good as d by weak liberalism. First, if this "socially at least as good as" is in fact "socially better than," then by transitivity of "better than" a is socially better than b. Since individual i prefers b to a and since weak liberalism gives her power over a and b, we should have that b is socially at least as good as a, which contradicts a socially better than b. Secondly, if this "socially at least as good as" is "there is an indifference between", then since a is socially better than c, c and d are socially indifferent and b is socially better than d, a is socially preferred to b by the properties of interval orders. Then we are exactly in the same situation as in the first case where b was socially as good as a. That is, having applied the assumption of weak liberalism to individual i and to social states a and b, we arrived at a contradiction.

It is shown by Salles (2008) that the results obtained for social welfare functions, semi-order valued functions and interval-order valued functions are very similar. The differences only pertain to the set of social states. For social welfare functions, the two social states over which individuals i and j have power must not be identical. For semi-order valued functions, we must add that there are at least four social states. For interval-order valued functions, the social states over which individual i and j have power must be distinct (so that there are at least four social states). As shown by the extended version of Sen's example regarding *Lady Chatterley's Lover* having four distinct social states is not a strong requirement. With two elements a and b, one can form four elements in the two-person Cartesian product structure: (a, b), (b, a), (a, a), (b, b).

4.2 The Choice-Theoretic Framework

In the choice-theoretic framework, the Pareto condition remains the same as what we described in Sect. 3. An option x Pareto-dominated by y will not be chosen in a set of options to which y belongs. On the other hand, the weak liberalism entails an important modification. As previously, two individuals i and j have a specific power over two options, a and b for i, and c and d for j. Let us consider individual i. Weak liberalism says that if individual i prefers one of the two options, say, a, to the other, b, then if it happens that b is chosen in a set to which a belongs then a has to be chosen too. For individual j, it says, of course that if j prefers one of the two options, say, c, to the other, d, then if it happens that d is chosen in a set to which c belongs, c has to be chosen too.

Let us consider an example that was previously described. The options a and b are identical social states except that in a individual i sleeps on the back and in b she sleeps on the right side. Options c and d are also identical social states except that in c individual j take a bath in any given morning and in d she takes a shower in the same given morning. Let us assume that individual i ranks the social states in the order d, a, b, c and individual j in the order b, c, d, a. To find a rationale behind these rankings, let us imagine the following story. Individual j is individual i's servant. Individual i knows that if individual j takes a bath in the morning she will be sleepy during all the day and, then, less efficient. Accordingly, she ranks d at the top of her preference and c at the bottom. Since she prefers to sleep on the back she ranks a before b. Individual j knows that sleeping on the back is not that recommended for a good rest and that when individual i is a little tired she is in a bad mood. Consequently, she ranks b at the top of her preference and a at the bottom. Since she prefers taking a bath rather than having a shower, she ranks c before d. This rationale shows very clearly the negative externality phenomenon. It also shows that it is not so easy to justify that people who are, in principle, unconcerned should be indifferent (here, for instance, individual i should be indifferent between c and d). It shows, in fact, the limits of the notion of personal sphere. If we consider a choice over the set composed of the four social states a, b, c and d, since both individuals prefer d to a and b to c, neither a nor c can be chosen by the Pareto condition. We are left with b and d. But since individual i prefers a to b, if b happens to be chosen then a has to be chosen too by weak liberalism applied to individual i. The fact is that a cannot be chosen so b cannot be chosen either. We are left with d. But since individual j prefers c to d, if d happens to be chosen, c has to be chosen too by weak liberalism. We know that c being chosen is impossible. In conclusion there is no choice at all. It is shown in Salles (2009) that we still have an impossibility when one social state a or b is either c or d (then a, b, c and d are not distinct) provided that there are at least four social states. When there are only three social states (in this case, of course, one of a or b is either c or d), we can still obtain an impossibility provided that the so-called *Weak Axiom of Revealed Preference* (WARP) is satisfied. WARP was introduced in the form presented here by Arrow (1959, 1984) and studied among others by Schwartz (1976), Sen (1971) and Suzumura (1976). We can explain WARP in a very elementary way. Let us suppose that you are making your weekly shopping in a supermarket. At the exit, in your shopping trolley there are goods from many different sections including the household products section. Now if we set all the goods aside and ask you to start again your shopping but with the possibility to uniquely visit the household products section, what you will choose will be exactly what you previously chose in the household products section. This is WARP!

What is remarkable with this result is that, except that we cannot deal with the case of only two social states and that for three-option case we need WARP, it is exactly the result obtained in Sect. 3. There is no need to consider rationality properties of the WARP type. Now, is there a justification for using this new – weak – form of liberalism? Although we have been criticized because choice can only be uniquely defined, on the basis that it is impossible to have two different social states being chosen, it seems to us that this is rather irrelevant since this is in complete contrast with the standard theory of choice as developed by economists, psychologists, philosophers, mathematicians etc. Furthermore, let us consider our previous example. Let us suppose that individual i slightly prefers a to b, that is she slightly prefers to sleep on the back. In the liberalism version of Sect. 3, b is then excluded if a can be chosen. If sleeping on the back is a possible option, sleeping on the right side is forbidden for i.[12] Since her preference is only slight, this means that she does not dislike sleeping on the right side and from time to time even take pleasure in sleeping also on her right side.[13] With weak liberalism, either the social state including "sleeping on the right side" is excluded or, if not excluded, then the social state including "sleeping on the back" is permissible. We can then truly see the condition of liberalism as a condition giving rights: if individual i has the right to sleep on the right side, she must also have the right to sleep on her back. One can develop the same kind of comments with the bath and shower variant. Individual j may prefer taking a bath to having a shower, but this preference may be very slight. It seems strange in this case that she has no right to have a shower. Weak liberalism says on the other hand that if she has the right to have a shower, she must also have the right to take a bath.

5 Discussion and Remarks

Salles (2008) draws a parallel between Arrovian theorems and Sen-type theorems.[14] From a technical point of view there are major differences. Arrovian theorems are obtained for finite societies (the set of individuals has to be finite) and this is not necessary for Sen-type theorems. Also, there is no need of the controversial condition of independence of irrelevant alternatives for Sen-type theorems. The main difference which is at the origin of the numerous researches in non-welfaristic issues in normative economics is that Sen-type theorems are non-welfaristic. The word *welfarism* is associated with the idea that the goodness of social states are evaluated only on the basis of individual utilities attached to these social states. This leads to the following observation. If we have four social states w, x, y and z and if each individual attributes the same utility to w and to x, and the same utility to y and to z, then the social ranking of w and y must be the same as the social ranking of x and z. This can be generalized to various properties which have been called neutrality properties for aggregation functions defined on lists of individual utility functions and can be extended to aggregation functions defined on lists of individual preferences in which case one obtains intra or inter lists neutrality.[15] For instance, if the preference restriction of each individual i to x and y is related to her preference restriction to z and w, in the sense that individual i prefers x to y if and only if she prefers z to w, she prefers y to x if and only if she prefers w to z and she is indifferent between x and y if and only if she is indifferent between z and w, then x is socially preferred to y if and only if z is preferred to w, y is socially preferred to

---

[12] If during her sleep, individual i turns to the right side while she was sleeping on the back, one must have a device to take her back to her back!

[13] This also calls our attention to problems related to indeterminacy and vagueness (Piggins & Salles, 2007).

[14] For Arrovian theorems see Blau (1979), Blair and Pollack (1979), Blair, Bordes, Kelly, & Suzumura (1976) and Suzumura (1983).

[15] A remarkable introduction to the non-welfaristic literature is Pattanaik (1994).

x if and only if w is socially preferred to z and there is a social indifference between x and y if and only if there is a social indifference between z and w. The roles of x and z are similar, as are the roles of y and w.[16] Intuitively, neutrality means that the names of social states do not matter. To give a simple voting example, if voters are asked to rank the candidates and the voting procedure gives an outcome that is also a ranking, and if candidate a is ranked before candidate b in the outcome ranking, then modifying all ballot papers by replacing the name a by the name c and the name b by the name d, given neutrality (which is, in general, satisfied by voting rules), will give an outcome where c will be ranked before d. The liberalism conditions obviously violate neutrality since specific social states are attached to specific individuals. Likewise, anonymity, a condition that says that the name of individuals do not matter, is also violated since some specific individuals have some specific power.

In the choice-theoretic framework, we obtained exactly the same kind of result as Sen's theorem (with the exception of the assumptions on the number of options and on the two options over which the individuals have some power, but we believe that these assumptions are not very constraining).

6 Conclusion

In this paper, we have described, in a rather intuitive way, the results obtained by Salles (2008, 2009). We have considered two frameworks. A framework where social preferences were obtained from individual preferences (an aggregation function setting) and a framework where, rather than a social preference, a choice was done over all subsets of possible social states (a social choice function setting – or social choice correspondence setting as it is called by people who do not like to use the word "function" when the values taken by the "function" are subsets of a given set). The intuitive presentation has been based on many, sometimes quite famous examples. These examples were totally absent in Salles's papers. We think that the choice-theoretic framework is particularly interesting in the sense that it offers a rather direct generalization of Sen's theorem. This is not the case in the aggregation function setting. The next step in our research will be to study rights within the social choice paradigm by using the concepts of possibility and necessity as introduced in modal logic.[17] We have previously outlined that the analysis of rights within social choice theory had two basic formal aspects: obligation and possibility. Modal logic deals with this kind of notions, and, in particular, deontic logic studies the normative use of language. We conjecture that, using these logics, we will get new results that should clarify the sort of problems we considered.

---

[16] Formally z is obtained from x and w is obtained from y by a permutation over the finite set of options.

[17] See Priest (2008).

Acknowledgments Financial support to the first author from the French ANR through contract NT05-1_42582 (3LB) is gratefully acknowledged. We are very grateful to the Editors of this volume for many stylistic suggestions.

References

Arrow, K. J. (1950). A difficulty in the concept of social welfare. *Journal of Political Economy, 58,* 328–346.

Arrow, K. J. (1951, 1963). *Social choice and individual values.* New York: Wiley.

Arrow, K. J. (1959). Rational choice functions and orderings. *Economica, 26,* 121–127.

Arrow, K. J. (1984). *Individual choice under certainty and uncertainty. Collected papers of Kenneth J. Arrow, Volume 3.* Oxford: Blackwell.

Barberá, S., Bossert, W., & Pattanaik, P. K. (2004). Ranking sets of objects. In: S. Barberá, P. J. Hammond, & C. Seidl (Eds.), *Handbook of utility theory* (Vol. 2). Dordrecht: Kluwer.

Blair, D. H., Bordes, G., Kelly, J. S., & Suzumura, K. (1976). Impossibility theorems without collective rationality. *Journal of Economic Theory, 13,* 361–379.

Blair, D. H., & Pollack, R. A. (1979). Collective rationality and dictatorship: The scope of the Arrow theorem. *Journal of Economic Theory, 21,* 186–194.

Blau, J. H., 1979. Semiorders and collective choice. *Journal of Economics Theory, 21,* 195–203.

Brunel, A., & Salles, M. (1998). Interpretative, semantic and formal difficulties of the social choice approach to rights. In: J.-F. Laslier, M. Fleurbaey, & A. Trannoy (Eds.), *Freedom in economics: New perspectives in normative economics.* London: Routledge.

Fishburn, P. C. (1985). *Interval orders and interval graphs.* New York: Wiley.

Gaertner, W., Pattanaik, P. K., & Suzumura, K. (1992). Individual rights revisited. *Economica, 59,* 161–177.

Gärdenfors, P. (1981). Rights, games and social choice. *Nous, 15,* 341–356.

Gärdenfors, P. (2005). *The dynamics of thought.* Heidelberg: Springer.

Gibbard, A. (1974). A Pareto consistent libertarian claim. *Journal of Economic Theory, 7,* 388–410.

Hammond, P. J. (1998). Some comments on Brunel and Salles. In: J.-F. Laslier, M. Fleurbaey, & A. Trannoy (Eds.), *Freedom in economics: New perspectives in normative economics.* London: Routledge.

Hausman, D. M., & McPherson, M. S. (2006). *Economic analysis, moral philosophy, and public policy* (2nd ed.). Cambridge: Cambridge University Press.

Karni, E. (1974). *Individual liberty, the Pareto principle and the possibility of social decision function.* Working Paper, The Foerder Institute for Economic Research, Tel-Aviv University.

Li, L., & Saari, D. G. (2008). Sen's theorem: Geometric proof, new interpretations. *Social Choice and Welfare, 31,* 393–413.

Luce, R. D. (1959). *Individual choice behavior. A theoretical analysis.* New York: Wiley.

Luce, R. D. (2000). *Utility of gains and losses. Measurement-theoretical and experimental approaches.* Mahwah, NJ: Lawrence Elbaum Associates.

Mill, J. S. (1859). *On liberty.* London: John W. Parker and Son.

Pattanaik, P. K. (1994). Some non-welfaristic issues in welfare economics. In: B. Dutta (Ed.), *Welfare economics.* Delhi: Oxford University Press.

Pattanaik, P. K. (1996). On modelling individual rights: Some conceptual issues. In: K. J. Arrow, A. K. Sen, & K. Suzumura (Eds.), *Social choice reexamined* (Vol. 2). London: MacMillan.

Pattanaik, P. K., & Xu, Y. (1990). On ranking opportunity sets in terms of freedom of choice. *Recherches Economiques de Louvain, 56,* 383–390.

Peleg, B. (1998). Effectivity functions, game forms, games, and rights. *Social Choice and Welfare, 15,* 67–80, and in: J.-F. Laslier, M. Fleurbaey, N. Gravel, & A. Trannoy (Eds.), *Freedom in economics: New perspectives in normative economics.* London: Routledge.

Piggins, A., & Salles, M. (2007). Instances of indeterminacy. *Analyse & Kritik, 29,* 311–328.

Priest, G. (2008). *An introduction to non-classical logic: From if to is* (2nd ed.). Cambridge: Cambridge University Press.

Saari, D. G., & Pétron, A. (2006). Negative externalities and Sen's liberalism theorem. *Economic Theory, 28,* 265–281.

Saari, D. G. (2008). *Disposing dictators, demystifying voting paradoxes: Social choice analysis.* Cambridge: Cambridge University Press.

Salles, M. (1996). Discussion of Pattanaik's paper. In: K. J. Arrow, A. K. Sen, & K. Suzumura (Eds.), *Social choice reexamined* (Vol. 2). London: MacMillan.

Salles, M. (2000). Amartya Sen. Droits et choix social. *Revue Economique, 51,* 445–457.

Salles, M. (2008). Limited rights as partial veto and Sen's impossibility theorem. In: P. K. Pattanaik, K. Tadenuma, Y. Xu, & N. Yoshihara (Eds.), *Rational choice and social welfare, theory and applications: Essays in honor of Kotaro Suzumura.* Heidelberg: Springer.

Salles, M. (2009). Limited rights and social choice rules. In: K. Basu & R. Kanbur (Eds.), *Arguments for a better world, essays in honor of Amartya Sen, Volume I, ethics, welfare, and measurement.* Oxford: Oxford University Press.

Schwartz, T. (1976). Choice functions, "rationality" conditions, and variations on the weak axiom of revealed preference. *Journal of Economic Theory, 13,* 414–427.

Sen, A. K. (1970a). The impossibility of a Paretian liberal. *Journal of Political Economy, 78,* 152–157.

Sen, A. K. (1970b). *Collective choice and social welfare.* San Francisco: Holden-Day.

Sen, A. K. (1971). Choice functions and revealed preference. *Review of Economic Studies, 38,* 307–317.

Sen, A. K. (1976). Liberty, unanimity and rights. *Economica, 49,* 217–245.

Sen, A. K. (1982). *Choice, welfare and measurement.* Oxford: Blackwell.

Sen, A. K. (2002). *Rationality and freedom.* Cambridge, MA: Harvard University Press.

Suppes, P., Krantz, D. H., Luce, R. D., & Tversky, A. (1989). *Foundations of measurement* (Vol. 2). New York: Academic Press.

Suzumura, K. (1976). Rational choice and revealed preference. *Review of Economic Studies, 43,* 149–158.

Suzumura, K. (1983). *Rational choice, collective decisions and social welfare.* Cambridge: Cambridge University Press.

Suzumura, K. (2006). Rights, opportunities, and social choice procedures. In: K. J. Arrow, A. K. Sen, & K. Suzumura (Eds.), *Handbook of social choice and welfare* (Vol. 2). Amsterdam: North-Holland.

Some General Results on Responsibility for Outcomes

Martin van Hees

1 Introduction

Consider a committee that has to decide on a particular issue. After some deliberation and exchange of information, the members come to a decision, possibly by means of a vote. The decision made – the outcome – is something we can attribute to the committee. Indeed, we say, for instance, that a court of law *hands down* a verdict, a government *adopts* a policy, or that a company's board *settles* for a new strategy. Moreover, we can say that the committee bears *responsibility* for the decision it made. To what extent can we also attach such attributions to the individuals constituting the committee? Are some of them responsible for the decision made? And, if so, can we hold *each* individual judge, cabinet minister, or company board member responsible for the outcome of the decision process in which she was engaged?

The answers to these questions are not obvious. One possibility, though, is to say that membership of a committee in itself is sufficient to incur responsibility for whatever decision the committee makes. In this view, one is responsible simply because one is formally involved in the decision making process. If your dissatisfaction with some outcome is so strong that you do not want to be responsible for its realization, then, so goes the argument, you should have withdrawn from the committee. By remaining you have committed yourself to whatever decision is being made, or you are at least are complicit in it, even if the decision is one with which you strongly disagree. It is this commitment which is then taken to create responsibility for the resulting outcome.

We may call this kind of responsibility *formal* because it does not depend on the specific behaviour of the individual within the committee of which she is a member, i.e. the way she voted; rather, it accrues to her simply by virtue of her participation in the decision process. Whether we indeed always have such formal responsibility is contestable, however. Opting out need not always be a feasible option and it is therefore not always reasonable to state that a member is responsible. Moreover,

M. van Hees (✉)
Faculty of Philosophy, University of Groningen, 9712 GL Groningen, The Netherlands
e-mail: Martin.van.Hees@rug.nl

A. Van Deemen, A. Rusinowska (eds.), *Collective Decision Making,*
Theory and Decision Library C 43, DOI 10.1007/978-3-642-02865-6_7,
© Springer-Verlag Berlin Heidelberg 2010

even when opting out is a possibility, the rationale of assigning responsibility to any member can be contested. Suppose, for instance, that you have accepted an invitation to become a member of an internal appointment committee because you think the hiring policy of the company you work for should be changed. Say you object strongly to the very unequal male/female ratio in the company's top positions. Furthermore, when accepting the invitation, you were justified in believing that the policy could only be changed if you were to join the committee. Now suppose that, despite all your best efforts within the committee, you cannot convince the other committee members that your most preferred candidate – a woman – should be appointed. A majority turns out to be in favour of another candidate and the majority gets its way: yet again a male candidate is appointed to a top position. In cases like these – that is, in situations where some member of the group did his utmost to try to prevent some decision from being taken – we may be reluctant to aver that he is nevertheless responsible for the outcome. And even if we were justified in holding the person responsible merely for his having partaken in the decision process, the example shows that formal responsibility does not cover all types of responsibility. We may also want to assess whether a person is responsible for the outcome because of *how* he fulfilled his membership of the decision making body.

This second, non-formal kind of responsibility concerns a member's responsibility insofar as it evolves from the specific way the person acted within the committee. We refer to such responsibility when we say, for instance, that the opposition in parliament is not to be held responsible for some particular decision made by the government parties, or that a judge who expresses a dissenting opinion is not responsible for the verdict of the court of which he is a member. More generally, it is the kind of responsibility that we implicitly invoke when we say that some members of the decision making body are and some are not responsible for the eventual outcome. This paper focuses on this kind of non-formal responsibility for outcomes which, to ease the readers' burden, we henceforth simply refer to as "responsibility".

Responsibility judgements are notoriously difficult when several agents have contributed to the outcome, a problem known as "the many hands problem" (Thompson, 1980). In fact, in an important recent paper, Philip Pettit (2007) suggests that there may be situations in which *none* of the members of a group can be held responsible in this way. In this paper we examine some general conditions under which we can indeed assign responsibility to one or more of the individuals involved in the decision making process.

To do so, we must of course adopt some particular theory of responsibility; that is, we must have an account of what it means to say that a person is or is not responsible for some outcome. Drawing on Braham and van Hees (2009b), we assume that a person is responsible only if two conditions are realized. First, the person should have made a *causal contribution* to the outcome. That is, his behaviour – say the way he voted – was one of the causal factors that led to the realization of the outcome. Secondly, the person should have had a *reasonable opportunity to do otherwise*. This expresses the idea that we do not hold a person responsible for some outcome if it would not be reasonable to say that he could have done otherwise. The unreasonableness of such a claim may result from the person's simply not having had any alternative (say when someone is physically forced to perform some particular act), or from his not having had a reasonable alternative (say when someone is threatened with great loss if some act is not performed).

Clearly, these are just the rough outlines of an account of responsibility.[1] In Braham and van Hees (2009a, 2009b) we have shown how this account of responsibility can be described in game-theoretical terms and how the resulting approach solves the many hands problem – the analysis gives a rigorous formulation of the conditions under which we hold an agent responsible. Sections 2 and 3 below present the main elements of that analysis.[2] In Sect. 4 we apply the framework to examine the conditions under which *responsibility voids* arise, that is, situations in which there is some aspect of the outcome (or the outcome itself) for which none of the members can be held responsible. We shall see that the possibility of such voids depends crucially on whether the game satisfies a certain weak requirement of transparency. In our two-pronged theory of responsibility, the second step (ascertaining the availability of an alternative opportunity) may be more difficult to apply than the first (ascertaining whether the person made a causal contribution). The difficulty of establishing whether a person is responsible or not would be greatly reduced if causal efficacy were to suffice for assigning responsibility. For this reason, in Sect. 5 we examine the conditions under which causal efficacy always coincides with responsibility. It turns out that such a reduction of moral responsibility to causal efficacy is indeed possible, provided the game satisfies a stronger requirement of transparency. Next, in Sect. 6, we examine the types of decision situations in which being "efficacious" for *some* aspect of an outcome always entails being responsible for *all* of its aspects. Clearly, in such situations the allocation of responsibility would be even easier – we simply have to check whether a person has made a causal contribution to some aspect of the outcome to ascertain that he is fully responsible, that is, responsible for all aspects. However, the class of games in which this is the case turns out to be rather restricted.

2 The Formal Framework

A game G is an $n+4$-tuple $(N, X, S_1, \ldots, S_n, \pi, \Gamma)$, where N (with cardinality n) is the set of players, X a set of alternatives, for each $i \in N$, S_i is a set of strategies, π is a mapping from the set of all strategy combinations (one for each individual) onto X, and Γ is an n-tuple of probability distributions Γ_i, each describing the probabilities that an agent justifiably assigns to the various strategy combinations the others could adopt.

Note that a game as defined here does not specify the preferences of the individuals and in that sense cannot properly be called a game. However, the beliefs that

---

[1] Neither of the two conditions is uncontested. See Braham and van Hees (2009b) for references to discussions.

[2] For related accounts, see Goldman (1999) and Vallentyne (2008).

agents have concerning the way the others will act, and which are given by Γ_i, may well be derived from such preference information. In fact, we are implicitly making such an assumption when we assume that each i is *justified* in believing that Γ_i is the correct description of those probabilities.

An *event* is any combination of individual strategies belonging to $\Pi_{i \in T} S_i$, where T is some non-empty subset of N. For any events s_U and s_T, s_U is called a *subevent* of s_T if $U \subseteq T$ and if each member of U has the same strategy in s_U as in s_T. The outcomes to which some event s_T can lead is given by $\pi(s_T) = \{\pi(s_N) \mid s_T$ is a subevent of $s_N\}$.

A *play* of the game is any event s_N and a *contingency* is an event in which the strategies of exactly $n-1$ individuals are specified. To simplify the reader's task, we shall often write s_{-i} and s_{-T} rather than $s_{N-\{i\}}$ or s_{N-T}, respectively. For the same reason, we write s_{T-i} instead of $s_{T-\{i\}}$. Given an event s_T, s_i denotes the strategy that $i \in T$ adopts in s_T, for event s_T', it is denoted by s_i', etc. Finally, for disjoint T and U we write (s_T, s_U) to denote the (sub)event consisting of the combination of the (mutually exclusive) events s_T and s_U.

Aspects of elements of X can be called states of affairs and are represented by (non-empty and proper) subsets A of X. Thus, to refer to the example given in the introduction, if $x \in X$ is the outcome of an appointment procedure, we may say that $x \in A$ describes the fact that x is a man, $x \in B$ describes him being younger than thirty, etc. Obviously, we often want to ascertain an individual's responsibility for the realization of some such state of affairs, say when we want to examine the responsibility of the members of an appointment committee for hiring a man rather than a woman. Hence, we are not only interested in a person's responsibility for the actual outcome x of the game but also for proper subsets of X containing x.[3]

3 Conditions for Responsibility

As explained in the introduction, our account of responsibility rests on two pillars. We assume one can only be held responsible for a state of affairs A if one was *causally effective* for its realization and if one had sufficient *opportunity to do otherwise*.

Braham and van Hees (2009a) argued that causal contributions can be analyzed game-theoretically in terms of the performance of an action which is a part of some minimally sufficient condition for A. The basic idea goes back to what is called the NESS-test in the theory of causation (Hart & Honoré, 1959; Mackie, 1974). According to the NESS-test ("Necessary Element of a Sufficient Set of conditions"), an event c is said to form a causal condition for another event e if, and only if, c is a member of a set of conditions which is sufficient for e but which, if c were not an

---

[3] In our formal analysis we shall restrict ourselves to subsets, whereby responsibility for some $x \in X$ is analyzed in terms of responsibility for the singleton set of which x is the sole member. Yet, to simplify notation, we often omit the set brackets when the outcome refers to such a singleton set.

element, would not have been sufficient. Formulated in terms of events, this yields the following definition of causal efficacy.

Definition 1 Given G and some play s_N of G, individual i is causally effective for A ("makes a causal contribution to A") if, and only if, there is some subevent s_T of s_N such that $\pi(s_T) \subseteq A$ and $\pi(s_{T-i}) \not\subseteq A$.

Note that the definition is in terms of i's action being "necessary" for some event to lead to A. Since i's action can only be so if there is a subevent in which *every* individual is necessary and in which i adopts the same action, we can say that i makes a causal contribution if, and only if, his action is part of some minimally sufficient condition for A.

To illustrate the definition, consider a three-person committee facing a choice between three alternatives x, y and z. Each individual strategy consists of a vote for exactly one of the three alternatives, and the procedure that is used is the plurality rule combined with the specification that the chair breaks ties (we do not need to specify exactly how he does so, stipulating only that (a) the outcome will be one of the alternatives that are tied, (b) if the chair voted for one of the tied alternatives, then the alternative for which he voted will be chosen). First, suppose there is unanimity – all players vote for x. Any combination of two votes for x is sufficient for x to be adopted. Clearly, such a combination is also minimally sufficient for x – a single vote for x is not sufficient for x to be chosen. Since each of the individual votes for x is a member of at least one such minimally sufficient combination, each player makes a causal contribution to x.

Next consider the case in which each individual votes for a different alternative, that is, there is a tie. Assuming the chair, i say, voted for x, the outcome is x. Applying the definition, we see that each individual is causally effective for x – the actual play is a minimally sufficient condition for x.[4] Moreover, it is easy to check that i is causally effective for $\{x, y\}$ and $\{x, z\}$ as well, whereas the individuals who voted for y and z are not effective for $\{x, z\}$ and $\{x, y\}$, respectively.

The second ingredient of our account of responsibility expresses the requirement that one should have had a reasonable opportunity to do otherwise. It can easily be seen that causal efficacy as defined here entails that one had at least one alternative opportunity; that is, one could have performed an alternative action which could have resulted in a different state of affairs. After all, if $\pi(s_{T-i}) \not\subseteq A$, then there must be some s_i' and s_{N-T}' such that $\pi(s_{T-i}, s_i', s_{N_T}') \notin A$. However, the kind of alternative opportunity that causal efficacy entails is too weak to ground moral responsibility. To see why, consider again the voting committee faced with a tie between x, y and z, with the chair's vote for x breaking the tie. We saw that each individual is causally effective for the realization of x. Yet we may not want to hold the individuals who voted for y or z responsible for the outcome. Suppose, for instance, that the players did not had any idea about how the others would vote and therefore assigned equal probability to each possible contingency. In this case,

---

[4] In formal terms, if s_N denotes the actual play, we have $\pi(s_N) = x$ but $\pi(s_{N-i}) \neq \{x\}$, for all $i \in N$.

not voting for x was the best they could do to prevent x from being chosen. More precisely, such a vote minimized the probability they would be effective for x. On the other hand, if one of them knew for sure that the chair would vote for x and the other player for z, then we can hold him responsible for the outcome x – even though he voted for y. After all, he knew that his vote would then lead to x. Causal efficacy is therefore not sufficient for moral responsibility: the beliefs the agents had about the impact of their alternative actions are also relevant.

But how do those beliefs matter? It will not do to say that we should focus on the probability that the outcome would have been prevented if the player had adopted some other strategy. To see why, consider a play of the game in which all three of the players voted for x. All players had a strict preference for x and they all knew so; they therefore each assigned a probability of one to the contingency in which the others vote for x. Clearly, given these probabilities, no individual could vote in such a way that the outcome x would result with a probability lower than one. Yet we do hold each of them responsible for the realization of x: a person may not have been able to lower the probability that x would result, but he could have lowered the probability that he would be *effective* for x.

We therefore assume that the kind of alternative possibility that is needed to hold a person responsible involves the existence of a strategy which he justifiably believed to be *less likely* to make him causally effective for A than the strategy he actually played. To make this precise, define for each individual i and each $s \in S_i$, $h_i(s, A) = \{s_{-i} \mid i$ is effective for A in $(s, s_{-i})\}$ and set the probability that i will be effective for A if he adopts s as:

$$p_i(A, s) = \sum_{s_{-i} \in h(s, A)} \Gamma_i(s_{-i}).$$

Combining the two elements – causal efficacy and opportunity to do otherwise – now yields the following criteria for the assignment of moral responsibility[5]:

Definition 2[6] Given G and a play s_N of G, an individual $i \in N$ is responsible for $A \subseteq X$ if and only if,

1. i is causally effective for A in s_N;
2. for some $s' \in S_i$: $p_i(A, s') < p_i(A, s_i)$.

---

[5] Note that Definition 2 takes the conditions to be necessary *and* sufficient. A fully fledged theory of responsibility would also include a condition referring to the minimum degree of autonomy needed for responsibility. In what follows we simply assume this third requirement is always satisfied.

[6] The definition is a simplified version of the one presented in Braham and van Hees (2009b). First, we here ignore the possibility that an alternative opportunity may not be *eligible*; that is, it may not be reasonable to demand that the agent performed it. We simply assume that any of the available strategies is eligible. For a normative defence of this assumption in the analysis of political decision making, see Dowding and van Hees (2007). Moreover, we here ignore the possibility that the individuals' strategies are correlated in the sense that the probability that an agent i assigns to a contingency s_{-i} may differ for his different strategies.

4 Responsibility Voids

In this section we turn to the analysis of responsibility voids, that is, situations in which there is some aspect of the outcome of the game for which none of the individuals can be held responsible.

Definition 3 A game G displays a responsibility void if, and only if, for some $A \neq X$ and some s_N: $\pi(s_N) \in A$ and no $i \in N$ bears responsibility for A in s_N.

It turns out that the possibility of such voids depends crucially on the transparency of the game, that is, on whether there is an appropriate fit between the adoption of certain strategies and the resulting outcome. We distinguish two types of transparency. Each is defined in terms of *minimal A-strategies*.

Definition 4 We call a strategy $s \in S_i$ a *minimal A-strategy* of i if $p_i(A, s) \leq p_i(A, s')$ for all $s' \in S_i$. An *A-minimal play* is a play in which each player adopts a minimal A-strategy.

The first notion of transparency that we discuss states that a play in which all individuals adopt an A-minimal strategy, that is, a play in which each individual minimizes the probability of being effective for A, will never lead to A.

Definition 5 A game G satisfies weak transparency if, and only if, for any $A \subseteq X(A \neq X)$ and any A-minimal play s_N: the outcome of s_N does not belong to A.

Proposition 1 *A game never displays responsibility voids if, and only if, it is weakly transparent.*

Proof
$\Rightarrow$. Follows directly from the definition of A-minimality and from having an alternative opportunity.

$\Leftarrow$. Assume some play s_N yields a void for some A. Let T be the set of all players who are causally effective for A. Any $i \in T$ must be playing a minimal A-strategy for he would otherwise be responsible for A. Clearly, if $T = N$, the play is A-minimal and the game thus violates weak transparency. Assume $T \neq N$, and let s'_N be the play in which all of the members of T adopt the same strategy as in s_N and in which all of the members of $N - T$ adopt an A-minimal strategy as well. Since only the members of T are causally effective for A in s_N, it must be the case that $\pi(s_T) \subseteq A$. We therefore must have $\pi(s'_N) \in A$. Since s'_N is, by construction, A-minimal, the game violates weak transparency. $\square$

Weak transparency is a reasonable demand and will be satisfied by most voting games. Yet it may be violated in some special cases. Consider the following amendment of the plurality voting game described earlier. Though the individuals can only vote for x, y or z, there is a fourth alternative, say u, which will be the outcome if all of the alternatives get exactly one vote. Suppose such a full-blown tie does indeed materialize. It is easy to check that each player is causally effective for the resulting outcome u. Yet, for almost any reasonable specification of the various probabilities involved, each of the individuals plays a minimal u-strategy.

Though violations of weak transparency are thus possible, they will only arise in specific voting games and therefore need not worry us too much. The mere absence of voids may, however, not dispel all concerns about the assignment of responsibility. One particular difficulty is that it may be difficult to establish whether an agent did indeed have a reasonable opportunity to do otherwise; we may, for instance, not have the required information about the various probabilities. In the next two sections we examine the possibility of defining games which would avoid responsibility voids and which would considerably simplify the analysis because in them causal efficacy would be a necessary *and* sufficient condition for responsibility.

5 Equivalence of Efficacy and Responsibility

If causal efficacy and moral responsibility were always to coincide, an assessment of whether a person is morally responsible for some A would only require an examination of whether he is causally effective for it. It turns out there is a straightforward way to characterize games in which the two concepts are equivalent.

Definition 6 A game is strongly transparent if, and only if, for any player i and any A: if i plays an A-minimal strategy, then i is not causally effective for A.

Proposition 2 *A game is strongly transparent if, and only if, causal efficacy always coincides with moral responsibility (that is, a person is causally efficacious for some A if and only if he is morally responsible for A).*

Proof
$\Rightarrow$. Let a game be strongly transparent. If i is responsible for some A then, by definition, he is effective for it. Assume he is effective for it. Strong transparency entails he does not play an A-minimal strategy, which means he is morally responsible for A.

$\Leftarrow$. Suppose the game violates transparency: some player is effective for A through the adoption of an A-minimal strategy. Clearly, he cannot be responsible for A. Hence, he is effective but not responsible: the equivalence of moral responsibility and causal efficacy does not hold.   □

Whereas the result in itself is not very surprising, it can be fruitfully applied. To establish whether some voter is responsible for some state of affairs A, we now only have to examine whether he was effective for it. In terms of voting theory, pivotality here suffices to establish responsibility: if a person's vote was pivotal for the realization of the state of affairs, the person is responsible for it.

6 Full Responsibility

We have seen that strong transparency entails that causal effectivity coincides with moral responsibility. Of course, this does not preclude a person's being responsible only in a very limited sense: there may be many states of affairs resulting from the game for which he cannot be held responsible. We could preclude this by additionally demanding that a person is always "fully" responsible or not responsible at all.

Definition 7 A game satisfies full responsibility if, and only if, for any play s_N and any $i \in N$, either i is morally responsible for any proper non-empty subset of X containing $\pi(s_N)$ or i is responsible for no such subset of X at all.

Clearly, if strong transparency as well as full responsibility are satisfied, it becomes very easy to determine whether a person is responsible or not. We only have to establish that a person is *causally effective* for *some* aspect of the outcome to infer that he is *morally responsible* for *all* aspects of it. Unfortunately, it turns out that the two conditions are only satisfied in a very restricted and unattractive class of games.

Definition 8 A game is dictatorial if, and only if, there is some $i \in N$ such that for all $x \in X$ there is some $s \in S_i$ for which $\pi(s) = x$.

Proposition 3 *Let* #$X \geq 3$. *Any game satisfying strong transparency and full responsibility is dictatorial.*

Proof Take any G satisfying strong transparency and full responsibility. The proof proceeds in three steps.

Step 1. We show that for any play s_N in which for each i there is an a_i such that s_i is an $X - a_i$-minimal strategy: if some s_T is a minimal sufficient condition for $\pi(s_N)$, then $T \subseteq \{i \mid s_i$ is an $X - \pi(s_N)$-minimal strategy$\}$. Furthermore, for all $i \in T$ and for all $y \neq \pi(s_N)$, s_i is not $X - y$-minimal.

Suppose some element of $X - \cup_{i \in N} A_i$ is the outcome, where each A_i is defined as $A_i = \{a_i \mid s_i$ is an $X - a_i$-minimal strategy$\}$. Since $\pi(s_N) \in \cap_{i \in N} X - A_i$, each i fails to be responsible for some $X - \{a_i\}$ containing $\pi(s_N)$. However, some i must be causally effective for $\pi(s_N)$ and by strong transparency and full responsibility must therefore be responsible for any proper subset of X containing $\pi(s_N)$. Hence, we must have $\pi(s_N) \in \cup_{i \in N} A_i$, that is, some i plays an $X - \pi(s_N)$-minimal strategy.

Take some i who does not play an $X - \pi(s_N)$-minimal strategy. Since s_i is $X - a_i$-minimal for some $a_i \neq \pi(s_N)$, i is not responsible for $X - \{a_i\}$. Hence, by strong transparency and full responsibility he is not effective for $\pi(s_N)$. Since this holds for all i who do not play an $X - \pi(s_N)$-minimal strategy, only individuals who play an $X - \pi(s_N)$-minimal strategy are effective for $\pi(s_N)$. Strong transparency and full responsibility implies that any such i is responsible for any A containing $\pi(s_N)$, which means that they do not play an $X - y$-minimal strategy if $y \neq \pi(s_N)$.

Step 2. Let s_T^* be a sufficient condition for some outcome x and assume there is no U having fewer members than T and for which there is an event s_U' which is sufficient for some (possibly different) element of X. We prove that T is a singleton set.

For any A and i, let s_i^A denote an A-minimal strategy of i. Assume N contains exactly two elements i and j, and consider the play (s_i^{X-x}, s_j^{X-y}) $(x \neq y)$. The result now follows immediately from step 1. Next assume N contains at least three elements, let s_T^* be as defined and let y, z be two elements distinct from x $(y \neq z)$. Take arbitrary $i \in T$ and consider the play $(s_{T-i}^{X-y}, s_i^{X-x}, s_{N-T}^{X-z})$. By Step 1 the outcome must be either x, y or z. If the outcome is y, step 1 entails that s_{T-i}^{X-y} is a sufficient condition for y, contradicting the way s_T^* was defined. If z is the outcome, we have $\pi(s_{N-T}) = z$ by step 1, contradicting $\pi(s_T^*) = x$. Hence, the outcome is x and, again by step 1, s_i^{X-x} is a sufficient condition for x. Hence, $T = \{i\}$.

Step 3. If i has a strategy s_i^* which is sufficient for x, then he has one for any $y \in X$.

Let s_i^* be as defined. Take two different elements y, z of $X - \{x\}$ and consider the play $(s_i^{X-y}, s_{N-i}^{X-z})$. By Step 1, we either have $\pi(s_i^{X-y}) = \{y\}$ or $\pi(s_{N-i}^{X-z}) = \{z\}$. However, $\pi(s_{N-i}^{X-z}) = \{z\}$ contradicts sufficiency of s_i^* for x.   □

If we want to avoid dictatorial games, we should thus either drop the requirement of strong transparency or full responsibility. Dropping full responsibility seems to be the natural candidate. Indeed, if we permit it to be weakened by demanding that at least some player is fully responsible for the outcome, then possibilities emerge. Consider again the plurality rule in which a chair breaks ties. In our discussion of the rule in Sect. 3 we saw that it is possible that some voters are responsible for some but not all aspects of the outcome. However, it is also true that in the two examples that we gave, the chair, person i, is responsible for *every* aspect of the outcome.

7 Conclusion

Though the analysis of this paper applies to decision processes in general, our particular interest lies in responsibility for the outcome of voting processes. To give just one illustration of why this is important, consider politicians' voting records. Clearly, the assessment of such records is very relevant in any well-functioning, representative democracy – we want to know which collective decisions we can justifiably hold our representatives responsible for.

Moreover, the results are relevant when decisions have to be made about which voting rules to adopt. For instance, if we want to avoid responsibility voids, we should have to ensure that the voting game is weakly transparent. Similarly, if we take an equivalence of moral responsibility and causal efficacy to be a desideratum, we should opt for voting rules that yield a strongly transparent game. Clearly, the results are general in the sense that they apply to games as such, and are not applied to particular voting rules. A natural next step would therefore be to examine the conditions under which particular voting games satisfy the conditions introduced. Indeed, such an analysis is necessary if we want to establish which particular voting rules are compatible (and which are not) with the importance we attach to the possibility of holding people responsible.

References

Braham, M., & van Hees, M. (2009a). Degrees of causation. *Erkenntnis, 71*, 323–344.
Braham, M., & van Hees, M. (2009b). *An anatomy of moral responsibility*. Working Paper.
Dowding, K., & van Hees, M. (2007). In praise of manipulation. *British Journal of Political Science, 38*, 1–15.
Goldman, A. I. (1999). Why citizens should vote: A causal responsibility approach. *Social Philosophy and Policy, 16*, 201–217.
Hart, H. L. A., & Honoré, A. M. (1959). *Causation in the law*. Oxford: Oxford University Press.
Mackie, J. L. (1974). *The cement of the universe*. Oxford: Oxford University Press.
Pettit, P. (2007). Responsibility incorporated. *Ethics, 117*, 171–201.
Thompson, D. F. (1980). Moral responsibility of public officials: The problem of many hands. *American Political Science Review, 74*, 905–916.
Vallentyne, P. (2008). Brute luck and responsibility. *Philosophy, Politics, and Economics, 7*, 57–80.

Existence of a Dictatorial Subgroup in Social Choice with Independent Subgroup Utility Scales, an Alternative Proof

Anna B. Khmelnitskaya

1 Introduction

In Arrow's (1951) famous impossibility theorem, individual preferences are ordinally measurable and interpersonally noncomparable. Building on the seminal work of Sen (1970), there is now an extensive literature that investigates the implications for social decision-making of alternative assumptions concerning the measurability and interpersonal comparability of individual preferences. See, for example, Roberts (1980a, 1980b), d'Aspremont (1985), Yanovskaya (1988, 1989), Tsui & Weymark (1997), and Bossert and Weymark (2004). These studies adapt mainly the welfarist approach to social choice and assume that only individual utilities matter for ranking a feasible set of social alternatives. In this case a social choice rule can be equivalently described in terms of a *social welfare ordering* – a social ordering of the admissible profiles of individual utilities (admissibility is understood as the satisfaction of several *a priori* appealing conditions), or in terms of a *social welfare function* – a function that represents a social welfare ordering and measures social welfare. Various assumptions concerning the measurability and interpersonal comparability of utility can be formalized by partitioning the set of feasible individual profiles and requiring the social welfare ordering to be constant over a cell of the partition. These studies show that under different measurability-comparability assumptions over individual utilities, i.e., in case when more democracy is adapted by the society, classes of nondictatorial social choice rules exist that satisfy all of Arrow's axioms (restated in terms of utility functions). In the aforecited publications the measurement scales of individual utilities are assumed to be of the same type across the entire society. An extension of this direction is a study of Arrovian social choice problems when individual utilities in disjoint subgroups of individuals are measured by different scale types, in other words, when separate subgroups of individuals admit different types of information. This situation is common in

A.B. Khmelnitskaya (✉)
St. Petersburg Institute for Economics and Mathematics, Russian Academy of Sciences, 191187 St. Petersburg, Russia
e-mail: a.khmelnitskaya@math.utwente.nl

A. Van Deemen, A. Rusinowska (eds.), *Collective Decision Making,*
Theory and Decision Library C 43, DOI 10.1007/978-3-642-02865-6_8,
© Springer-Verlag Berlin Heidelberg 2010

real decision making. A typical example is the partitioning of a human society into families which in turn consist of individuals. If an outsider is making the comparisons based on reports from individuals, it is reasonable to suppose that the kind of information available within and between families will be different in general. Indeed, the kinds of utility comparisons that can be made within a family cannot be made between people who do not know each other. A number of publications of the author (Khmelnitskaya, 1996, 2002; Khmelnitskaya & Weymark, 2000) is devoted to study of Arrovian social choice problems with different scales of individual utility measurement in disjoint subgroups of individuals. In particular, in Khmelnitskaya and Weymark 2000 it is shown that for ordinally or cardinally measurable subgroup utility when levels (and in the case of cardinal utilities, differences) of utility may or may not be interpersonally comparable while no utility comparisons between subgroups are possible, every continuous social welfare ordering that meets the weak Pareto principle depends on the utilities of only one of the subgroups and is determined in accordance with the scale type admissible to this dictatorial subgroup. Here we introduce another proof[1] for this statement restated in equivalent terms of a social welfare function. This proof is longer but completely self-contained different to the proof in Khmelnitskaya and Weymark (2000) which is based on the employment of Bossert-Weymark (2004) continuous analogue of both – Arrow's (1951) impossibility theorem and Sen's (1970) variant of Arrow's theorem for cardinally measurable utilities. Moreover, being based on the study of level surfaces of a social welfare function this proof provides also extra deep insight into the structure of possible interrelations between utilities of different individuals, while the proof in Khmelnitskaya and Weymark (2000) allows only to state existence of a dictatorial subgroup.

In Sect. 2, we introduce basic definitions and notation and provide a formal statement of the problem. Section 3, provides the proof of the existence of a dictatorial subgroup for different combinations of mutually independent subgroup scales restated in terms of a social welfare function.

2 The Framework

Consider a society consisting of a finite set $N = \{1, \ldots, n\}$ of $n \geq 2$ individuals. Let X be a finite set of at least three alternatives and let $\mathcal{R}$ denote the set of all possible preference orderings over X. The members of $\mathcal{R}$ are assumed to be weak orders, i.e., complete, reflexive and transitive binary relations. A *social choice problem* is a triple $< X, N, \{R_i\}_{i \in N} >$, where $\{R_i\}_{i \in N}$ is a profile of individual preferences $R_i \in \mathcal{R}$, $i \in N$. To introduce measurability/comparability assumptions, we consider individual preferences represented as individual utilities, which may be interpreted as measurements of these preferences. So, let U be the set of all real-valued functions defined on $X \times N$: for any $u \in U$, let $u(x, i)$ denote the ith individual utility at the

---

[1] This proof circulated before in Khmelnitskaya's unpublished manuscript (Khmelnitskaya, 1999).

alternative $x \in X$. By a solution to a social choice problem we understand a *social welfare functional*, which is a mapping $f : \mathcal{D} \to \mathcal{R}$ where $\mathcal{D} \subseteq U$ is the domain of f. We assume f satisfies three welfarism axioms:

Unrestricted Domain. $\mathcal{D} = U$, i.e., f is defined for all $u \in U$.

Independence of Irrelevant Alternatives. For any $u, u' \in \mathcal{D}$ and $A \subseteq X$, if $u(x, i) = u'(x, i)$ for all $x \in A$ and $i \in N$, then $R : A = R' : A$ where $R = f(u)$ and $R' = f(u')$. ($R : A$ denotes the restriction of R to $A \subseteq X$.)

Pareto Indifference. For any pair $x, y \in X$ and for all $u \in \mathcal{D}$, if $u(x, i) = u(y, i)$ for all $i \in N$ then $x I y$, where I denotes the indifference relation corresponding to $R = f(u)$.

According to the welfarism theorem (D'Aspremont & Gevers, 1977; Hammond, 1979), these three axioms ensure that only individual utilities matter when ranking social alternatives, so any vector $u = (u_1, \ldots, u_n)$ in the n-dimensional Euclidian space $\mathbb{R}^n$ can be considered as a profile of individual utilities for the society N; here u_i is the utility of ith individual. From this perspective, a solution to a social choice problem can be regarded as a *social welfare ordering* (SWO), which is a weak order R^* on $\mathbb{R}^n$, the set of possible profiles of utility vectors. We assume that R^* also satisfies the Weak Pareto property.

Weak Pareto (WP). For all $u, v \in \mathbb{R}^n$, if $u_i > v_i$ for all $i \in N$, then $u P^* v$, where P^* denotes the strict preference relation corresponding to R^*.

A function $W : \mathbb{R}^n \to \mathbb{R}^1$ *represents* the SWO R^* if for all $u, v \in \mathbb{R}^n$

$$u R^* v \iff W(u) \geq W(v).$$

The representation W is called a *social welfare function* (SWF). By WP, any SWF W is strictly increasing, i.e., for all $u, v \in \mathbb{R}^n$

$$u \gg v \implies W(u) > W(v).$$

We impose one more restriction on an SWO R^* requiring R^* to be continuous.

Continuity (C). For all $u \in \mathbb{R}^n$, the sets $\{v \in \mathbb{R}^n \mid v R^* u\}$ and $\{v \in \mathbb{R}^n \mid u R^* v\}$ are closed in $\mathbb{R}^n$.

Continuity guarantees the existence of a continuous SWF (Debreu, 1954).

In the sequel by D_n, we denote the diagonal of $\mathbb{R}^n$. Let for any real $c \in \mathbb{R}^1$, c_N be a vector in $\mathbb{R}^n$ with all components equal to c and let $\gamma(c) = \{u \in \mathbb{R}^n \mid W(u) = c\}$ be a c-level surface of the SWF W; obviously, for every $u \in \mathbb{R}^n$, $\gamma(W(u))$ is a level surface of W containing u.

Remark 1 Because of continuity and strict monotonicity of all SWF, every level surface of any SWF meets a diagonal D_n of $\mathbb{R}^n$ and moreover, this meet of set is a singleton. Hence, a natural scale for the meanings of SWF arises: since every SWF W is defined up to monotonic strictly increasing transforms, then without loss of generality it may be assumed that for any $u \in \mathbb{R}^n$, $W(u) = c$, with c defined by the equality $\gamma(W(u)) \cap D_n = \{c_N\}$.

In the classic case of Arrow utilities were ordinally measurable and interpersonally non-comparable. More generally, within the SWO framework, the degree of measurability and comparability of utility inside the society N can be specified by a class of invariance transforms Φ, where each transform $\phi \in \Phi$ is a list of functions $\phi = \{\phi_i\}_{i \in N}$, $\phi_i : \mathbb{R}^1 \to \mathbb{R}^1$, with the property: for all $u, v \in \mathbb{R}^n$

$$u R^* v \Longleftrightarrow (\phi u) R^* (\phi v), \tag{1}$$

where $\phi u = \{\phi_i u_i\}_{i \in N}$. In what follows we use the notation Φ_N, when we need to specify to which particular society N the transforms of a class Φ apply; when no ambiguity appears, the index N will be omitted.

Under conditions imposed, the Arrovian social choice problem in the informational environment introduced by an invariance class Φ can be equivalently described in terms of SWF W which

(1) *is a continuous real-valued function $W : \mathbb{R}^n \to \mathbb{R}^1$, such that for any $c \in \mathbb{R}^1$, $W(c_N) = c$;*
(2) *is nondecreasing,[2] i.e., for all $u, v \in \mathbb{R}^n$,*

$$u \geq v \Longrightarrow W(u) \geq W(v);$$

(3) *is invariant under invariance transforms of class Φ, i.e., for any $\phi \in \Phi$ and for all $u, v \in \mathbb{R}^n$,*

$$W(u) \geq W(v) \Longrightarrow W(\phi u) \geq W(\phi v). \tag{2}$$

For an invariance class Φ to be a scale in the sense of the standard theory of measurement it has to satisfy the stronger condition of being a group (see Phanzagl, 1971). Different scale types for individual utility measurement have been examined in the literature (Roberts, 1980; d'Aspremont, 1985; Bossert & Weymark, 2004). Next we list the scales to be considered.

Ordinal Measurability (OM). $\phi \in \Phi$ iff ϕ is a list of independent strictly increasing transforms ϕ_i, $i \in N$.

Ordinal Measurability and Full Comparability (OFC). $\phi \in \Phi$ iff ϕ is a list of identical strictly increasing transforms, i.e., for any real t and all $i \in N$, $\phi_i(t) = \phi_0(t)$ where ϕ_0 is a strictly increasing function independent of i.

Cardinal Measurability (CM). $\phi \in \Phi$ iff ϕ is a list of independent strictly positive affine transforms, i.e., for any real t and all $i \in N$, $\phi_i(t) = \alpha_i + \beta_i t$ for some real α_i and real $\beta_i > 0$.

---

[2] This holds because W is continuous and strictly increasing.

Cardinal Measurability and Unit Comparability (CUC). $\phi \in \Phi$ iff ϕ is a list of strictly positive affine transforms with common unit, i.e., for any real t and all $i \in N$, $\phi_i(t) = \alpha_i + \beta t$ for some real α_i and $\beta > 0$ with β independent of i.

Cardinal Measurability and Full Comparability (CFC). $\phi \in \Phi$ iff ϕ is a list of identical strictly positive affine transforms, i.e., for any real t and all $i \in N$ $\phi_i(t) = \alpha + \beta t$ for some real α and $\beta > 0$, both independent of i.

The main concern of this paper is the situation when the entire society N is partitioned into m disjoint subgroups of individuals, i.e., $N = N_1 \cup N_2 \cup \cdots \cup N_m$ with $N_i \cap N_j = \emptyset$ for $i \neq j$. It is assumed that a SWF W defined on $\mathbb{R}^n$ for different subgroups of variables indexed by N_k, $k \in \{1, \ldots, m\}$, may admit invariance transforms of different invariance classes Φ_{N_k}, which amounts to W being invariant under transforms of a class Φ_N such that $\Phi_N = \{\Phi_{N_k}\}_{k=1}^m$, i.e., for every $\phi \in \Phi_N$ for all $k \in \{1, \ldots, m\}$, $\phi_{N_k} = \{\phi_i\}_{i \in N_k} \in \Phi_{N_k}$. In other words Φ_N is the Cartesian product of the subgroup classes of transforms Φ_{N_k}. Notice that the class Φ_N meets the condition (1). But, in general, even if all invariant classes Φ_{N_k} are scales, Φ_N is not necessarily a scale: the condition of being a group may no longer hold. For example, a combination of CFC scales with a common zero is not a scale. In what follows we concentrate on mutually independent subgroup scales. The subgroup scales Φ_{N_k}, $k = 1, \ldots, m$, are *mutually independent*, if for any distinct $k_1, k_2 \in \{1, \ldots, m\}$, for all $i \in N_{k_1}$ and $j \in N_{k_2}$, there exist $\phi_i \in \Phi_{N_{k_1}}$ and $\phi_j \in \Phi_{N_{k_2}}$ such that $\phi_i(t) = \alpha_i + \beta_i t$ with $\beta_i > 0$ and $\phi_j(t) = \alpha_j + \beta_j t$ with $\beta_j > 0$, where $\alpha_i \neq \alpha_j$ and $\beta_i \neq \beta_j$. Note that since OM and CM include the positive affine transforms, these classes are covered by the above definition as well. Mutual Independence preserves the group property and guarantees Φ_N to be the direct product of groups Φ_{N_k} when each of the Φ_{N_k} is a group, i.e., it guarantees Φ_N to be a scale, if all Φ_{N_k} are scales. It should also be stressed that Mutual Independence is a property of the set of subgroup classes of transforms $\{\Phi_{N_1}, \ldots, \Phi_{N_m}\}$, not of individual transforms within these classes.

Introduce now some extra notation. By n_k we denote the cardinality of N_k. It is obvious that $\sum_{k=1}^m n_k = n$. Let for any $u \in \mathbb{R}^n$ and all $k \in \{1, \ldots, m\}$, u_{N_k} be a subvector of u that belongs to $\mathbb{R}^{n_k}$ and is composed of components u_i, $i \in N_k$. $\mathbb{R}^{N_k}$ is a coordinate subspace of $\mathbb{R}^n$ induced by coordinates with indices from N_k, i.e.

$$\mathbb{R}^{N_k} = \{v \in \mathbb{R}^n \mid v_i = 0, i \notin N_k\}.$$

For any $u \in \mathbb{R}^n$ and $k \in \{1, \ldots, m\}$, let

$$\mathbb{R}^{N_k}(u) = \{u' \in \mathbb{R}^n \mid u'_{N \setminus N_k} = u_{N \setminus N_k}\}$$

be a hyperplane of dimension n_k parallel to coordinate subspace $\mathbb{R}^{N_k}$ and containing u. Obviously, $\mathbb{R}^{N_k} = \mathbb{R}^{N_k}(\mathbf{0})$ and $\mathbb{R}^{N_k}(u) = u + \mathbb{R}^{N_k}$.

Denote by

$$D_{N_k} = \{u \in \mathbb{R}^{N_k} \mid u_i = u_j, i, j \in N_k, \& u_i = 0, i \notin N_k\}$$

the diagonal of a coordinate subspace $\mathbb{R}^{N_k}$, and let L^D be a subspace of $\mathbb{R}^n$ spanned by the diagonals D_{N_k}, $k \in \{1, \ldots, m\}$. It is easy to see that every $u \in L^D$, $u = \{u_i\}_{i \in N}$, has the form $u_i = v_{k(i)}$, for some $v = v(u) \in \mathbb{R}^m$ and $k(i)$ defined by the relation $i \in N_{k(i)}$, i.e., all variables in L^D indexed by the same subgroup of indices have the same value.

For any vector $u \in \mathbb{R}^n$ and any real c, denote by $u\|c_{N_k}$ the vector in $\mathbb{R}^n$ with components

$$(u\|c_{N_k})_i = \begin{cases} u_i, & i \in N\setminus N_k, \\ c, & i \in N_k. \end{cases}$$

It is easy to see that $u\|c_{N_k}$ is an orthogonal projection of u on the hyperplane $\mathbb{R}^{N\setminus N_k}(c_{N_k})$. For any real c, let $(c_{N_k}, \mathbf{0}_{N\setminus N_k})$ denote the vector in $\mathbb{R}^n$ with components

$$(c_{N_k}, \mathbf{0}_{N\setminus N_k})_i = \begin{cases} c, & i \in N_k, \\ 0, & i \in N\setminus N_k. \end{cases}$$

We denote an orthogonal projection of the level surface $\gamma(c)$ to the hyperplane $\mathbb{R}^{N_k}(c_N)$ by $\gamma_{N_k}(c)$. For any two points $u, u' \in \mathbb{R}^n$, $u \neq u'$, let $l(u, u')$ and $r[u, u')$ be respectively a straight line passing through both points, u and u', and a ray starting from u and passing through u'; moreover, by $r(u, u') = r[u, u')\setminus\{u\}$ we denote an open ray without its origin.

As usual, $\mathbb{R}^n_+ = \{u \in \mathbb{R}^n | u_i \geq 0, i \in N, \& u \neq \mathbf{0}\}$ is the nonnegative orthant in $\mathbb{R}^n$. For the mean value of a vector $u \in \mathbb{R}^n$ we use the standard notation $\bar{u}$, i.e. $\bar{u} = (\sum_{i=1}^n u_i)/n$. Following (Bossert & Weymark, 2004), for any vector $u \in \mathbb{R}^n$, the *fan generated by* u is

$$Y(u) = \{u \in \mathbb{R}^n | u = \theta 1_n + \lambda u, \theta \in \mathbb{R}, \lambda \in \mathbb{R}_+\}.$$

A subset Y of $\mathbb{R}^n$ is a *fan*, if it is a fan generated by some $u \in \mathbb{R}^n$.

3 Existence of a Dictatorial Subgroup

Clearly, every continuous nondecreasing n-dimensional function that is determined only by variables with indices from one of the subgroups and that is invariant under invariance transforms proper to this subgroup of variables is a SWF. Below we study the situations for which such a form of a SWF is the only possible one, or equivalently, for which a dictatorial subgroup, i.e., a decisive coalition equal to one of the subgroups of individuals, must exist. The social ordering is then determined in accordance with the scale type of this dictatorial subgroup.

Theorem 1 *Let* $N = N_1 \cup N_2 \cup \cdots \cup N_m$, $N_i \cap N_j = \emptyset$ *for all* $i \neq j$, *and let a continuous nondecreasing function* $W : \mathbb{R}^n \to \mathbb{R}^1$ *with respect to variables indexed* *by N_k be invariant under one of scales OM, OFC, CM, CUC, or CFC. Moreover, the subgroup scales are assumed to be mutually independent. Then there exists a unique integer $k \in \{1, \ldots, m\}$, such that for all $u \in \mathbb{R}^n$, W has the form*

$$W(u) = W(u_{N_k}),$$

i.e., W is determined only by variables indexed by N_k, and besides is fully characterized by the scale type proper to this subset of variables.

Remark 2 Notice that any CFC transform at the same time is a transform of any of the OM, OFC, CM and CUC invariant classes. Hence, it is possible to simplify the statement of Theorem 1 by requiring only that the function $W(u)$ with respect to variables indexed by N_k, $k \in \{1, \ldots, m\}$, be invariant under mutually independent CFC transforms.

Theorem 1 allows us to construct a SWF characterization for various combinations of OM, OFC, CM, CUC and CFC independent subgroup utility scales on the basis of well-known results for social choice problems with the same measurement scales of individual utilities for the entire society.

In terms of level surfaces, the statement of Theorem 1 means that for any function $W(u)$, there exists a unique $k \in \{1, \ldots, m\}$ such that every level surface $\gamma(c)$ is parallel to the coordinate subspace $\mathbb{R}^{N \setminus N_k}$. The latter is tantamount to $\mathbb{R}^{N \setminus N_k}(u) \subset \gamma(W(u))$, for all $u \in \mathbb{R}^n$. It is not difficult to see that for the proof of the last inclusion, it is sufficient to show that every meet of set $\gamma(W(u)) \cap \mathbb{R}^{N_k}(u)$, $k \in \{1, \ldots, m\}$, except one is a hyperplane of dimension n_k. For different combinations of mutually independent OM, CM and CUC scales, the result may be easily obtained based on the admissibility of the transform $\phi = \{\phi_i\}_{i \in N}$:

$$\phi_i(t) = \begin{cases} t, & S = N_k, \\ (1 - \alpha)a_i + \alpha t, & \alpha > 0, \ i \in N \setminus N_k. \end{cases}$$

Indeed, for all combinations of OM, CM and CUC scales, for all $k \in \{1, \ldots, m\}$, every meet of set $\gamma(W(u)) \cap \mathbb{R}^{N_k}(u)$ together with any two points contains the whole straight line passing through these points, and therefore has to be a hyperplane. So, for this case the proof of Theorem 1 is rather simple. However, if we append OFC and CFC scales, then the defined above transform ϕ is inadmissible for all combinations of scales, and not every meet of set $\gamma(W(u)) \cap \mathbb{R}^{N_k}(u)$ is a hyperplane.

To prove Theorem 1, first, we show that every level surface $\gamma(c)$ contains its own orthogonal projection $\gamma_{N_k}(c)$ on the hyperplane $\mathbb{R}^{N_k}(c_N)$, $k \in \{1, \ldots, m\}$, which in turn coincides with the meet of set $\gamma(c) \cap \mathbb{R}^{N_k}(c_N)$ (Lemma 1). Next, in terms of these projections we derive a necessary and sufficient condition for a function $W(u)$ to be fully determined only by variables indexed by some fixed subgroup N_k (Lemma 2). And finally, we prove that this condition holds under the hypothesis of the theorem (Lemma 3 and Lemma 4).

Lemma 1 *Any level surface $\gamma(c)$ for all $k \in \{1, \ldots, m\}$ contains its own orthogonal projection on the hyperplane $\mathbb{R}^{N_k}(c_N)$, i.e.,*

$$\gamma_{N_k}(c) \subset \gamma(c), \tag{3}$$

moreover, either $\dim \gamma_{N_k}(c) = n_k$ *or* $\dim \gamma_{N_k}(c) = n_k - 1$ *and*

$$\gamma_{N_k}(c) = \gamma(c) \cap \mathbb{R}^{N_k}(c_N). \tag{4}$$

Proof Fix some $k \in \{1, \ldots, m\}$. To prove (3) it will suffice to show that for every $u \in \gamma(c)$, $u \| c_{N \setminus N_k} \in \gamma(c)$. Let $u \in \gamma(c)$. If $u \in \mathbb{R}^{N_k}(c_N)$, then $u \| c_{N \setminus N_k} = u$ and obviously, $u \| c_{N \setminus N_k} \in \gamma(c)$. Assume $u \notin \mathbb{R}^{N_k}(c_N)$. Due to Remark 1, $c_N \in \gamma(c)$. Take an admissible transform $\phi = \{\phi_i\}_{i \in N}$:

$$\phi_i(t) = \begin{cases} t, & i \in N_k, \\ (1 - \alpha)c + \alpha t, & \alpha > 0, \ i \in N \setminus N_k. \end{cases}$$

By (2) for all $\alpha > 0$, $W(\phi u) = W(\phi c_N)$. But for any $\alpha > 0$, $\phi c_N = c_N \in \gamma(c)$. Hence, for all $\alpha > 0$, $\phi u \in \gamma(c)$, and moreover, since $u \notin \mathbb{R}^{N_k}(c_N)$, ϕu corresponding to different α are different. If $\alpha = 1$, $\phi u = u$, whence $r(u \| c_{N \setminus N_k}, u) \subset \gamma(c)$. Therefore, every neighborhood of $u \| c_{N \setminus N_k}$ has a nonempty meet with $\gamma(c)$. Whence by continuity of W, $u \| c_{N \setminus N_k} \in \gamma(c)$. Since $W(u)$ is defined for every $u \in \mathbb{R}^n$, $W(u \| c_{N \setminus N_k})$ is well defined. Assume $W(u \| c_{N \setminus N_k}) = a \neq c$. Because of continuity of W, there exists a neighborhood S of $u \| c_{N \setminus N_k}$ such that $|W(u') - a| < |c - a|/2$, for all $u' \in S$, wherefrom $|W(u') - c| > |c - a|/2$, for every $u' \in S$. Hence, $W(u') \neq c$, for all $u' \in S$. The obtained contradiction proves (3).

From the definition of orthogonal projection it follows directly that

$$\gamma_{N_k}(c) \subset \mathbb{R}^{N_k}(c_N) \tag{5}$$

and

$$\gamma(c) \subset \gamma_{N_k}(c) + \mathbb{R}^{N \setminus N_k}.$$

Whence,

$$\dim \gamma_{N_k}(c) \leq n_k$$

and

$$\dim \gamma(c) \leq \dim \gamma_{N_k}(c) + (n - n_k).$$

Combining the last inequalities together with the equality $\dim \gamma(c) = n - 1$, we obtain

$$n_k - 1 \leq \dim \gamma_{N_k}(c) \leq n_k.$$

From the definition of orthogonal projection it also follows that

$$\gamma(c) \cap \mathbb{R}^{N_k}(c_N) \subset \gamma_{N_k}(c).$$

From which together with (3) and (5), (4) follows immediately.   □

Remark 3 Lemma 1 remains true under a coarser partition of N into disjoint subgroups when a few subgroups N_k, $k \in \{1, \ldots, m\}$, may merge into one. It is worth noting that this remark concerns all subsequent propositions as well.

Remark 4 Due to the admissibility of the transform $\{\phi_i(t) = \alpha + t\}_{i \in N}$ for all real α, the level surfaces $\gamma(c)$ relevant to different c can be obtained from each other by parallel shifts along the diagonal D_n. (This property was mentioned earlier in Roberts (1980)). Wherefrom together with (4) it follows that for all real c and c',

$$\gamma_{N_k}(c') = \gamma_{N_k}(c) + (c' - c)_N, \tag{6}$$

i.e., all projections $\gamma_{N_k}(c)$ relevant to the same k and different c can be obtained from each other by parallel shifts along D_n.

Remark 5 Observe that $\gamma_{N_k}(c)$ is a cone in $\mathbb{R}^{N_k}(c_N)$ with a top in c_N. Indeed, if $u' \in \gamma_{N_k}(c)$ and $u' \neq c_N$, then there exists $u \in \gamma(c)$, $u \neq c_N$, such that $u' = u\|c_{N \setminus N_k}$. Since $c_N \in \gamma(c)$ and because of the admissibility of the transform $\{\psi_i(t) = (1 - \alpha)c + \alpha t\}_{i \in N}$ for all $\alpha > 0$, $r[c_N, u) \subset \gamma(c)$. But the ray $r[c_N, u')$ is a projection of the ray $r[c_N, u)$ onto the hyperplane $\mathbb{R}^{N_k}(c_N)$. Thus, for every $u' \in \gamma_{N_k}(c)$ such that $u' \neq c_N$, $r[c_N, u') \subset \gamma_{N_k}(c)$, which proves that $\gamma_{N_k}(c)$ is a cone. In particular, a cone $\gamma_{N_k}(c)$ with dim $\gamma_{N_k}(c) = n_k$ may coincide with $\mathbb{R}^{N_k}(c_N)$. If dim $\gamma_{N_k}(c) = n_k - 1$, it may be a hyperplane in $\mathbb{R}^{N_k}(c_N)$ passing through c_N.

Denote by $H_{N_k}(c)$ the cylinder $\gamma_{N_k}(c) + \mathbb{R}^{N \setminus N_k}$.

Remark 6 As it was already noted in the proof of Lemma 1, for any real c and all $k \in \{1, \ldots, m\}$,

$$\gamma(c) \subset H_{N_k}(c). \tag{7}$$

Lemma 2 *A function W for any $u \in \mathbb{R}^n$ has the form*

$$W(u) = W(u_{N_k}), \qquad \text{for some} \qquad k \in \{1, \ldots, m\},$$

i.e. depends only on the variables u_i with indices $i \in N_k$, if and only if there exists real c such that dim $\gamma_{N_k}(c) = n_k - 1$.

Proof I. Necessity. Clearly, for every real c

$$\gamma(c) \cap \mathbb{R}^{N_k}(c_N) = \{u \in \mathbb{R}^{N_k}(c_N) \mid W(u) = c\}.$$

By hypothesis, for all $u \in \mathbb{R}^n$ and, in particular, for all $u \in \mathbb{R}^{N_k}(c_N)$, $W(u) = W(u_{N_k})$. But for $u \in \mathbb{R}^{N_k}(c_N)$, the variables u_{N_k} are intrinsic coordinates in

$\mathbb{R}^{N_k}(c_N)$. Therefore and because of (4), the projection $\gamma_{N_k}(c)$, being a subset of the n_k-dimensional hyperplane $\mathbb{R}^{N_k}(c_N)$, is characterized by the unique equality $W(u_{N_k}) = c$ in the intrinsic coordinates of $\mathbb{R}^{N_k}(c_N)$, whence it follows that for every c, $\dim \gamma_{N_k}(c) = n_k - 1$.

II. Sufficiency. From (6) for all real c and c',

$$H_{N_k}(c') \cap \mathbb{R}^{N_k}(c_N) = \gamma_{N_k}(c) + ((c' - c)_{N_k}, \mathbf{0}_{N \setminus N_k}),$$

i.e., for all $c' \neq c$, every meet of set $H_{N_k}(c') \cap \mathbb{R}^{N_k}(c_N)$ is obtained from $\gamma_{N_k}(c)$ by a parallel shift along the diagonal $D_{N_k}(c)$ of the hyperplane $\mathbb{R}^{N_k}(c_N)$,

$$D_{N_k}(c) = \{u \in \mathbb{R}^n \mid u_i = u_j, \ i, j \in N_k \ \& \ u_i = c, \ i \notin N_k\}.$$

If we show that for every $k \in \{1, \ldots, m\}$ such that $\dim \gamma_{N_k}(c) = n_k - 1$, all parallel shifts of $\gamma_{N_k}(c)$ along $D_{N_k}(c)$ in $\mathbb{R}^{N_k}(c_N)$ do not meet each other and cover the whole $\mathbb{R}^{N_k}(c_N)$, it will follow that cylinders $H_{N_k}(c)$ relevant to different c do not meet and cover $\mathbb{R}^n$. On the other hand, since W is defined on the entire $\mathbb{R}^n$, for every $u \in \mathbb{R}^n$, there exists a level surface of W containing u. Hence, because of (7) for every real c, $\gamma(c) = H_{N_k}(c)$, which is the same as for all $u \in \mathbb{R}^n$, $W(u) = W(u_{N_k})$. Thus, to complete the proof of sufficiency, it is enough to show that for every $k \in \{1, \ldots, m\}$ for which $\dim \gamma_{N_k}(c) = n_k - 1$, the parallel shifts of $\gamma_{N_k}(c)$ along $D_{N_k}(c)$ in $\mathbb{R}^{N_k}(c_N)$ do not meet each other and cover $\mathbb{R}^{N_k}(c_N)$.

First, we show that for every $k \in \{1, \ldots, m\}$, the parallel shifts of $\gamma_{N_k}(c)$ along $D_{N_k}(c)$ in $\mathbb{R}^{N_k}(c_N)$ cover $\mathbb{R}^{N_k}(c_N)$. For any $u \in \mathbb{R}^n$ the level surface $\gamma(W(u))$ passes through u. Whence and because of Remark 1, every $\gamma(W(u))$ is a cone with a top in $\{W(u)\}_N \in D_n$ and all level surfaces may be obtained from each other by parallel shifts along D_n. Therefore, through every point in any two-dimensional half-plane with a boundary D_n, denoted in the sequel by $\mathbb{R}^2_\pm(D_n)$, passes a ray that starts in some $c_N \in D_n$ and belongs completely to $\gamma(c)$. Moreover, since different level surfaces do not meet and are obtained from each other by parallel shifts along D_n, from every point $c_N \in D_n$, in any half-plane $\mathbb{R}^2_\pm(D_n)$, there emanates a unique ray that belongs to $\gamma(c)$ and that does not meet other level surfaces $\gamma(c')$, $c' \neq c$. Parallel rays starting from different $c_N \in D_n$ and belonging to some half-plane $\mathbb{R}^2_\pm(D_n)$ cover the entire $\mathbb{R}^2_\pm(D_n)$. Hence, for every $c_N \in D_n$, in any two-dimensional plane $\mathbb{R}^2(D_n)$ passing through D_n there are exactly two rays starting from c_N and located in distinct half-planes of $\mathbb{R}^2(D_n)$ separated by D_n, i.e., in $\mathbb{R}^2_+(D_n)$ and $\mathbb{R}^2_-(D_n)$ respectively; in particular, these two rays may form a straight line meeting D_n in c_N. A collection of mutually non-overlapping pairs of rays relevant to different level surfaces $\gamma(c)$ covers $\mathbb{R}^2(D_n)$. Since every $u \in \mathbb{R}^{N_k}(c_N) \setminus D_{N_k}(c)$ and a straight line $D_{N_k}(c)$ determine unambiguously a two-dimensional plane, a set of all two-dimensional planes $\mathbb{R}^2(D_{N_k}(c)) \subset \mathbb{R}^{N_k}(c_N)$ containing the diagonal $D_{N_k}(c)$ of $\mathbb{R}^{N_k}(c_N)$ covers $\mathbb{R}^{N_k}(c_N)$. Any plane $\mathbb{R}^2(D_{N_k}(c))$ may be considered as a projection of a cylinder $\mathbb{R}^2(D_{N_k}(c)) + \mathbb{R}^{N \setminus N_k}$ on $\mathbb{R}^{N_k}(c_N)$. Since $D_n \subset \mathbb{R}^2(D_{N_k}(c)) + \mathbb{R}^{N \setminus N_k}$, every cylinder $\mathbb{R}^2(D_{N_k}(c)) + \mathbb{R}^{N \setminus N_k}$ is covered by a set of all two-dimensional planes

$\mathbb{R}^2(D_n) \subset \mathbb{R}^2(D_{N_k}(c)) + \mathbb{R}^{N\setminus N_k}$. Observe that $D_n \| c_{N\setminus N_k} = D_{N_k}(c)$. There-fore, for each plane $\mathbb{R}^2(D_n) \subset \mathbb{R}^2(D_{N_k}(c)) + \mathbb{R}^{N\setminus N_k}$ that is not orthogonal to $\mathbb{R}^2(D_{N_k}(c))$, a projection of $\gamma(c) \cap \mathbb{R}^2(D_n)$ on $\mathbb{R}^{N_k}(c_N)$ consists of exactly two rays $\tilde{r}_1, \tilde{r}_2 \subset \gamma_{N_k}(c)$ starting from $c_N \in D_{N_k}(c)$ and belonging to the different half-planes $\mathbb{R}^2_+(D_{N_k}(c))$ and $\mathbb{R}^2_-(D_{N_k}(c))$ of the plane $\mathbb{R}^2(D_{N_k}(c))$ that are separated by $D_{N_k}(c)$, i.e., $\tilde{r}_1 \subset \mathbb{R}^2_+(D_{N_k}(c))$, $\tilde{r}_2 \subset \mathbb{R}^2_-(D_{N_k}(c))$. Any plane orthogonal to $\mathbb{R}^2(D_{N_k}(c))$ maps completely on $D_{N_k}(c)$. Under parallel shifts along $D_{N_k}(c)$, rays $\tilde{r}_1$ and $\tilde{r}_2$ cover the entire plane $\mathbb{R}^2(D_{N_k}(c))$, while the collection of all shifts of $\gamma_{N_k}(c)$ along $D_{N_k}(c)$ covers the hyperplane $\mathbb{R}^{N_k}(c_N)$.

To show that for every $k \in \{1, \ldots, m\}$ for which $\dim \gamma_{N_k}(c) = n_k - 1$, parallel shifts of $\gamma_{N_k}(c)$ along $D_{N_k}(c)$ in $\mathbb{R}^{N_k}(c_N)$ do not meet, it suffices to show that every half-plane $\mathbb{R}^2_\pm(D_{N_k}(c))$ contains a ray belonging to $\gamma_{N_k}(c)$ and solely one. Assume the contrary, and let at least two rays $r_1, r_2 \subset \gamma_{N_k}(c) \cap \mathbb{R}^2_\pm(D_{N_k}(c))$. Then due to continuity of the level surface $\gamma(c)$ and continuity of the projection mapping $\text{Pr}\colon \mathbb{R}^n \to \mathbb{R}^{N_k}(c_N)$, the piece of a half-plane $\mathbb{R}^2_\pm(D_{N_k}(c))$ between rays r_1 and r_2 also belongs to $\gamma_{N_k}(c)$ as well, which is impossible since by hypothesis, $\dim \gamma_{N_k}(c) = n_k - 1$. □

Remark 7 The necessary and sufficient condition in Lemma 2 may be restated equiv-alently in terms of cylinders $H_{N_k}(c)$. Indeed, the equality

$$\dim \gamma_{N_k}(c) = n_k - 1, \qquad \text{for some } k \in \{1, \ldots, m\},$$

is tantamount to the equality

$$\gamma(c) = H_{N_k}(c), \qquad \text{for the same } k. \tag{8}$$

Lemma 3 *For every level surface $\gamma(c)$, if for some $k \in \{1, \ldots, m\}$*

(1) $\dim \gamma_{N_k}(c) = n_k - 1$, then $\gamma_{N\setminus N_k}(c) = \mathbb{R}^{N\setminus N_k}(c_N)$ and for all $k' \in \{1, \ldots, m\}$, $k' \neq k$, $\gamma_{N_{k'}}(c) = \mathbb{R}^{N_{k'}}(c_N)$;
(2) $\dim \gamma_{N_k}(c) = n_k$, then $\gamma_{N\setminus N_k}(c) \neq \mathbb{R}^{N\setminus N_k}(c_N)$,

and furthermore, if $\gamma_{N_k}(c) = \mathbb{R}^{N_k}(c_N)$, then $\dim \gamma_{N\setminus N_k}(c) = n - n_k - 1$, while if $\gamma_{N_k}(c) \neq \mathbb{R}^{N_k}(c_N)$, then $\dim \gamma_{N\setminus N_k}(c) = n - n_k$.

Proof To prove the first statement, assume that $\dim \gamma_{N_k}(c) = n_k - 1$, for some $k \in \{1, \ldots, m\}$. By (4) and (8), for all $k \in \{1, \ldots, m\}$

$$\gamma_{N\setminus N_k}(c) = \gamma(c) \cap \mathbb{R}^{N\setminus N_k}(c_N) = H_{N_k}(c) \cap \mathbb{R}^{N\setminus N_k}(c_N) = \mathbb{R}^{N\setminus N_k}(c_N).$$

Similarly for all $k' \in \{1, \ldots, m\}$, $k' \neq k$,

$$\gamma_{N_{k'}}(c) = \gamma(c) \cap \mathbb{R}^{N_{k'}}(c_N) = H_{N_k}(c) \cap \mathbb{R}^{N_{k'}}(c_N) = \mathbb{R}^{N_{k'}}(c_N).$$

Prove now the second one. Assume the contrary that $\gamma_{N\setminus N_k}(c) = \mathbb{R}^{N\setminus N_k}(c_N)$. Then because of (3), $\mathbb{R}^{N\setminus N_k}(c_N) \subset \gamma(c)$, which is equivalent to $W(u) = W(u_{N_k})$. Whence, by Lemma 2, $\dim \gamma_{N_k}(c) = n_k - 1$, which contradicts to the hypothesis.

Next, from Lemma 1 and Remark 3 it follows that either $\dim \gamma_{N\setminus N_k}(c) = n - n_k$, or $\dim \gamma_{N\setminus N_k}(c) = n - n_k - 1$. If $\dim \gamma_{N\setminus N_k}(c) = n - n_k - 1$, then by the Remark 7, $\gamma(c) = H_{N\setminus N_k}(c)$. Obviously,

$$H_{N\setminus N_k}(c) \cap \mathbb{R}^{N_k}(c_N) = \mathbb{R}^{N_k}(c_N),$$

i.e.,

$$\gamma(c) \cap \mathbb{R}^{N_k}(c_N) = \mathbb{R}^{N_k}(c_N),$$

whence by (4), $\gamma_{N_k}(c) = \mathbb{R}^{N_k}(c_N)$.

Further, if we suppose $\gamma_{N_k}(c) = \mathbb{R}^{N_k}(c_N)$ and repeat the latter arguments, then because of (3) and Lemma 2, we arrive at $\dim \gamma_{N\setminus N_k}(c) = n - n_k - 1$. □

Remark 8 Because of Remark 3, the validity of the second statement in the second point of Lemma 3 can be obtained directly from the first point as well.

From the first statement of Lemma 3 applying the induction argument with respect to the number m of subgroups N_k in the partition of N, we derive the next corollary.

Corollary 1 *For any level surface $\gamma(c)$ not every projection $\gamma_{N_k}(c)$, $k \in \{1, \dots, m\}$, coincides with the corresponding hyperplane $\mathbb{R}^{N_k}(c_N)$.*

Lemma 4 *For every level surface $\gamma(c)$, for any $k \in \{1, \dots, m\}$, a projection $\gamma_{N_k}(c)$ either coincides with a hyperplane $\mathbb{R}^{N_k}(c_N)$ or $\dim \gamma_{N_k}(c) = n_k - 1$.*

Proof From the first statement of Lemma 3, if $\dim \gamma_{N_k}(c) = n_k$ and $\gamma_{N_k}(c) \neq \mathbb{R}^{N_k}(c_N)$, then $\dim \gamma_{N\setminus N_k}(c) = n - n_k$. It follows that there exist a real $\varepsilon > 0$ and two points $u_1 \in \gamma_{N_k}(c)$, $u_2 \in \gamma_{N\setminus N_k}(c)$, such that $u_1^\varepsilon = u_1 + (\varepsilon_{N_k}, \mathbf{0}_{N\setminus N_k}) \in \gamma_{N_k}(c)$ and $u_2^\varepsilon = u_2 + (\mathbf{0}_{N_k}, \varepsilon_{N\setminus N_k}) \in \gamma_{N\setminus N_k}(c)$. Moreover, by Lemma 1 and Remark 3 , $u_1, u_1^\varepsilon, u_2, u_2^\varepsilon \in \gamma(c)$. Consider the admissible transform $\phi = \{\phi_i\}_{i\in N}$:

$$\phi_i(t) = \begin{cases} t + \varepsilon, & i \in N_k, \\ t, & i \in N\setminus N_k. \end{cases}$$

By (2), $W(\phi u_1) = W(\phi u_2^\varepsilon)$. Then notice that $\phi u_1 = u_1^\varepsilon \in \gamma(c)$. Hence, $\phi u_2^\varepsilon \in \gamma(c)$. But $\phi u_2^\varepsilon = u_2 + \varepsilon_N$, whence since $u_2 \in \gamma(c)$ and since all level surfaces $\gamma(c')$ for different c' can be obtained from each other by parallel shifts along D_n, $\phi u_2^\varepsilon \in \gamma(c + \varepsilon)$. But for $\phi u_2^\varepsilon \in \gamma(c)$, the latter is impossible. □

Remark 9 From Remark 4 it follows that, if for some c and $k \in \{1, \dots, m\}$, the statement of Lemma 3 or of Lemma 4 holds true, then for the same k it holds true for all $c' \neq c$.

Proof of Theorem 1 From Corollary 1 and Lemma 4 it follows that for some $k \in \{1, \ldots, m\}$, $\dim \gamma_{N_k}(c) = n_k - 1$. Moreover, by the first statement of Lemma 3, this k is unique. Whence together with Lemma 2 we obtain the validity of Theorem 1.   □

Acknowledgments The paper was partially written during the author's 2008 research stay in Tilburg Center for Logic and Philosophy of Science (TiLPS, Tilburg University) whose hospitality and support are highly appreciated.

References

Arrow, K. J. (1951). *Social choice and individual values* (2nd ed., 1963). New York: Wiley.

Bossert, W., & Weymark, J. A. (2004). Utility in social choice. In: Barberá, S., Hammond, P. J., & Seidl, C. (Eds.), *Handbook of utility theory* (Vol. 2, pp. 1099–1178). Boston: Kluwer Academic Publishers.

d'Aspremont, C. (1985). Axioms for social welfare orderings. In: Hurwicz, L., Schmeidler, D., & Sonnenschein, H. (Eds.), *Social goals and social organizations: Essays in memory of Elisha Pazner* (pp. 19–76). Cambridge: Cambridge University Press.

d'Aspremont, C., & Gevers, L. (1977). Equity and the informational basis of collective choice. *Review of Economic Studies, 44*, 199–209.

Debreu, G. (1954). Representation of a preference ordering by a numerical function. In: Thrall, R. M., Coombs, C. H., & Davis, R. L. (Eds.), *Decision processes* (pp. 159–165). New York: Wiley.

Hammond, P. J. (1979). Equity in two person situations: Some consequences. *Econometrica, 47*, 1127–1135.

Khmelnitskaya, A. B. (1996). Social choice problems with different scales of individual welfares measurement for different subgroups of individuals. In: Kleinschmidt, P., Bachem, A., Derigs, U., Fischer, D., Leopold-Wildburger, U., & Möring, R. (Eds.), *Operations research proceedings 1995* (pp. 252–257). Berlin: Springer-Verlag.

Khmelnitskaya, A. B. (1999). *Social welfare orderings for different subgroup utility scales.* Discussion Paper #198, Center for Rationality and Interactive Decision Theory at The Hebrew University of Jerusalem.

Khmelnitskaya, A. B. (2002). Social welfare functions for different subgroup utility scales. In: Tangian, A., & Gruber, J. (Eds.), *Lecture notes in economics and mathematical systems* (vol. 510, pp. 515–530). Berlin: Springer-Verlag.

Khmelnitskaya, A. B., & Weymark, J. A. (2000). Social choice with independent subgroup utility scales. *Social Choice and Welfare, 17*, 739–748.

Phanzagl, J. (1971). *Theory of measurement* (2nd ed.). Würzburg–Wien: Physica-Verlag.

Roberts, K. W. S. (1980a). Possibility theorems with interpersonally comparable welfare levels. *Review of Economic Studies, 47*, 409–420.

Roberts, K. W. S. (1980b). Interpersonal comparability and social choice theory. *Review of Economic Studies, 47*, 421–439.

Sen, A. K. (1970). *Collective choice and social welfare.* San Francisco: Holden-Day.

Tsui, K.-Y., & Weymark, J. A. (1997). Social welfare orderings for ratio-scale measurable utilities. *Economic Theory, 10*, 241–256.

Yanovskaya, E. B. (1988). Social choice functions for different scales of individual preference measurement (in Russian). *Annals of VNIISI* (All-Union Research Institute for System Studies, Moscow), *6*, 64–76.

Yanovskaya, E. B. (1989). Group choice rules in problems with comparisons of individual preferences. *Automation and Remote Control, 50*, 822–830 (translated from the 1989 Russian original that appeared in *Avtomatika i Telemekhanika, 6*, 129–138).

Making (Non-standard) Choices

Wulf Gaertner

1 Introduction

Imagine a person who, given three alternatives x, y and z, chooses x over y, y over z, and z over x. This person's choices definitely are not transitive. What we encounter instead is a case of cyclical choice. There have been quite a few experiments which reveal that a non-negligible number of individuals exhibits cycles of binary choice, for one reason or another.[1] Simple mistakes but also a high degree of complexity of the alternatives at stake have frequently been given as reasons for cyclical choice behaviour.

A constituent element of the standard model of rational choice is the "weak axiom of revealed preference" WARP (Samuelson, 1938) which says that if some alternative x is picked when another alternative y is available, then y is never chosen from a set of alternatives including both x and y. The WARP axiom is equivalent to the following requirement: If for two sets X and Y with $X \subset Y$, $C(Y) \cap X$ is nonempty, where $C(Y)$ is the choice from Y, then the choice from X is $C(X) = C(Y) \cap X$ (Arrow, 1959).

There is wide agreement that WARP, together with its stronger version, the "strong axiom of revealed preference" (Houthakker, 1950), and Arrow's requirement are the central consistency conditions of economic behaviour. Individuals who satisfy either of these requirements are viewed as acting "fully rationally". The

W. Gaertner (✉)
Department of Philosophy, Logic and Scientific Method, London School of Economics,
London, UK
e-mail: Wulf.Gaertner@uni-osnabrueck.de

[1] In an experiment of choice behaviour among gray jays, Waite (2001), reported in Manzini and Mariotti (2007), finds that all the birds preferred option a to b and b to c, but no bird preferred a to c, where all alternatives, characterized by (n, l), consisted in getting n raisins at the end of an l cm long tube, with $a = (1$ raisin; 28 cm$)$, $b = (2;42)$ and $c = (3;56)$. Apparently, many birds showed an intransitive choice behaviour in this experiment.

A. Van Deemen, A. Rusinowska (eds.), *Collective Decision Making,*
Theory and Decision Library C 43, DOI 10.1007/978-3-642-02865-6_9,
© Springer-Verlag Berlin Heidelberg 2010

question then arises how one should describe the behaviour of those agents who violate these conditions. Are they behaving irrationally?

Sen (1993) has argued that a violation of WARP or Arrow's condition is by no means sufficient to claim that an agent's choices have to be viewed as irrational. Sen writes that "we cannot determine whether the person is failing in any way without knowing what he is trying to do, that is, without knowing something external to the choice itself" (1993, p. 501). Sen makes a distinction between purely internal grounds which are confined to the choice itself, and the environment or context within which the choice act has taken place. Here, motivations, goals, and principles play a role and only when this "external reference" has been specified, does it become reasonable to discuss the issue of rational versus irrational behaviour. In the conventional case or the case that standard microeconomics textbooks discuss, choices are induced by preference optimization and this external reference provides justification for the conditions described above.

Let us briefly mention some other cases; we shall discuss them in more detail in the main body of this paper. Consider the following situation depicted by Manzini and Mariotti (2007). Let there be three alternatives a, b and c. Suppose that c Pareto dominates a while no other comparisons are possible according to the Pareto criterion. Assume now that the choosing individual considers a to be fairer than b and b fairer than c. The individual decides first according to the Pareto principle and only then, when Pareto is not decisive, according to fairness. Consequently, the individual's choice function C is such that $C(\{a, b, c\}) = \{b\}$. First a is eliminated by c due to the Pareto principle and then c is eliminated by b due to the fairness criterion. As the reader can see, two criteria are consecutively applied in this choice situation.

If we consider binary choices, we obtain $C(\{a, b\}) = \{a\}$ and $C(\{b, c\}) = \{b\}$ due to fairness and $C(\{c, a\}) = \{c\}$ due to Pareto. So we get a pairwise cyclical choice pattern as in our very first example and also a violation of WARP since a was chosen against b while b was picked from a set where both a and b were present. Or, according to Arrow's choice axiom, b was chosen from the superset $\{a, b, c\}$ but not picked from the subset $\{a, b\}$. Can the described choice behaviour be termed irrational? Obviously not though it violates the standard axioms of rational choice, i.e., WARP and Arrow's axiom of choice consistency.

Sen (1993) and Baigent and Gaertner (1996) considered the choice of the second largest element as the most preferred choice. So let there be three pieces of cake with a being largest and c being smallest with b lying in between. Then an individual who has internalized the above principle will choose c from $\{a, c\}$ and c from $\{b, c\}$ but will pick b from $\{a, b, c\}$. Such choice behaviour violates Arrow's choice axiom and also a condition called expansion. The latter says that if an alternative x is chosen from a set S and from a set T, then it must also be chosen from $S \cup T$. Again, do we have an instance of irrational choice in front of us? The person who follows the principle of choosing the second largest and not the largest element would clearly deny this.

Finally, let us consider a person who always picks the median element (see Gaertner & Xu, 1999). So let there be seven elements a, b, c, d, e, f and g arranged according to their price from highest to lowest. The individual chooses c from $\{a, b, c, d, e\}$ and picks c from $\{a, b, c, f, g\}$ but chooses d from $\{a, b, c, d, e, f, g\}$. The reader realizes immediately that Arrow's choice axiom is again violated and also the requirement that we called expansion is not fulfilled. Again, does the individual described show any trace of inconsistency?

The purpose of this paper is twofold. First, as has become "visible" above, we argue that choice situations that do not fulfil the standard rationality conditions by no means imply that individuals are behaving irrationally. On the contrary, they are very rational, following particular external references. Second, if the standard requirements are not satisfied as shown above, the question is which the conditions are that characterize various types of non-standard behaviour. In other words, how do the axioms look like that entail such types of choice behaviour?

In Sect. 2 we shall discuss in more detail the three choice functions briefly introduced above. Note again that they all violate the standard axioms of rational choice. In Sect. 3, we depict other choice functions that are non-standard. Section 4 offers some concluding remarks.

2 Three Particular Choice Functions

2.1 Sequential Rationalizability

Manzini and Mariotti (2007) have proposed a choice function that they call a rational shortlist method which works as follows. It is assumed that a decision maker uses sequentially two rationales to discriminate among the given alternatives. These rationales are applied in a fixed order, independently of the set of available alternatives, to remove inferior alternatives. The authors assert that this procedure sequentially rationalizes a choice function if, for any feasible set, "the process identifies the unique alternative specified by the choice function" (2007, p. 1824). An example of such a procedure has already been given in the introduction, the first rationale being the Pareto principle, the second rationale being the fairness criterion.

Let us become more formal now. Let X be a set of alternatives, with at least three elements. Given $S \subseteq X$ and an asymmetric binary relation $P \subseteq X \times X$, let us denote the set of P-maximal elements of S by $\max(S; P) = \{x \in S : \nexists y \in S$ with $(y, x) \in P\}$. Let χ be the set of all nonempty subsets of X. A choice function on X picks one alternative from each possible element of χ. In other words, it is a function $C : \chi \to X$ with $C(S) \in S$ for all $S \in \chi$. In the standard model of rational choice, a choice function C maximizes according to an acyclic binary relation P such that $C(S) = \max(S; P)$ for all $S \in \chi$. The new concept by Manzini and Mariotti uses two asymmetric binary relations P_1 and P_2 from $X \times X$ in order to eliminate alternatives via two sequential rounds.

Definition 1 (Manzini & Mariotti, 2007) A choice function C is a rational shortlist method (RSM) whenever there exists an ordered pair (P_1, P_2) of asymmetric relations, with $P_i \subseteq X \times X$ for $i \in \{1, 2\}$, such that $C(S) = \max(\max(S; P_1); P_2)$

for all $S \in \chi$. (P_1, P_2) are said to sequentially rationalize C. Each P_i is called a rationale.

In the first round the decision maker retains only those elements that "survive" according to rationale P_1. In the second round, he retains only the element that is maximal according to rationale P_2. And this is the final choice. The authors emphasize that it is crucial that the rationales and the sequence in which they are applied are invariant with respect to the choice set. Note that in the authors' example with the Pareto condition and the fairness requirement, discussed in the introduction, the outcome of the two-stage procedure would be different if the fairness criterion had been applied first.

We now introduce a more formal definition of the weak axiom of revealed preference.

Definition 2 WARP. If an alternative x is chosen when y is available then y is not chosen when x is available. More formally, for all $S, T \in \chi : [\{x\} = C(S), y \in S, x \in T] \rightarrow [\{y\} \neq C(T)]$.

WARP is a necessary and sufficient condition such that choice is rationalized by an ordering (a complete and transitive binary relation). Note again that WARP is violated both by the criterion of choosing the second largest element and by the method of picking the median element, and is not satisfied by RSM either.

Definition 3 Weak WARP (Manzini & Mariotti, 2007). If an alternative x is chosen both when only y is also available and when y and other alternatives $\{z_1, \ldots, z_k\}$ are available, then y is not chosen when x and a subset of $\{z_1, \ldots, z_k\}$ are available. Formally, for all $S, T \in \chi : [\{x, y\} \subset S \subset T, \{x\} = C(\{x, y\}) = C(T)] \rightarrow [\{y\} \neq C(S)]$.

Note that the maxim of picking the second largest element satisfies Weak WARP. However, the choice of the median violates this condition. This can be seen from the following example. Let there be seven elements q, v, w, x, y, z, and r with q having the highest price and r having the lowest. Let us further assume, without loss of generality, that in the case of only two objects, the higher priced object is chosen. Then $C(\{x, y\}) = \{x\}$, $C(\{q, v, w, x, y, z, r\}) = \{x\}$ but $C(\{w, x, y, z, r\}) = \{y\}$.

Let us next formally define the expansion condition which was already described in the introduction.

Definition 4 Expansion. An alternative which is picked from each of two sets is also chosen from their union. Formally, for all $S, T \in \chi : [\{x\} = C(S) = C(T)] \rightarrow \{x\} = C(S \cup T)]$.

The following result now holds.

Result 1 (Manzini & Mariotti, 2007) *Let X be any (not necessarily finite) set. A choice function C on X is an RSM iff it satisfies Expansion and Weak WARP.*

As already mentioned, both the principle of picking the second largest element and the principle of choosing the median do not satisfy the expansion condition.

Both rules focus on positions and therefore, the choice may change when the menu changes. Picking the largest element or the smallest element as the best choice would always satisfy Expansion.

Consider the following weakening of the expansion condition. Manzini and Mariotti call it "always chosen".

Definition 5 Always Chosen. If an alternative is chosen in pairwise choices over all other alternatives in a set, then it is chosen from the set. Formally, for all $S \in \chi$: $[\{x\} = C(\{x, y\})$ for all $y \in S - \{x\}] \to [\{x\} = C(S)]$.

A binary cyclical choice pattern was manifest in the example with the two criteria of Pareto and fairness. The following property excludes such cycles.

Definition 6 No Binary Cycles. There are no pairwise cycles of choice. Formally, for all $x_1, \ldots, x_{n+1} \in X$: $[C(\{x_i, x_{i+1}\}) = \{x_i\}, i \in \{1, \ldots, n\}] \to [\{x_1\} = C(\{x_1, x_{n+1}\})]$.

Manzini and Mariotti assert that the class of choice functions that do not satisfy WARP can be classified in the following way. There are three subclasses: choice functions that violate exactly one of No Binary Cycles or Always Chosen, and those that violate both. Therefore, the following result can be formulated.

Result 2 *A choice function that violates WARP also violates Always Chosen or No Binary Cycles.*

The rational shortlist method can be generalized to more than two rationales. Manzini and Mariotti call this sequential rationalizability.

Definition 7 (Manzini & Mariotti, 2007) A choice function C is sequentially rationalizable whenever there exists an ordered list $P_1, \ldots, P_k$ of asymmetric relations, with $P_i \subseteq X \times X$ for $i \in \{1, \ldots, k\}$, such that, defining recursively, $M_o(S) = S, M_i(S) = \max(M_{i-1}(S; P_i)), i \in \{1, \ldots, k\}$, we have $C(S) = M_k(S)$ for all $S \in \chi$.

We say that $(P_1, \ldots, P_k)$ sequentially rationalize C; each P_i is called a rationale.

For each S, there are sequential rounds of elimination of alternatives. At each round, only those elements that are maximal according to a round-specific rationale carry over to the next round. Again, the rationales and the sequence are invariant with respect to the choice set.

Result 3 (Manzini & Mariotti, 2007) *If a choice function is sequentially rationalizable, it satisfies Always Chosen.*

The intuition behind this result is very simple. If an alternative x, let's say, survives in binary contests on each stage i, given rationale $P_i, i \in \{1, \ldots, k\}$, then it eliminates all the other alternatives and is eliminated by no other rationale. So it is always chosen.

Since WARP is violated if there is a binary cycle, the following result follows from Results 2 and 3.

Result 4 (Manzini & Mariotti, 2007) *A sequentially rationalizable choice function violates WARP iff it exhibits binary cycles.*

Manzini and Mariotti call the violations of Always Chosen and No Binary Cycles two elementary pathologies of choice to which "*all* violations of 'rationality' can be traced back" (2007, p. 1832). Since the principle of choosing the second largest element as well as the maxim of picking the median element both violate Always Chosen, they cannot be sequentially rationalizable. Furthermore, they reveal an elementary pathology of choice according to the two authors. Do they really? We shall look at them more closely in the following two sections.

2.2 Picking the Second Largest

Baigent and Gaertner (1996) were the first to characterize axiomatically the choice of the second largest element (or piece of cake, if you wish), thereby following an example by Sen (1993) expressing a norm of politeness or the attitude of not being too greedy. Let q denote a linear order on X; q can be seen as representing the relevant "quality" – ordering over the given set of alternatives. In other words, q may represent an ordering in terms of size or length (from highest to lowest, let's say), in terms of a specified quality such as speed or acceleration, and so on. In contrast to the authors' original approach and for reasons of simplification, we only consider objects of unequal size or length, for example. Therefore, a linear ordering (complete, transitive and asymmetric) will do. Now in order to characterize the choice of the second largest, let $M(S, q)$ denote the maximal elements of $S \in K$ according to q, where K is the set of all subsets of X, including the empty set. So in contrast to the analysis in Sect. 2.1, we shall also consider situations where the choice set will be the empty set. We shall be more specific in due course. Note that according to our assumption above, $M(S, q)$ is always unique. The standard approach of optimization would now postulate that for all S, $C(S) = M(S, q)$. The Baigent–Gaertner–Sen choice function in contrast is, for all $S \in K$,

$$C(S) = M(S - M(S, q), q). \tag{1}$$

This means that if there are m elements arranged by q according to size, let's say, the maximal element is deleted from S and in a second step, the maximal element is chosen from the remaining $m - 1$ objects. Note that according to its construction, $C(S)$ is the empty set for one-element sets and $C(\emptyset) = \emptyset$.

The characterization that we now present is not the original one from the Baigent–Gaertner article but a more recent one proposed by Xu (2007). It is somewhat simpler and also differs from the earlier one in so far as choice sets can be empty, as mentioned above. Here are the axioms.

Definition 8 Emptiness of Singleton Choice Situations (ESCS).
For all $x \in X$, $C(\{x\}) = \emptyset$.

Definition 9 Non-Emptiness of Non-Singleton Choice Situations (NENCS). For all $S \in K$ with $\sharp S \geq 2$, $C(S) \neq \emptyset$.

Definition 10 Constrained Contraction Consistency (CCC). For all $S \in K$ with $\sharp S \geq 3$, there exists $s^* \in S$ with $\{s^*\} \neq C(S)$ such that, for all $S_1, S_2 \subseteq S$, if $s^* \in S_1 \subseteq S_2$ and $C(S_2) \subseteq S_1$, then $C(S_1) = C(S_2)$.

Definition 11 Anti-Expansion (AE). For all distinct $x, y, z \in X$, if $\{x\} = C(\{x, y\}) = C(\{x, z\})$, then $\{x\} \neq C(\{x, y, z\})$.

Definition 12 Consistency of a Revealed Norm (CRN). For all $S \in K$ and all $x \in S$, if $\{x\} \neq C(S)$ and $\{x\} \neq C(\{x \cup C(S)\})$, then, for all $y \in S - \{x\}$, $\{x\} \neq C(\{x, y\})$.

Let us give some brief explanations of the five axioms above. ESCS just states that the choice from single-element choice situations is "choosing nothing" or abstaining from picking the only element that is given. It may be another expression of politeness. This is in conformity with Sen's (1993) example of not choosing the last apple in the fruit basket. Where there is more than one apple left, NENCS says that a "genuine" choice will be made.

Axiom CCC is a contraction consistency condition in the vein of Arrow's (1959) requirement of choice consistency, though weaker. It says that if there is some focal alternative s^* that is not chosen from the grand set (for example, the largest object), and this alternative is also included in subsets S_1 and S_2, then the choice from S_2, if it is contained in S_1, is also the choice from S_1. Note that the latter part of this argument is what Arrow required in his consistency condition.

Definition 11, i.e. Anti-Expansion, is the opposite of Expansion in Definition 4, here defined in a binary way. An element that is picked in all binary contests is not chosen from the union of these elements. Finally, axiom CRN requires that if an element x is not picked from set S, neither from a set which consists of x and the chosen element from S, then x should not be chosen in any pairwise contest between itself and any element from S.

Here is Xu's (2007) characterization.

Result 5 *A choice function C that reflects the norm of never picking the largest element is in this sense rationalizable iff it satisfies axioms ESCS, NENCS, CCC, AE and CRN.*

Given the Baigent–Gaertner–Sen choice function in (1), any choice function C on X is rationalizable according to (1) iff there exists an ordering q on X that satisfies (1).

Does the choice function just characterized show any signs of elementary pathology? If the expansion condition or its weakening, viz. Always Chosen, are viewed in such a way that any violation of either of these two requirements is pathological, then the answer should definitely be "yes". On the other hand, the norm which is behind the maxim of never choosing the largest element as the first best choice is very clear and intuitive, though not every agent is, of course, supposed to follow this rule. The anti-expansion axiom mirrors a fundamental feature of this choice behaviour, viz. that the individual position of objects within an overall arrangement of these objects counts. The addition as well as subtraction of alternatives matters a lot, and does change an individual's choice, a feature that will also become manifest in the third choice function that we shall discuss now.

2.3 The Choice of the Median Element

Gaertner and Xu (1999) offered a characterization of the choice of the median as the best alternative. Picking the median makes a lot of sense in various contexts. Choosing a median-priced gift manifests a good balance between the extremes of appearing as a miser and showing off. The pursuit of balancedness can be found in classic Chinese philosophy. However, as mentioned at the end of our introduction, picking the median-sized element violates Arrow's consistency requirement and Expansion.

Let us again become more formal. We assume that q once more represents the relevant "quality" – ordering over a given set of alternatives. For example, q linearly orders the party spectrum from left to right (or right to left, if preferred); q may order objects according to their price or size or weight.

For all $S \in \chi$, the set of all nonempty subsets of X, and all $x \in S$, we define
$U(x, S, q) = \{a \in S : aqx\}$, and
$L(x, S, q) = \{a \in S : xqa\}$.

Then, for all $S \in \chi$, define $G(S, q)$ as

$$\begin{cases} \{x \in S : |U(x, S, q)| = |L(x, S, q)|\}, \text{ if } |S| \text{ is odd}, \\ \{x \in S : |U(x, S, q)| - 1 = |L(x, S, q)|\}, \text{ if } |S| \text{ is even}. \end{cases} \quad (2)$$

$|S|$ stands for the cardinality of set S. Note that in the case of an even number of objects, there are two median elements "theoretically". In the original Gaertner–Xu paper we defined both these elements as median elements. In the present version, a decision in the sense of uniqueness is made, defining the right of the two objects as the median element. We now wish to say that a choice function is median-type rationalizable iff there exists a linear ordering q on X such that $C(S) = G(S, q)$, for all $S \in \chi$.

Again we do not present the original set of axioms put forward by Gaertner and Xu (1999), but use the recent set of axioms from Xu (2007).

Definition 13 Non-Emptiness of Singleton Choice Situations (NESCS). For all $x \in X, C(\{x\}) = \{x\}$.

Definition 14 Independence of Rejected Alternatives (IRA). For all $S \in \chi$ with $\#S \geq 3$, there exist distinct $x, y \in S$ such that $C(S) \cap \{x, y\} = \emptyset$ and $C(S') = C(S' - \{x, y\})$ for all $S' \subseteq S$.

Definition 15 Minimal Consistency of Rejection (MCR). For all distinct $x, y, z \in X$, if $\{x\} \neq C(\{x, y, z\})$ and $\{x\} \neq C(\{x, y\})$, then $\{x\} \neq C(\{x, z\})$.

These three axioms together with two earlier ones from Sect. 2.2 will give us our result. But before that, let us briefly explain the new axioms.

Axiom NESCS says that the choice from a singleton set is always the single element. Axiom IRA states that in the case of at least three alternatives, there is always a pair of alternatives that is choice-irrelevant (i.e. each of them is never chosen) and this also holds for all subsets of the considered set. Axiom MCR specifies that if x is rejected from a triple of alternatives, it is also rejected in pairwise contests.

Here is the characterization result given by Xu (2007).

Result 6 *A choice function C that reflects the norm of picking the median element is in this sense rationalizable iff it satisfies axioms NESCS, NENCS, AE, IRA and MCR.*

We see that the characterization results 5 and 6 have two axioms in common, and it is the anti-expansion condition in particular to which we want to draw the reader's attention. We mentioned earlier that the maxim of picking the median element neither satisfies the latter condition nor Manzini and Mariotti's Weak WARP axiom. The issue of pathology comes up again. By no means do we want to claim that the two rules from the present and preceding section are THE rules to follow. But making a balanced choice is a deeply rooted principle that looks for the center of gravity, as advocated by the Confucian school. So many people seem to have internalized it in order to apply it under various circumstances. And, fortunately, many people follow certain rules of modesty and politeness.

3 Some Other Non-Standard Choice Functions

Does non-standard choice "automatically" mean that one of the standard rationality or consistency conditions is violated? Not necessarily. Consider, for example, the so-called "Mother Teresa" choice function.

If q again stands for the relevant "quality" – ordering over a given set of objects, let's say that q orders the elements according to their size or weight or value, a person who always picks the lowest or smallest object according to q perfectly satisfies the standard consistency condition. WARP and Arrow's consistency requirement are "easily" fulfilled.

Consider a choice procedure where at stage 1, the largest and the smallest elements according to ordering q are eliminated, and where at stage 2 the then largest element is picked. This two-stage choice procedure does not satisfy Arrow's consistency as can be seen from the following example. Let $S = \{a, b, c, d, e, f, g\}$ with a being largest and g being smallest according to q. Then elements a and g are deleted at stage 1 and b is picked at stage 2. Next, consider $S' = \{b, c, d, e, f\}$. Elements b and f are now deleted at stage 1 and c is chosen at stage 2. Clearly, b which was chosen from S is still available under S' but not picked.

Recently, Salant and Rubinstein (2008) considered various choice functions "with frames" which they call extended choice functions. A frame represents "observable information that is irrelevant in the rational assessment of the alternatives, but nonetheless affects choice" (2008, p. 1287). A frame can be a status-quo bias, an aspiration level or a deadline for making a choice. In the latter case, the decision maker needs time to process the information relevant to each alternative available for choice. However, a deadline has been set before which the choice has to be performed. In the sequel, we consider a choice procedure which is based on two orderings, viz. an attention ordering and a preference ordering.

The attention ordering O with respect to X, the set of alternatives, determines the objects the decision maker focuses on. The preference ordering P represents the decision maker's preferences. Given (A, n) where n is the number of objects the decision maker can actually consider, the decision maker chooses the best element according to P among the first min $\{n, |A|\}$ elements in A based on ordering O.

Salant and Rubinstein formulate three properties that characterize the class of all extended choice functions $C_{o,p}(A, n)$.

Definition 16 Attention 1. If $C(\{a, b\}, 1) = a$, then for every set A that contains a and b, $C(A, 1) \neq b$.

This property says that if alternative a is more accessible to the decision maker than object b, then for every set A that contains a and b, the decision maker will not pick b if the amount of attention devoted to the choice problem is small.

Definition 17 Attention 2. If $C(\{a, b\}, 2) = a$, then for every set A, $C(A, |A|) \neq b$.

This property states that if object a is picked when the decision maker considers both a and b, then for every set A that contains a and b, the decision maker will not choose b when he considers all the elements of set A.

Definition 18 Attention 3. If $C(A, k) = a$ and $C(\{x, y\}, 1) = y$ for every $y \in A$, then $C(A \cup \{x\}, k) = a$.

This property says that adding an element x to a set A, where x is less accessible than all the elements of A, does not alter the choice as long as the amount of attention k, devoted to the deliberation process remains constant.

Note that for this class of extended choice functions, the two relations P and O are treated completely symmetrically though P expresses the preferences of the decision maker and O merely reflects the degree of attention devoted to the choice procedure. Note also that this class of choice functions violates Arrow's consistency condition. If for three elements x, y and z, we have $xOyOz$ but $zPyPx$, then $C(\{x, y, z\}, 2) = y$, while $C(\{y, z\}, 2) = z$.

4 Concluding Remarks

In the foregoing sections, we discussed a larger number of – what we have called – non-standard choice functions which except for the Mother Teresa choice function have the property that standard consistency conditions are violated. Are simple mistakes or a high degree of complexity of the underlying options the reason for this? Not at all. We argued that all these choice functions appear reasonable under specified circumstances.

We would like to make it very clear that standard utility maximization plays a very productive role in certain environments, for example in consumer theory when commodities are narrowly defined. If what counts are the characteristics of certain consumer goods, characteristics which are clearly identifiable and measurable and not properties such as the last apple in a fruit basket or the largest or the most gorgeous piece of cake or the shiniest chair at a garden-party, then ordinary utility maximization can be the appropriate tool. This is so because the external reference is confined to the derivation of a maximum amount of "utils" generated by different combinations of commodity characteristics. We would never claim, for example, that choosing the median element in such situations makes a lot of sense. However, when individual-based internalized norms or societal norms play an important role, the picture can change drastically as we have seen. Unfortunately, since there exists a multitude of norms of different kinds, it appears highly unlikely that a larger set of properties will be satisfied by *all* choice functions based on norms (see Baigent, 2007).

At the end of this paper, we would like to add one more thought. We have described the individual alternatives for choice in a narrow sense. So if one set of objects contains two identically looking apples and the second set just contains one of these apples and not the other, we have "tacitly" assumed that the latter is a strict subset of the former. Consider the following situation where the host of the evening presents a basket S containing two identical pears and two identical apples to one of his guests, i.e., $S = \{p, p; a, a\}$. Assume that the guest picks one of the apples so that $\{a\} = C(S)$. Now reduce the fruit basket from S to S' such that $S' = \{p, p; a\}$. If the guest now picks a pear, i.e., $\{p\} = C(S')$, Arrow's contraction consistency condition is violated since $a \in S' \subset S, a \in C(S)$, but $\{p\} = C(S')$. If, however, the last or only apple in set S' is considered to be essentially different from one of the two identically looking apples in S, we do not have $S' = \{p, p; a\}$ but $S'' = \{p, p; \hat{a}\}$ so that it is no longer true that $S'' \subset S$. Object $\hat{a}$ is different from $a \in S$ since $\hat{a}$ is the only apple left in the fruit basket. If alternatives are defined in such a comprehensive way, one can argue that for a given set S, there are no proper subsets at all. Each set S' which no longer contains one or several elements from S is a set of its own, with new characteristics so to speak. Apple a as the last remaining apple in the fruit basket and apple a among several identical apples are no longer the same. Clearly, in such a world, contraction and expansion consistency conditions are trivially satisfied. Comprehensively describing alternatives or states of the world can be done, if at all, without any clearly defined limits but to say the least, this is not the path that general economic analysis pursued in the past (see also Baigent & Gaertner, 1996, p. 241).

Acknowledgments It is a great pleasure to dedicate this paper to Harrie de Swart who for many years has been *spiritus rector* of stimulating social choice seminars in the Netherlands. Many thanks to Nick Baigent and Yongsheng Xu for long discussions on rationality and choice and to the two editors of this book for their comments. The hospitality of Queen Mary College London is also gratefully acknowledged.

References

Arrow, K. J. (1959). Rational choice functions and orderings. *Economica, 26*, 121–127.

Baigent, N. (2007). Choices, norms and preference revelation. *Analyse & Kritik, 29*, 139–145.

Baigent, N., & Gaertner, W. (1996). Never choose the uniquely largest: A characterization. *Economic Theory, 8*, 239–249.

Gaertner, W., & Xu, Y. (1999). On rationalizability of choice functions: A characterization of the median. *Social Choice and Welfare, 16*, 629–638.

Houthakker, H. S. (1950). Revealed preference and the utility function. *Economica* (New Series), *17*, 159–174.

Manzini, P., & Mariotti, M. (2007). Sequentially rationalizable choice. *American Economic Review, 97*, 1824–1839.

Salant, Y., & Rubinstein, A. (2008). (A, f): Choice with frames. *The Review of Economic Studies, 75*, 1287–1296.

Samuelson, P. A. (1938). A note on the pure theory of consumer's behaviour. *Economica, 5*, 61–71.

Sen, A. K. (1993). Internal consistency of choice. *Econometrica, 61*, 495–521.

Waite, Th. A. (2001). Intransitive preferences in hoarding gray jays (Perisoreus canadensis). *Behavioral Ecology and Sociobiology, 50*, 116–121.

Xu, Y. (2007). Norm-constrained choices. *Analyse & Kritik, 29*, 329–339.

Puzzles and Paradoxes Involving Averages: An Intuitive Approach

Scott L. Feld and Bernard Grofman

1 Three Insights into Aggregation

Before we proceed to a discussion of specific issues involving weighted averages, we wish to make two broad points derived from our reading of the aggregation literature, and then state the third insight that is at the heart of this essay

Insight 1: if data is broken into different pieces, the properties of the whole may be different from a summation performed on each of its parts, and exactly how we divide something into parts can matter a great deal.

Here we are not making any kind of metaphysical claim about "emergent properties." Rather we are simply observing that how we divide things up into pieces matters for the results, and, thus in particular, aggregating information from some of the possible piecewise divisions need not give us the same result as looking at the whole.

Most of the social choice discussion of this insight involves properties of majority rule and related voting rules such as so-called paradoxes like the *paradox of cyclical majorities, Hillinger's paradox, Anscombe's paradox, Ostrogorski's paradox*, the *referendum paradox*, and the *paradox of compound elections* (see e.g., Saari, 1994, 1995; Nurmi, 1999; Saari & Sieberg, 2001). But in this essay we will be looking at the majority rule preference aggregation process only in passing. Instead, we will illustrate the insight above with a familiar mathematical operation, the *median*, since this illustration makes many of the same points, but without the "philosophic baggage" that comes with discussing terms like democracy or majority rule.

Consider the sequence of numbers 1 through 9. The median is, of course, 5. If we take these nine numbers and divide them into the three sets of three numbers each: {1, 2, 3}, {4, 5, 6} and {7, 8, 9}, the three medians are 2, 5, and 8, and thus the "median median" is again 5. But now, divide the set into groups as {1, 2, 3}, {4, 6, 8} and {5, 7, 9}. Now the medians are 2, 6 and 7, and so the median median is 6. We can also readily create groups whose median median is 4, e.g., {1, 2, 5}, {3, 4, 6}

S.L. Feld (✉)
Department of Sociology, Purdue University, West Lafayette, IN 47907, USA
e-mail: sfeld@purdue.edu

A. Van Deemen, A. Rusinowska (eds.), *Collective Decision Making,*
Theory and Decision Library C 43, DOI 10.1007/978-3-642-02865-6_10,
© Springer-Verlag Berlin Heidelberg 2010

and $\{7, 8, 9\}$. The alert reader will notice, however, that there are constraints on how far away the median median can be from the overall median in this example, and we can work out the mathematics to define those constraints.

It is useful to consider the limiting case. Imagine a very large set from 1 to n, n odd, to be divided into k still very large equally sized pieces, with k a divisor of n, such that each piece has $s = n/k$ elements, with s also an odd number.[1] Let us put the $s(k-1)/4$ smallest numbers into the first $(k-1)/2$ pieces, and let us put the next $s(k-1)/4$ smallest numbers into the remaining $(k-((k-1)/2) = (k+1)/2$ pieces, with the same number of elements in each piece. Now none of the smallest $s(k-1)/2$ elements can be a median median, since the median median will be a median in the last set of pieces, and in each of those the median element must be some element with a larger value, since a *minority* of the elements in each such piece come from the smaller numbers. But, with this "trick" in mind we can construct a partition in which the median median is simply the median among the largest $(sk - (s(k-1)/2) = s(k+1)/2$ numbers. But that means that, for n large, we can construct examples where the median median is $((n+1)/2+n)/2 = (3n+1)/4 \cong 3n/4$. In a similar manner, we can work out a partition in which the median median is $((n+1)/2+0)/2 = (n+1)/2 \cong n/4$.

More generally, we can "force" the median median to be (essentially) any number in the range from the first quartile to the third quartile in the distribution by choosing our partition appropriately. (With small n and k values we cannot quite get to these limits, as shown in the example we looked at earlier.)

Insight 2: the results we get when some portion of the information about the data is not available to us, need not be the same as when we have all the data to examine.

What we have identified as insight 2 seems like such an obvious point that one might wonder why we have listed it as a fundamental insight. But in fact there are examples where we can get unexpected insights from realizing this simple point (though usually only after doing a lot more thinking and sophisticated theoremizing about its implications).

Consider, for example, the work of van der Hout, de Swart and ter Veer (2006). They axiomatize properties of pure list systems of proportional representation in terms of what they call the *plurality ranking rule*, namely one which "assigns to each combination of individual preference orderings of the parties a social ordering of those parties, where a party higher (receives more seats) when it is the first preference of more voters (receives more first votes)" (2006, p. 460) They look at a property they call consistency which says, very roughly speaking, that if a party "does better" in two disjoint subsets than does another party, then it should still do better than the other party when the subsets are combined into one, a key question in studying aggregation. They prove some theorems about what kinds of procedures satisfy consistency and some other properties generally thought to be normatively desirable such as neutrality, anonymity, and faithfulness (which looks

---

[1] We restrict ourselves to odd numbers so as to avoid complications caused by finding *the* median for an even number of cases.

at what would happen if there is only one voter, and requires that that voter's preferences be honored). For present purposes, however, their most important result has to do with party fragmentation. Roughly speaking, they show (2006, p. 466) that only proportional representation rules that make use of only first preference information are *party fragmentation proof*, i.e., such that splitting a party into two separate lists can never improve its summed seat allocation. Thus, they argue that a normative case can be made for rules that "throw away" information.[2]

On the other hand, Saari (1994, 1995) has made a strong case for the Borda rule to be used in choosing a single winner because that rule is the most attractive of all the "scoring rules" and scoring rules, unlike pairwise comparisons, take into account the entire structure of voter preferences and do *not* "throw away" information by only looking at pairwise comparisons. Moreover, by recognizing that pairwise comparisons throw away information, Saari argues that results such as Arrow's Theorem which require the condition of independence of (so-called) irrelevant alternatives, should not be regarded as either paradoxical or problematic for democratic theory.

Insight 3: while the whole is not the simple sum of its parts, sometimes we can reconstruct the whole from the parts by appropriately weighting the parts.

2 Parts and Wholes

How can it be that most households in the United States are headed by unmarried adults, yet most adults are married? How can family income be going down even though per capita income is going up? How can standardized achievement test scores (e.g. SAT scores) be going down over time even though the scores of every racial and ethnic group taking the test is going up? How can most people think that roads are crowded even though most of the time there may be hardly any cars on the road? How can it be that most classes at a university are small and yet nearly all the students find that most of their classes are large? How can George Bush win the Electoral College even though he got fewer votes than his opponent?

It might appear as if these puzzles have nothing in common. Certainly, they deal with totally different substantive arenas. Yet, as we show below, each of these apparent paradoxes can be resolved by understanding the notion of average in two different ways, (1) as an average over a whole, and (2) as an averaged average, i.e., an average over a set of parts. Since these parts are not necessarily equal to one another, we may think of an "averaged average" as a "weighted" average – where the weights are related to the relative sizes of the parts. The two types of averages, weighted and

---

[2] I might also note that, when van der Hout, de Swart and ter Veer (2006) use the term 'plurality ranking rule' to characterize list PR the implicit linkage they draw between plurality voting rules and list PR voting is at odds with how these systems are commonly treated in political science. In the electoral systems literature, with only a handful of exceptions (see Kurrild-Klitgard, 2008; Grofman, forthcoming) list PR systems and plurality systems are regarded as at opposite ends of a proportionality continuum, and their great similarity in focusing on only first place preferences tends to be overlooked.

unweighted, need not coincide and, indeed, can be very far apart.[3] Each type of average gives us a different "perspective" that helps us make sense of the world.[4]

2.1 Types of Households

How can we explain that almost half of the households in the United States are headed by unmarried adults, yet most adults are married? Well, it's not really very complicated once we realize that every marriage has two partners. Consider a simple example: suppose that there are 15 single adults and 10 married couples, composing 25 households in a very small town. Here households either contain single persons or married persons. The majority of households (15/25) are headed by single people, but the majority of the people are married and dwelling in households headed by married people (20 married out of 35 adults). We can think of this in weighted average terms as follows: if we count people, then most are married; if we look at units (households), then to convert back to people we must weight the proportions of household containing married persons by the number of married persons in such households, and then normalize by the ratio of households to people (25/35). In other words, the proportion of adults who are married

$$= 20/35$$
$$= (2^*10 + 0^*15)/35$$
$$= 2^*(10/25)^*(25/35) + 0^*(15/25)^*(25/35).$$

So to convert back from averages based on units, here the proportions of units headed by a married person, to an average for the society as a whole, here the

---

[3] Because Simpson (1951) was perhaps the first to clearly state the apparent paradox of different outcomes for averages (or other features) of parts and whole, compositional paradoxes of the sort we review here are often known generically as *Simpson's paradox* (see e.g., Wainer & Brown, 2004). However, the statistical intuition goes back at least as far as Yule (1903), and the basic intuition has been well known for hundred of years, showing up for example in Eldbidge Gerry's manipulation of constituency boundaries in early 19th century Massachusetts to yield a majority of the seats with less than a majority of the votes, a now classic instance of what has of what has come to be called in the U.S., in Gerry's (dis)honor, the *gerrymander*. Nurmi (1999) refers to gerrymandering as a special case of what he calls the *referendum paradox*. We prefer to think of both gerrymandering and the *referendum paradox* as special cases of paradoxes involving weighted averages, and thus as special cases of what we might think of as the *generalized Simpson's paradox*. (See also our earlier discussion of compositional effects involving the median.) There are numerous essays that touch on Simpson's paradox. Some look at how Simpson's paradox is related to causal inference (in particular, the problem of confounding variables: see e.g., Pearl, 2000), or at other statistical issues (see e.g., Blyth, 1972; Samuels, 1993), while some look at instances of the paradox in various substantive domains (see e.g., Baker & Kramer, 2001; Wainer, 1986).

[4] Also, depending upon how we weight there can be different types of weighted averages for the same data.

proportion of married persons in the society, we weight the units containing married persons by $2*(25/35)$ and we weight the units containing unmarried persons by $0*(25/35)$.

Note that we are not claiming that one type of average is correct and the other wrong. A sociologist studying marriage and divorce would certainly need to know the proportion of people who are married. For real estate agents, on the other hand, the fact that most households are headed by unmarried adults is what matters, because that tells them an important fact about the mature of the clientele for real estate rentals and sales.[5]

2.2 Family and per Capita Income

How can family income be going down even though per capita income is going up? Well, once again the key is to understand that units (here families) come in different sizes. Imagine a simple world. In the beginning, there are 15 families of mean size six, giving us a population of size 90, and average per capita income is $5,000. Here, average family income is $30,000. Some years later, there are 25 families of mean size four, giving us a population of 100 persons, and average per capita income is $7,000. In this second time period, average family income is $28,000. Even though society is getting much richer – in the sense that total GDP has gone up by 56% (from $450,000 to $700,000) and per capita income has increased by 40% – if we look at families they appear poorer. Why is that? Well, basically families are smaller in period two than they were to start, so when we convert per capita income to family income we would need to take into account family size.

We can again think of this in weighted average terms as follows: to convert from family income to per capita income, we simply weight family income by the ratio of families to persons. In other words, per capita income in time one

$$= \$5,000$$
$$= (\$30,000)^*(15/90).$$

Similarly, per capita income in time two

$$= \$7,000$$
$$= (\$28,000)^*(25/100).$$

Once again both per capita income and family income are meaningful numbers. But, if we compare family incomes for time periods when families are very different in average size, we are in effect, comparing apples and oranges. Also, if per capita

---

[5] Also relevant to real estate agents is the average size of household. We would expect average size of household to differ between households head by someone married and those not.

income is increasing, but family size is going down at an even faster rate, so that the ratio of per capita income to persons per family declines, then we will observe a decline in family income even though the society may well be getting richer (as in the example above)! So we must be very careful to understand why the two indices of income don't need to go up (or down) in sync.

2.3 Standardized Test Scores

How can SAT (standardized test) scores be going down even though the SAT scores of every racial and ethnic group taking the test is going up? Well, what we have here is a compositional effect that can easily be understood in terms of weighted averages. The average SAT score is given by the scores of the various groups taking the test multiplied by (i.e., weighted by) the proportion of test takers coming from that group.

Consider a simplified world where we divide test takers into two groups, Hispanic and non-Hispanics and compare two different points in time. Imagine that, the SAT test scores for both Hispanics and non-Hispanics increased from time one to time two, but that in both periods the SAT scores of Hispanics are lower than those of non-Hispanic test takers. Imagine further that the proportion of Hispanic test takers increased between the two test periods. To make this example concrete, let us imagine that, at time one, Hispanic SAT Verbal scores are, say, 500, while non-Hispanic SAT Verbal scores are 600, and that 5% of the test-takers are Hispanic; while at time two, Hispanic SAT Verbal scores are 520 and non-Hispanic SAT Verbal scores are 610, but now 20% of the test-takers are Hispanic. The mean SAT score in the first period is $0.95*600+0.05*500 = 595$; while the mean SAT score in the second period is $0.8*610+0.2*520 = 592$. How could average scores in to go down even though performance within each group of test-takers was going up? Well, quite simply, a higher proportion of the lower test-scoring group was now taking the exam. Overall average scores here are given by the *weighted* average of the scores of each of the groups taking the test, with the weights the proportion of test takers coming from that group.

There are numerous variants of this kind of compositional effect. Imagine, for example, that in a given university, within each graduate department, men and women are equally likely to be accepted relative to their proportions in the applicant pool. Yet overall, it still might be the case that, say, more women than men are accepted to the university if women and men do not apply to all departments in equal proportions, and if the acceptance rate is higher in the units where mostly women are applying. We can even construct hypothetical examples in which the GPA (or GRE) score of students who are not admitted for graduate study in a given university is higher than the GPA (or GRE) of students who are accepted to that university All we need to do is to find a case in which the departments that admit (substantially) more students have (substantially) lower thresholds of acceptance in terms of undergraduate GPAs or GREs.

2.4 Crowded Roads

How crowded are the roads? Well, if we took a snapshot of the roads at various times of day, we would find that a large part of the time the roads are (nearly) empty, and, thus, from this perspective, we would probably conclude that, on average, roads weren't very crowded. But now look at things from the perspective of the drivers. When they are out, it is likely that they will be on the road when it is crowded; thus, most drivers will experience crowded roads.

To see how this works imagine a very simplified example. Imagine that the roads are either empty, which they are 22/24ths of the time, or every driver is on the road (rush hour, coming and going), which occurs 2/24ths of the time. Now the average crowdedness of the roads is 8.3% relative to the total number of cars that might be there (= $1^* 2/24 + 0^* 22/24$), but every driver thinks the roads are 100% crowded because that is their only experience! When the roads are empty there are no drivers on the road to experience that emptiness!

2.5 Class Sizes

Assume, for simplicity, that, at a given university, each of its m faculty teaches the same number of courses, say k, and that the total enrollment in all courses taught in some semester is E. Clearly we have n, the number of courses, equal to mk. The average class taught by faculty, $\bar{s}$, thus contains E/n students. It must also be the case that, if the ith class is of size s_i, then

$$\bar{s} = \Sigma \, s_i/n. \tag{1}$$

But, how large is the class size experienced by the average student? Well, if the ith class is of size s_i, then exactly s_i students experience a class of that size. Thus, the average class size experienced by students is the student-weighted class average, i.e.,

$$\Sigma \, s_i^2 / \Sigma \, s_i. \tag{2}$$

In general, these two numbers, weighted and unweighted averages (given by Eqs. (1) and (2) respectively), will not be the same, and they can be very far apart. Feld and Bernard (1977) used data from the classes at the State University of New York at Stony Brook to analyze this ratio for several different majors and for the university as a whole. For example, for the university as a whole, classes had a mean size of 40.5 with a standard deviation of 65.8. While faculty thought (correctly) that they were teaching classes with an average of just under 41 students in each, students thought (correctly, as well) that they were taking classes which averaged over 150 students![6] {See text box below for mathematical details.)

---

[6] See also Feld and Grofman (1980).

The well known Herfindahl-Hirschman (H-H) index of concentration (Hirschman, 1945; Herfindahl, 1950; cf. Taagepera & Grofman, 1981), $1 - \Sigma\ p_i^2$, is a special case of a weighted average. In effect it is simply a size-weighted average, i.e., if the proportions in each of the various units are given by p_i, then the H-H index gives the average proportion weighted by *itself*, and then subtracted from one. Here, the larger the size of the bigger components in the distribution the smaller will be the H-H index. The paradox of class sizes discovered by Feld and Bernard (1977, 1980) is closely related to the Herfindahl-Hirschman index.

While the Feld and Bernard (1977) calculations are in terms of raw numbers, it is easy to convert their formulae to percentages. In particular, if we divide through by E, the total enrollment, then we get the average class size as a proportion of total class enrollment, $\bar{p}$, as being given by

$$\bar{p} = \Sigma\ p_i/n = 1/n. \tag{1'}$$

Similarly, the class size proportion experienced by the average student is given by

$$\Sigma\ p_i^2/\Sigma\ p_i = \Sigma\ p_i^2 \tag{2'}$$

Feld and Grofman (1980) show that R, which is the ratio of Eq. (2) to (1), or of Eq. (2)$'$ to (1)$'$, is given by

$$R = 1 + \sigma^2/\mu^2. \tag{3}$$

Thus, the class size paradox (and also, we should note, the H-H index) can be directly linked to familiar ideas in statistics; namely the mean and the variance of a distribution (cf. Feld & Grofman, 2007).

A professor with a six course load who finds herself teaching, say, six classes with 75 students each may think it better to teach one 400 person class to allow her to offer five seminars to 10 students each. However, in her "improved" situation, almost all her former students (400 of the 450) are enrolled in a 400-person class, and the average class size from the perspective of the students is a whopping 356, even though the professor sees herself with the same average class size she had before, namely 75 students per class! Many universities, in part at the urging of their faculty, have "changed" their course offerings in this way, apparently without recognizing the very large consequences for their students, who see themselves at a multiversity despite the seemingly large number of small seminars the faculty (correctly) insist are being offered the student body!

2.6 Bush v. Gore: The 2000 US Presidential Election

In addition to the claim that George W. Bush (and/or the U.S. Supreme Court) stole the election from Al Gore because of what happened in the Florida recount process, a frequent claim about the 2000 US presidential election has been that Bush won the Electoral College vote despite Gore having won a plurality of the popular vote because of the biases in the Electoral College introduced by overweighting the small states. The Electoral College is a form of weighted voting, with states as units. Each state gets a number of Electoral College votes equal to the combined size of its House and Senate delegations. Of course, while House seats are allocated proportional to a state's population,[7] each state gets two Senate seats regardless of population.

It is true that, in the 2000 presidential contest, Bush did better than Gore in the smallest states, and Gore did better than Bush in the largest states,[8] which makes blaming the discrepancy between Electoral College and popular vote outcome plausible.[9] But even if (a) states were equipopulous and (b) each state's share of Electoral College votes had been perfectly proportional to its population, it is still possible for Bush to have won the Electoral College while losing the popular vote. Such an outcome could have happened under a winner take all rule for each state's electoral college vote if, Gore's *average* margin of victory in the minority of states that Gore won was much larger than Bush's average margin of victory in the majority of states that Bush won. Had this occurred, Gore would have wasted more votes than did Bush.[10]

To see how this could work consider the simplest possible example. Imagine that we have just three equipopulous districts, with equal turnout in each. Republicans win two with 60% of the vote, Democrats win one with 85% of the vote. The Democrats won more votes, yet capture a minority of the seats.[11] The knowledgeable reader will immediately recognize that what we have here is a form of gerrymandering (Grofman, 1990).

---

[7] Still, because of lumpiness effects due to rounding and the fact that no state can be given less than one seat in the House of Representatives regardless of its size, the U.S. House apportionment is only approximately proportional to state populations (Balinski & Young, 1982).

[8] The correlation between state size (measured by the size of its congressional delegation in 2000) and the Bush share of the two party presidential vote in 2000 was only -0.16.

[9] For the record, we should note that Bush's 2000 presidential victory was overdetermined, i.e., can be "blamed" on many factors, from failure by Gore to hold his home state of Tennessee, to excessive wasted votes by Gore in the Electoral College, to felon disfranchisement that disproportionately froze out potential Democratic-leaning voters (especially minority voters) from political participation in 2000, to Gore's legal team's mismanagement of the legal issues in Florida, to the "spoiler" candidacy of Ralph Nader.

[10] We can make the story more complicated by allowing for apportionment *and* turnout effects (Grofman, Koetzle, & Brunell, 1997; cf. Grofman, Brunell, & Campagna, 1997).

[11] In actuality, however, Bush won his 31 states with an average of 58% of the two-party vote; while Gore won his 19 states (plus the District of Columbia) with an average of 57% of the vote.

The 2000 House of Representatives was apportioned based on the 1990 census. Had the apportionment used in 2002 (based on the 2000 Census, and thus closer to the actual population figures in the states ca. 2000) been available for use instead, i.e., had the Electoral College allocation that will be used in 2004 been used in 2000, then Bush would have increased his Electoral College share from 50.5% to 51.8%. Indeed, even had the 2000 Electoral College allocated votes based just on the 2002 House seats (with no bonus for Senate seats), but again using a statewide winner take all system, then (putting Florida into the Bush column, as before), Bush would still have won the 2000 election with 50.1% of the votes. Thus, if all other things were equal, Bush might have been predicted (ca. 2002) to do better in 2004 than he did in 2000! And, of course, in fact he did.[12]

2.7 Friendship Networks

Most of us find that we have fewer friends than some of our friends do. In fact, Feld (1991) shows why we ought to expect that the average person's average friend has a friendship network that is larger than her own. That is because the relatively few people with many friends include many of us in their large friendship nets. Consequently, we number among our own friends a disproportionately high proportion of people with many friends. When we "average in" the size of their very large friendship networks with those of our other friends with smaller rolladexes, we can still expect to find that, on average, friends of ours have a large friendship network than we do.

3 Different Types of Averages

Besides the distinction between weighted and unweighted averages we have emphasized here, there are other types of averages than every social scientist should know about.

3.1 Median

Consider the *median*, the value such that half or more of the items in a distribution are at or above that value while half or more of the items in that same distribution are at or below it as well. In addition to playing a central role in models of party competition over a single policy or ideological dimension (see e.g., Downs, 1957), there are useful things to say about the median versus the mean highly relevant to social science theory.

---

[12] Indeed, in 2004, even were there no Senate two seat "bonus", Bush could still carry a weighted majority of the states.

For example, Seymour Martin Lipset's famous thesis (Lipset, 1959) that rich countries are more likely to be democratic than poor countries is almost always tested with data on *mean* income (Diamond, 1992). But that's nonsense. The appropriate test is *median* income; otherwise you fall prey to the "Abu Dhabi fallacy" of thinking that a county with a few billionaires and lots of poor people is a rich country. In fact, unpublished work by one of the present authors has shown that essentially all of the current counterexamples to rich countries being democratic are countries where there are huge differences between mean and median income.[13]

3.2 Geometric Mean

Another neglected type of average is the *geometric mean*, the square root of the product of the values to be averaged. Statisticians regard the geometric mean as appropriate when losses or gains can best be expressed in percentage terms; when rapid growth is involved in the development of a bacterial or viral population, or when the data span several orders of magnitude (Good & Hardin, 2003, p. 96). Consider competing claims about the value of some quantitative variable where one side has an incentive to lie on the high side and the other side to lie on the low side, and the two claims are orders of magnitude apart. The physicist turned electoral systems specialist Rein Taagepera (personal communication, September 5, 2003) has proposed that. rather than taking the arithmetic average of the two values, we are more likely to come closer to the truth if we take the geometric mean instead.

Taagepera tells an amusing story to illustrate this point. While still a high school student in Morocco, Professor Taagepera heard two quite different estimates of the number of people killed in an incident involving French troops and Moroccan protesters. The protestors claimed that roughly 4,000 were killed; the French officials that only 40 were. Taagepera did not believe either estimate but he did believe that they provided bounds on the feasible range. If we simply took the arithmetic average of the two estimates to get a "best" estimate, we would get 2,020, far closer to the "official" than to the "local" estimates. However, we might more plausibly assume that each estimate is off by the same proportion, x, i.e., $4,000/x = x/40$. Thus, $x^2 = 4,000*40$ and the "best estimate" of the number of protesters killed is simply the square root of 16,000, i.e., 400. Hence, assuming each estimate is off by the same *proportion* gives us the rule that the "best estimate" is the square root of the product of the estimates, a.k.a. the *geometric mean*. As it turns out, the young Taagepera had a friend in the police force who was in a position to provide a more

---

[13] Some scholars have tried to "save" the Lipset thesis by restating it as one where countries that are rich and which *become* democratic are likely *to stay* so. But if we look at median income rather than mean income there is no need to "rescue" the thesis in this way. Moreover, the principal underlying mechanism implied by Lipset, namely the greater likelihood of there being a substantial middle class in wealthier countries than in poorer countries, makes far more sense if operationalized in terms of median income (or of other related features of the income distribution) than when it is operationalized by per capita income.

reliable estimate of deaths than the public estimate, and this estimate proved to be very close to the geometric mean calculated above.[14]

3.3 Harmonic Mean

Lastly, we consider a useful use of the harmonic mean, the simplest case of which, for two values, s_1 and s_2, is defined as $1/(1s_1 + 1/s_2)$ perhaps the most obscure mean of all. We illustrate the uses of the harmonic mean with a Mother Goose tale. As is well known, Jack and Jill went up the hill to fetch a pail of water. Jack fell down and broke his crown and Jill came tumbling after. Now, imagine the hill is one mile high and Jack and Jill went up the hill at only two miles per hour, but they came tumbling down the hill at 6 miles per hour. What was their average speed on the hill? Let d be distance and s be speed. The answer is based on the harmonic mean of 2 and 6 (see Fig. 1), and is given by the formula.

$$d/(1/s_1 + 1/s_2) = 2/(1/2 + 1/6) = 3 \text{ miles per hour}$$

Thus 3 miles per hour is the correct answer, not, the simple average – four miles per hour.[15]

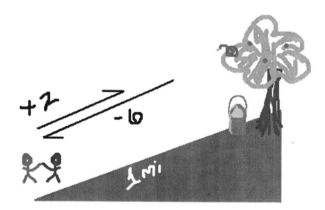

Fig. 1

---

[14] For other uses of the geometric mean see Taagepera (2001).
[15] The figure below was drawn by a student, Gaelan Lloyd, in Professor Grofman's three quarter undergraduate statistics course to illustrate Lloyd's answer to a "Jack and Hill homework assignment" in the section of the course dealing with different types of averages. We are indebted to Mr. Lloyd for permission to reproduce the figure.

4 Discussion

Understanding the idea of weighted average helps us make sense of many sociological and social psychological puzzles of the sort discussed above, as well as puzzles in other social science disciplines – such as how a majority can be outvoted on a majority of issues if we vote, not on policies one at a time, but instead on policy platforms combining multiple issues (Anscombe, 1976; Nurmi, 1999; Saari & Sieberg, 2001); or how a minority of the voters can control a majority of the seats in a legislature (see Grofman, 1990 and discussion of the Electoral College above). Moreover, the notion of weighted averages shows up in a number of places where you might not expect it, e.g., in the Hirschman-Herfindahl measure of concentration, which can be thought of as a "self-weighted" average. In sum, issues of aggregation and so-called aggregation paradoxes and the many varieties of average are all topics that should be part of the common wisdom of the educated social scientist.

Acknowledgments This research was supported by the Jack W. Peltason (Bren Foundation) Endowed Chair at the University of California, Irvine. We are indebted to Clover Behrend-Gethard and Sue Ludeman for library assistance. The listing of authors is alphabetical.

References

Anscombe, G. E. M. (1976). On frustration of the majority by fulfillment of the majority's will. *Analysis, 36*, 161–168.

Baker, S. G., & Barnett, S. K. (2001). Good for women, good for men, bad for people: Simpson's paradox and the importance of sex-specific analysis in observational studies. *Journal of Women's Health and Gender-Based Medicine, 19*(9), 867–872.

Balinski, M. L., & Young, H. P. (1982). *Fair representation: Meeting the idea of one man, one vote.* New Haven: Yale University Press.

Blyth, C. (1972). On Simpson's paradox and the sure-thing principle. *Journal of the American Statistical Association, 67*, 364–366.

Diamond, L. (1992). Economic development and democracy reconsidered. *American Behavioral Scientist, 35*, 450–499.

Downs, A. (1957). *An economic theory of democracy.* New York: Harper & Row.

Feld, S. L. (1991). Why your friends have more friends than you do. *American Journal of Sociology, 96*(May), 1464–1477.

Feld, S. L., & Bernard, G. (1977). Variation in class size, the class size paradox, and some consequences for students. *Research in Higher Education, 6*(3), 215–222.

Feld, S. L., & Grofman, B. N. (1980). Conflict of interest between faculty, students and administrators: Consequences of the class size paradox. In G. Tullock (Ed.), *Frontiers of economics* (Vol. 3, pp. 111–116). Blacksburg, VA: Center for Study of Public Choice.

Feld, S. L., & Grofman, B. (2007). The Laakso-Taagepera index in a means and variance framework. *Journal of Theoretical Politics, 19*(1), 101–106.

Good, P. I., & Hardin, J. W. (2003). *Common errors in statistics (and how to avoid them).* New York: Wiley-Interscience.

Grofman, B. (Ed.). (1990). *Political gerrymandering and the courts.* New York: Agathon Press.

Grofman, B.. (Forthcoming). Electoral rules and ethnic representation and accommodation: Combining social choice and electoral system perspectives. In B. O'Leary (Ed.), *Power sharing in deeply divided societies: Progress and regression.* Philadelphia: University of Pennsylvania Press.

Grofman, B., Brunell, T., & Campagna, J. (1997). Distinguishing between the effects of swing ratio and bias on outcomes in the U.S. Electoral College, 1990–1992. *Electoral Studies, 16*(4), 471–487.

Grofman, B., Koetzle, W., Brunell, T. (1997). An integrated perspective on the three potential sources of partisan bias: Malapportionment, turnout differences, and the geographic distribution of party vote shares. *Electoral Studies, 16*(4), 457–470.

Grofman, B. N., & Owen, G. (Eds.). (1986). *Information pooling and group decision making.* Greenwich, CT: JAI Press.

Herfindahl, O. C. (1950). Concentration in the Steel Industry. Unpublished Ph.D. dissertation, Columbia University.

Hirschman, A. O. (1945). *National power and structure of foreign trade.* Berkeley: University of California Press.

King, G. (1997). *A solution to the ecological inference problem.* Princeton, NJ: Princeton University Press.

Kurrild-Klitgard, P. (2008). Voting paradoxes under proportional representation: Evidence from eight danish elections. *Scandinavian Political Studies, 31*(3), 242–267.

Lipset, S. M. (1959). Some social requisites of democracy: Economic development and political legitimacy. *American Political Science Review, 53*, 69–105.

Nurmi, H. (1999). *Voting paradoxes and how to deal with them.* Berlin: Springer Verlag.

Pearl, J. (2000). *Causality: Models, reasoning, and inference.* New York: Cambridge University Press.

Saari, D. G. (1994). *Geometry of voting.* Berlin and New York: Springer Verlag.

Saari, D. G. (1995). *Basic geometry of voting.* Berlin and New York: Springer Verlag.

Saari, D. G., & Sieberg, K. K.. (2001). The sum of the parts can violate the whole. *American Political Science Review, 95*(June), 415–433.

Samuels, M. (1993). Simpson's paradox and related phenomena. *Journal of the American Statistical Association, 88*(March), 81–88.

Simpson, E. H. (1951). The interpretation of interaction in contingency tables. *Journal of the Royal Statistical Society, Ser. B, 13*, 238–241.

Taagepera, R. (2001). Party size baselines imposed by institutional constraints: Theory for simple electoral systems. *Journal of Theoretical Politics, 13*(4), 331–354.

Taagepera, R., & Grofman, B. (1981). Effective size and number of components. *Sociological Methods & Research, 10*(1), 63–81.

Van der Hout, E., de Swart, H., ter Veer, A. (2006). Characteristic properties of list PR systems. *Social Choice and Welfare, 27*, 459–475.

Wainer, H. (1986). Minority contributions to the SAT score turnaround: An example of Simpson's paradox. *Journal of Educational and Behavioral Statistics, 11*(4), 239–244.

Wainer, H., & Brown, L. (2004). Statistical paradoxes in the interpretation of group differences. *American Statistician, 58*(2), 117–123.

Yule, G. U. (1903). Notes on the theory of association of attributes in statistics. *Biometrika, 2*, 121–134.

Voting Weights, Thresholds and Population Size: Member State Representation in the Council of the European Union

Madeleine O. Hosli

1 Introduction

Voting rules influence policy outcomes. This is true for national electoral procedures, decisions within domestic parliaments as well as policy results generated by supranational institutions. Of course, voting rules and procedures are not the only factors influencing policy outcomes, but they certainly do have crucial repercussions.

Voting in European Union (EU) institutions has not been of much interest as long as, especially in the framework of the Council of Ministers (now the Council of the EU), decisions were taken almost exclusively on the basis of unanimity. The increased role of qualified majority votes (QMV), however, has changed the practical relevance of the decision quota.

This contribution aims at clarifying trade-offs related to voting rules, notably as regards the decision quota and the distribution of votes in the Council of the EU. Although voting is not always conducted formally in the Council, there is little doubt that the distribution of voting weights and the QMV threshold within this institution influence the way coalitions between EU member states are built, and the bargaining processes leading to collective decisions.

Of course, the decision quota – i.e. the threshold in terms of the percentage of votes required to make decisions – is not the only relevant "voting rule". The order on which issues are voted, respective agenda-setting power and the overall inter-institutional framework certainly do affect policy results. Nonetheless, QMV and the distribution of votes affect both representation of EU member states in EU institutions and the negotiation process leading to policy decisions. Over time, decision quotas – in terms of the required number of votes needed to support a proposal – have been adapted for the Council and new voting rules have been implemented, such as the triple majority rule incorporated into the Treaty of Nice and the double-majority clause encompassed in the Lisbon Treaty. However, these decision quotas

M.O. Hosli (✉)
Department of Political Science, Leiden University, 2333 AK, Leiden, The Netherlands
e-mail: hosli@fsw.leidenuniv.nl

A. Van Deemen, A. Rusinowska (eds.), *Collective Decision Making,*
Theory and Decision Library C 43, DOI 10.1007/978-3-642-02865-6_11,
© Springer-Verlag Berlin Heidelberg 2010

also have important repercussions as regards the minimum fraction of total EU population needed to either support or block a decision as taken by the Council. These latter effects can nicely be shown on the basis of graphical presentations.

This chapter focuses on Council decision thresholds, vote distributions and implied minimal fractions of EU population, and is structured as follows. The next section shows the trade-off between adverse external effects of decision rules based on a low decision threshold as compared to high decision-making costs under more inclusive voting provisions. Section three provides an overview of the distribution of votes in the Council as compared to EU members' population size in the past, partially by resorting to graphical tools. Section four discusses government preferences for the Council decision threshold in the framework of the negotiations on the European Constitution. Section five shows the currently applicable rules on the basis of the Treaty of Nice and the Lisbon Treaty, respectively. Again, using graphical tools, partially unexpected consequences of these provisions are shown. The conclusion summarizes and briefly discusses the main findings of the chapter.

2 Characteristics of Voting Rules

In terms of thresholds, three major categories of decision rules within a voting body can be distinguished: simple majority, special majority rules – including QMV – and unanimity. In addition, there may be voting rules determining, for example, the order on which issues are voted.[1] Generally, a trade-off exists between the external effects of a decision on the individual voter (or committee member) and the collective costs of decision-making. The unanimity rule minimizes the first type of costs, i.e. the risk of a member being negatively affected by a decision not reflecting his or her own preferences, but it maximizes the latter type of costs. By comparison, the simple majority rule minimizes costs of collective decision-making, but encompasses enhanced risks for individuals to be outvoted and hence, to be negatively affected by a collective decision.

This trade-off can be shown graphically on the basis of an illustration used by Buchanan and Tullock (1962).[2] Figure 1 shows external costs of decision-making, whereas Fig. 2 reflects the collective costs of reaching the required threshold (the decision quota). Figure 3 adds the two curves graphically to derive the total costs of a specific voting rule. The point representing minimum total costs of decision-making, consequently, is point K in Fig. 3, showing an "optimal" quota or threshold for collective decisions.

In theory, it is possible to find an "optimal decision threshold" for a committee (see point K in Fig. 3). An institution such as the Council of the EU, for example,

---

[1] For a thorough discussion on the importance of the order on which issues are voted, see for example Rasch (2000).

[2] Figures 1, 2, and 3 are based on Buchanan and Tullock (1962), pp. 65 and 70–71. This representation has also been applied by Torsten Peters (1996) in an analysis of EU decision rules.

Fig. 1 Expected external costs

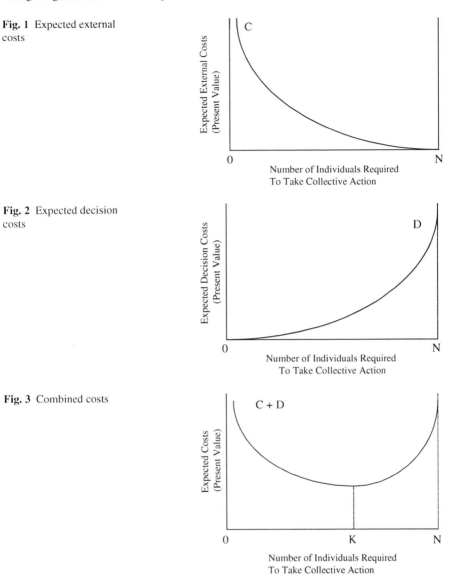

Fig. 2 Expected decision costs

Fig. 3 Combined costs

might potentially benefit from such a "search". However, it is not easy to assess the two types of costs in practice, as it is difficult to locate point K on the basis of empirical information. First, evaluating the external costs of a decision to an individual is a complex endeavor.[3] Second, assessing the costs of decision-making on the basis of

---

[3] For example, individuals can have incentives to overstate the external costs of a decision to themselves in order to obtain bargaining concessions from other committee members. The same is true for governments as represented in the Council of the EU.

the decision rule, combined with the number of individuals involved in the decision process, certainly is a challenging task. Costs involved in this process are, for example, costs of bargaining and possible "side-payments" among actors. Nonetheless, the graphical illustrations (Figs. 1, 2, and 3) help clarifying potential costs involved in reaching decisions within a committee, including within an institution such as the Council of the EU. It shows that a decision rule close to unanimity helps to attain an outcome unlikely to be detrimental to an individual actor's interests, but is likely to maximize the costs of finding a suitable solution for the group as a whole.

As far as the Council of the EU is concerned, trade-offs exist for member states as regards the protection of their individual interests in the case of QMV, but in addition to this, the capacity of the Council of the EU to act is clearly influenced by the definition of the threshold.[4] This trade-off, in fact, was at the core of heated discussions in recent years among EU heads of state and government as regards the decision thresholds that should be applicable in the Council. Clearly, several member states feared that if the quota would be too low, their risk of being outvoted – potentially violating substantial national interests – would be considerable. However, governments also realized that the Council of the EU would have to maintain a reasonable capacity to act, in spite of considerable EU enlargement.

In the representation by Buchanan and Tullock, the trade-off related to the definition of the quota is essentially based on the "one person, one vote" approach. However, in the EU, a second matter complicates the situation: in recent years, apart from the discussion on the appropriate QMV threshold to be used, there was considerable debate as regards the distribution of votes among individual EU states. In other words, it seems that two – partially interrelated – problems came to the fore simultaneously in political bargaining processes. The next section focuses on the issue of representation (voting weights) by EU states in the Council.

3 Former Vote Allocations in the Council

Past enlargements of the EU have been accompanied by relative changes in the distribution of votes in the Council, but they were not usually paralleled by adaptations in the absolute number of members' voting weights. With the exception of the first, 1973 enlargement – in which the UK, Denmark and Ireland joined the European Community (EC) – member states' voting weights were not usually modified. Similarly, the definition of the QMV threshold did not experience much change over time. In fact, up until the Treaty of Nice, in all stages of membership in the EU's past, the QMV threshold was located at a level of approximately 71% of the total.[5] Maintenance of this fraction for several different constellations of membership suggests that the voting system may not have been set up "coincidentally"

---

[4] On voting weights in the EU and the capacity of the Council to act, e.g. see Leech (2002) and de Swart (2008).

[5] See Hosli (1993).

Table 1 The distribution of votes and the decision quota in the council, 1958–1995 (total number of votes; percentages in brackets)

Member	1958–1972	1973–1980	1981–1985	1986–1994	Since 1995
Austria	–		–	–	4 (4.6)
Belgium	2 (11.8)	5 (8.6)	5 (7.9)	5 (6.6)	5 (5.7)
Denmark	–	3 (5.2)	3 (4.8)	3 (3.9)	3 (3.4)
Finland		–	–	–	3 (3.4)
France	4 (23.5)	10 (17.2)	10 (15.9)	10 (13.2)	10 (11.5)
Germany	4 (23.5)	10 (17.2)	10 (15.9)	10 (13.2)	10 (11.5)
Greece	–	–	5 (7.9)	5 (6.6)	5 (5.7)
Ireland	–	3 (5.2)	3 (4.8)	3 (3.9)	3 (3.4)
Italy	4 (23.5)	10 (17.2)	10 (15.9)	10 (13.2)	10 (11.5)
Luxembourg	1 (5.9)	2 (3.4)	2 (3.2)	2 (2.6)	2 (2.3)
Netherlands	2 (11.8)	5 (8.6)	5 (7.9)	5 (6.6)	5 (5.7)
Portugal	–	–	–	5 (6.6)	5 (5.7)
Spain	–	–	–	8 (10.5)	8 (9.2)
Sweden	–	–	–	–	4 (4.6)
United Kingdom	–	10 (17.2)	10 (15.9)	10 (13.2)	10 (11.5)
Total	17 (100)	58 (100)	63 (100)	76 (100)	87 (100)
Qualified Majority	12 (70.6)	41 (70.7)	45 (71.4)	54 (71.1)	62 (71.3)
Blocking Minority	6 (35.3)	18 (31.0)	19 (30.2)	23 (30.3)	26 (29.9)

Source: adapted from Hosli (1993).

(or on the basis of political bargaining), but may have implied some more exact "thinking behind the stage".[6] Nonetheless, equal vote allocations were maintained for the largest states (including Germany and France) throughout all enlargements, up until the more recent changes envisaged by the Treaty of Nice. Table 1 shows the distribution of votes, the requirement for QMV and the implicit threshold to form "blocking minorities" over time.

The number of votes for the largest member states was increased from four to ten in the context of the 1973 enlargement. Similarly, the number of votes allocated to the middle-sized states, Belgium and the Netherlands, was then raised from two to five. After the 1973 enlargement, voting weights, however, remained constant for all EC states and new member states obtained shares corresponding to the ones held by EC members of similar size.[7] For example, in the 1981 enlargement, Greece obtained five votes – the same number of votes as Belgium and the Netherlands had. Similarly, in 1986, Portugal received five votes, but Spain eight (as its population size was between that of the largest members and the middle-sized ones). Up until the 1995 enlargement – with the exception of the first constellation of membership – no country obtained four votes. This allocation occurred, however, for Austria and Sweden when they joined the EU in 1995.

---

[6] On the specific reasons for the definition of the quota in different constellations of membership and the relationship between the voting weights of larger and smaller members, e.g. see Moberg (1998), Midgaard (1999) and Best (2000).

[7] See Moberg (1998).

Table 2 Population size and votes in the council, 1958, 1973, 1986 and 1995

	Population 1958 (in million)[a]	Number of votes 1958–1972	Population 1973 (in million)	Number of votes 1973–1980	Population 1986 (in million)	Number of votes 1986–1994	Population 1995 (in million)	Number of votes 1995–2004
Austria	–	–	–	–	–	–	8.0	4
Belgium	9.2	2	9.7	5	9.9	5	10.1	5
Denmark	–	–	5.0	3	5.1	3	5.2	3
Finland	–	–	–	–	–	–	5.1	3
France	46.5	4	52.1	10	55.4	10	57.5	10
Germany[b]	54.0	4	62.0	10	60.9	10	80.6	10
Greece	–	–	–	5	9.9	5	10.3	5
Ireland	–	–	3.1	3	3.6	3	3.6	3
Italy	50.5	4	54.8	10	57.2	10	56.9	10
Luxembourg	0.3	1	0.4	2	0.4	2	0.4	2
Netherlands	11.5	2	13.4	5	14.5	5	15.2	5
Portugal	–	–	–	–	10.3	5	9.9	5
Spain	–	–	–	–	38.9	8	39.1	8
Sweden	–	–	–	–	–	–	8.7	4
United Kingdom	–	–	56.3	10	56.6	10	58.0	10
Total	172.0	17	256.8	63	322.7	76	368.5	87
Average (Non-weighted)	28.67	2.83	28.53	7.0	26.89	6.33	24.57	5.8

[a]The figures are for the population censuses of the following years: 1960 (Luxembourg and the Netherlands), 1961 (Belgium, Germany and Italy) and 1962 (France).
[b]Federal Republic of Germany for 1958, 1973 and 1986.
Sources: Eurostat: Basic Statistics of the EU; United Nations Statistical Yearbook; World Bank World Tables.

In order to show the relation between population size and number of votes in the Council in the past, Table 2 gives population figures for member states at the inception of the Community, its first enlargement in 1973, the "Iberian" enlargement by Portugal and Spain in 1986 and the 1995 enlargement.

Hence, the relation between population size and the number of votes allocated to member states, up until the 1995 enlargement, varied somewhat within groups. For example, in the context of the first constellation of membership, the population size of the large members ranged from 46.5 million (France) to 54 million (Germany). As of 1986, the respective range was from 55.4 million (France) to 60.9 million (Germany). Nevertheless, vote allocation to both states was on an equal basis: both held four votes starting in 1958, and ten since 1973.

Generally, the distribution of votes in a comparison between smaller and larger members can be illustrated nicely by the means of "Lorenz curves".[8] In the case

---

[8] Lorenz curves graphically illustrate the cumulative shares of two variables as compared to a proportional relationship. They are particularly useful, for example, to show patterns of income distribution among a country's citizens (with the share in population shown on one axis and the

of the Council, they can show the distribution of votes compared to population size for different constellations of EU membership. Of specific interest in these graphs are the relative changes in "proportionality" over time, but these curves can also be used for another purpose: the graphs not only show the relative degree of "inequality" – compared to a proportional distribution – but they can also illustrate the (minimal) fraction of total population required to either reach the QMV threshold in the Council or to constitute a "blocking minority": the intersection of the curve with a horizontal line at the decision threshold (in percent) of the total vote (given on the vertical axis) shows – on the horizontal axis, read off from the right-hand side – the minimal EU population as represented in the Council that can prevent a QMV decision from being accepted (point x_1). These graphs, then, provide some information that is relevant in terms of the trade-off related to decision quotas as shown by Buchanan and Tullock: expected external costs to individuals will increase if QMV in the Council is at a level requiring a relatively small fraction of the population to support a decision – paralleled by a relatively high "blocking minority" as a percentage of total population – whereas expected decision costs increase if the QMV threshold is high (also in terms of the required fraction of EU population needed to support a decision), paralleled by a small share of EU population able to block a Council decision.

In Figs. 4 and 5, the intersection of the Lorenz curve with a (horizontal) line at 100% minus the decision threshold shows the minimal share of EU population necessary to support a proposal (at point x_2, again read off from the right-hand side).

Figures 4 and 5 show that the distribution of votes in the Council in both 1958 and 1995, in terms of representation based on population size, favored smaller member states. But the relative advantage for smaller states appears to be more pronounced in 1995 than it was in the beginning of the European Community (EC): the Lorenz curve shifted "outwards" and away from a proportional distribution.[9] These trends are largely due to the increased number of small and medium-sized member states in 1995 as compared to 1958.

In earlier stages of the EC, a common assumption was that the QMV quota could, in an extreme case, be attained by a fraction of less than 50% of the EU's total population (as represented in the Council). However, on the basis of population figures, Moberg (1998) demonstrated that this was not the case in practice. Figures 4 and 5 graphically support Moberg's finding: the minimal required share of EU population to obtain QMV ($100 - x_2$) was about 62% in the first constellation of Community membership, and decreased to about 54% by 1995. However, due to actual member state representation, the largest three states could carry a proposal (1958); in 1995, the largest eight states (representing about 88% of EU population) were needed. The

---

share in total income on the other), or an overview of political parties' share of votes received in domestic elections as compared to seats obtained in the national parliament. The degree of inequality can subsequently be expressed by the Gini-index: in a two-dimensional setup, the Gini-index measures the size of the area between the resulting Lorenz curve and the 45-degree line that represents pure proportionality.

[9] In fact, the Gini-Index for the 1958 constellation of membership, is 0.085, as compared to 0.14 in 1995. A Gini-Index of 0 indicates an entirely proportional distribution.

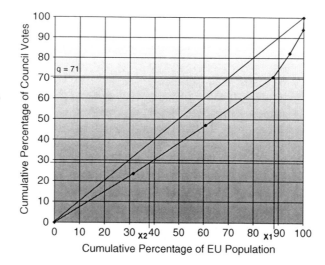

Fig. 4 Share in votes and share in total population: European Community, Council 1958

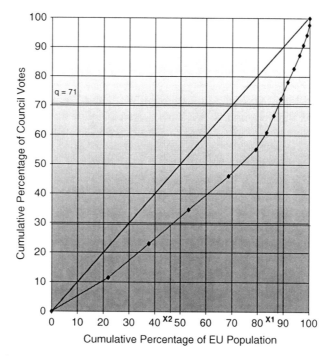

Fig. 5 Share in votes and share in total population: Council of the European Union 1995

smallest four states (including one 4-vote state) could block a proposal, whereas the smallest nine could do so in 1995. In terms of the trade-off related to external and decision-making costs, this means that in the phase following the 1995 EU enlargement, as compared to the first constellation of membership, potential external costs to individual member states increased (with the QMV quota in population terms decreasing from 62 to 54%), whereas the costs of decision-making decreased. The minimum blocking minority in percentage terms of total population, however, remained fairly constant.

4 Government Preferences for the Council Decision Threshold

In the 2003 negotiations on the European Constitutional Treaty – in the aftermath of the 2002–2003 Convention on the Future of Europe – EU member state governments negotiated, *inter alia,* the new Council decision rules, to be applicable in view of then considerable prospective EU enlargement. In fact, during the December 2003 EU summit meeting, the voting threshold and the vote allocation to EU member states in the Council constituted one of the most intensively discussed items in the intergovernmental bargaining processes.

Table 3 shows options discussed towards the end of 2003. This is the point in time that interviews were held with official representatives of the various EU member states in the framework of the research project "Domestic Structures and European

Table 3 Official government positions of European Union member states as regards the preferred decision threshold for the council

Preferred decision threshold (answer categories in brackets)	The Nice Treaty model: (1) 72% of the qualified-majority votes; (2) a majority of member states; (3) 62% of the population. (Category 1)	75% or more of member states and a specific majority of the population (Category 2)	A 60/60 threshold (Category 3)	A simple majority of member states and three-fifth of the population (Category 4)	A simple majority of member states and a simple majority of the population (Category 5)
Member state	Estonia Hungary Malta Poland Slovakia Spain Sweden		Czech Republic Lithuania	Cyprus Denmark France Germany Ireland Italy Luxembourg Netherlands United Kingdom	Austria Belgium Finland Greece Latvia Portugal Slovenia

Source: DOSEI data collection, answers as regards official government positions to question 8 ("Which voting threshold does the government prefer for qualified majority voting in the Council?").

Integration" (DOSEI).[10] DOSEI Question 8 asked experts about the preferred rule regarding the QMV threshold in the Council. It gave respondents five choices, ranging from the option that decisions be taken by a simple majority of member states and of EU population (option 5) up to the triple majority clause as encompassed in the Treaty of Nice (option 1). In practice, however, only answer categories 1, 3, 4, and 5 were chosen by experts, with option 4 denoting the possibility of a simple majority of member states and three-fifths of the population being required for decisions in the Council to pass – a proposal resulting from the Convention on the Future of Europe.

Table 3 gives the official government positions as regards the preferred Council decision threshold. A plurality of member states (nine) preferred option four, whereas the number of member states favoring the options reflected by categories one and five was also considerable (seven each). Only two states preferred option three. Option four – a majority of member states and 60% of EU population – was indeed the option that came out of the negotiations on the Convention on the Future of Europe. The actual decision thresholds, however, were adapted and increased to 55% (member states) and 65% (EU population) respectively, in the context of the subsequent EU summit meeting.

5 Recent Adaptations: Nice and Lisbon Treaty Provisions

The recent changes, first due to the Treaty of Nice and then the more recent Lisbon Treaty, have essentially led to a re-weighting of votes, in addition to the introduction of triple-majority provisions (Treaty of Nice) and a double-majority clause (Convention and later the Lisbon Treaty), respectively. What is the current distribution of votes in the Council and what are the consequences as regards relative proportionality in a comparison of population size and voting weights? Table 4 shows the distribution of votes and decision thresholds encompassed by these more recent provisions.

Clearly, as Table 4 shows, the Treaty of Nice introduced a triple-majority clause that implemented a fairly high decision threshold (almost 74%) based on the new voting weights, in addition to the requirement of a majority of EU member states and 62% of population. Clearly, this raised collective costs of decision-making. The population threshold (62%) implies that the distribution of population as compared to voting weights ("proportionality") brought the EU back close to the 1958 situation. But as seen graphically (see Fig. 6), the minimal required share of EU population to obtain the 73.9% threshold was about 58%, implying a blocking minority threshold of about 12% of EU population. These are fairly high decision quotas. As Felsenthal and Machover (2001) have demonstrated, however, the third threshold – the required majority of EU member states – was in fact void, as there was no

---

[10] The DOSEI project was funded under the 5th framework programme of the European Commission. For detailed project information see http://dosei.dhv-speyer.de.

Table 4 Population size and votes in the council: Treaty of Nice, European Convention and Lisbon Treaty

Member states	Population 2007 (in million)	Treaty of Nice (27 EU States) — Voting weights	European Convention (27 EU States) — Number of states	Lisbon Treaty (27 EU States) — Population 2007 (in percent)[a]	Number of states	Population 2007 (in percent)[a]	Number of states	Population 2007 (in percent)[a]
Austria	8.30	10	1	1.68	1	1.68	1	1.68
Belgium	10.58	12	1	2.14	1	2.14	1	2.14
Bulgaria	7.68	10	1	1.55	1	1.55	1	1.55
Cyprus	0.78	4	1	0.16	1	0.16	1	0.16
Czech Republic	10.29	12	1	2.08	1	2.08	1	2.08
Denmark	5.45	7	1	1.10	1	1.10	1	1.10
Estonia	1.34	4	1	0.27	1	0.27	1	0.27
Finland	5.28	7	1	1.07	1	1.07	1	1.07
France	63.39	29	1	12.80	1	12.80	1	12.80
Germany	82.31	29	1	16.62	1	16.62	1	16.62
Greece	11.17	12	1	2.26	1	2.26	1	2.26
Hungary	10.07	12	1	2.03	1	2.03	1	2.03
Ireland	4.31	7	1	0.87	1	0.87	1	0.87
Italy	59.13	29	1	11.94	1	11.94	1	11.94
Latvia	2.28	4	1	0.46	1	0.46	1	0.46
Lithuania	3.38	7	1	0.68	1	0.68	1	0.68
Luxembourg	0.48	4	1	0.10	1	0.10	1	0.10
Malta	0.41	3	1	0.08	1	0.08	1	0.08

Table 4 (continued)

Member states	Population 2007 (in million)	Treaty of Nice (27 EU States)			European Convention (27 EU States)		Lisbon Treaty (27 EU States)	
		Voting weights	Number of states	Population 2007 (in percent)[a]	Number of states	Population 2007 (in percent)[a]	Number of states	Population 2007 (in percent)[a]
Netherlands	16.36	13	1	3.30	1	3.30	1	3.30
Poland	38.13	27	1	7.70	1	7.70	1	7.70
Portugal	10.60	12	1	2.14	1	2.14	1	2.14
Romania	21.57	14	1	4.36	1	4.36	1	4.36
Slovakia	5.39	7	1	1.09	1	1.09	1	1.09
Slovenia	2.01	4	1	0.41	1	0.41	1	0.41
Spain	44.47	27	1	8.98	1	8.98	1	8.98
Sweden	9.11	10	1	1.84	1	1.84	1	1.84
United Kingdom	60.85	29	1	12.29	1	12.29	1	12.29
Total	495.12	345	27	100.00	27	100.00	27	100.00
QMV	–	255	14	306.98	14	297.08	15(55%)	321.83
Theresold		(73.9%)		(62%)		(60%)		(65%)

Source: Adapted from Hosli (2008); population figures from Eurostat.

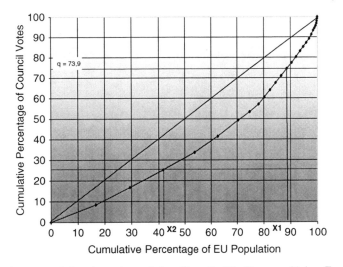

Fig. 6 Share in votes and share in total population: Council of the European Union, Treaty of Nice, 27 member states

winning coalition meeting the voting weight threshold and the population threshold without also meeting the majority of EU member state criterion.

The European Convention was comparatively radical by proposing a 50% of member state and 60% of EU population threshold as the future Council decision rule. In the subsequent EU Summit meeting, these thresholds were adapted to 55 and 65%, respectively – the provisions actually implemented in the Lisbon Treaty.

Clearly, the Convention proposal would have increased expected external costs to individual governments, but lowered the collective costs of decision-making for the Council. Expressed in terms of Fig. 3, they would have located the sum of expected external and of collective decision costs towards the left as compared to the situation reflected in the Nice Treaty.

How did these newer provisions affect the distribution of votes as compared to EU population size? Figure 7 shows that the double-majority clause according to the Lisbon Treaty implies a QMV threshold of only about 13% of EU population (derived from the 55% of member state provision), whereas the blocking minority threshold has decreased to about 8%. This decrease corresponds with the fact that the Council's capacity to act, under the provisions of the Lisbon Treaty, clearly increased.[11] In terms of the trade-off related to decision rules, expected external costs increase quite significantly by the implementation of this provision, with collective decision costs being much lower – a shift even more to the left on the combined costs curve (Fig. 3).

Figure 7 also shows that the official decision thresholds in terms of EU population size integrated into the most recent provisions, do not always reflect the "minimal

---

[11] On respective calculations, e.g. see de Swart (2008).

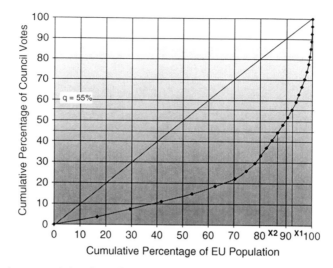

Fig. 7 Share in votes and share in total population: Council of the European Union, Lisbon Treaty, 27 member states

blocking minority threshold" in terms of the share of EU population needed to attain QMV: implied in one of the other quotas can be another threshold in terms of population size that may in fact be lower (and with this, expected decision costs may increase, with the effects not necessarily being transparent to the general public). In fact, the minimal population blocking minority threshold has remained approximately stable when comparing the 1958, 1995 and Nice Treaty situations, with six, 15 and 27 member states, respectively. Somewhat counter-intuitively, it is the Lisbon Treaty provisions, which enhance the Council's overall capacity to act, that have lowered the implicit requirement in terms of the minimal share of EU population that can block a decision: this share used to be about 12%. In the Lisbon Treaty situation, calculated on the basis of 2007 population figures, it has decreased to approximately 8%. The relatively favorable representation of smaller members is also expressed by the fact that the Lorenz curve, just comparing the "one state, one vote" provision based on a 55 threshold with the (implicit) population threshold, has moved away from the proportional 45-degree line: the Gini-index (Lisbon provisions) is highest as compared to earlier stages of Council representation.

Finally, what do the decision thresholds imply in terms of the minimum number of member states required to support a QMV decision? Figure 8 shows the situation for the Nice Treaty provisions (27 member states): the minimum requirement in terms of the 50% of member state quota is 14 states; the minimum requirement in terms of the 62% of EU population clause is 10 states and finally, the minimum requirement in terms of the 73.9% of weighted vote criterion is 7 states. This implies that for the 27-member EU under the Nice provisions, the minimal blocking criterion in terms of member states is 14 states (majority of member state threshold).

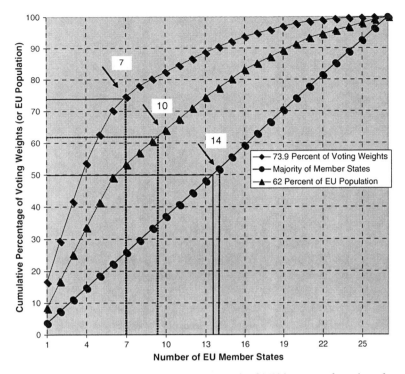

Fig. 8 Nice treaty provisions: Minimum requirements for QMV in terms of number of member states according to three decision quotas

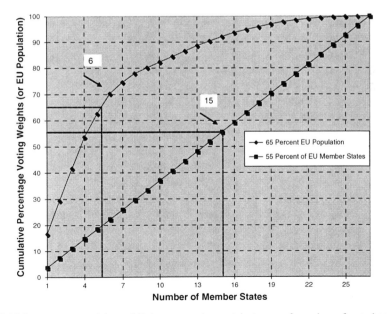

Fig. 9 Lisbon treaty provisions: Minimum requirement in terms of number of member states according to two decision quotas

For the Lisbon Treaty, the situation is similar. However, as there are only two decision quotas, the figure looks slightly different. Figure 9 shows the situation for the Lisbon Treaty (27 EU states), based on 2007 population figures.

In terms of minimum requirements, the 65% of EU population provision implies that QMV can be attained by a minimum of 6 member states (with the minimal blocking threshold of the smallest states being 22), whereas the 55 of member state threshold leads to a QMV minimal requirement of 15 states (or conversely, a minimum blocking minority of the smallest 13 EU member states).

6 Conclusions

Voting rules in a committee generally embody an important trade-off: the more inclusive they are – that is, the more members they require for the passage of a proposal – the higher are the costs of decision-making. But the more inclusive they are, the lower are the possible external effects of a decision for individual members. The simple majority rule has the advantage of generating relatively low costs of collective decision-making and with this, improving a committee's capacity to act, but it implies potentially high (external) costs of collective decisions to individual members, due to the risk for them to be outvoted and hence to be negatively affected by a collective decision.

This contribution started out by a graphical demonstration of this trade-off. Subsequently, it showed the relationship between population and representation of EU member states in the Council of the EU. Clearly, QMV thresholds and related minimum blocking minority requirements, expressed in terms of total EU population, have important repercussions as regards the trade-offs related to decision rules (costs of decision-making and expected external costs). The chapter then demonstrated ways to assess effects of the voting threshold in terms of proportionality of respective minimum requirements for QMV and blocking minorities.

The most recent changes to the Council's patterns of representation and decision thresholds, as incorporated into the Treaty of Nice and the recent Lisbon Treaty, have changed the Council's capacity to act (with the Lisbon Treaty clearly increasing this capacity and clearly lower expected Council decision costs). But implicitly, the effects in terms of required fractions of population size show that the Nice Treaty caused a minimal blocking minority in terms of population size of as little as about 12% of total EU population (caused by the 73.9 of weighted vote threshold), whereas the minimal fraction of population able to carry a decision (due to the voting weight threshold) was about 58% of EU population. This blocking minority threshold, in fact, was at about the same level as in 1958 (six members, weighted voting system) and the situation reached with the 1995 enlargement (15 EU states, weighted votes). The Lisbon Treaty decreases the blocking minority threshold: QMV needs support by 65% of EU population as represented in the Council. But implied in the 55% member state threshold is a minimal blocking minority in terms of EU population of just about 8%. Accordingly, the smallest

13 EU states, constituting approximately 8% of total EU population, can block a Council decision (27 EU states). Clearly, although expected decision costs appear to be low – due to the relatively low formal decision threshold – the small percentage of EU population needed to block a proposal, implicit in the 55% of member state provision, potentially enhances decision-making costs (and with this, lowers expected external effects to individual EU governments, notably those of the smallest member states).

According to the Nice Treaty provisions, collective decision costs for the Council are high, but potential external effects to individual governments are comparatively low. Whereas the Lisbon Treaty clearly enhances the Council's collective capacity to act – and with this, lowers the institution's decision costs while containing the potential risk of enhancing external costs to individual EU states – it has, somewhat counter-intuitively, lowered the minimum share of EU population needed to block a collective Council decision. For the 27-member EU, this minimal blocking minority consists of just about 8% of total EU population. This is the lowest threshold reached in the course of the various EU enlargements. Accordingly, the Lisbon Treaty, while increasing the leverage of larger states in EU decision-making due to the explicit integration of the population size threshold, still provides considerable protection to the EU's smallest member states, notably allowing them to prevent decisions on the basis of the 55% of member states clause.

References

Best, E. (2000). The debate over the weighting of votes: The mis-presentation of representation?. In E. Best, M. Gray, & A. Stubb (Eds.), *Rethinking the European Union: IGC 2000 and Beyond* (pp. 105–130). Maastricht: European Institute of Public Administration.

Buchanan, J., & Tullock, G. (1962). *The calculus of consent.* Ann Arbor: University of Michigan Press.

de Swart, H. (2008). Over de Machtsverhoudingen in de Europese Unie. *Nieuw Archief voor Wiskunde*, 268–272.

Felsenthal, D., & Machover, M. (2001). The treaty of nice and qualified majority voting. *Social Choice and Welfare, 18*(3), 431–464.

Hosli, M. O. (1993). Admission of European free trade association states to the European community: Effects on voting power in the European Community council of ministers. *International Organization, 47*, 629–643.

Hosli, M. O. (2008). Council decision rules and European Union constitutional design. *AUCO Czech Economic Review, 2*(1), 76–96.

Leech, D. (2002). Designing the voting system for the council of the European Union. *Public Choice, 113*(3–4), 437–464.

Midgaard, K. (1999). *Schemes of voting weight distributions in the EU: Possible and actual justifications.* ARENA Working Paper, WP 99/25.

Moberg, A. (1998). The voting system in the council of the European Union: The balance between large and small countries. *Scandinavian Political Studies, 21*(4), 437–465.

Peters, T. (1996). Decision making after the EU Intergovernmental Conference. *European Law Journal, 2*(3), 251–266.

Rasch, B.-E. (2000). Parliamentary floor voting procedures and power indices. *Legislative Studies Quarterly, 25*(1), 3–23.

Stabilizing Power Sharing

Steven J. Brams and D. Marc Kilgour

1 Introduction

Power sharing has been problematic from time immemorial. Children have difficulty sharing toys and desserts. Couples have difficulty dividing responsibilities.

In the corporate world, it is rare for two CEOs to share power without crossing swords. After a merger, quarrels between the CEOs of the merged companies are common; sometimes they become so fierce that one CEO is forced out. Such a power struggle is almost always detrimental to the new company, occasionally leading to its collapse.

At the national level, no country in the world officially has two presidents or two prime ministers. When two party leaders agree to share the prime ministership, then one typically holds this position for one period followed by the other's taking the reins for another period.[1] But power sharing in the sense of ensuring that different factions are represented in a government has proved successful in many countries (Norris, 2008).

When there is power sharing among political parties in parliamentary democracies because no party wins a majority of seats in the parliament, it is most often of cabinet ministries. Usually the largest party is awarded the prime ministership, and there is no simultaneous sharing of this prize.

At the international level, it is quite common for countries to rotate offices in an international organization. A new secretary-general of the United Nations never comes from the same country and almost never from the same region of the world as his or her predecessor, just as the presidency of the Council of Ministers of the European Union rotates every six months among its 27 members. Still, the largest

---

S.J. Brams (✉)
Department of Politics, New York University, New York, NY 10012, USA
e-mail: steven.brams@nyu.edu

[1] This happened, for example, when a national-unity government, comprising the two largest parties in Israel, assumed power over the 4-year period from 1983 to 1986. Itzhak Shamir of the Likud Party was prime minister for the first two years, and Shimon Peres of the Labor Party for the next two years.

A. Van Deemen, A. Rusinowska (eds.), *Collective Decision Making,*
Theory and Decision Library C 43, DOI 10.1007/978-3-642-02865-6_12,
© Springer-Verlag Berlin Heidelberg 2010

countries in these organizations often exercise veto power – de facto or de jure – and sharing is anything but equal among the members of these organizations.

We focus in this paper on two-party power-sharing agreements and ask which factors make them stable. In a previous paper (Brams & Kilgour, 2008), we developed game-theoretic models in which players could agree to share power or engage in a duel. Each player had an unlimited number of bullets to expend, round by round.

By firing at an opponent and, with a specified probability, eliminating it, a player could capture all the assets. But because we assumed that the players were not perfect shots, shooting was not a surefire strategy to acquire these assets.

Ominously, we found that power sharing was almost never rational, however the assets were divided and however they were discounted in repeated play. Because the players almost always had an incentive to shoot, there was a "race to preempt."

The only way we found to slow down this race was to postulate that shooting would cause damage in each period that it occurred. But even this damage was often insufficient to deter the players from shooting, because they still received benefits in each period they survived.

If only one player survived, it benefited the most, because it received all the remaining assets. Because these assets were discounted or damaged more heavily the longer play continued, a player did best by eliminating its opponent early, which was abetted by its being a good shot.

In this paper, we assume that the game the duelists play is different from the ones we analyzed earlier. While repeated, it does not bestow payoffs on the players in each period that shooting occurs and neither is eliminated. Instead, there is a single prize, awarded at the end of play, which goes to

- *both players* if they agree to share it; or
- *one or neither player* if they refuse to share it and instead fire at each other until one or both is eliminated.

Thus, the context of power-sharing is a situation in which one player faces another in a duel. Unlike most duels, in which one or both players end up wounded or dead, the duel we propose is one the players can opt out of by refusing to shoot; doing so means sharing some prize that one player alone would receive if it were the sole survivor. We say that the players *share power* – and ultimately win some prize that they divide – when neither shoots the other in the duel.

We admit that this is an unusual outcome for a duel, and that our usage of the term "duel" might be considered inappropriate. Our work is adapted from mathematical models of duels; we conceive of power sharing as a game in which two opponents confront each other and must choose whether to reconcile – and share the resulting benefits, which we call "power" – or to fight and try to eliminate the other. We will give conditions in which it is rational for neither player to shoot and, instead, for both to share power.

We consider two possibilities for shooting – that it may occur either sequentially or simultaneously. Although power sharing can occur for each possibility, the power-sharing region is considerably enlarged when shooting is simultaneous.

Simultaneity also makes more sharing arrangements stable, so players have greater opportunity to design an agreement without fear that it will be abrogated.

2 Notation and Assumptions

Assume there are two players, P and Q. Power is a prize that both players may share at any time and has an initial value of 1.[2] If P and Q decide to share the prize, they do so in the ratio of $a : (1 - a)$, which is a ratio that we assume was set before play commenced. If the value of the prize when the players agree to share it is v, then P receives a payoff of av, and Q a payoff of $(1 - a)v$.

Alternatively, P and Q may attempt to eliminate one another. If P fires at Q, Q is eliminated with probability p; if Q fires at P, P is eliminated with probability q. When a player is eliminated, its payoff is 0. The survivor, if any, wins the entire prize. We assume that there is no disgrace or other penalty incurred from firing and missing an opponent.

Once started, firing proceeds in rounds as long as both players survive. If one or both players are eliminated, the game terminates, and the survivor, if any, receives the prize at that time.

In any round, both players have one opportunity to eliminate their opponent. A round of shooting in which neither player is eliminated reduces the value of the prize by a factor of $1 - s$, which reflects the damage caused by firing. Consequently, the prize is worth 1 in the first round, s in the second round, s^2 in the third round, and so on. If there are n rounds of fighting in which neither player is eliminated, and if the prize is then won during the $(n + 1)^{st}$ round, then it is worth s^n.

The payoff to a player is the expected value of the prize it receives. The players value nothing else, and firing has no cost.[3]

To avoid trivial cases, we usually assume that $0 < a < 1, 0 < s < 1$, $0 < p < 1$, and $0 < q < 1$, and their values are common knowledge. While a may be related to the other parameters, including p, q, or s, we assume no specific relationship in our models. Later, we study which values of a (in terms of p, q, and s) make sharing the prize – as opposed to fighting for it – a rational choice of the players.

Unlike our earlier models (Brams & Kilgour, 2008), we assume there are no interim rewards – in particular, there is no accumulation of payoffs, round by round,

---

[2] Power is often conceptualized as a relationship between players, not a good they may share. Because it is not apparent what sharing means in a power relationship, we posit a divisible good (prize) that the players agree to share or, by shooting, try to capture entirely.

[3] This no-cost assumption differs from that in most economic models, in which players use up resources when they attack one another. We do not develop such a model here in order to focus on the conditions that discourage fighting when it is not costly. But cost considerations come into play indirectly – fighting makes the prize less valuable.

as long as the players survive.[4] In particular, neither player receives anything until (i) each agrees to share the prize (once and for all), or (ii) at least one player is eliminated.

While time plays no direct role in our models, the players know that play cannot continue indefinitely (see note 4). The damage parameter, s, is effectively a discount parameter, whereby the prize shrinks in value as fighting continues. Consequently, even winning all of it in some later round will be less advantageous than sharing it at the start of play.

We turn next to assessing the effects of sequential versus simultaneous shooting. As we will show, simultaneous shooting is more likely to deter the players from firing, because it is more fearsome: It may cause more damage early; and it may eliminate both players on any round, which sequential shooting can never do.

3 Sequential Interaction

We assume the players act in sequence:[5] Either the players agree at the outset to share the prize, or one of them fires at its opponent. If, say, P eliminates Q, P receives the prize, which has value 1. If P fails, Q responds by firing at P. If Q eliminates P, Q receives the prize, still worth 1. But if Q also fails, the players are in the same position as at the start, except that the value of the prize has been reduced from 1 to s.

We search for Nash equilibria in stationary strategies, which means that a player's strategy depends only on its strategic possibilities at the moment and not on the history of the players' interaction. Thus, a stationary strategy that calls for a player to try to eliminate its opponent in the first round must, if both players survive the first round, call for the player to try to eliminate its opponent on the second round, and so on in future rounds.[6]

In analyzing sequential firing, we do not assume any particular firing order. Instead, we search for divisions of power that each player prefers to its most favorable sequential duel. It is easy to show that, in a sequential contest, a player does

---

[4] If anything, costs rather than rewards accumulate as play continues. Firing uses up ammunition and other limited resources. The models we develop probably apply best to situations in which P and Q have more or less equal resources, so a war of attrition would not favor either player. While fighting always ends in a finite number of rounds because p and q are positive, one cannot say exactly when it will end, except in probabilistic terms.

[5] This assumption underlies the theory of moves (Brams, 1994), the graph model (Fang, Hipel, & Kilgour, 1993), and other variants of non-cooperative game theory. Whether "launch on warning" should be considered a simultaneous or sequential move is discussed in Sect. 6.

[6] Why is this plausible? Because the only feature that has changed in the second and subsequent rounds is the value of the prize, which has decreased, so the strategic incentives remain the same because there is nothing in our model that relates the size of the prize to these incentives. To illustrate a nonstationary strategy, assume that after one round of firing, P chooses not to fire to try to induce its opponent to share the prize. Because P's behavior changes in the course of play, history matters, rendering its strategy nonstationary.

better if it shoots first. We search for a division of power in which each player prefers its share to the expected share it will receive if it, rather than its opponent, opens fire. Varying the probability that P, say, fires first produces a spectrum of sequential contests: A division of power is *stable* iff each player finds it at least as preferable as every possible sequential contest.

To determine whether sharing and receiving the fixed amount, a, or firing first is better for P, we calculate P's expected reward, V_P, if P fires at Q. If Q survives, Q will fire back at P in the same round, as Q has nothing to lose, and will gain if it eliminates P. Because both players survive with probability $(1 - p)(1 - q)$, we have

$$V_P = V = p(1) + [(1-p)q](0) + [(1-p)(1-q)](sV) = p + [(1-p)(1-q)](sV),$$

where the factor sV on the right side reflects the continuation of the game to a second round in which V is reduced to sV. Solving for V produces

$$V_P = \frac{p}{1 - [(1 - p)(1 - q)]s}. \tag{1}$$

P is rationally deterred from initiating the firing if and only if (iff) $V_P \leq a$, which is equivalent to

$$p \leq \frac{a - as(1 - q)}{1 - as(1 - q)}. \tag{2}$$

The fraction on the right side of (2) is the threshold value of p for deterrence to occur – that is, for P to prefer its share of the prize, a, to what it obtains, on average, from fighting.

Note that the numerator of the right side of (2) is $a[1 - s(1 - q)]$. Since

$$[1 - s(1 - q)] < [1 - as(1 - q)]$$

because $a < 1$, it follows that, independent of the values of s and q, if P is rationally deterred, then $p < a$. In other words, (2) implies that if $p \geq a$, a rational P will always prefer to initiate the firing.

Similarly, Q will be rationally deterred from initiating the firing iff its expected value, V_Q, is not greater than $1 - a$, the value it receives from sharing. Analogous to (2), the condition for deterrence of Q is

$$q \leq \frac{1 - a - s(1 - a)(1 - p)}{1 - s(1 - a)(1 - p)}. \tag{3}$$

Just as P is rationally deterred when the right side of (2) is less than a, Q is rationally deterred when the right side of (3) is less than $1 - a$. In particular, if $q \geq 1 - a$, a rational Q will never be deterred from initiating the firing.

Rewriting (3) as a condition on p and combining it with (2) shows that (2) and (3) both hold iff p satisfies

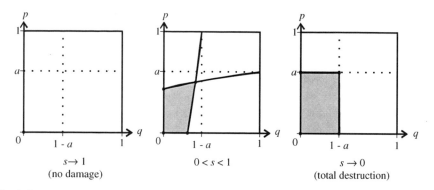

Fig. 1 Sequential-interaction model. s = damage parameter. Power-sharing region *shaded*

$$\frac{a - (1 - q) + s(1 - a)(1 - q)}{s(1 - a)(1 - q)} \le p \le \frac{a - as(1 - q)}{1 - as(1 - q)} \tag{4}$$

and, of course, $0 < p < 1$. The points (q, p) defined by these conditions are shown as the shaded region in Fig. 1 for three cases: s approaches 0; $0 < s < 1$; and s approaches 1.

Inequality (4) provides both lower and upper bounds on p. The upper bound on p always lies between 0 and a, and is strictly decreasing in s and increasing in q. It approaches a as s approaches 0 or as q approaches 1, and it approaches 0 as s approaches 1 and q approaches 0.

The lower bound for p given by (4) is nonpositive when

$$q \le \frac{(1 - s)(1 - a)}{1 - s(1 - a)},$$

which explains why the additional condition, $p > 0$, may come into play. When

$$\frac{(1 - s)(1 - a)}{1 - s(1 - a)} < q < 1 - a,$$

this lower bound is positive, increasing in q and decreasing in s.

As q approaches 1, the numerator on the right side of (4) approaches a, and when $q = 1 - a$, the numerator on the left side of (4) equals 1. Thus, for example, as q approaches 0, P is rationally deterred from firing iff

$$0 < p \le \frac{a - as}{1 - as}.$$

As Fig. 1 shows, for any fixed (positive) value of s, deterrence is possible if p and q are sufficiently small. Deterrence is maximal when damage is nearly total (i.e., s is near 0), and occurs when both $p < a$ and $q < 1 - a$. The rectangular area defined by these inequalities is greatest when $a = 1 - a = 1/2$, rendering the deterrence region a square of area 1/4. In some sense, players that share the prize equally are least likely to prefer to fire.

Deterrence is impossible when $s = 1$, i.e., firing inflicts no damage. Therefore, for a power-sharing arrangement to be stable, unsuccessful firing must produce some damage, and the players' probabilities of eliminating their opponents must not be too high.

In the special case when $a = 1/2$ and the players share the prize equally, the deterrence region – the set of (q, p) values where both players are rationally deterred from firing – is symmetric (it becomes a square as s approaches 0). The corner point of the deterrence region opposite the origin $(0, 0)$ is (x, x), where

$$x = \frac{s - 1 + \sqrt{s - s^2}}{s}.$$

Note that x is a decreasing function of s and approaches 0 as s approaches 1; it approaches 1/2 as s approaches 0. When $a = \frac{1}{2}$ and s approaches 0, the area of the deterrence region is maximal at 1/4 of the (q, p) unit square. Thus, even in the best case of total damage and equal sharing, both players' shooting accuracies cannot exceed 1/2 for deterrence to occur.

4 Simultaneous Interaction

We now assume that the players act simultaneously (or that if one player fires first, its opponent can return fire, regardless of whether the first shot hits its mark). Since there is only one variant of sequential firing, we simply define a *stable* division $(a, 1-a)$ as one that is Pareto-superior to fighting. Thus, either the players agree at the outset to share the prize, or they fire at each other. In the latter case, it is possible for both shots to be successful, eliminating both players in any round, so each would receive a payoff of 0.

If the first shot is successful and a player is therefore eliminated, it would appear inconsistent to allow the eliminated player to return fire. However, there are instances of people who are fatally shot but, while taking their dying breath, manage to kill an assailant. At the international level, a "doomsday machine" also works in this manner, enabling state A to destroy B even as A itself is destroyed. By contrast, instantaneous reciprocation cannot happen in the sequential-interaction model, because an eliminated player cannot subsequently eliminate its opponent.

As in the sequential-interaction model, the value of the prize in the simultaneous-interaction model is reduced by the factor of $1 - s$ on each round if both players fire and neither is eliminated. Also as before, we restrict our analysis to stationary strategies.

To determine whether sharing or firing is better for P, we calculate P's expected payoff, W_P, if P fires at Q. P will receive a positive payoff if P's shot succeeds and Q's (simultaneous) shot fails, whereas P will receive a payoff of 0 if Q's shot succeeds. If neither player's shot hits the mark, which will occur with probability

$(1 - p)(1 - q)$, both players will survive and the game will continue to a new round:

$$W_P = [p(1-q)](1) + q(0) + [(1-p)(1-q)]s W = p(1-q) + [(1-p)(1-q)]s W.$$

This equation can be rewritten as

$$W_P = \frac{p(1 - p)}{1 - [(1 - p)(1 - q)]s}. \tag{5}$$

P is rationally deterred from initiating the firing iff $W_P \leq a$, which is equivalent to

$$p \leq \frac{a - as(1 - q)}{(1 - q) - as(1 - q)}. \tag{6}$$

The fraction on the right side of (6) is the threshold value of p for deterrence. This threshold is always positive; it is less than 1 iff $a - as(1 - q) < (1 - q) - as(1 - q)$, which reduces to $q < 1 - a$. Hence, if $q \geq 1 - a$, P is rationally deterred from firing no matter what the value of p is.

Analogous to (6), Q is rationally deterred from firing iff

$$q \geq \frac{1 - a - s(1 - a)(1 - p)}{(1 - p) - s(1 - a)(1 - p)}. \tag{7}$$

The threshold value of q, given by the right side of (7), is always positive, and it is less than 1 iff $p < a$. Hence, if $p \geq a$, Q is rationally deterred from firing no matter what the value of q is.

It is rational for P and Q to share the prize iff both (6) and (7) hold. Rewriting (7) as a lower bound on p (rather than an upper bound on q) shows that power sharing in the ratio $a : (1 - a)$ is rational for both players iff

$$\frac{a - (1 - q) + s(1 - a)(1 - q)}{q + s(1 - a)(1 - q)} \leq p \leq \frac{a - as(1 - q)}{(1 - a) - as(1 - q)}, \tag{8}$$

and, of course, $0 < p < 1$. The deterrence region, which are the points of the (q, p) unit square defined by (8), is shaded in Fig. 2 for three cases: s approaches 0, $0 < s < 1$, and s approaches 1.

Note that for any value of a, there are always some (q, p) values for which both players prefer to share the prize in the ratio $a : (1 - a)$ rather than fight. The deterrence region includes all points where $p \geq a$ and $q \geq 1 - a$; in particular, it includes points where the values of p and q are both near 1. Unlike the sequential-interaction model, both players benefit from sharing when they have high probabilities of eliminating each other.

The deterrence region also includes points where the values of q and p are near 0, but those points are much more confined, as Fig. 2 makes clear. But as s falls, the damage caused by firing increases, and the deterrence region near $(q, p) = (0, 0)$ grows larger.

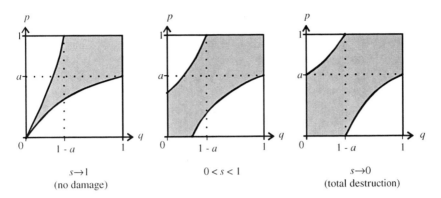

Fig. 2 Simultaneous-interaction model. s = damage parameter. Power-sharing region *shaded*

Figure 2 also shows that as s approaches 0, the deterrence region includes the rectangle with opposite corners $(0, 0)$ and $(1 - a, a)$, and the rectangle with opposite corners $(1 - a, a)$ and $(1, 1)$. In other words, in a broad band around the 45° line from $(0, 0)$ to $(1, 1)$, both players will be deterred.

Note that for any fixed s with $0 < s < 1$ (the middle case of both Figs. 1 and 2), the intersections of the curved lines in Figs. 1 and 2 with the q- and p-axes are identical. This shows that at any (q, p) where deterrence is rational in the sequential-interaction model (Fig. 1), it is also rational in the simultaneous-interaction model (Fig. 2).

5 How Should Power Be Shared to Induce Stability?

We now take a different approach to power sharing, asking a design question: When power is to be shared in the ratio $a : (1 - a)$, what values of a render power sharing stable? More specifically, given p and q, what are the stabilizable values of a, if any, and for each of these, what values of s support power sharing? As we will see, the answers to these questions depend fundamentally on whether the interaction is sequential or simultaneous.

5.1 Sequential Interaction

Suppose that P and Q are interacting sequentially (SQ). Then P will rationally be deterred from initiating the firing iff $V_P \leq a$. From (1),

$$V_P = f_{SQ}(p,q,s) = \frac{p}{1 - (1 - p)(1 - q)s} \leq a. \qquad (9)$$

Analogously, Q will rationally be deterred from initiating the firing iff

$$V_Q = \frac{q}{1 - (1 - p)(1 - q)s} \leq 1 - a. \tag{10}$$

Inequality (10) is equivalent to

$$a \leq g_{SQ}(p,q,s) = \frac{1 - q - (1 - p)(1 - q)s}{1 - (1 - p)(1 - q)s}. \tag{11}$$

Combining (9) and (11), power sharing in the ratio $a : (1 - a)$ is stable – neither P nor Q will initiate the firing – for all values of a that satisfy the double inequality,

$$f_{SQ}(p,q,s) \leq a \leq g_{SQ}(p,q,s). \tag{12}$$

Now suppose that $p > 0$ and $q > 0$ are fixed and consider the behavior of the functions, $f_{SQ}(p,q,s)$ and $g_{SQ}(p,q,s)$, as s increases from 0 to 1. It is easy to verify that P's expected reward is bracketed by a lower bound of p and an upper bound that is a function of p and q,

$$f_{SQ}(p, q, 0) = p \leq f_{SQ}(p,q,s) \leq \frac{p}{p + q - pq} = f_{SQ}(p,q,1), \tag{13}$$

for any value of s satisfying $0 \leq s \leq 1$. Furthermore, from (9), $f_{SQ}(p,q,s)$ is strictly increasing in s. From (10), $g_{SQ}(p,q,s)$ is strictly decreasing in s, and, analogous to (13),

$$g_{SQ}(p, q, 0) = 1 - q \geq g_{SQ}(p,q,s) \geq \frac{p - pq}{p + q - pq} = g_{SQ}(p,q,1) \tag{14}$$

for any value of s satisfying $0 \leq s \leq 1$.

Comparing the two right-hand expressions in (13) and (14), we find

$$g_{SQ}(p,q,1) = p - pq < p = f_{SQ}(p,q,1), \tag{15}$$

because of our assumptions that $p > 0$ and $q > 0$. Inequality (15) contradicts inequality (12), so (12) cannot be true when $s = 1$.

Thus, when there is no damage, there is no possibility of power sharing when interaction is sequential. One player will initiate the shooting, which will continue until one player is eliminated and the other player obtains all the (undamaged) value.

Note that the difference, $g_{SQ}(p,q,s) - f_{SQ}(p,q,s)$, is a strictly decreasing function of s, because both g_{SQ} and $-f_{SQ}$ are strictly decreasing functions of s. From (12) it follows that power sharing is possible if and only if this strictly decreasing difference is nonnegative, allowing for values of a that would stabilize power sharing. This implies that if power sharing is possible for some specific value of s, say $s = s_0$, then it is also possible for all $s < s_0$, and in particular for $s = 0$.

But from (13) and (14) we know that $g_{SQ}(p, q, 0) - f_{SQ}(p, q, 0) \geq 0$ iff $(1-q) - p \geq 0$, or, equivalently, $p + q \leq 1$. Therefore, there is no possibility for power sharing (with sequential interaction) when $p + q > 1$. In other words, if the sum of the elimination probabilities is too high, each player will have an incentive to get in the first shot.

Next suppose that p and q satisfy $p + q = 1$. Then

$$g_{SQ}(p, q, 0) - f_{SQ}(p, q, 0) = 1 - q - p = 0,$$

which implies that power sharing is possible, but only for $s = 0$. In addition, because a must satisfy (12), power can be shared only in the ratio $a : (1 - a) = p : q$. In conclusion, power can be shared if $p + q = 1$, but only if damage is total ($s = 0$) and the power-sharing agreement exactly reflects the elimination-probability ratio ($p : q$).

The case $p + q < 1$ is all that remains. By (12), power-sharing can be stabilized for any value of s that satisfies $f_{SQ}(p, q, s) \leq g_{SQ}(p, q, s)$, which is equivalent to

$$s \leq \frac{1 - p - q}{(1 - p)(1 - q)} = s_{max}(p, q).$$

If $s = 0$, power can be shared in the ratio $a : (1 - a)$ iff a satisfies the inequality $p \leq a \leq 1 - q$. But, as can be verified directly, if $s = s_{max}(p, q)$, power must be shared in the ratio $a_0 : (1 - a_0)$, where

$$a_0 = a_0(p, q) = \frac{p}{p + q},$$

which is the limiting case discussed in the previous paragraph.

The possibilities for power sharing are illustrated in Fig. 3. Note that all values of a such that $p \leq a \leq 1 - q$ induce stability if $s = 0$, but the interval of stabilizable values of a (shaded area in Fig. 3) diminishes in length as s increases. When s reaches $s_{max}(p, q)$, the interval contains only the single point $a_0(p, q)$, and it vanishes entirely as s increases further. In fact, it can be shown that the length of this interval decreases at an increasing rate as s increases.

We conclude that sequential interaction offers relatively few opportunities to stabilize power sharing. First, players will not be deterred from shooting unless their combined probabilities of eliminating their opponents on any round are relatively low; otherwise, each player will find it advantageous to try to eliminate its opponent at the start. Second, even when this condition is met, the ratio of their power shares, $a : (1 - a)$, must more or less reflect the ratio of their elimination probabilities, $p : q$, for the players to be deterred from firing; in fact, only this ratio stabilizes power sharing if $s = s_{max}(p, q)$.

Finally, the damage caused by firing on any round must be substantial. Indeed, if the value of the prize that the players seek is relatively undiminished on each round they shoot (i.e., if s is high), power sharing may be impossible, even when all other conditions for stability are met.

Fig. 3 Sequential
stabilization (*shaded area*)

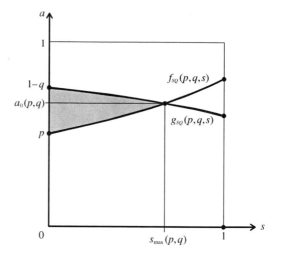

5.2 Simultaneous Interaction

Now suppose that P and Q are interacting simultaneously. Then P will be rationally
deterred from initiating the firing if $W_P \leq a$. From (5),

$$W_P = f_{SM}(p,q,s) = \frac{p(1-q)}{1-(1-p)(1-q)s} \leq a$$

and, analogously for Q,

$$W_Q = f_{SM}(p,q,s) = \frac{q(1-p)}{1-(1-p)(1-q)s} \leq 1-a.$$

The latter inequality is equivalent to

$$a \leq g_{SM}(p,q,s) = \frac{1-(1-p)q-(1-p)(1-q)s}{1-(1-p)(1-q)s}.$$

Therefore, power sharing in the ratio $a : (1-a)$ is stable for all values of a that
satisfy the double inequality,

$$f_{SM}(p,q,s) \leq a \leq g_{SM}(p,q,s). \tag{16}$$

Now suppose that $p > 0$ and $q > 0$ are fixed, and consider the behavior of the
functions, $f_{SM}(p,q,s)$ and $g_{SM}(p,q,s)$, as s increases from 0 to 1. As in the case of
sequential interaction, it is easy to verify that

$$f_{SM}(p,q,0) = p - pq \leq f_{SM}(p,q,s) \leq \frac{p-pq}{p+q-pq} = f_{SM}(p,q,1)$$

for any value of s satisfying $0 \leq s \leq 1$, and that $f_{SM}(p,q,s)$ is strictly increasing in s. Similarly, $g_{SM}(p,q,s)$ is strictly decreasing in s, and

$$g_{SM}(p,q,0) = 1 - q + pq \leq g_{SM}(p,q,s) \leq \frac{p}{p+q-pq} = g_{SM}(p,q,1),$$

for any value of s satisfying $0 \leq s \leq 1$.

Observe that $g_{SM}(p,q,1) > f_{SM}(p,q,1)$, which implies that inequality (16) is true (for appropriate values of a) when $s = 1$. Moreover, $g_{SM}(p,q,s) - f_{SM}(p,q,s)$ is a strictly decreasing function of s. Therefore, for any values of p and q, power sharing (with simultaneous interaction) is possible for every value of s – that is, power sharing in some ratio is feasible, whatever the level of damage shooting causes.

As in the sequential-interaction case, the length of the interval of stabilizable values of a diminishes, at an increasing rate, as s increases. This is shown in Fig. 4 for the same values of p and q that were used in Fig. 3.

The values of s and a that make sequential stabilization possible (darker shade in Fig. 4) can be shown to be a subset of those that make simultaneous stabilization possible (lighter shade). Note in Fig. 4 that

$$f_{SM}(p,q,1) = g_{SM}(p,q,1) \text{ and } f_{SQ}(p,q,1) = g_{SQ}(p,q,1).$$

However, the interval between these points stabilizes power sharing in the case of simultaneous interaction but not in the case of sequential interaction.

Clearly, simultaneous interaction is much more potent a tool than sequential interaction for stabilizing power sharing. More specifically,

- simultaneous stabilization is possible for any values of p and q, whereas sequential stabilization is possible only if $p + q \leq 1$;

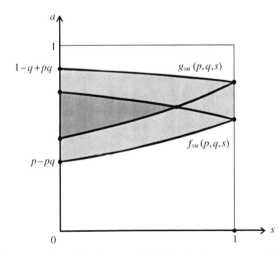

Fig. 4 Stabilization comparison. Simultaneous (*light shading*) versus sequential (*light shading*)

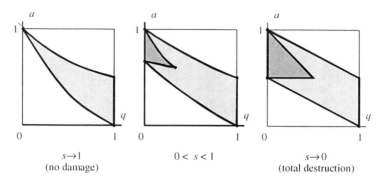

Fig. 5 Stabilizable values of a when $p = 1/2$. Simultaneous: *light shading*; Sequential: *dark shading*

- if $p + q \leq 1$, simultaneous stabilization is possible for every value of s, whereas sequential stabilization is possible only if $s \leq s_{max}(p, q)$;
- if $p + q \leq 1$ and $s \leq s_{max}(p, q)$, simultaneous stabilization produces a wider interval of values of a than does sequential stabilization.

The superior ability of simultaneous interaction to stabilize power sharing is made even more evident in Fig. 5, which fixes $p = 1/2$ and asks how the stabilizable power-haring ratios depend on q. The figure includes three cases, $s = 0$ (total damage), $s = 1/2$, and $s = 1$ (no damage).

Observe that as q increases from 0, the stabilizable values of a decrease. For example, when $s = 0$ and stabilization is simultaneous, values of a from 1/2 to 1 can be stabilized if $q = 0$, but at $q = 1$ the stabilizable values of a run from 0 to 1/2. If interaction is sequential, the situation is bleaker: There are no stabilizable values of a when q exceeds 1/2. Thus, it is apparent that simultaneous interaction is far more efficacious at stabilizing power sharing than sequential interaction, especially when the elimination probability of a player increases.

Increasing s (i.e., decreasing damage) diminishes the possibility of stabilization in both the simultaneous and sequential cases. As suggested by the three cases in Fig. 5, if a particular point (q, a) is stabilizable (for either sequential or simultaneous interaction) for any particular value of s, then it is also stabilizable for any smaller value of s. For instance, any point, (q, a), that is shaded (either light or dark) when $s = 1/2$ is also shaded when $s = 0$. Thus, the more the damage caused by shooting, the more players will try to avoid it.

6 Conclusions

Why are the incentives to share power in the simultaneous-interaction case greater than in the sequential-interaction case? The former allows for the possibility that both players will be eliminated and, consequently, receive none of the prize, whereas the latter model allows for at most one player to be eliminated. This makes the prospect of fighting more unsavory if interaction is simultaneous, raising the value to the players of sharing the prize.[7]

To deter players from firing and encourage power sharing, therefore, it helps if the players can respond rapidly, if not immediately, to firing by an opponent and so, potentially, wreak more damage. A hair trigger, despite the risks of accidental firing, therefore strengthens deterrence. So does the doctrine of "launch on warning," given good intelligence and surveillance, because it enables the attacked player to retaliate before it is hit.

The near-simultaneity of possible retaliation by the superpowers during the Cold War arguably benefited deterrence, Wohlstetter's (1959) warning of the "delicate balance of terror" notwithstanding. Of course, mutual assured destruction (MAD) was never entirely assured, because the doomsday machines the superpowers put in place were not certain to work.

Failures of either command and control or political will were a constant concern, making the doomsday machines at best probabilistic (Brams, 1985, p. 36; Brams & Kilgour, 1988, pp. 50–52). However, as each side developed second-strike capability – primarily through its submarine-launched nuclear missiles, which could not be destroyed in a first strike despite the increased accuracy of ICBMs – MAD became more secure and, perhaps, less mad. Each side could ride out a first strike and still wreak destruction on the other side.

The simultaneous-interaction model mirrors this second-strike capability. Although firing may not literally be simultaneous, a player can respond to an attack, even if devastated by it, so a successful shot in simultaneous interaction does not "eliminate" an opponent entirely.

Put differently, even when great damage is inflicted on a player, it may be able to respond. What makes power sharing a rational strategy in this situation is the damage that both sides incur if both are eliminated at once (e.g., possibly a "nuclear winter" in the case of a nuclear exchange).

Unlike nuclear warfare, the damage caused by terrorist acts tends not to be highly destructive, except over long periods of time. Thus low damage, as well as sequentiality, may make terrorists reluctant to share power; instead, they do better by slowly wearing down the government. Indeed, the government may hasten its own demise if it fights back heavy-handedly, alienating the populace and, ultimately, losing its support if it is unable to detect and destroy many terrorist targets.

To increase the damage factor for terrorists, the best counterstrategy would seem to be to dry up their sources of support, especially financial, that derive from the populace. This, of course, is easier said than done. But we emphasize that the main lesson of our models is that the s factor – specifically, diminishing the value of the

---

[7] The demise of dueling in the early 20th century seems to have been largely a function of the moral repugnance that came to be associated with it. But it also may have been due to the greater possibility that both players would be killed or wounded as pistols became more accurate. For a review of recent books on dueling, see Krystal (2007).

prize by making shooting (attacks) as damaging as possible – is the key to making power sharing attractive to both sides.

Can our models be extended to n-person power-sharing games, starting with truels, or 3-person extensions of duels (Kilgour & Brams, 1997; Bossert, Brams, & Kilgour, 2002)? The combinatorial possibilities of shooting rapidly multiply as the players increase, but so do the potential benefits of not shooting, so we think this question is well worth exploring in today's multipolar world.

Acknowledgments We thank Eric S. Dickson, Agnieszka Rusinowska, and Adrian Van Deemen for valuable comments on an earlier version of this paper.

References

Bossert, W., Brams, S. J., & Kilgour, D. M. (2002, August). Cooperative vs. non-cooperative truels: Little agreement, but does that matter? *Games and Economic Behavior, 40*(2), 185–202.

Brams, S. J. (1985). *Superpower games: Applying game theory to superpower conflict*. New Haven, CT: Yale University Press.

Brams, S. J. (1994). *Theory of moves*. Cambridge, UK: Cambridge University Press.

Brams, S. J., & Kilgour, D. M. (1988). *Game theory and national security*. New York: Basil Blackwell.

Brams, S. J., & Kilgour, D. M. (2008). The instability of power sharing. In M. Braham & F. Steffen (Eds.), *Power, freedom, and voting: Conceptual, formal, and applied dimensions* (pp. 227–243). Heidelberg, Germany: Springer.

Fang, L., Hipel, K. W., & Kilgour, D. M. (1993). *Interactive decision making: The graph model for conflict resolution*. New York: Wiley.

Kilgour, D. M., & Brams, S. J. (1997, December). The truel. *Mathematics Magazine, 70*(5), 315–326.

Krystal, A. (2007, March 12). En Garde! *New Yorker*, 80–84.

Norris, P. (2008). *Driving democracy: Do power-sharing institutions work?* Cambridge, UK: Cambridge University Press.

Wohlstetter, A. (1959, January). The delicate balance of terror. *Foreign Affairs, 37*, 209–234.

Different Approaches to Influence Based on Social Networks and Simple Games

Michel Grabisch and Agnieszka Rusinowska

1 Introduction

1.1 Aim of the Paper

The existence of influence between agents in collective decision-making situations, in which individual agents are to choose among a number of alternatives, may have a considerable impact on the collective decision, and consequently, on the performance of the collective body. Investigating appropriate tools to measure influence is of importance in every organization, at the individual, group and macro levels. The capacity to influence others seems to be as old as the world, since already the biblical story of Adam and Eva can be modeled in terms of influence, and the consequences of this "first" influence are experienced constantly in the world. Since influence is present practically everywhere, in all kinds of structures where, e.g., personal, social, economic, and political decisions are to be made, it is not surprising that different approaches to the influence issues can be and have been applied. For a short overview of theoretical and empirical studies of political influence and power in groups presented in the political economic literature, we refer, e.g., to van Winden (2004).

The aim of the present paper is to deliver an overview of the key investigations of our research on influence. The model presented in this paper is a game theoretical model and contributes to the literature of cooperative game theory and network theory on interactions and influence between agents. Since there are many worthwhile research on this framework, delivering an overview of research conducted on the influence model is of importance. It helps to realize what has been done on this subject and to which direction it is good to navigate. In the following subsection, we give a short overview of both cooperative and noncooperative approaches to influence, with a particular focus on our own research on this topic.

M. Grabisch (✉)
Centre d'Economie de la Sorbonne, Université Paris I Panthéon-Sorbonne, 75013 Paris, France
e-mail: michel.grabisch@univ-paris1.fr

A. Van Deemen, A. Rusinowska (eds.), *Collective Decision Making,*
Theory and Decision Library C 43, DOI 10.1007/978-3-642-02865-6_13,
© Springer-Verlag Berlin Heidelberg 2010

1.2 Overview of Research on Influence

Already more than 50 years ago, Isbell (1958) introduced the concept of influence relation to qualitatively compare the a priori influence of voters in a simple game. In a voting game, where players vote either "yes" or "no", voter k is said to be at least as influential as voter j, if whenever j can transform a losing coalition into a majority by joining it, voter k can achieve the same *ceteris paribus*. This influence relation is extended in Tchantcho, Diffo Lambo, Pongou, and Mbama Engoulou (2008) to voting games with abstention. Grabisch and Roubens (1999) analyze the concept of interaction among agents. Players in a coalition are said to exhibit a positive (negative) interaction when the worth of the coalition is greater (smaller) than the sum of the individual worths.

The cooperative game theoretical approach to interaction is also used in Hu and Shapley (2003a, 2003b), where the authors apply the command structure of Shapley (1994) to model players' interaction relations by simple games. For each player, boss sets and approval sets are introduced, and based on these sets, a simple game called the *command game* for a player is built. Given a set of command games, the *command function* is defined, which assigns to each coalition the set of all players that are "commandable" by that coalition.

A different approach, related to noncooperative game theory, is applied in Koller and Milch (2003), where the so called multi-agent influence diagrams are introduced. These diagrams are a graphical representation for noncooperative games, and represent decision problems involving multiple agents.

One of the concepts naturally related to influence is the concept of leadership. DeMarzo (1992) examines the set of outcomes sustainable by a leader with the power to make suggestions which are important even if players can communicate and form coalitions. van den Brink, Rusinowska, and Steffen (2009) define the satisfaction and power scores for opinion leaders – followers structures and examine common properties of these scores.

As mentioned in Hojman and Szeidl (2006), individual decisions and strategic interaction are both embedded in a social network. Social networks are therefore particularly useful in analyzing influence. In Lopez-Pintado (2008), where the author stresses the fact that decisions of individuals are often influenced by the decisions of other individuals, a network of interacting agents whose actions are determined by the actions of their neighbors is studied.

The point of departure for our research on influence is a framework originally introduced in Hoede and Bakker (1982). The model concerns influence in a social network in which agents are to make an acceptance/rejection decision on a certain proposal. Each agent has an inclination to say either "yes" or "no" on the proposal, but agents may influence the decisions of others, and consequently the agents' decisions may differ from their preliminary inclinations. Such a transformation from the inclinations to the decisions is represented by an influence function. In Hoede and Bakker (1982) the concept of decisional power (called later in some related papers the Hoede–Bakker index) is introduced. Some properties of this index are studied in Rusinowska and de Swart (2007), where the authors examine if the Hoede–Bakker index satisfies some postulates for power indices, like the monotonicity postulate, the donation postulate, and the bloc postulate (see e.g., Felsenthal & Machover, 1998), and if the Hoede–Bakker index displays some voting power paradoxes, like the redistribution paradox (Fischer & Schotter, 1978; see also Schotter, 1981), the paradox of new members (Brams, 1975; Brams & Affuso, 1976), and the paradox of large size (Brams, 1975). Following a probabilistic approach to power indices (see e.g., Laruelle & Valenciano, 2005), Rusinowska and de Swart (2006) investigate a generalization of the Hoede–Bakker index that coincides with the Penrose measure (Penrose, 1946; see also Banzhaf, 1965), and some modifications of this index that coincide with other well known power indices, like the Rae index (Rae, 1969), the Coleman indices (Coleman, 1971, 1986), and the König–Bräuninger index (König & Bräuninger, 1998). Analogous modifications of the Hoede–Bakker index to the Shapley–Shubik index (Shapley & Shubik, 1954) and the Holler–Packel index (Holler & Packel, 1983) are presented in Rusinowska (2009). In Rusinowska (2008) the not-preference based version of the Hoede–Bakker index is investigated.

As noticed in our first paper on influence (Grabisch & Rusinowska 2009b), the Hoede–Bakker index does not give a full description of the influence, in the sense that it hides the actual role of the influence function. This observation has initiated our larger project on the model of influence in a social network, with the aim to investigate measures of influence and other tools to deal with this phenomenon. In Grabisch and Rusinowska (2009b), the concept of a weighted influence index of a coalition on an individual is defined. We consider different influence functions, like the majority function, the guru function, the identity function, the reversal function, the mass psychology function, and study their properties. In particular, the set of followers, the kernel of an influence function, and a purely influential function are analyzed.

As mentioned above, another framework which models players' interactions is the framework of command games introduced by Hu and Shapley (2003a, 2003b). In Grabisch and Rusinowska (2009a), we study the relation between this framework and the influence model and show that the model of influence is more general than the command games. In particular, we define several influence functions which capture the command structure. Moreover, we propose a more general definition of the influence index and show that under some assumptions several well-known power indices coincide with some expressions of the weighted influence indices.

In Grabisch and Rusinowska (2008), we study the exact relation between two central concepts of the influence model: the influence function and the follower function. We deliver sufficient and necessary conditions for a function to be a follower function, and describe the structure of the set of all influence functions that lead to a given follower function. Moreover, we investigate the exact relations between the key concepts of the command games and of the influence model. A sufficient and necessary condition for the equivalence between an influence function and a command game is delivered. We also find sufficient and necessary conditions for a function to be a command function, and describe the minimal sets generating a command game.

In Grabisch and Rusinowska (2009d), the yes/no model is extended to the influence model in which each agent has a totally ordered set of possible actions. The generalized influence indices and other tools related to the multi-choice model are investigated and the results are compared to the ones obtained in the yes/no model of influence. In Grabisch and Rusinowska (2010), we consider another generalized model of influence in which each player has a continuum of actions.

1.3 Structure of the Paper

In the remaining parts of the paper, we present a formal description of our investigations on the selected influence issues. Section 2 concerns the yes/no model of influence. We describe the model and recapitulate some results on the key concepts of the influence model. In Sect. 3 the framework of command games and some of the relations between this framework and the yes/no influence model are presented. In Sect. 4 we mention the generalized model of influence in which agents have a totally ordered set of possible actions. Section 5 gives some reflections on the problem of identifying the model of influence in a practical situation. Section 6 is devoted to concluding remarks on our future research on the influence issues.

2 The Model of Influence in a Social Network

2.1 Description of the Model and Weighted Influence Indices

We consider a social network with a set of agents (players, actors, voters) denoted by $N := \{1, 2, \ldots, n\}$ who are to make a certain acceptance-rejection decision on a specific proposal. Each agent has an *inclination* either to say "yes" (denoted by $+1$) or "no" (denoted by -1). By the inclination of an agent we mean an action that the agent would choose being completely "on his own", that is, without any interaction with other agents and not being influenced by others. Let $i = (i_1, i_2, \ldots, i_n)$ denote an *inclination vector* and $I := \{-1, +1\}^n$ be the set of all inclination vectors. For convenience, $(1, 1, \ldots, 1) \in I$ and $(-1, -1, \ldots, -1) \in I$ are denoted by 1_N and -1_N, respectively, and also for mixed cases like $(-1_{N \setminus S}, 1_S)$.

Agents in such a social network may influence each other, and due to the influences, the final decision of an agent may be different from his original inclination. Formally, each inclination vector $i \in I$ is transformed into a *decision vector* $Bi = ((Bi)_1, (Bi)_2, \ldots, (Bi)_n)$, where $B : I \to I, i \mapsto Bi$ is the *influence function*. The set of all influence functions will be denoted by $\mathcal{B}$.

What do we mean by *influence* and how is it modeled in our framework? In our most general statement, we say that an agent is *influenced* if the decision of the agent is different from his (original) inclination. In Grabisch and Rusinowska (2009b) we distinguish between a *direct influence* and an *opposite influence*. The direct influence of a unanimous coalition on an agent, that is, a coalition of players with the same inclination, means that the agent's inclination is different from the inclination of that coalition, but his decision coincides with the inclination of the coalition. Under the opposite influence of a coalition on an agent, the inclination of the agent coincides with the inclination of the coalition, but his decision is different from the inclination of the coalition. In the case of direct influence, which is the most common, the agent changes his opinion because he may be convinced by the arguments of the influencing coalition, or for some political, hierarchical or more personal reason, he feels obliged to follow that coalition. On the other hand, the opposite influence is a kind of reactive behavior. The agent, again for some political or personal reason, systematically decides for the opposite opinion of the influencing coalition. In the present paper, we consider for simplicity only the notion of the direct influence, and hence, in all following definitions we will omit the word "direct".

Let us introduce several notations for convenience. Cardinality of sets $S, T, \ldots$ will be denoted by the corresponding lower case $s, t, \ldots$. We omit braces for sets, e.g., $\{k, m\}$, $N \setminus \{j\}$, $S \cup \{j\}$ will be written km, $N \setminus j$, $S \cup j$, etc. For any $S \subseteq N$, $|S| \geq 2$, we introduce the set I_S of all inclination vectors under which all members of S have the same inclination

$$I_S := \{i \in I \mid \forall k, j \in S \, [i_k = i_j]\} \tag{1}$$

and $I_k := I$, for any $k \in N$. By i_S we denote the value i_k for some $k \in S, i \in I_S$. Let for each $S \subseteq N$ and $j \in N \setminus S$, $I_{S \to j}$ denote the set of all inclination vectors of *potential influence of S on j*, that is,

$$I_{S \to j} := \{i \in I_S \mid i_j = -i_S\} \tag{2}$$

and additionally, for each $B \in \mathcal{B}$, let $I^*_{S \to j}(B)$ denote the set of all inclination vectors of *observed influence of S on j under $B \in \mathcal{B}$*, that is,

$$I^*_{S \to j}(B) := \{i \in I_{S \to j} \mid (Bi)_j = i_S\}. \tag{3}$$

In Grabisch and Rusinowska (2009b), we introduce the *weighted influence indices*, whose main idea is to give a relative importance to the different inclination vectors. For each $S \subseteq N$, $j \in N \setminus S$ and $i \in I_S$, we introduce a *weight* $\alpha_i^{S \to j} \in [0, 1]$ *of influence of coalition S on $j \in N \setminus S$ under the inclination vector $i \in I_S$*. There is no normalization on the weights, but we assume that for each $S \subseteq N$ and $j \in N \setminus S$, there exists $i \in I_{S \to j}$ such that $\alpha_i^{S \to j} > 0$. Moreover, we impose the *symmetry* *assumption* that $\alpha_i^{S \to j}$ depends solely on the number of agents having the same inclination as S under $i \in I_S$.

Given $B \in \mathcal{B}$, for each $S \subseteq N$, $j \in N \setminus S$, the *weighted influence index* of coalition S on player j is defined as

$$d_\alpha(B, S \to j) := \frac{\sum_{i \in I^*_{S \to j}(B)} \alpha_i^{S \to j}}{\sum_{i \in I_{S \to j}} \alpha_i^{S \to j}} \in [0, 1]. \qquad (4)$$

It is the (weighted) proportion of situations of observed influence among all situations of potential influence. Two particular ways of weighting lead to the *possibility influence index* $\overline{d}(B, S \to j)$, under which any possibility of influence is taken into account, and the *certainty influence index* $\underline{d}(B, S \to j)$, where we take into account only the situations in which all agents outside $S \cup j$ have the inclination different from the inclination of S. We have for each $S \subseteq N$, $j \in N \setminus S$ and $B \in \mathcal{B}$

$$\overline{d}(B, S \to j) = d_{\overline{\alpha}}(B, S \to j), \text{ where } \overline{\alpha}_i^{S \to j} = 1 \text{ for each } i \in I_S$$

and

$$\underline{d}(B, S \to j) = d_{\underline{\alpha}}(B, S \to j), \text{ where for each } i \in I_S$$

$$\underline{\alpha}_i^{S \to j} = \begin{cases} 1, & \text{if } \forall p \notin S \cup j, i_p = -i_S \\ 0, & \text{otherwise.} \end{cases}$$

Consequently, we can write

$$\overline{d}(B, S \to j) = \frac{|I^*_{S \to j}(B)|}{|I_{S \to j}|} \in [0, 1] \qquad (5)$$

$$\underline{d}(B, S \to j) = \frac{|\{i \in I^*_{S \to j}(B) \mid \forall p \notin S [i_p = -i_S]\}|}{2} \in \{0, \frac{1}{2}, 1\}. \qquad (6)$$

The possibility influence index gives therefore the fraction of potential influence situations that happen to be situations of observed influence indeed. The certainty influence index measures also such a fraction, except that it focuses only on situations in which the coalition in question is the only one which (directly) influences the agent.

2.2 Follower Functions and Influence Functions

The key concept of the influence framework is the concept of *follower* of a given coalition, that is, an agent who always follows the inclination of that coalition when all members of the coalition have the same inclination. The *follower function* of $B \in \mathcal{B}$ is a mapping $F_B : 2^N \to 2^N$ defined as

$$F_B(S) := \{k \in N \mid \forall i \in I_S, (Bi)_k = i_S\}, \quad \forall S \subseteq N, S \neq \emptyset \qquad (7)$$

and $F_B(\emptyset) := \emptyset$. We say that $F_B(S)$ is the *set of followers of S under B*. The set of all follower functions is denoted by $\mathcal{F}$. In Grabisch and Rusinowska (2009b), it is shown that

$$d_\alpha(B, S \to j) = 1, \quad \forall j \in F_B(S) \setminus S.$$

Another important concept of the influence model is the concept of *kernel* of an influence function, which is the set of "truly" influential coalitions. Assume F_B is not identically the empty set. The *kernel* of B is defined as

$$\mathcal{K}(B) := \{S \in 2^N \mid F_B(S) \neq \emptyset, \text{ and } S' \subset S \Rightarrow F_B(S') = \emptyset\}. \qquad (8)$$

As defined before, in order to model influences between players, that is, to represent a transformation between agents' inclinations and their decisions, an influence function is used. We like to recapitulate definitions and some basic properties of some of the influence functions defined in Grabisch and Rusinowska (2009b) that model different types of influence. Four functions will be mentioned: the identity function (which models the absence of any influence), the reversal function (which depicts a systematic reversal of inclination), the guru function (which describes following the guru by each agent in every situation, assuming such a guru exists), and the majority function (under which if a majority of agents has the positive inclination, then all agents choose the yes-option, otherwise all agents choose the no-action). Let us recall definitions of these influence functions.

- *The identity function* $\mathsf{Id} \in \mathcal{B}$ is defined by

$$\mathsf{Id} i = i, \quad \forall i \in I. \qquad (9)$$

- *The reversal function* $-\mathsf{Id} \in \mathcal{B}$ is defined by

$$(-\mathsf{Id}) i = -i, \quad \forall i \in I. \qquad (10)$$

- Let $\widetilde{k} \in N$ be a particular player called the guru.
  The *guru influence function* $\mathsf{Gur}^{[\widetilde{k}]} \in \mathcal{B}$ is defined by

$$(\mathsf{Gur}^{[\widetilde{k}]} i)_j = i_{\widetilde{k}}, \quad \forall i \in I, \quad \forall j \in N. \qquad (11)$$

- Let $n \geq t > \lfloor \frac{n}{2} \rfloor$, and for any $i \in I$ we define $i^+ := \{k \in N \mid i_k = +1\}$. The *majority influence function* $\mathsf{Maj}^{[t]} \in \mathcal{B}$ is defined by

$$\text{Maj}^{[t]}_i := \begin{cases} 1_N, & \text{if } |i^+| \geq t \\ -1_N, & \text{if } |i^+| < t \end{cases}, \quad \forall i \in I. \tag{12}$$

In Grabisch and Rusinowska (2009b), we prove that the follower functions of these influence functions, for each $S \subseteq N$, are equal to

$$F_{\text{Id}}(S) = S, \quad F_{-\text{Id}}(S) = \emptyset, \quad F_{\text{Gur}^{[\tilde{k}]}}(S) = \begin{cases} N, & \text{if } \tilde{k} \in S \\ \emptyset, & \text{if } \tilde{k} \notin S, \end{cases}$$

$$F_{\text{Maj}^{[t]}}(S) = \begin{cases} N, & \text{if } s \geq t \\ \emptyset, & \text{if } s < t \end{cases}$$

and the kernels of these influence functions are

$$\mathcal{K}(\text{Id}) = \{\{k\}, k \in N\}, \quad \mathcal{K}(-\text{Id}) = \emptyset, \quad \mathcal{K}(\text{Gur}^{[\tilde{k}]}) = \{\tilde{k}\},$$
$$\mathcal{K}(\text{Maj}^{[t]}) = \{S \subseteq N \mid |S| = t\}.$$

In Grabisch and Rusinowska (2008), we establish the exact relation between the influence function and the follower function. In particular, we find sufficient and necessary conditions for a function to be the follower function of some influence function. Moreover, given a follower function, we find the smallest and greatest influence functions that lead to this follower function.

First of all, note that while there is no restriction on an influence function $B : 2^N \to 2^N$, any follower function $F_B : 2^N \to 2^N$ should satisfy some conditions. The mapping $\Phi : \mathcal{B} \to (2^N)^{(2^N)}$, defined by $B \mapsto \Phi(B) := F_B$ is neither a surjection nor an injection (that is, several different B's may have the same follower function, and there are functions in $(2^N)^{(2^N)}$ which cannot be the follower function of some influence function). We have $\Phi(\mathcal{B}) = \mathcal{F}$. In Grabisch and Rusinowska (2008), we prove that a function $F : 2^N \to 2^N$ is a follower function of some $B \in \mathcal{B}$ (i.e., $F_B = F$, or $\Phi(B) = F$) if and only if it satisfies the following three conditions:

- $F(\emptyset) = \emptyset$;
- F is an isotone function ($S \subseteq S'$ implies $F(S) \subseteq F(S')$);
- If $S \cap T = \emptyset$, then $F(S) \cap F(T) = \emptyset$.

Moreover, the smallest and greatest influence functions belonging to $\Phi^{-1}(F)$ are respectively the influence functions $\underline{B}_F$ and $\overline{B}_F$, defined by, for all $i \in I$ and all $k \in N$:

$$(\underline{B}_F i)_k := \begin{cases} +1, & \text{if } k \in F(S^+(i)) \\ +-1, & \text{otherwise} \end{cases},$$

$$(\overline{B}_F i)_k := \begin{cases} -1, & \text{if } k \in F(S^-(i)) \\ +1, & \text{otherwise} \end{cases},$$

where $S^{\pm}(i) := \{j \in N \mid i_j = \pm 1\}$.

For instance, if $F(S) = \emptyset$ for all $S \subseteq N$, then $\underline{B} \equiv -1_N$ and $\overline{B} \equiv 1_N$.

If $F = \mathsf{Id}$, then $\Phi^{-1}(\mathsf{Id}) = \{\mathsf{Id}\}$.

In Grabisch and Rusinowska (2008), we also find the (algebraic) structure of $\Phi^{-1}(F)$, i.e., the set of all influence functions that lead to the follower function F and we indicate how to compute it. This structure happens to be a distributive lattice.

2.3 Example

In order to illustrate the concepts introduced in the previous subsections, let us consider a three-agent network, i.e., $N = \{1, 2, 3\}$, with the following principles of the decision-making process:

(i) Agent 1 follows himself;
(ii) Agent 2 follows agent 1;
(iii) Agent 3 follows the majority (i.e., he decides according to the inclination of at least two agents).

Figure 1 shows a social network for this example. An arc from player j to k means that j influences player k.

The set of all inclination vectors is $I = \{-1, +1\}^3$, $|I| = 8$. Table 1 presents the influence function B for the example. Please note that B is a kind of a mixture of the three influence functions mentioned in Sect. 2.2: agent 1 uses the identity function Id, agent 2 decides according to his guru $\tilde{k} = 1$, and agent 3 applies the majority function $\mathsf{Maj}^{[t]}$ with $t = 2$.

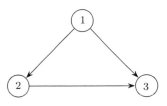

Fig. 1 Three-agent social network

Table 1 The influence function B

$i \in I$	$(1, 1, 1)$	$(1, 1, -1)$	$(1, -1, 1)$	$(-1, 1, 1)$	$(1, -1, -1)$	$(-1, 1, -1)$
Bi	$(1, 1, 1)$	$(1, 1, 1)$	$(1, 1, 1)$	$(-1, -1, 1)$	$(1, 1, -1)$	$(-1, -1, -1)$

$i \in I$	$(-1, -1, 1)$	$(-1, -1, -1)$
Bi	$(-1, -1, -1)$	$(-1, -1, -1)$

Table 2 The sets of followers under B

$S \subseteq N$	$\emptyset$	1	2	3	12	13	23	N
$F_B(S)$	$\emptyset$	12	$\emptyset$	$\emptyset$	N	N	3	N

Table 2 shows the set of followers under B of each coalition. Obviously, the conditions for a follower function recapitulated in Sect. 2.2 are satisfied by F_B.

From Table 2 we get the kernel of the influence function B

$$K(B) = \{1, 23\}$$

and using Table 1, we can calculate the influence indices. Note that for each weighted influence index, we have

$$d_\alpha(B, 1 \to 2) = d_\alpha(B, 13 \to 2) = d_\alpha(B, 12 \to 3) = 1$$

which illustrates the property of the weighted influence index mentioned in Sect. 2.2, and moreover

$$d_\alpha(B, 2 \to 1) = d_\alpha(B, 3 \to 1) = d_\alpha(B, 23 \to 1) = 0.$$

Table 3 presents the possibility and certainty influence indices $\left(\overline{d}(B, S \to j), \underline{d}(B, S \to j)\right)$ for each $\emptyset \neq S \subset N$ and $j \in N \setminus S$.

Note that in this example the certainty influence index is either 0 or 1, but is never equal to $\frac{1}{2}$. This is related to the neutrality of the influence function B defined in Table 1 which states that $B(-i) = -Bi$ for each $i \in I$.

Table 3 The possibility and certainty influence indices $\left(\overline{d}(B, S \to j), \underline{d}(B, S \to j)\right)$

$S \to$ $j \downarrow$	1	2	3	12	13	23
1	—	$(0, 0)$	$(0, 0)$	—	—	$(0, 0)$
2	$(1, 1)$	—	$(\frac{1}{2}, 0)$	—	$(1, 1)$	—
3	$(\frac{1}{2}, 0)$	$(\frac{1}{2}, 0)$	—	$(1, 1)$	—	—

3 The Command Games

3.1 Command Games and Command Functions

The framework of *command games* has been introduced in Hu and Shapley (2003a, 2003b), and later analyzed in Grabisch and Rusinowska (2008, 2009a). Let us recall the key concepts of this model. Let $N = \{1, \ldots, n\}$ be the set of players. For $k \in N$ and $S \subseteq N \setminus k$:

- S is a *boss set* for k if S determines the choice of k;

- S is an *approval set* for k if k can act with an approval of S.

For each $k \in N$, a simple game $(N, \mathcal{W}_k)$ is built, called the *command game for k*, with the set of winning coalitions defined by

$$\mathcal{W}_k := \{S \mid S \text{ is a boss set for } k\} \cup \{S \cup k \mid S \text{ is a boss or approval set for } k\}. \quad (13)$$

The boss and approval sets for k can be recovered by

$$\mathsf{Boss}_k = \{S \subseteq N \setminus k \mid S \in \mathcal{W}_k\} = \mathcal{W}_k \cap 2^{N \setminus k}$$
$$\mathsf{App}_k = \{S \subseteq N \setminus k \mid S \cup k \in \mathcal{W}_k \text{ but } S \notin \mathcal{W}_k\}.$$

We have $\mathsf{Boss}_k \cap \mathsf{App}_k = \emptyset$. In particular, if $\mathsf{App}_k = 2^{N \setminus k}$, then k is called a *free agent*, since he needs no approval ($\emptyset \in \mathsf{App}_k$) and nobody can boss him ($\mathsf{Boss}_k = \emptyset$). If $\mathsf{App}_k = \emptyset$, then k is called a *cog*.

Given a set of command games $\{(N, \mathcal{W}_k), k \in N\}$, the *command function* $\omega : 2^N \to 2^N$ is defined as

$$\omega(S) := \{k \in N \mid S \in \mathcal{W}_k\}, \quad \forall S \subseteq N. \quad (14)$$

$\omega(S)$ is the *set of all members that are "commandable" by S*.

As noticed in Grabisch and Rusinowska (2008), any set of command games $\{(N, \mathcal{W}_k), k \in N\}$ can be viewed as a mapping $\Omega : N \times 2^N \to \{0, 1\}$, with

$$(k, S) \mapsto \Omega(k, S) = \begin{cases} 1, & \text{if } S \in \mathcal{W}_k \\ 0, & \text{otherwise} \end{cases}.$$

Recall that for any $S \subseteq N$, the *principal filter* of S is defined as $\uparrow S := \{T \subseteq N \mid T \supseteq S\}$. A *normal command game* Ω is a set of simple games $\{(N, \mathcal{W}_k), k \in N\}$ satisfying the two conditions:

- For each $k \in N$, there exists a minimal nonempty family of nonempty subsets $S_1^k, \ldots, S_{l_k}^k$ (called the *generating family of $\mathcal{W}_k$*) such that $\mathcal{W}_k = \uparrow S_1^k \cup \ldots \cup \uparrow S_{l_k}^k$.
- For each $k \in N$, $S_1^k \cap \cdots \cap S_{l_k}^k \neq \emptyset$.

The last condition is motivated by the following fact: if there exist two disjoint boss sets for agent k, then there will be a conflict if the boss sets have a different opinion. We denote by $\mathcal{G}$ the set of all normal command games. There exists a bijection $\Psi : 2^{N \times 2^N} \to (2^N)^{(2^N)}$ defined by

$$\Psi(\Omega) = \omega, \quad \text{with } \omega(S) := \{k \in N \mid \Omega(k, S) = 1\}, \quad \forall S \subseteq N$$
$$\Psi^{-1}(\omega) = \Omega, \quad \text{with } \Omega(k, S) = 1 \text{ iff } k \in \omega(S). \quad (15)$$

In Grabisch and Rusinowska (2008), we show the exact relation between command games and command functions. We prove that $\omega \in (2^N)^{(2^N)}$ corresponds to some normal command game, i.e., $\omega \in \Psi(\mathcal{G})$, if and only if the following conditions are satisfied:

- $\omega(\emptyset) = \emptyset, \omega(N) = N$;
- ω is isotone;
- If $S \cap S' = \emptyset$, then $\omega(S) \cap \omega(S') = \emptyset$.

Note the similarity between the sufficient and necessary conditions for a function to be the command function of some command game, and those for a function to be the follower function of some influence function. We can conclude that comparing the command framework with the influence model should be based on comparing command games with influence functions, and will be closely related to the relation between command functions and follower functions.

3.2 Command Games and Influence Functions

We investigate the relation between command games and influence functions. In particular, we are interested in equivalence between command games and influence functions. An influence function B and a command game Ω are said to be *equivalent* if $\omega \equiv F_B$.

In Grabisch and Rusinowska (2008), we show that if B is an influence function, then there exists a unique normal command game Ω equivalent to B if and only if $F_B(N) = N$. Moreover, if Ω is a normal command game, then any influence function in $\Phi^{-1}(\omega)$ is equivalent to Ω.

Let us present command games equivalent to the four influence functions recapitulated in Sect. 2.2. In Grabisch and Rusinowska (2009a), we prove the following:

- The identity function $\mathsf{Id} \in \mathcal{B}$ is equivalent to the set of command games $\{(N, \mathcal{W}_k^{\mathsf{Id}}) \mid k \in N\}$, where

$$\mathcal{W}_k^{\mathsf{Id}} = \{S \subseteq N \mid k \in S\}, \ \forall k \in N.$$

- There is no set of command games equivalent to the reversal function $-\mathsf{Id} \in \mathcal{B}$.
- The guru function $\mathsf{Gur}^{[\tilde{k}]} \in \mathcal{B}$ is equivalent to the set of command games $\{(N, \mathcal{W}_k^{\mathsf{Gur}^{[\tilde{k}]}}) \mid k \in N\}$, where

$$\mathcal{W}_k^{\mathsf{Gur}^{[\tilde{k}]}} = \{S \subseteq N \mid \tilde{k} \in S\}, \ \forall k \in N.$$

- The majority function $\mathsf{Maj}^{[t]} \in \mathcal{B}$, where $n \geq t > \lfloor \frac{n}{2} \rfloor$, is equivalent to the set of command games $\{(N, \mathcal{W}_k^{\mathsf{Maj}^{[t]}}) \mid k \in N\}$ with

$$\mathcal{W}_k^{\mathsf{Maj}^{[t]}} = \{S \subseteq N \mid s \geq t\}, \ \forall k \in N.$$

Note that the existence of a unique normal command game equivalent to $B \in \{\text{Id}, \text{Gur}^{[\tilde{k}]}, \text{Maj}^{[t]}\}$ could be already concluded from Sect. 2.2, where it is straightforward to see that $F_B(N) = N$ for $B \in \{\text{Id}, \text{Gur}^{[\tilde{k}]}, \text{Maj}^{[t]}\}$. On the other hand, we note that $F_{-\text{Id}}(N) = \emptyset$.

3.3 Example Continued

We turn to the example presented in Sect. 2.3, and model it in terms of a command structure. Hence, we have a three-agent game $N = \{1, 2, 3\}$, in which agent 1 follows himself, agent 2 follows agent 1, and agent 3 follows the majority. The command game Ω for the example is defined as follows:

$$W_1 = W_2 = \{1, 12, 13, 123\}$$
$$W_3 = \{12, 13, 23, 123\}.$$

Hence, we have

$$\text{Boss}_1 = \emptyset, \quad \text{Boss}_2 = \{1, 13\}, \quad \text{Boss}_3 = \{12\}$$
$$\text{App}_1 = \{\emptyset, 2, 3, 23\}, \quad \text{App}_2 = \emptyset, \quad \text{App}_3 = \{1, 2\}.$$

Note that agent 1 is a free agent, and agent 2 is a cog.
The command function ω for this example is presented in Table 4.
Note that the influence function B defined in Sect. 2.3 and the command game Ω of the present example are equivalent, because $\omega \equiv F_B$.

Table 4 The command function ω

$S \subseteq N$	$\emptyset$	1	2	3	12	13	23	N
$\omega(S)$	$\emptyset$	12	$\emptyset$	$\emptyset$	N	N	3	N

3.4 Power and Influence Indices

In Grabisch and Rusinowska (2009a), a more general version of the weighted influence index is defined which can cover all imaginable types of influence, in particular, the direct influence, the opposite influence, an influence of a coalition on its member, etc. First of all, it is assumed that only a coalition with all members unanimous in inclinations may influence an agent. An influence of a coalition S on a player j takes place if $(Bi)_j = \lambda$, where $\lambda \in \{-i_j, i_S, -i_S, +1, -1\}$. Hence, the *set $I_{S \to j, \lambda}(B)$ of all inclination vectors of influence of S on j under B* is defined as

$$I_{S \to j, \lambda}(B) := \{i \in I_S \mid (Bi)_j = \lambda\} \tag{16}$$

and given $B \in \mathcal{B}$, for each $S \subseteq N$, $j \in N$, the *general weighted influence index of coalition S on player j under B* is defined as

$$\psi_{\alpha,\lambda}(B, S \to j) := \frac{\sum_{i \in I_{S \to j,\lambda}(B)} \alpha_i^{S \to j}}{\sum_{i \in I_S} \alpha_i^{S \to j}}. \tag{17}$$

In particular, the weighted (direct) influence index defined in the previous section is recovered as

$$\psi_{\alpha,\lambda}(B, S \to j) = d_\alpha(B, S \to j) \text{ if } \lambda = -i_j \text{ and } \alpha_i^{S \to j} = 0 \text{ for } i_j = i_S.$$

For an arbitrary set of command games, we construct several equivalent (command) influence functions. This shows that the model of influence is broader than the framework of the command games. Moreover, we apply several power indices to the command games and prove that these power indices coincide with some expressions of the general weighted influence indices under the command influence functions. One of the (command) influence functions that we define is the influence function with abstention, related to an extended three-action model of influence recapitulated in Sect. 4.1. In this model, each agent has three options for his decision: "yes" (denoted by $+1$), "no" (denoted by -1), or "abstain" (denoted by 0), that is, $B(I) \subseteq \{-1, 0, +1\}^n$.

Given a set of command games $\{(N, \mathcal{W}_k) \mid k \in N\}$, the *command influence function* Com is defined for each $k \in N$ and $i \in I$ by

$$(\text{Com}i)_k := \begin{cases} +1, & \text{if } \{j \in N \mid i_j = +1\} \in \mathcal{W}_k \\ -1, & \text{if } \{j \in N \mid i_j = -1\} \in \mathcal{W}_k \\ 0, & \text{otherwise} \end{cases} \tag{18}$$

According to Com, for each agent k and each inclination vector, if all players with the same inclination forms a winning coalition in his command game, the agent k follows the inclination of this winning coalition. Otherwise, k abstains.

We have shown that for each set of command games $\{(N, \mathcal{W}_k) \mid k \in N\}$, the command influence function Com is equivalent to this set of command games (in the sense of Sect. 3.2).

We prove that if $\{(N, \mathcal{W}_j) \mid j \in N\}$ is a set of command games, and Com is the command influence function defined in (18), then for each $j, k \in N$

$$Sh_k(N, \mathcal{W}_j) = \psi_{\alpha(Sh), \lambda=i_k}(\text{Com}, k \to j) - \psi_{\alpha(Sh), \lambda=-i_k}(\text{Com}, k \to j)$$

where $Sh_k(N, \mathcal{W}_j)$ is the Shapley–Shubik index of player k in the command game for j, $\psi_{\alpha(Sh), \lambda}$ is the weighted influence index defined in (17), and for each $i \in I$

$$
\alpha_i^{(Sh)k \to j} = \begin{cases} \dfrac{1}{n\binom{n-1}{|i|-1}}, & \text{if } i_k = +1 \\[2ex] \dfrac{1}{n\binom{n-1}{n-|i|-1}}, & \text{if } i_k = -1 \end{cases} \tag{19}
$$

and $|i| := |\{m \in N \mid i_m = +1\}|$. Moreover,

$$
Bz_k(N, \mathcal{W}_j) = \psi_{\alpha^{(Bz)}, \lambda = i_k}(\text{Com}, k \to j) - \psi_{\alpha^{(Bz)}, \lambda = -i_k}(\text{Com}, k \to j)
$$

where $Bz_k(N, \mathcal{W}_j)$ is the Banzhaf index of player k in the command game for j, $\psi_{\alpha^{(Bz)}, \lambda}$ is the weighted influence index defined in (17) with

$$
\alpha_i^{(Bz)k \to j} = 1, \ \forall i \in I.
$$

This means that both the Shapley–Shubik index and the Banzhaf index of player k in the command game for j are equal to the difference between the weighted influence index in which agent j is said to be influenced by k if he follows k, and the weighted influence index in which the influence of k on j means that agent j's decision is opposite to the inclination of k. Both weighted influence indices are measured under the command influence function Com. The difference between the results on these power indices lies only in the weights: while for the Shapley–Shubik index the weights are defined in (19), the weights for the Banzhaf index are always equal to 1.

4 Enlarging the Set of Possible Yes/No Actions

4.1 The Influence Model with an Ordered Set of Possible Actions

In Grabisch and Rusinowska (2009d), we extend the yes/no model of influence to the framework in which each agent has a totally ordered set of possible actions. We recapitulate in this section the main concepts and results of this work. We investigate the generalized influence indices and other tools related to the multi-choice model.

Let us recapitulate a simplified version of this model. We consider a social network with the set of agents denoted by $N = \{1, \dots, n\}$. There is a totally ordered (finite) set of possible actions denoted by $\mathcal{A}$. A real number is assigned to each action in $\mathcal{A}$, so that the ordering of these numbers reflect the ordering of the actions (ordinal scale). Let A denote the set of these numbers. Assuming there are no two actions with the same rank, we have a bijection between $\mathcal{A}$ and A, so that we can deal only with A. A particular example is to allow abstention (see, e.g., Braham & Steffen, 2002; Felsenthal & Machover, 1997, 2001), and to consider the yes/no-abstention model of influence with $A = \{-1, 0, +1\}$, with 0 denoting the action "to abstain". The yes/no model of influence considered in the previous sections is obviously covered by this generalized framework with $A = \{-1, +1\}$.

Each player has an *inclination* to choose one of the actions. Let i denote an *inclination vector* and $I = A^n$ be the set of all inclination vectors.[1] As in the yes/no model, it is assumed that agents may influence each others, and due to the influences, the final decision of a player may be different from his original inclination. Let $B : I \to I, i \mapsto Bi$ denote the influence function, and Bi a *decision vector*. The set of all influence functions will be denoted by $\mathcal{B}$. We introduce for any $\emptyset \neq S \subseteq N$

$$I_S := \{i \in I \mid \forall k, j \in S \, [i_k = i_j]\}, \tag{20}$$

which is the set of inclination vectors under which all players in S have the inclination to choose the same action.

We analyze *positive influence* which measures how much a coalition pulls the agent's decision closer to the inclination of the coalition. A player who has an inclination different from the inclination of a given coalition is said to be influenced by this coalition if his decision is closer to the inclination of the coalition than his inclination was. A direct influence in the yes/no model is therefore a particular case of positive influence. We also investigate *negative influence*. For each inclination vector in which the members of a given coalition have the same inclination, there is one (or two) action(s) which is (are) the most extreme action(s). These actions lie farthest from the inclination of the coalition. If the inclination of a player is different from such actions, and his decision comes "closer" to the extreme action, we say that there is a negative influence of the coalition on the player. An opposite influence in the yes/no model is a particular case of negative influence. In the present paper we recapitulate only the positive influence. Let for each $S \subseteq N$ and $j \in N \setminus S$

$$I_{S \to j} := \{i \in I_S \mid i_j \neq i_S\} \tag{21}$$

denotes the set of all inclination vectors of *potential positive influence* of S on j. Given coalition $S \subset N$, agent $j \in N \setminus S$, and inclination vector $i \in I_{S \to j}$, there is a certain distance $|i_j - i_S|$ between i_j and i_S. Under the influence, the decision $(Bi)_j$ of agent j may be different from his inclination, and we can also measure the distance $|(Bi)_j - i_S|$ between the decision of the agent and the inclination of the coalition. For each $S \subseteq N$, $j \in N \setminus S$, and $B \in \mathcal{B}$, we define the *set of all inclination vectors of influence of S on j under B* as

$$I^*_{S \to j}(B) := \{i \in I_{S \to j} \mid |(Bi)_j - i_S| < |i_j - i_S|\}. \tag{22}$$

For each $S \subseteq N$, $j \in N \setminus S$ and $i \in I_{S \to j}$, we introduce a *weight* $\alpha_i^{S \to j} \in [0, 1]$ *of influence of coalition S on $j \in N \setminus S$ under the inclination vector* $i \in I_{S \to j}$. We assume that for each $S \subseteq N$ and $j \in N \setminus S$, there exists $i \in I_{S \to j}$ such that $\alpha_i^{S \to j} > 0$.

---

[1] We keep for the set of inclination vectors the same notation as in the yes/no model. This should cause no confusion.

Given $B \in \mathcal{B}$, for each $S \subseteq N$, $j \in N \setminus S$, the *generalized weighted influence index of coalition S on agent j* is defined as

$$D_\alpha(B, S \to j) := \frac{\sum_{i \in I^*_{S \to j}(B)} \left[|i_j - i_S| - |(Bi)_j - i_S| \right] \alpha_i^{S \to j}}{\sum_{i \in I_{S \to j}} |i_j - i_S| \alpha_i^{S \to j}} \in [0, 1]. \quad (23)$$

We can recover the *generalized possibility influence index of coalition S on player j* as

$$\overline{D}(B, S \to j) = D_{\overline{\alpha}}(B, S \to j), \quad \text{where } \overline{\alpha}_i^{S \to j} = 1 \text{ for each } i \in I_{S \to j}$$

that is,

$$\overline{D}(B, S \to j) = \frac{\sum_{i \in I^*_{S \to j}(B)} \left[|i_j - i_S| - |(Bi)_j - i_S| \right]}{\sum_{i \in I_{S \to j}} |i_j - i_S|}. \quad (24)$$

A *follower* of a coalition in the generalized influence model is defined as an agent whose decision is never farther from the inclination of the coalition than his inclination was. An agent who always decides according to the inclination of the coalition in question is called a *perfect follower* of that coalition. Formally, the *follower function* of $B \in \mathcal{B}$ is a mapping $F_B : 2^N \to 2^N$ defined as

$$F_{B(S)} := \{ j \in N \mid \forall i \in I_S \, [[i_j \neq i_S \Rightarrow |(Bi)_j - i_S| < |i_j - i_S|]$$
$$\wedge \, [i_j = i_S \Rightarrow (Bi)_j = i_S]]\}, \quad (25)$$

where $F_B(\emptyset) := \emptyset$, and the *perfect follower function* $F_B^{\mathrm{per}} : 2^N \to 2^N$ is defined as

$$F_B^{\mathrm{per}}(S) := \{ j \in N \mid \forall i \in I_S \, [(Bi)_j = i_S]\}. \quad (26)$$

Of course, each perfect follower is also a follower, i.e., for each $B \in \mathcal{B}$ and $S \subseteq N$, $F_B^{\mathrm{per}}(S) \subseteq F_B(S)$.

It is important to note that all the above definitions coincide with the ones of the yes/no model if we put $A = \{-1, +1\}$. We show that some of the properties of the follower function in the yes/no model remain valid also in the extended model of influence. In particular,

- F_B is an isotone function;
- $F_B(S) \cap F_B(T) = \emptyset$ whenever $S \cap T = \emptyset$;
- $D_\alpha(B, S \to j) = 1$ for each $j \in F_B^{\mathrm{per}}(S) \setminus S$.

In the yes/no model, the last property is satisfied for the set of followers $F_B(S)$, but in the multi-choice game it remains valid only for the set of perfect followers $F_B^{\mathrm{per}}(S)$.

Assume F_B is not identically the empty set. The *kernel* of B is defined similarly as in the yes/no model of influence, i.e.,

$$\mathcal{K}(B) := \{S \in 2^N \mid F_B(S) \neq \emptyset, \text{ and } S' \subset S \Rightarrow F_B(S') = \emptyset\}.$$

Next, we generalize several influence functions $B \in \mathcal{B}$ (defined in the yes/no model) for the multi-choice framework. We investigate the properties of these functions and compare them with the results on the analogous functions in the yes/no model. Let us recapitulate the majority influence function $\widetilde{\mathsf{Maj}^{[t]}}$ defined in the extended model, which differs from the majority function $\mathsf{Maj}^{[t]}$ presented in Sect. 2.

Let $n \geq t > \lfloor \frac{n}{2} \rfloor$, and introduce for any $i \in I$ and $a \in A$, the set

$$i^a := \{k \in N \mid i_k = a\}.$$

The *majority influence function* $\widetilde{\mathsf{Maj}^{[t]}} \in \mathcal{B}$ is defined by

$$\left(\widetilde{\mathsf{Maj}^{[t]}}i\right)_j := \begin{cases} a, & \text{if } \exists a \in A \left[|i^a| \geq t\right] \\ i_j, & \text{otherwise} \end{cases}, \quad \forall i \in I, \quad \forall j \in N. \quad (27)$$

If a majority of players have an inclination a, then all agents decide for a, and if not, then each agent decides according to his own inclination.

We prove that the follower function of this majority function, for each $S \subseteq N$, is equal to

$$F_{\widetilde{\mathsf{Maj}^{[t]}}}(S) = \begin{cases} N, & \text{if } s \geq t \\ S, & \text{if } n - t < s < t \\ \emptyset, & \text{if } s \leq n - t, \end{cases}$$

and the kernel is $\mathcal{K}(\widetilde{\mathsf{Maj}^{[t]}}) = \{S \subseteq N \mid |S| = n - t + 1\}$. The results on the set of followers and the kernel for the majority function in the multi-choice model are different from the ones obtained for the yes/no model of influence, which is rather not surprising, since the definitions of the majority influence function in the two models differ from each other.

4.2 Example Continued

We turn again to the example presented in Sect. 2.3, i.e., $N = \{1, 2, 3\}$, but assume that the agents have a third option to choose, the abstention. We have $A = \{-1, 0, +1\}$, and there are 27 possible inclination vectors, $|I| = 27$.

For all inclination vectors with inclinations "yes" or "no", the extended influence function B in the 3-action model coincides with the influence function B presented in Sect. 2.3. We have still to define B when at least one agent has the inclination to abstain. Roughly speaking, in this example we assume the abstention to weaken the influence and independence of agent 1 and to increase the independence of agents 2 and 3. For instance, if agent 1 is inclined to abstain, and the remaining agents are unanimous, he will decide according to their inclination. Agent 2 follows agent 1 except for the situations where agent 1 is inclined to abstain, and agents 2 and 3 are unanimous. When there is at least one "abstention", agent 3 will follow himself, except the situations when he is inclined to abstain, and the remaining agents are unanimous. In this case agent 3 will decide according to their inclination. Table 5 shows the influence function B.

Table 6 presents the generalized possibility influence indices. Note that, for instance, the cases $B(0, -1, 1) = (0, 0, 1)$ and $B(0, 1, -1) = (0, 0, 1)$ count for the influence of agent 3 on agent 2, since the distance between the inclinations of agents 2 and 3 was 2, and the distance between the decision of agent 2 and the inclination of agent 3 becomes 1.

Indeed, when comparing Tables 3 and 6, we can see that in the 3-action model the influence indices of agent 1 on agents 2 and 3, and the influence index of coalition $\{1, 2\}$ on agent 3 decreased, while the influence of coalition $\{1, 3\}$ on agent 2 is still equal to 1. The influence of coalition $\{2, 3\}$ on agent 1 increased.

Table 5 The influence function B

$i \in I$	Bi	$i \in I$	Bi	$i \in I$	Bi
$(-1,-1,-1)$	$(-1,-1,-1)$	$(0,0,0)$	$(0,0,0)$	$(1,1,1)$	$(1,1,1)$
$(-1,-1,0)$	$(-1,-1,-1)$	$(0,0,-1)$	$(0,0,-1)$	$(1,1,-1)$	$(1,1,1)$
$(-1,0,-1)$	$(-1,-1,-1)$	$(0,-1,0)$	$(0,0,0)$	$(1,-1,1)$	$(1,1,1)$
$(0,-1,-1)$	$(-1,-1,-1)$	$(-1,0,0)$	$(-1,-1,0)$	$(-1,1,1)$	$(-1,-1,1)$
$(-1,-1,1)$	$(-1,-1,-1)$	$(0,0,1)$	$(0,0,1)$	$(1,1,0)$	$(1,1,1)$
$(-1,1,-1)$	$(-1,-1,-1)$	$(0,1,0)$	$(0,0,0)$	$(1,0,1)$	$(1,1,1)$
$(1,-1,-1)$	$(1,1,-1)$	$(1,0,0)$	$(1,1,0)$	$(0,1,1)$	$(1,1,1)$
$(-1,0,1)$	$(-1,-1,1)$	$(0,-1,1)$	$(0,0,1)$	$(1,-1,0)$	$(1,1,0)$
$(-1,1,0)$	$(-1,-1,0)$	$(0,1,-1)$	$(0,0,-1)$	$(1,0,-1)$	$(1,1,-1)$

Table 6 The generalized possibility influence indices $\overline{D}(B, S \to j)$

$S \to$ $j \downarrow$	1	2	3	12	13	23
1	—	$\dfrac{1}{9}$	$\dfrac{1}{9}$	—	—	$\dfrac{1}{3}$
2	$\dfrac{8}{9}$	—	$\dfrac{4}{9}$	—	1	—
3	$\dfrac{2}{9}$	$\dfrac{2}{9}$	—	$\dfrac{2}{3}$	—	—

Table 7 The sets of followers under B

$S \subseteq N$	$\emptyset$	1	2	3	12	13	23	N
$F_B(S)$	$\emptyset$	$\emptyset$	$\emptyset$	$\emptyset$	12	N	3	N

Finally, we calculate the sets of followers under B of each coalition. They are presented in Table 7.

One can see from comparing Tables 2 and 7 that agent 1 as well as coalition $\{1, 2\}$ lost (some of) their followers when allowing the abstention. Moreover, the kernel of the influence function B contains all two-agent coalitions, that is,

$$\mathcal{K}(B) = \{12, 13, 23\}.$$

From the comparison of $\mathcal{K}(B)$ in the yes/no model and in the three-action model, we can see that when extending the model to the three-action framework, coalition $\{2, 3\}$ remains the "truly" influential coalition, while agent 1 is not "truly" influential on his own anymore, but he needs one of the remaining agents to belong to the kernel.

Our conclusions on influence indices, followers, and kernels, are obviously valid only for this example, when we specifically "weaken" the position of agent 1 by allowing the abstention. However, we like to stress the fact that for an arbitrary example one can apply the same approach and draw conclusions on the impact of enlarging the set of possible actions on agents' influence position.

4.3 The Influence Model with a Continuum of Actions

In Grabisch and Rusinowska (2010), we consider another generalized model of influence in which each player has a continuum of actions. The set of actions is assumed to be a real interval $[a, b]$. Each player has an *inclination* to choose one of the actions, i.e., by the inclination of a player we mean the particular action from $[a, b]$ the player wants to choose. For the continuum case, we have defined and studied, in particular, the influence index of a coalition on a player, several influence functions, the set of followers and perfect followers, and the kernel of an influence function. The main difference between the two generalized models of influence lies naturally in the definitions of the influence indices. While in the previous model (i.e., the model with a totally ordered set of actions), the influence index has been defined by the sums of some expressions over the particular sets, in the continuum case the sums are replaced by integrals. These integrals are calculated over particular sets of inclination vectors which are of a smaller dimension than the set of n-inclination vectors. We show the equivalence between the influence index of a coalition on a player and the corresponding influence index in which the coalition in question is treated as one player. For a more detailed analysis of this model we refer to Grabisch and Rusinowska (2010).

5 Levels of Knowledge and the Identification Problem

Let us come back for simplicity to the yes/no model. So far we have taken for granted that the function B is known, so that influence indices, the follower function, kernels, command games, etc., can be computed. In practice this is too strong an assumption, since the knowledge of B requires the observation of $n2^n$ values, which are 0 or 1. Specifically, supposing that the inclination vector i is known (there are 2^n different such vectors), we observe the final decision of each agent (n values).

Let us first try to establish a kind of hierarchy of knowledge. At the top level of this hierarchy lies the influence function B. Its complete definition requires $n2^n$ binary values, and these values are free, i.e., we actually have $n2^n$ degrees of freedom. Knowing B permits to compute all quantities defined in this paper. At the second level lie follower functions. They also require $n2^n$ binary values to be defined, but due to properties that characterize follower functions (see Sect. 2.2), there are less than $n2^n$ degrees of freedom. In fact, this point is completely elucidated since we know all possible influence functions that give rise to a given follower function: they are given by the function Φ^{-1} (see Sect. 2.2). Now, due to the equivalence between command functions of command games and follower functions (up to the condition that $F(N) = N$), and moreover between command functions and boss sets and approval sets (see Sect. 3.1), we can say that the knowledge of boss sets and approval sets lies on the same second level as follower functions.

On the next third level we presumably find indices of influence, although their exact position with respect to follower functions is not known, nor is known their exact relation with influence functions (similarly as in the case of follower functions, one would like to know the set of influence functions giving rise to a given set of values for the influence indices). The number of different values for the influence indices is equal to the number of $S \to j$, for $S \subseteq N, S \neq \emptyset, N$, and $j \notin S$. This gives

$$\sum_{S \subseteq N, S \neq \emptyset, N} (n - s) = (2^n - 2)n - \sum_{s=1}^{n-1} s \binom{n}{s} < n2^n.$$

Therefore, the knowledge of the indices does not permit to recover B.

On the fourth level we find influence graphs (social networks), as the one given to explain the example in Sect. 2.3. An influence graph is only a qualitative description of influence among agents, and does not specify what happens in case of conflict (i.e., when two arrows arrive on the same agent), nor it permits to distinguish between the influences when the inclination of influencing agents is "yes" or "no". The kernel is another type of qualitative information, but which does not seem comparable to influence graphs. The kernel identifies the minimal influencing coalitions, but does not tell whom they influence.

Let us assume that in some experimental situation, observing the behavior of agents, the ultimate knowledge we would like to get is the influence function B. However, we can only know it partly, hence what can we do in order to have the most complete possible knowledge on it? We give some thoughts on this problem below.

A first general remark is that we are concerned here with the vast area of machine learning (and therefore optimization, interpolation), and also hypothesis testing and the theory of estimation. We use the generic term of *identification* for obtaining the complete definition of some function or quantity, as for example the influence function. In any problem of identification, it is important to define what should be done in case of lack of knowledge. In our context, the answer for this is fairly obvious: if there is no observation of influence, by invoking the principle of insufficient reason, just say there is no influence, and therefore $B = \mathsf{Id}$. This defines the general philosophy one should take: use the available knowledge of any kind to construct B, and for the regions where B is not known, just put $B = \mathsf{Id}$. The same holds for any kind of notions so far introduced: in case of absence of observation/knowledge, the follower function is identical to the empty set, all influence indices are 0, etc.

What can we observe in an experimental situation? The direct observation of inclinations and decisions of agents defines B on a small part of its domain. However, a priori information can be used to complete the model, for instance:

(i) It is likely (or well known, often observed, etc.) that coalition S strongly influences agents $j, k, \ldots$;

(ii) We suppose that the underlying model is of the majority type, or of the guru type where agent j plays the rôle of the guru, or of the mass psychology type, etc.

In the first case, we use the mathematical properties underlying our concepts to find the set of functions B compatible with the information we have on the followers, degrees, and so on (inverse function problem, completely solved for the case of follower functions). In the second case, the procedure is quite different since this is typically a problem of hypothesis testing and estimation, and therefore the appropriate statistical tools should be used. For example: "Is player k a guru?" is a hypothesis, and an appropriate test should be defined for this. Now, "Is the model of the majority type?" is both a hypothesis testing (yes or no) and an estimation problem, since the threshold t has to be measured. For each hypothesis, there should exist a minimal subset $I_0 \subseteq I$ of all inclination vectors, so that, if observing decisions for this set I_0, the test can be done with a given probability of success/failure. The estimation problem proceeds similarly. Note that the same methodology can be applied to derive a model on lower levels of knowledge, that is, for the follower function (equivalently, the boss and approval sets), the degrees, the influence graph and so on. It should be possible to test for example: "Is S a boss set for agent k?" and so on.

In summary, the problem of identification of an influence model in a practical situation is a difficult one, and should initiate a new area of research.

6 Future Research on Influence

As one can conclude from this short overview, the influence issues create very complex problems that can be recognized in everyday life situations. Consequently, there are still many open questions that should be answered and many possibilities to continue the project on influence. We would like to finish the paper by mentioning some of our future research plans on these issues.

- The influence framework that we have studied so far is the one-step model, where a decision of an agent may be influenced by opinions of other players, but no possibility of iterating influence is assumed. In reality, the mutual influence does not stop necessarily after one step, as modeled by the influence framework studied by us so far, but may iterate. We intend to introduce dynamic aspects in the model, to study the behavior of the series of (different) influence functions, and to look for the convergence conditions for such series.
- We have compared our approach to influence based on social networks with the cooperative game theoretic approach based on command games. We are also going to compare the dynamic model of influence with the command games. In the framework of command games, an authority distribution over an organization was defined, and the power transition matrix of the organization was created. A Markov chain was used to describe the organization's long-run authority. In our future investigations, we could introduce the authority distribution based on the influence indices.
- In order to measure influence between agents in a social network, we defined, in particular, the influence indices. However, we did not focus either on properties of these indices nor on their axiomatization. Consequently, in our future research on the influence topics, an axiomatic characterization of the influence indices should be provided.
- In our work on influence, we paid a lot of attention to the concept of influence function. In particular, we determined the exact relation between influence functions and follower functions. While we defined several influence functions and studied their properties, only deterministic functions were considered. Hence, it would be interesting to assume that the influence function is a probabilistic function. Such an assumption will model the reality in a more adequate way than restricting the analysis to deterministic functions.
- Our research on influence conducted so far was only theoretical. In order to get a deeper insight into the process of influence between agents, we would like to conduct some experiments on this issue, and to address the difficult problem of identification of the model, as presented in Sect. 5.

References

Banzhaf, J. (1965). Weighted voting doesn't work: A mathematical analysis. *Rutgers Law Review, 19*, 317–343.

Braham, M., & Steffen, F. (2002). Voting power in games with abstentions. In: M. J. Holler, H. Kliemt, D. Schmidtchen, & M. E. Streit (Eds.), *Power and fairness* (pp. 333–348). Tübingen: Mohr-Siebeck.

Brams, S. J. (1975). *Game theory and politics*. New York: Free Press.

Brams, S. J., & Affuso, P. (1976). Power and size: A new paradox. *Theory and Decision, 7*, 29–56.

Coleman, J. S. (1971). Control of collectivities and the power of a collectivity to act. In: B. Lieberman (Ed.), *Social choice* (pp. 269–300). New York: Gordon and Breach.

Coleman, J. S. (1986). *Individual interests and collective action: Selected essays*. Cambridge: Cambridge University Press.

DeMarzo, P. M. (1992). Coalitions, leadership, and social norms: The power of suggestion in games. *Games and Economic Behavior, 4*, 72–100.

Felsenthal, D., & Machover, M. (1997). Ternary voting games. *International Journal of Game Theory, 26*, 335–351.

Felsenthal, D., & Machover, M. (1998). *The measurement of voting power: Theory and practice, problems and paradoxes*. London: Edward Elgar Publishers.

Felsenthal, D., & Machover, M. (2001). Models and reality: The curious case of the absent abstention. In: M. J. Holler & G. Owen (Eds.), *Power indices and coalition formation* (pp. 87–103). Dordrecht: Kluwer.

Fischer, D., & Schotter, A. (1978). The inevitability of the paradox of redistribution in the allocation of voting weights. *Public Choice, 33*, 49–67.

Grabisch, M., & Roubens, M. (1999). An axiomatic approach to the concept of interaction among players in cooperative games. *International Journal of Game Theory, 28*, 547–565.

Grabisch, M., & Rusinowska, A. (2008). Influence functions, followers and command games. GATE Working Paper, 2008-31.

Grabisch, M., & Rusinowska, A. (2009a). Measuring influence in command games. *Social Choice and Welfare, 33*, 177–209.

Grabisch, M., & Rusinowska, A. (2009b). A model of influence in a social network. *Theory and Decision*, Forthcoming.

Grabisch, M., & Rusinowska, A. (2010). A model of influence with a continuum of actions. GATE Working Paper, 2010-04.

Grabisch, M., & Rusinowska, A. (2009d). A model of influence with an ordered set of possible actions. *Theory and Decision*, Forthcoming.

Hoede, C., & Bakker, R. (1982). A theory of decisional power. *Journal of Mathematical Sociology, 8*, 309–322.

Hojman, D., & Szeidl, A. (2006). Endogenous networks, social games, and evolution. *Games and Economic Behavior, 55*, 112–130.

Holler, M. J., & Packel, E. W. (1983). Power, luck and the right index. *Journal of Economics, 43*, 21–29.

Hu, X., & Shapley, L. S. (2003a). On authority distributions in organizations: Controls. *Games and Economic Behavior, 45*, 153–170.

Hu, X., & Shapley, L. S. (2003b). On authority distributions in organizations: Equilibrium. *Games and Economic Behavior, 45*, 132–152.

Isbell, J. R. (1958). A class of simple games. *Duke Mathematical Journal, 25*, 423–439.

Koller, D., & Milch, B. (2003). Multi-agent influence diagrams for representing and solving games. *Games and Economic Behavior, 45*, 181–221.

König, T., & Bräuninger, T. (1998). The inclusiveness of European decision rules. *Journal of Theoretical Politics, 10*, 125–142.

Laruelle, A., & Valenciano, F. (2005). Assessing success and decisiveness in voting situations. *Social Choice and Welfare, 24*, 171–197.

Lopez-Pintado, D. (2008). Diffusion in complex social networks. *Games and Economic Behavior, 62*, 573–590.

Penrose, L. S. (1946). The elementary statistics of majority voting. *Journal of the Royal Statistical Society, 109*, 53–57.

Rae, D. (1969). Decision-rules and individual values in constitutional choice. *American Political Science Review, 63*, 40–56.

Rusinowska, A. (2008). On the not-preference-based Hoede–Bakker index. In: L. Petrosjan & V. Mazalov (Eds.), *Game theory and applications* (Vol. 13). New York: Nova Science Publishers, Inc., Chapter 9, pp. 127–141.

Rusinowska, A. (2009). The Hoede–Bakker index modified to the Shapley–Shubik and Holler–Packel indices. *Group Decision and Negotiation.* Forthcoming.

Rusinowska, A., & de Swart, H. (2006). Generalizing and modifying the Hoede–Bakker index. In: H. de Swart, E. Orlowska, G. Schmidt, & M. Roubens (Eds.), *Theory and applications of relational structures as knowledge instruments II LNAI 4342* (pp. 60–88). Heidelberg: Springer-Verlag.

Rusinowska, A., & de Swart, H. (2007). On some properties of the Hoede–Bakker index. *Journal of Mathematical Sociology, 31*, 267–293.

Schotter, A. (1982). The paradox of redistribution: Some theoretical and empirical results. In: M. J. Holler (Ed.), *Power, voting, and voting power.* Wurzburg–Wien: Physica-Verlag.

Shapley, L. S. (1994). A Boolean model of organization authority based on the theory of simple games. *Mimeo.*

Shapley, L. S., & Shubik, M. (1954). A method for evaluating the distribution of power in a committee system. *American Political Science Review, 48*, 787–792.

Tchantcho, B., Diffo Lambo, L., Pongou, R., & Mbama Engoulou, B. (2008). Voters' power in voting games with abstention: Influence relation and ordinal equivalence of power theories. *Games and Economic Behavior, 64*, 335–350.

van den Brink, R., Rusinowska, A., & Steffen, F. (2009). Measuring power and satisfaction in societies with opinion leaders: Dictator and opinion leader properties. *Homo Oeconomicus, 26*, in print.

van Winden, F. (2004). Interest group behavior and influence. In: C. K. Rowley & F. Schneider (Eds.), *The encyclopedia of public choice* (pp. 118–129). Heidelberg: Springer.

Networks, Information and Choice

René Janssen and Herman Monsuur

1 Introduction

In several scientific disciplines, like sociology, biology and economics, interaction between individual entities are formulated in terms of networks. In sociology these interactions may indicate friendship, in biology they may represent an ecological food web, while in economics these interactions may be alliances. In the literature one may find several illustrations of this social, biological and economic network approach. For comprehensive introductions see, for example, Barabási (2003), Dutta and Jackson (2003), Goyal (2007), Jackson (2009), Wasserman and Faust (1994) or Watts (1999). The network approach is interesting and has been fruitful due to the analytical tractability: there are several ways of expressing and measuring relevant features of networks such as power, centrality, clustering, robustness or domination. These features, or network statistics, can be used to make explicit how actions of actors, rather than determined by norms and values, can be viewed as consequences of the system of relations by which they are constrained and/or empowered. For a first illustration, in a strategic and political context, we refer to Delver and Monsuur (2001), where norms, or (von Neumann–Morgenstern) standards of behaviour, are derived from a dominance network on a set of strategic options, economic doctrines or other lasting intellectual conceptions with regard to a certain issue. In that model, domination between a pair of alternatives is assumed to be generated by at least one effective coalition. An effective coalition will be inclined to apply its binary dominance, but, in the larger context of the dominance relation, it may have strategic reasons for not exercising its power. We refer to Delver and Monsuur (2001) for (behavioral) axioms that characterize these standards. A second illustration of the use of various network statistics is the study of dynamic evolution of interactions between a fixed set of homogeneous actors. For various

R. Janssen
Netherlands Defence Academy, 1780 CA Den Helder, The Netherlands
e-mail: RHP.Janssen@NLDA.NL

A. Van Deemen, A. Rusinowska (eds.), *Collective Decision Making,*
Theory and Decision Library C 43, DOI 10.1007/978-3-642-02865-6_14,
© Springer-Verlag Berlin Heidelberg 2010

reasons, nodes form and terminate links, thereby rearranging the network, see Dutta and Jackson (2003) and Jackson (2009) for an overview of this literature where local, binary decisions shape global network structures. In Monsuur (2007b) we introduced a mechanism that formalizes a possible incentive that guides nodes in constructing their local network structure, see Sect. 5 for more details. Reiteration of this mechanism, based on the so-called cover relation (Monsuur & Storcken, 2004) that only uses local network features, results in just a few types of emergent, stable network topologies. Examples are uni-polar networks, bi-polar networks and ring-networks.

In management and also military sciences, the concept of networked operations has attained considerably attention. There the issue is how operations are affected by the topology and architecture of information, physical and also social networks. The idea of networked operations is that it offers decisive advantage through the timely provision and exploitation of (*feedback*) information and intelligence to enable effective decision-making and agile actions. Clearly, the latent power of networks is not new, but technological advances over time have enabled better exchange of information. These advances will continue and must be optimized through the parallel development of new procedures and concepts of operation, see Cares (2005, 2006), Darilek, Perry, Bracken, Gordon, Nichiporuk (2001), Grant (2006), Monsuur (2007a) or Perry and Moffat (2004) for illustrations in the military domain. For example, consider the ancient Chinese game of "GO" in which players capture stones and occupy territory. The board on the left of Fig. 1 shows a traditional grid, while the board on the right shows a grid designed for a complex network. There are large hubs, clusters and long distance connections. It is clear that in order to win this game, new strategies will have to be developed. On the left, a traditional strategy creates advantage from a great number of adjacent stones, while new strategies have to take into consideration hubs and long distance connections between cleverly placed clusters (Cares, 2006). An appealing property of these "battles of networks" is that complex networks prevent competitors from guessing the specifics of their strategies.

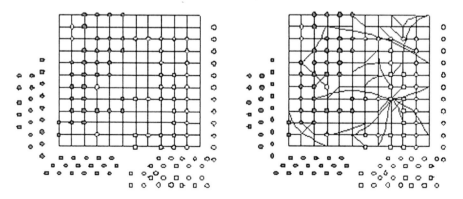

Fig. 1 The game of GO on a regular and complex network structure (Modification of a figure from Cares (2006)

Of course, a great challenge is the development of a clear notion of the value that operating in an networked manner may generate. In management science, market forces determine value: winners emerge and losers fade away. Here serendipity, trial and error abound, see Cares (2005). But, from a national security point of view, speculation and experimentation may generate unnecessary human sacrifice. This implies that the need for validating and quantifying (in advance) the benefits of various ways of networked operations is extremely important. This identification and measurement of networked effects may be identified as a third potential use of various relevant network features. In this paper, we therefore focus on the aspect of information sharing in collaboration networks and discuss a feedback model for situational awareness, that combines exogenously given characteristics of nodes with their positioning within the network topology. Here, situational awareness is generally understood to mean "knowing what is going on", implying the possession of knowledge and understanding to achieve a certain goal. Using this model, one may identify the contribution of the network topology to the situational awareness of individual nodes and also to the network as a whole. In Sect. 2, we give an overview of methods for measuring network value, which are based on feedback in a network. In Sect. 3, we introduce and discuss our model for situational awareness and consider two stochastic variations that reflect incentives and choices of the nodes regarding transferring or uploading information along the links. Next, in Sect. 4, we return to the more general problem of identifying and measuring network effects. In Sect. 5, we discuss a choice mechanism that guides nodes in deciding on the deletion and forming of links in a network. In the final section, we present some conclusions.

2 Network Value of Nodes

A network G is a pair (V, E) where $V = \{v_1, v_2, \ldots, v_n\}$ with $n \geq 2$ is a finite set of *nodes* and E is a subset of $\{(x, y) : x, y \in V, x \neq y\}$, the set of *ordered* pairs of V. An element (a, b) of E is called a *link* from a to b. In the context of information networks, a link (a, b) assumes that information flows from node a to b.

The networks we have in mind in this contribution connect autonomous nodes, where a link between two nodes indicates a formal or informal agreement of some kind of cooperation. Examples of such networks are social networks, networks of alliances between firms or (international) military networks exchanging information. We assume that networks generate value for the network as a whole, but also for the individual nodes that are connected through operational links of the network. In a social network for example, network value of a particular node may be something like status or prestige that a node derives from characteristics of its local network structure: perhaps it is in a brokery position, meaning that the network becomes disconnected if it severs links. An important characteristic of a social network is that if a node somehow succeeds in gaining extra status, this also adds to the status of neighboring nodes, so status is transferable. Generally speaking, network value is the valuation of any "good" or "asset" a node is supposed to control based on its position within the network topology (and its exogenous characteristics).

For the information networks we have in mind, network value is taken to be the so-called *situational awareness*. The concept of situational awareness is generally understood to mean "knowing what is going on", implying the possession of knowledge and understanding to achieve a certain goal. It is the *perception* of the elements in the environment, the *comprehension* of their meaning and the *projection* of their status in the near future, see Endsley (1995). We assume that this situational awareness is transferable and, in addition, the extent of transferability depends on the strength of the tie between the two nodes.

We let A be the adjacency matrix, where $a_{ij} \in [0, 1]$ is the extent to which value from node j is *usable* or *transferable* to node i regarding the improvement of i's situational awareness. We take $a_{ii} = 0$ for each node i. To determine the usability or transferability a_{ij} for a link (j, i), we may use an approved method, the Analytic Hierarchy Process (AHP), introduced in Saaty (1980). To this end, we suggest to use just 4 independent dimensions that cover the attribute usability, see the hierarchy in Fig. 2.

Relevance is the extent to which the information is applicable and helpful for the task at hand. *Timeliness* is the extent to which information is sufficiently up-to-date and current for the task at hand. *Concise* is the extent to which information is compactly represented without being overwhelming. Finally, *Reputation* is the extent to which information is highly regarded in terms of source and content. This way, the receiving node is able to evaluate the quality of the transferred situational awareness, given its own uncertainties, tasks and range of decisions considered.

To motivate and validate our choice for these dimensions, one could carry out a principal component or factor analysis, starting with 20 or more dimensions for information quality, like accurate, timely and concise, see Knight and Burn (2005) and Wang and Strong (1996). This factor analysis is an effective statistical technique to suppress redundant data and dimensions and provide in only a few independent *factors* (combinations of the existing dimensions) most of the data/information (Gorsuch, 1983). Our choice of the four dimensions is based on the observation that a factor analysis typically returns factors concerning: *evaluation* ("good-bad"), *potency* ("strong-weak"), and *activity* ("dynamic-static"). This factorial structure makes intuitive sense. To match this with our dimensions, observe that "reputation" has to do with evaluation. "Relevance" is related to potency, while "timeliness" is identified with activity. To also address the issue of information overload, we include the dimension "concise".

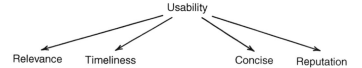

Fig. 2 Hierarchy for measurement of usability of information

Now, given a (directed) link from node j to node i, one has to come up with a scalar s_k^{ij} between 0 and 1 for each dimension k, $k = 1, \ldots, 4$. For example, the scalar s_4^{ij} measures the "reputation" of information flowing from node j to node i: s_4^{ij} is between 0 (no effect, bad reputation) and 1 ("ideal" or "very reliable"). These estimates are from the point of view of the receiving node i. To aggregate these 4 estimates into one scalar we have to determine the *relative importance* of the dimensions for usability of information that flows along a link. To this end, a 4×4 reciprocal matrix R is constructed:

$$
\begin{array}{c}
\\
\text{Relevance} \\
\text{Timeliness} \\
\text{Concise} \\
\text{Reputation}
\end{array}
\begin{array}{cccc}
\text{Relevance} & \text{Timeliness} & \text{Concise} & \text{Reputation} \\
\left(\begin{array}{cccc}
1 & R_{12} & R_{13} & R_{14} \\
1/R_{12} & 1 & R_{23} & R_{24} \\
1/R_{13} & 1/R_{23} & 1 & R_{34} \\
1/R_{14} & 1/R_{24} & 1/R_{34} & 1
\end{array}\right),
\end{array}
$$

where R_{uv} indicates the relative importance of dimension u with respect to v. The AHP uses a nine point (semantic) scale resulting in a reciprocal matrix R, meaning that $R_{uv} = 1/R_{vu}$. The six relative importances may be provided using expert opinions and express the point of view of an arbitrary node that receives information through links of the network. (We assume that this is the same for each receiving node.) Using techniques from the AHP, a vector $w = (w_1, w_2, w_3, w_4)$ of relative weights (summing to 1) for the dimensions is derived from this matrix R. For internal consistency reasons in the matrix R, the number of dimensions must not exceed 4, see Monsuur (1997). Finally, one then may compute the expression $\sum_{k=1}^{4} w_k s_k^{ij}$, which can be used as an estimate for the entry a_{ij} of the adjacency matrix A, indicating the usability of the information flowing from node j to node i

Now, given a network $G = (V, E)$ and adjacency matrix A, one may distinguish several approaches for the determination of network value of nodes in an information network. Here we only consider approaches that are based on some notion of *feedback of operational links*. The reason that we focus on feedback of links that transfer information is that, from an informational point of view, just one specific arrangement of links and nodes creates value: sub-networks that form a cycle, see Cares (2005). These cycles make possible to react to one another, share ideas, adjust views and act accordingly.

We consider the following approaches:

- *The iterated feedback.* Feedback is made operational through iteration of the adjacency matrix:

$$x^t = Ax^{t-1}$$

thereby updating the (previously obtained) situational awareness. In most cases, one takes $x^0 = e$, a vector of 1's.

- *The weighted average of direct and indirect updates.* To this end, we consider infinite sums:

$$x = \sum_{k=0}^{\infty} (\alpha A)^k x_0,$$

where $\alpha < 1/\lambda$ to assure convergence. Here λ is the principal eigenvalue of A.
- *The recursive, mutual dependence of situational awareness.* This recursive dependence is expressed as an eigenvalue problem for the adjacency matrix A:

$$\lambda c_i = \sum_j a_{ij} c_j$$

or

$$c_i = \sum_j \frac{a_{ij}}{\lambda} c_j$$

where λ is the principal eigenvalue. If the components of c sum to 1, it is called the Perron vector. So, we let the value c_i of node i be proportional to the combined values of nodes it is linked to. This is a sum of independent contributions of the type $a_{ij} c_j$, consisting of usability a_{ij}, times the network value c_j. As the network is connected, any nonnegative eigenvector of A is a multiple of c, see for example Berman and Plemmons (1979). The scalar $1/\lambda$ may be interpreted as follows. If we take into consideration just one isolated link, the extent of transferability equals a_{ij}. But, if we go beyond this dyadic level, taking into account all incoming links, this aggregates to $\frac{1}{\lambda} a_{ij}$. Similar phenomena of smoothening data occur if one tries to extract a ranking profile from a matrix of intransitive or inconsistent data. For example, in the AHP the estimate R_{uv} is aggregated into w_u / w_v.
- *Balancing incoming and outgoing interactions.* Consider the vector of fair bets f, discussed and axiomatized in Slutzki and Volij (2005): for each node i, we let

$$\sum_j a_{ij} f_j = \sum_j a_{ji} f_i.$$

The first part may be seen as a measure of the value transfered to node i, given the usabilities a_{ij} and values f_j. The second part then measures the total amount of value that is transfered from node i. These two are supposed to be the same. This corresponds to a kind of steady state of the process of information flow through the network. To compute this vector of fair bets, one has to solve the equation $v = C_A^{-1} A v$, where C_A is the diagonal matrix with the column sums of A on the diagonal.

Note that the redistribution of value, if properly normalized, results in the eigenvector.

We next consider two other approaches for the determination of situational awareness, which are defined for arbitrary networks. The first one combines operational feedback with local informational potential, while the second one combines operational feedback with exogenous values:

- *Combining operational feedback links with local informational potential.* In Herings, van der Laan, and Talman (2005), network value of a node i is the unique (positive) solution of the equation

$$x_i = \sum_{j:(j.i)\in E} (1 + \frac{1}{n}x_j).$$

In this model, a node receives 1 point for each (direct) incoming link, representing the possibility of receiving information, plus $1/n$ times the value of the sending node.
- *Combining operational feedback links with exogenous value.* In this model, first introduced in Monsuur (2007a), given a scalar α and a vector of exogenous characteristics b, the value v is the unique solution of the equation:

$$v = \alpha Av + b.$$

So, the vector v is the sum of two components. First of all, the vector b, the "stand-alone" value. Secondly, the improvement that results form transferred value, αAv, of this final vector v itself. We therefore say that v is "confirmed" by the network structure and b. Note that in taking the sum, we tacitly assume that the value contributions of nodes to a common adjacent node are independent: each node has unique characteristics and their transfered network value can be summed at the receiving node.

The scalar $\alpha > 0$ may be interpreted as the balance between exogenous values b and the influence of the network topology, Av. It also relates to the transition from the local, dyadic level to the aggregate level of information flowing through the network. We discuss this model in more detail in the following two sections.

3 Situational Awareness in Networks

Consider a military network where nodes exchange information they have gathered and processed. Then network value may be the situational awareness in the area of operation that results from the functioning of this information exchange network. Transferability depends on usability of information: is the information that is relayed to a particular node relevant, timely, concise, and is it highly regarded in terms of source and content. The concept of situational awareness is generally understood to mean "knowing what is going on", implying the possession of knowledge and understanding to achieve a certain goal. There are at least two factors that influence situational awareness of nodes, where nodes represent decision facilities, informa-tion fusion centers, combat units and so on. Firstly, it depends on characteristics of the individual decision-makers themselves, such as experience and training, qual-ity of information fusion facilities and rate at which information can be processed, the location within the area of operation, the psycho-social environment, organiza-tion, prior knowledge, etc. In this contribution, we assume that these characteristics are given and fixed. We focus on another, second factor, which is the positioning of nodes within the network and the network topology. As networks provide an opportunity for cooperating entities to share information, situational awareness of a particular node also depends on the local network topology.

3.1 Deterministic Behaviour of Nodes

We assume that through exchanging information, cooperating nodes in a network are able to increase their situational awareness. In this subsection we assume that individual nodes are always in a position to receive information or hand over infor-mation to others if possible *and* they are always prepared to do so. This assumption states that the nodes behave fully deterministically.

Let the nodes are labeled from 1 to n. For a node i, a real nonnegative number b_i, which is called the "stand-alone" situation awareness of this particular node, represents its experience and training, location within the area of operation, its prior knowledge, etc. The vector b contains all the individual values b_i.

If there is a link from node j to node i, we say that node j is an adjacent node of node i. As explained in Sect. 2, we then associate a real nonnegative number, a_{ij}, with this link which represents the usability of the information flowing from node j to node i from the point of view of the receiving node i. If there is no link from node j to node i, we put $a_{ij} = 0$. The $n \times n$ matrix A with the entries a_{ij} is called the adjacency matrix.

Next we introduce a discount factor α, $0 < \alpha < 1$, which brings in the fact that the usability of information which is flowing along links will decay over time, i.e. information will lose its usability if it is getting older. Before sharing information, the situational awareness of the nodes is given by the vector b. After each node has received information *only* from its adjacent nodes, the new situational awareness of the nodes is given by $b + \alpha A b$. By iteration information can be updated through the network, so that nodes also receive information from nodes which are not adjacent nodes, but which are two, three, or more steps away. Updating information in m steps yields the situation awareness v_m, which for $m \geq 1$ is defined recursively as follows:

$$v_0 = b; \quad v_1 = b + \alpha A v_0 \quad \ldots \quad v_m = b + \alpha A v_{m-1}$$

Taking the limit of m to infinity, we get

$$v = \lim_{m \to \infty} v_m = \lim_{m \to \infty} \sum_{k=0}^{m} \alpha^k A^k b = (I - \alpha A)^{-1} b$$

We call v the situational awareness of the nodes after sharing information. This vector v satisfies the equation

$$v = \alpha A v + b$$

In this sense we can say that v is "confirmed" by the network structure and the "stand-alone" situational awareness of the nodes, b: if we add to b the transferred situational awareness $\alpha A v$ due to v itself, we again obtain v.

For example consider the network of Fig. 3 with

$$b = \begin{pmatrix} b_1 \\ b_2 \\ b_3 \\ b_4 \\ b_5 \end{pmatrix} = \begin{pmatrix} 1.00 \\ 0.50 \\ 0.85 \\ 1.00 \\ 0.30 \end{pmatrix} \quad A = \begin{pmatrix} 0 & 0.5 & 0 & 0 & 0 \\ 0 & 0 & 0 & 0.5 & 0 \\ 0 & 0.5 & 0 & 0 & 0.5 \\ 0.5 & 0 & 0.5 & 0 & 0 \\ 0.5 & 0 & 0 & 0.5 & 0 \end{pmatrix} \quad \alpha = 0.25$$

Solving the equation $v = \alpha A v + b$ yields the following situational awareness:

$$v = \begin{pmatrix} v_1 \\ v_2 \\ v_3 \\ v_4 \\ v_5 \end{pmatrix} = \begin{pmatrix} 1.08 \\ 0.66 \\ 1.01 \\ 1.26 \\ 0.59 \end{pmatrix}$$

So we can conclude that, compared to b, for each node the situational awareness has increased.

We next show that the situational awareness derived with our model that includes exogenous characteristics, is similar to the Perron eigenvector c of Sect. 2 in case we let α approach $1/\lambda$ from below. (A matrix A is primitive if $A^k > 0$ for some positive k.)

Theorem 1 *Suppose that A is primitive. Then*

$$\lim_{\alpha \uparrow 1/\lambda} (1 - \alpha \lambda) v = (d^T b) c.$$

Here, d is the (positive) eigenvector of A^T corresponding to λ with $d^T c = 1$.

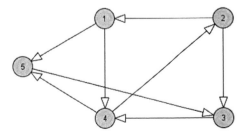

Fig. 3 A communication network

Proof Note that the principal eigenvalue of αA equals $\alpha\lambda < 1$. As A is primitive, $\alpha\lambda$ has multiplicity 1 and is larger than any other eigenvalue. Suppose that the eigenvalue of A with second largest modulus is μ, so, the second largest eigenvalue for αA is $\alpha\mu < \alpha\lambda$. Without loss of generality, we assume that to $\alpha\mu$ corresponds a $m \times m$ Jordan block and that these are the only eigenvalues, so αA is an $(1 + m) \times (1 + m)$- matrix, with two Jordan blocks, corresponding to the two eigenvalues $\alpha\lambda$ and $\alpha\mu$. We then have $\alpha A = SJS^{-1}$, and

$$
J^k = \begin{pmatrix}
(\alpha\lambda)^k & 0 & \cdots & \cdots & 0 \\
0 & (\alpha\mu)^k & \binom{k}{1}(\alpha\mu)^{k-1} & \cdots & \binom{k}{m-1}(\alpha\mu)^{k-m+1} \\
0 & 0 & (\alpha\mu)^k & \binom{k}{1}(\alpha\mu)^{k-1} & \cdots \\
\vdots & \vdots & \vdots & & \binom{k}{1}(\alpha\mu)^{k-1} \\
0 & 0 & 0 & & (\alpha\mu)^k
\end{pmatrix}.
$$

Straightforward calculations show that

$$
\sum_{k=0}^{\infty} J^k = \begin{pmatrix}
1/(1-\alpha\lambda) & 0 & \cdots & \cdots & 0 \\
0 & 1/(1-\alpha\mu) & 1/(1-\alpha\mu)^2 & \cdots & 1/(1-\alpha\mu)^m \\
0 & 0 & 1/(1-\alpha\mu) & \cdots & 1/(1-\alpha\mu)^{m-1} \\
\vdots & \vdots & \vdots & & 1/(1-\alpha\mu)^2 \\
0 & 0 & 0 & & 1/(1-\alpha\mu)
\end{pmatrix}.
$$

Therefore, $D = \lim_{\alpha \uparrow \frac{1}{\lambda}}(1 - \alpha\lambda)\sum_{p=0}^{\infty} J^p$ is a matrix with all entries equal to 0, except for $d_{11} = 1$. Furthermore, $\lim_{\alpha \uparrow \frac{1}{\lambda}}(1 - \alpha\lambda)\sum_{p=0}^{\infty}(\alpha A)^p = SDS^{-1}$. As $\alpha AS = SJ$, we let the first column of S be the Perron vector c of αA, which is the Perron vector of A. Let d^T be the first row of S^{-1}, meaning that d is a multiple of the Perron vector of A^T. As $S^{-1}S = I$, we know that $d^T c = 1$, so d is a positive vector. Therefore, $SDS^{-1} = cd^T$, proving our claim.

It is quite easy to investigate the effect of changes in the matrix A on the situational awareness. For example, consider upgrading the network by increasing usabilities of all existing links:

$$
A(t) = A + tG,
$$

where the matrix G is defined by $G_{ij} = 1$ if $A_{ij} \neq 0$ and $G_{ij} = 0$ otherwise. Then one easily derives:

$$
v'(0) = \alpha BGv,
$$

where $B = (I - \alpha A)^{-1}$. For the Perron vector c, in the model without exogenous values, this is much more complicated. Then one may prove for symmetric A, adapting the approach presented in Deutsch and Neumann (1985):

Proposition 1 $c'(0) = M^+ Gc - \frac{1}{n}(e^T M^+ Gc)c$, where M^+ is the Moore-Penrose inverse of the matrix $\lambda I - A$.

3.1.1 A Network Performance Metric

Next we introduce a network performance metric which combines given characteristics of the nodes with the network topology (NT) in order to compare different network configurations. As stated before, updating information in m steps yields situation awareness v_m. For $m \geq 1$ we define the network performance metric NTb_m by

$$NTb_m = \frac{e^T v_m}{e^T b} = \frac{e^T \sum_{k=0}^{m} \alpha^k A^k b}{e^T b} = \sum_{k=0}^{m} \alpha^k \frac{e^T A^k b}{e^T b}$$

where e is a vector of $1's$. Taking the limit of m tending to infinity, we get

$$NTb = \lim_{m \to \infty} NTb_m = \frac{e^T v}{e^T b} = \frac{e^T (I - \alpha A)^{-1} b}{e^T b}$$

This means that we take the quotient of the total situational awareness after updating, and the total value of exogenously given characteristics as expressed in the vector b.

3.2 Stochastic Behaviour of Nodes

In the former subsection we assumed that individual nodes are always in a position to receive information from adjacent nodes or hand over information to other nodes if possible *and* they are always prepared to do so. However as may be experienced in practice, the process of updating information not only depends on given characteristics of the nodes itself and the network structure. It also depends on the *uncertain* willingness or possibility of individual nodes to receive and transfer information. We will now take into account this uncertainty.

At each stage $k, k \geq 1$, of the process of updating information within the network, the uncertain behaviour of the nodes is modelled by a collection of independent and identically distributed random variables $\varepsilon_{k,ij} : \Omega \to [0, 1]$, $1 \leq i, j \leq n$, such that $\varepsilon_{k,ij} = 1$ if an information flow between node j and i is possible and $\varepsilon_{k,ij} = 0$ otherwise. So from the viewpoint of a receiving node i we can say that all its adjacent nodes j are willing to send information to node i but because of uncertain external factors it is not always possible or some nodes j do not want to send information to node i although an information flow is possible. So we can say that from the viewpoint of a receiving node i that all its adjacent nodes j behave in a random manner. For a fixed outcome ω in the sample space Ω the process of updating information in m steps yields the situation awareness $v_m(\omega)$, which for $m \geq 1$ is defined recursively by

$$v_0(\omega) = b; \quad v_1(\omega) = b + \alpha A_1(\omega)v_0(\omega) \quad \ldots \quad v_m(\omega) = b + \alpha A_m(\omega)v_{m-1}(\omega)$$

where the matrices A_k have the entries $a_{ij}\varepsilon_{k,ij}$. Note that we obtain the former, deterministic expression for the situation awareness v_m if all the matrices $A_k(\omega)$ are equal to A. The network performance metric that combines the given characteristics of the nodes with the network topology is defined by

$$NTb_m = \frac{E\left(e^T v_m\right)}{e^T b} = 1 + \sum_{k=1}^{m} \alpha^k \frac{E\left(e^T \left(\prod_{s=0}^{k-1} A_{m-s}\right) b\right)}{e^T b}$$

where $E\left(\cdot\right)$ denotes the expectation and e is a vector of $1's$.

Most of all we are interested in the case when m tends to infinity. So let $\{D_1, \ldots, D_N\}$ be the collection of all outcomes of $A_1(\omega)$. Notice that this collection is always finite, because $N \leq 2^n$. Suppose $\alpha \leq \left(\max_j \sum_{i=1}^{n} a_{ij}\right)^{-1}$. Then the network performance that combines the given characteristics of the nodes with the network topology is defined by

$$NTb = \frac{\int e^T x \, d\mu(x)}{e^T b}$$

Here μ is the unique probability measure which satisfies the equation

$$\mu = \sum_{m=1}^{N} P\left(A_1 = D_m\right) \mu \circ f_m^{-1},$$

where f_m is the affine mapping $f_m : x \mapsto b + \alpha D_m x$. The existence and uniqueness of this probability measure follows from the fact that

$$\{f_1, \ldots, f_N; P\left(A_1 = D_m\right), \ldots, P\left(A_1 = D_N\right)\}$$

is an iterated function system with probabilities. In order to determine and compute NTb we use the following theorem:

Theorem 2 *Fix a sequence of matrices $\{A_k(\omega)\}_{k\geq 1}$ for some outcome ω in the sample space Ω. Let the orbit $\{x_n\}_{n=0}^{\infty}$ be defined by $x_0 = b$ and $x_{n+1} = b + \alpha A_{n+1}x_n$. Then with probability one*

$$NTb = \lim_{n \to \infty} \frac{1}{n+1} \left(1 + \sum_{k=1}^{n} \frac{e^T x_k}{e^T b}\right)$$

Proof The integral $\int e^T x \, d\mu(x)$ in the expression of *NTb* can be determined by applying Elton's theorem (Elton, 1987). This means that

$$\lim_{n \to \infty} \frac{1}{n+1} \sum_{k=0}^{n} e^T x_k = \int e^T x \, d\mu(x)$$

with probability one. By dividing both sides of this expression by $e^T b$, the theorem is proved.

3.2.1 Observing the Choices of Other Nodes

In the previous discussion we assumed that for the process of updating information within the network, the uncertain behaviour of the nodes is modelled by a collection of independent and identically distributed random variables $\varepsilon_{k,ij}, k \geq 1, 1 \leq i, j \leq n$. In this simple model the behaviour of a node does not depend on the behaviour of other nodes, i.e. if a node i did not receive any information from its adjacent nodes in step $k - 1$, it does not have any effect on the willingness of this node i to send information to other nodes in step k. In order to incorporate this kind of behaviour of nodes, we have to adjust our model, i.e. the random variables $\varepsilon_{k,ij}$, $k \geq 1, 1 \leq i, j \leq n$ will not be i.i.d. anymore. A reasonable assumption is that the probability distribution of the random 0–1 variables $\varepsilon_{k,ij}, 1 \leq i, j \leq n$ is completely determined once the outcomes of the 0–1 random variables $\varepsilon_{k-1,ij}, 1 \leq i, j \leq n$ are known.

Fix an arbitrary node i and an adjacent node of this node i, say node j. From the point of view of a receiving node i, we suppose that at each stage $k, k \geq 1$, node j behaves in the following way. With probability $p_{ij}(1)$ node j sends information to node i and with probability $p_{ij}(0)$ it does not send information to node i, *independently of the state of the system* at stage $k - 1$. So with probability $1 - p_{ij}(1) - p_{ij}(0)$ the decision of node j to send information depends on the outcomes of the 0-1 random variables $\varepsilon_{k-1,ij}, 1 \leq i, j \leq n$. But how does this dependence look like? We say that at step k the probability that node j sends information to node i depends on two factors: (1) is it true that j has sent information to node i at the former step $k - 1$? (2) is it true that node j received information from its own adjacent nodes at step $k - 1$?

Analogous to the interaction model with network structure, see Jackson (2009), we suggest the following (Markov) model which takes into account these factors:

$$P\left(\varepsilon_{k,ij} = 1 | \varepsilon_{k-1,ij} = \beta_{ij}, \varepsilon_{k-1,jt} = \beta_{jt}, t \in N_j\right) =$$

$$p_{ij}(1) + \left(1 - p_{ij}(1) - p_{ij}(0)\right) \frac{1}{\gamma + (1-\gamma)|N_j|} \left(\gamma \beta_{ij} + (1-\gamma) \sum_{t \in N_j} \beta_{jt}\right)$$

and

$$P\left(\varepsilon_{k,ij} = 0 | \varepsilon_{k-1,ij} = \beta_{ij}, \varepsilon_{k-1,jt} = \beta_{jt}, t \in N_j\right) =$$
$$1 - P\left(\varepsilon_{k,ij} = 1 | \varepsilon_{k-1,ij} = \beta_{ij}, \varepsilon_{k-1,jt} = \beta_{jt}, t \in N_j\right)$$

where node j is an adjacent node of node i, N_j is the set containing all indices of the adjacent nodes of node j, the parameter $0 \leq \gamma \leq 1$ measures the balance between the contribution of the adjacent nodes of node j and the behaviour of node j itself at the previous step and finally the random 0–1 variables $\varepsilon_{k,ij}$, $1 \leq i, j \leq n$ are conditionally independent given $\varepsilon_{k-1,ij}$, $1 \leq i, j \leq n$. If node j is not an adjacent node of node i we take

$$P\left(\varepsilon_{k,ij} = 0\right) = 1$$

4 Network Dynamics

As stated in the introduction, a great challenge is the development of a clear notion of the value that operating in an networked manner may generate. To this end, the so-called NEC value chain has been introduced. Here, NEC stands for Network Enabled Capabilities. The claims are that a robustly, secure and more extensive networked organization generates shared, accurate, timely, relevant information, which improves information sharing. This in turn results in better shared understanding. This enables better decisions and agile and adaptable actions. Eventually, this results in better effects. The defence organization has introduced five Maturity Levels (ML's) that provide a framework for defining or describing the capabilities of an organization, with ML1 being the lowest and ML5 being the highest level. The fourth and fifth ML may be briefly described as follows:

- *ML4: Collaborate.* Organizations demonstrate collective development and execution of a shared common plan that establishes independent relationships. A unified infrastructure based on a single network allows the seamless sharing of data. Advanced horizontal and vertical interactive collaboration facilitates planning and execution. Major organizational and process changes are evident, with rich and continuous interactions between partners. The whole organization can readily adapt to any mission, rapidly planning and synchronizing to execute a common intent.
- *ML5: Coherent effects.* At the highest level of maturity, coalitions or alliances can rapidly plan and execute missions as if they were one homogeneous team. Complete situational awareness is possible through a proliferation of sensors and continuous interaction between partners. Information is transparently available regardless of location. Decision making is extremely fast and responses are agile.

To also include network statistics into the measurement tools for these ML's, we may use the model of Sect. 3. This way, one may compute the informational advantage that a node derives from its positioning within the network. But, we also may try to quantify the total networked effects. In the literature, one may find several models. In the model described in Cares (2005) it is assumed that just one specific arrangement of links and nodes creates value. These arrangements are sub-networks that form a cycle. In a cycle, the functions of nodes flow into each other over a path that revisits at least one node once. To give an indication of the magnitude of networked effects, it is suggested to use the largest eigenvalue of the adjacency matrix, which is a measure of the multiplicity of internal paths:

$$\lambda = \max_{x>0} \min_i \frac{(Ax)_i}{x_i}.$$

A drawback of this model is that it does not take into consideration the various network values of the nodes; the nodes are assumed to be homogeneous. A second model is the model introduced in Ling, Moon, and Kruzins (2005). They introduce a time-dependent connectivity measure given by

$$C_M(t) = \sum_{\mu=1}^{N_T} K_\mu(t) \sum_{v=1}^{N_\mu} \sum_{\gamma=1}^{N_{\mu v}} L_\gamma^{\mu v}(d, t),$$

where K_μ, the value of the node μ, is used to express the inhomogeneity of the nodes, while $L_\gamma^{\mu v}(d, t)$ is the value of the route γ connecting neighbors μ and v. For example, take L to be equal to the product of the values of A along the route, divided by its length. This measure $C_M(t)$ then is normalized to obtain a measure of *network reach*. Although this model takes into account the inhomogeneity of the nodes, these values K_μ are fixed and have been determined in advance. So the positioning of the nodes does not matter. To also take this into account, one may substitute for K_μ the network value discussed previously in Sect. 3. Then, using $C_M(t)$, the topology of the network is represented using two more or less independent components: nodes and their values $K_\mu(t)$ due to the positioning within the network, and the information flow parameter $L_\gamma^{\mu v}(d, t)$ of routes γ connecting nodes μ and v. As a final model, in Sect. 3.1.1, we suggested an alternative network performance metric that combines given characteristics b of nodes with the Network Topology. It is the quotient of two values measured on the same scale:

$$NTb = \frac{\sum_i v_i}{\sum_i b_i} = \frac{e^T (I - \alpha A)^{-1} b}{e^T b},$$

where e is a vector of 1's. It is easy to verify that NTb does not depend on the *unit* of the scale on which values of b are measured. An advantage of our model is that it also makes possible to identify and quantify

- the contribution of the network to the network value v: this is equal to $\alpha A v$;
- the percentage of network value v that is not due to value emanating from other nodes, which we call the powerbase: As v_i equals $\sum_j (\sum_{p=0}^{\infty} (\alpha A)^p)_{ij} b_j$, for node i, this percentage $PB(i, \alpha)$, is equal to

$$PB(i, \alpha) = \frac{\sum_j (\sum_{p=0}^{\infty} (\alpha A)^p)_i{}_j \overline{b}_j}{\sum_j (\sum_{p=0}^{\infty} (\alpha A)^p)_{ij} b_j},$$

where $\overline{b}_j = 0$ for $j \neq i$ and $\overline{b}_i = b_i$.

By multiplying numerator and denominator by $(1 - \alpha \lambda)$, we then may prove (Monsuur, 2008):

Theorem 3 *Suppose that A is primitive. Then, for any given vector b of exogenously given characteristics, we have*

$$\lim_{\alpha \uparrow \frac{1}{\lambda}} PB(i) = \frac{d_i b_i}{d^T b},$$

where d is the left eigenvector of A.

To obtain a large network value v, one has to invest in incoming links; to obtain a large powerbase, one also has to maintain outgoing links, that transfers value to other nodes of the network. Of course, for symmetric networks, where an incoming link goes hand in hand with an outgoing link with the same strength, the powerbase also equals $\frac{c_i b_i}{c^T b}$.

5 A Choice Mechanism for Network Evolution

In the Maturity Levels described in the previous section, social networks may play an important role. As may be observed in practice, social networks change over time. In this section, we describe a model that can be used to study the dynamic evolution of networks. This model falls within the category of game-theoretic models, or to be more precise within the class of pairwise stability models (Jackson, 2009). Nodes re-arrange their local network structure, attempting to improve their position.

In this section we only consider symmetric networks. To be more specific, we let E be a subset of $\{(x, y) : x, y \in V, x \neq y\}$, the set of *non-ordered* pairs of V. Next, $P = < c_0, c_1, \ldots, c_k >$ is a *path* in G from c_0 to c_k, if $\{c_0, c_1, \ldots, c_k\} \subset V$ and $(c_i, c_{i+1}) \in E$ for all $i \in \{0, \ldots, k - 1\}$. We tacitly assume that networks are *connected*: between any two nodes there is a path connecting the two nodes. A *cycle* in a network G is a path $< v_1, v_2, \ldots, v_{k-1}, v_k >$ of $k - 1 \geq 3$ distinct nodes, with $v_k = v_1$. A *tree-network* is a network without cycles. Finally, a *complete* network is a network that has a link for each pair of nodes.

5.1 The Uncovered Set

In Monsuur & Storcken (2004) we introduced the so-called *cover relation*, based on the original formulation of the cover relation for tournaments in Miller (1980).

Let a, b be nodes in V, $a \neq b$. Then a covers b in $G = (V, E)$ if (1) for all $x \in V \setminus \{a\}$, $(x, b) \in E$ implies $(x, a) \in E$, and (2) there exists at least one node $c \notin \{a, b\} \subset V$ such that $(c, a) \in E$ while $(c, b) \notin E$. This means that node a covers node b if all nodes linked to b are also linked to a and node a has at least one extra link. Note that we do not require that $(b, a) \in E$. Intuitively speaking, a outperforms b. If the network is a social network or a network of alliances, then it also is clear that a's position is more advantageous: every social link of b can be covered by one of a and a has at least one extra link. The cover relation is a generalization of the cover relation defined for tournaments as introduced in Miller (1980). We let U or $U(G)$ be the uncovered set: $U = \{v \in V$: there is no node $w \in V$ that covers v in the network $G\}$. In Monsuur & Storcken (2004), we characterized this non-empty set U of uncovered nodes by three independent axioms. There we use the concept of a *center* ϕ that assigns to any network $G = (V, E)$ a non-empty subset $\phi(G) \subset V$. The center ϕ_{uc} assigns to a network G the set of uncovered nodes.

Theorem 4 *The center set U is the only inclusion minimal set of nodes that is compatible with structural equivalence, has the mediator property and is stable.*

Here a center ϕ of nodes is *compatible with structural equivalence* if for two nodes a and b that are structurally equivalent, $a \in \phi(G)$, if and only if $b \in \phi(G)$. Next, a center ϕ has the *mediator property* if for each pair of distinct nodes a and b, there is a shortest path connecting these nodes, such that any node in between a and b on this path is in $\phi(G)$. The third condition is on stability. A center ϕ is *stable* if for each (noncentral) node $s \notin \phi(G)$ and each node $t \notin V$, there is a (central) node $w \in \phi(G)$ such that $s \notin \phi(G')$, where $G' = (V \cup \{t\}, E \cup \{(s, t), (w, t)\})$. This condition may be interpreted as follows: a node s not belonging to the central nodes, in trying to become central, may develop a relation with a new node t. However, the set of current central nodes is assumes to be able to neutralize this effort by selecting a node of the center to also connect to this new node t.

5.2 Forming or Severing Links

In order to be able to introduce and explain the notion of *pairwise stable networks*, in Monsuur (2007b) we used the following dichotomy: A node is either covered or it is uncovered. We further assume that the status "uncovered" is ranked higher than the status "covered".

The mechanism. Each step consists of taking, randomly, two distinct nodes a and b from V. Then for the link (a, b):

- if $(a, b) \in E$, it is deleted by a if the network remains connected and the status of node a does not decrease,
- if $(a, b) \notin E$, it is added if both a and b achieve a higher status.

To motivate the deletion of links, note that a node a is able to *unilaterally* sever any existing link $(a, x), x \in V$. If, for example, a is covered and therefore is in a subdued position, the link (a, x) is possibly severed as a's status can not decrease any further (and costs are less). The link is also possibly severed if a is uncovered, and afterward it still is uncovered. Note that a link (a, b) is not deleted if this results in a disconnected network. As afterwards, a and b are not able to communicate anymore, directly nor indirectly, this seems a reasonable decision. Regarding the addition of links, as both nodes must agree to establish the link, it is assumed that both have to gain in terms of *achieving* the status of being uncovered. The structural mechanism embodies the idea that nodes have the discretion to form or sever links. The formation of a link requires the consent of both nodes involved, while severance can be done unilaterally.

A network G is called pairwise stable if the mechanism described before never leads to changes. If $G' = (V, E')$ differs from $G = (V, E)$ by just one link (a, b) and, starting with G this difference is the result of the mechanism described before, then G' is said to be a successor network of G. We have the following theorem, see Monsuur (2007b):

Theorem 5 *Let G be a network with $|V| > 2$. Suppose that there is at least one node c that is covered. Then there exists a sequence of successor networks that transforms G into one of the following pairwise stable networks*

- *a uni-polar network,*
- *a bi-polar network,*
- *a ring-network,*

(see Fig. 4), where a uni-polar network is a network with $|V| > 3$ and $E = \{(s, v_i) : v_i \in V \setminus \{s\}\}$ for some node s; a bi-polar network is a tree-network with $|U| = 2$ and $|C| > 2$; and finally, a ring-network is a network (V, E) with $V = \{v_1, v_2, \ldots, v_k\}$, $k > 2$ and $E = \{(v_1, v_2), (v_2, v_3), \ldots, (v_k, v_1)\}$ (so $U = V$).

In van Klaveren, Monsuur, Janssen, Schut, and Eiben (2009) we conducted a simulation study that shows that, starting with a randomly generated network, one almost always ends up with a ring-network. So, ring-networks are very dominant and have a large "basin of attraction". Further research will involve nonhomogeneous actors and more sophisticated "agent"-behaviour, combining social choice theory, (social) network theory and artificial intelligence.

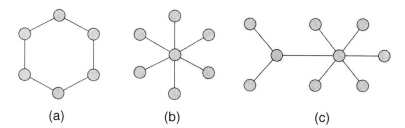

$$(a) \qquad\qquad (b) \qquad\qquad (c)$$

Fig. 4 Types of pair-wise stable network topologies: (**a**) ring, (**b**) uni-polar, (**c**) bi-polar

6 Conclusions

In military network sciences, several major research challenges have been formulated. One of these challenges, see National Research Council, Committee on Network Science for Future Army Applications (2005), is the study on

> *Dynamics, spatial location, and information propagation in networks.* A major need in network science is a better understanding of the relationship between the architecture of the network and its function. This is particularly important in networks where dynamics plays an important role, either through the flow of information around the network or through changes in the network structure (by evolution or adaptation). How the structure of a network relates to the behavior of the system is still not well-understood and will be a major impediment to progress in many applications.

To this end, in this contribution, we investigated a model for situational awareness that combines the network topology with exogenous characteristics of nodes. We also discussed a model for network evolution. A more sophisticated version of that model, is currently under investigation to be included in the tools for measuring the Maturity Levels, as described in Sect. 4. Altogether, the results presented here may be useful to increase our understanding of the role of social, information and physical networks in complex operations.

References

Barabási, A.-L. (2003). *Linked: The new science of networks*. Cambridge, MA: Plume Books.

Berman, A., & Plemmons, R. J. (1979). Nonnegative matrices in the mathematical sciences. New York: Academic Press.

Cares, J. (2005). *Distributed networked operations*. New York: Universe, Inc.

Cares, J. (2006). Battle of the networks. *Harvard Business Review, 84*, 40–41.

Darilek, R., Perry, W., Bracken, J., Gordon, J., & Nichiporuk, B. (2001). *Measures of effectiveness for the information-age army*. Santa Monica, CA: RAND Cooperation.

Delver, R., & Monsuur, H. (2001). Stable sets and standards of behaviour. *Social Choice and Welfare, 18*, 555–570.

Deutsch, E., & Neumann, M. (1985). On the first and second order derivatives of the Perron vector. *Linear Algebra and its Applications, 71*, 57–76.

Dutta, B., & Jackson, M. O. (Eds.). (2003). *Networks and groups, models of strategic formation*. Heidelberg: Springer.

Elton, J. H. (1987). An ergodic theorem for iterated maps. *Ergodic Theory and Dynamical Systems, 7*, 481–488.

Endsley, M. R. (1995). Toward a theory of situation awareness in dynamic systems. *Human Factors, 37*(1), 32–64.

Gorsuch, R. L. (1983). *Factor analysis*. Hillsdale, NJ: Lawrence Erlbaum.

Goyal, S. (2007). *Connections. An introduction to the economics of networks*. Princeton, NJ: Princeton University Press.

Grant, T. J. (2006). *Measuring the potetential benefits of NCW: 9/11 as case study*. Proceedings of the 11th ICCRTS Conference. Washington, DC: US DoD C&C Research Program (CCRP).

Herings, P. J.-J., van der Laan, G., & Talman, D. (2005). The positional power of nodes in digraphs. *Social Choice and Welfare, 24*(3), 439–454.

Jackson, M. O. (2009). *Social and economic networks*. Princeton, NJ: Princeton University Press.

Knight, S., & Burn, J. (2005). Developing a framework for assessing information quality on the world wide web. *Informing Science Journal, 8,* 159–172.

Ling, M. F., Moon, T., & Kruzins, E. (2005). Proposed network centric warfare metrics: From connectivity to the OODA cycle. *Military Operations Research Society Journal, 10,* 5–13.

Miller, N. R. (1980). A new solution set for tournament and majority voting: Further graph-theoretical approaches to the theory of voting. *American Journal of Political Science, 24,* 68–96.

Monsuur, H. (1997). An intrinsic consistency threshold for reciprocal matrices. *European Journal of Operational Research, 96*(2), 387–391.

Monsuur, H., & Storcken, T. (2004). Centers in connected undirected graphs: An axiomatic approach. *Operations Research, 52,* 54–64.

Monsuur, H. (2007a). Assessing situation awareness in networks of cooperating entities: A mathematical approach. *Military Operations Research, 12*(3), 5–15.

Monsuur, H. (2007b). Stable and emergent network topologies: A structural approach. *European Journal of Operational Research, 183*(1), 432–441.

Monsuur, H. (2008). Network-induces power base: The appreciation of contributing to the value of other nodes. In: H. L. Schneider & L. M. Huber (Eds.), *Social networks: Developments, evaluation and influence* (pp. 179–200). New York: Nova Science Publishers.

National Research Council, Committee on Network Science for Future Army Applications. (2005). *Network science.* Washington, DC: The National Academies Press.

Perry, W. L., & Moffat, J. (2004). *Information sharing among military headquarters: The effects on decisionmaking.* Santa Monica, CA: RAND Corporation.

Saaty, T. L. (1980). *The analytic hierarchy process.* New York: McGraw-Hill.

Slutzki, G., & Volij, O. (2005). Ranking participants in generalized tournaments. *International Journal of Game Theory, 33,* 255–270.

van Klaveren, P. D., Monsuur, H., Janssen, R. H. P., Schut, M. C., & Eiben, A. E. (2009). *Exploring stable and emergent network topologies.* Proceedings of the 21st Benelux Conference on Artificial Intelligence, to appear.

Wang, Y., & Strong, D. M. (1996, Spring). What data quality means to data consumers. *Journal of Management Information Systems, 12*(4), 5–33.

Wasserman, S., & Faust, K. (1994). *Social network analysis: Methods and applications.* Cambridge: Cambridge University Press.

Watts, D. J. (1999). *Small worlds: The dynamics of networks between order and randomness.* Princeton Studies in Complexity. Princeton, NJ: Princeton University Press.

Characterizations of Bargaining Solutions by Properties of Their Status Quo Sets

Hans Peters

1 Introduction

In the classical axiomatic approach to bargaining as initiated by Nash (1950), solutions are characterized by properties that focus on how the solution outcome changes if the feasible set changes. This is in particular the case for the main distinguishing properties, such as "independence of irrelevant alternatives" for the Nash bargaining solution, and "individual monotonicity" for the Kalai–Smorodinsky solution. Among the first papers that focus more explicitly on the role of the status quo point (or disagreement point) is (the hitherto unpublished paper) Peters (1986). Parts of it have been published in a modified and extended version by Peters and van Damme (1991). In Sects. 2–9 of this chapter the results of Peters (1986) are quite accurately reproduced: the only somewhat more substantial change is the characterization of the Continuous Raiffa Solution, which has benefitted from later insights. The chapter is concluded by an added section (Sect. 10), which provides a brief overview of later related literature.

2 Bargaining and Status Quo

Many economic situations that involve a (potential) conflict between two parties may be modelled as two-person bargaining games. One distinguishing feature of such situations is the presence of some alternative which results if no agreement between the two parties is reached. Some possible candidates for this alternative are: (i) maintenance of the status quo; (ii) the carrying out of threats by one or both parties; (iii) a decision made by an outside arbitrator; . . . An example of (i) is, in dividing a fixed amount of money: if no agreement is reached then no party gets anything. In the case of (ii), we may think of economic (or real) warfare if no

H. Peters (✉)
Department of Quantitative Economics, Maastricht University, 6200 MD Maastricht,
The Netherlands
e-mail: h.peters@maastrichtuniversity.nl

A. Van Deemen, A. Rusinowska (eds.), *Collective Decision Making,*
Theory and Decision Library C 43, DOI 10.1007/978-3-642-02865-6_15,
© Springer-Verlag Berlin Heidelberg 2010

agreement is attained. Legal decisions are often instances of (iii). A conflict between an industry or firm and a union may result in a strike (case (ii)) or in governmental or legal arbitration (case (iii)).

A *bargaining game* (S, d) consists of a subset S of the plane, and a point d in S called the *status quo point* (mathematical details are given in the next section). Its interpretation is that there are two parties (bargainers, *players*), who bargain over the outcomes in S. If they agree on some $x = (x_1, x_2) \in S$, then players 1 and 2 receive (e.g., von Neumann–Morgenstern) utilities x_1 and x_2, respectively. Otherwise, they receive d_1 and d_2, respectively. So, in a bargaining game, the original nature of the status quo point is abstracted from (indeed, the point d may be called, alternatively, the disagreement point or threat point). Further, it is implicitly assumed that an agreement $x \in S$ can be enforced in some way or another, e.g., collusion in duopoly by some legal contract. In other words (in the language of game theory) a bargaining game (S, d) of this kind is a *cooperative game*.

The usual "axiomatic" approach to bargaining is to specify some map or bargaining solution f, assigning to each bargaining game (S, d) a point of S, by requiring it to satisfy certain properties ("axioms"). (For convenience, we adopt here a manner of speech which corresponds to a *normative* point of view but, in principle, one might take a *positive* standpoint.) One would expect the point $f(S, d)$ to depend properly on d, so *individual rationality* (i.e., $f(S, d) \geq d$ always) is the least to require. Indeed, the status quo point plays a prominent role in the definitions of most well-known bargaining solutions (see, e.g., Kalai & Smorodinsky, 1975; Nash, 1950); but in most properties characterizing these solutions, its role is only implicit. Consider, for instance, the well-known property called *independence of irrelevant alternatives*, proposed by Nash in his seminal paper (Nash, 1950). This property requires two bargaining problems to have the same solution outcome whenever (i) they have a common status quo point; (ii) the outcomes in one game are a subset of the outcomes in the other game; and (iii) the solution outcome in the larger game is also feasible in the smaller game. So in the description of this property – and of many other properties in the literature – the status quo point is kept fixed while the set of (other) outcomes is varied. In this chapter we shall take the opposite approach: we shall propose some properties in which the set of outcomes of a bargaining game, or subsets of it depending in obvious ways on the status quo point, are kept fixed as much as possible, and the status quo point is varied. In particular, if two status quo points d and e give rise to the same solution outcome, i.e., $f(S, d) = f(S, e)$, we shall say that d and e belong to the same *status quo set*. We shall characterize bargaining solutions by properties of their status quo sets.

This approach will result in alternative characterizations of the bargaining solutions of Nash (1950), Kalai and Rosenthal (1978), Kalai & Smorodinsky (1975), Raiffa (1953), and of the Egalitarian solution (e.g. Kalai, 1977). These results are presented in Sects. 4–7, respectively. The paper on which this chapter is based (Peters, 1986), originated from an attempt to characterize another solution proposed by Raiffa (1953), called here the *Continuous Raiffa solution*; the result of that attempt is presented in Sect. 8.

It will be seen that all these different solutions are characterized by different subsets of the same large set of properties. Every single one of these properties is satisfied by at least two, and often more than two of the mentioned solutions. This indicates that there is a closer relationship between these solutions than one would expect at first sight. It also shows that the properties considered in this chapter are not "tailor made" for particular solutions. We shall elaborate on these points in Sect. 9. Further, we shall also give a "sensitivity analysis" of our results.

In Sect. 10 we provide a brief overview of later literature.

In the next section we give the basic definitions and discuss the announced properties of bargaining solutions.

3 Basic Definitions and Properties

For elements $x, y \in \mathbb{R}^2$ we use the following vector inequalities: $x > y$, meaning that $x_i > y_i$ for $i = 1, 2$; and $x \geq y$, meaning that $x_i \geq y_i$ for $i = 1, 2$. The inequalities $x < y$ and $x \leq y$ are defined similarly.

For a non-empty subset T of $\mathbb{R}^2$ we denote the *comprehensive hull of* T by

$$\mathrm{com}(T) := \{y \in \mathbb{R}^2 \mid y \leq x \text{ for some } x \in T\}.$$

If $T = \mathrm{com}(T)$, we say that T is *comprehensive*.

A *two-person bargaining game* or simply a *game* is a pair (S, d) with $d \in \mathrm{int}(S) \subseteq \mathbb{R}^2$ (where $\mathrm{int}(S)$ is the interior of S) such that

$$S \text{ is closed and convex,} \tag{1}$$
$$g_i(S) := \max\{x_i \mid x = (x_1, x_2) \in S\} \text{ exists for } i = 1, 2, \tag{2}$$
$$S \text{ is comprehensive.} \tag{3}$$

Closedness of S is required for mathematical convenience. Convexity of S may follow, for instance, from the use of lotteries and von Neumann-Morgenstern utility functions in some underlying bargaining situation. The point $g(S)$ in (2) is called the *global utopia point* of S: (2) requires its existence. Comprehensiveness of S can be interpreted as the possibility of free disposal of utility. The set S is the *set of feasible outcomes* and d is the *status quo point*. For the game-theoretic interpretation of a bargaining game we refer to Sect. 2. By $\mathcal{B}$ we denote the set of all two-person bargaining games.

A *two-person bargaining solution* or simply a *solution* is a map $f : \mathcal{B} \to \mathbb{R}^2$ which assigns to each $(S, d) \in \mathcal{B}$ a feasible outcome.

Let S be a subset of $\mathbb{R}^2$ satisfying (1), (2), and (3), let x be a point in S, and let f be a solution. The *status quo set of S with respect to f and x* is the set

$$D(S, f, x) := \{d \in \mathrm{int}(S) \mid f(S, d) = x\}.$$

Although the status quo set plays a central role in this chapter, we shall avoid using the notation $D(\cdot, \cdot, \cdot)$ whenever possible: most of the properties in this section in particular can be formulated at least as clearly without the use of this notation.

Other important subsets of S, for a game (S, d), are: the *Pareto optimal subset of S*, denoted

$$P(S) := \{x \in S \mid \text{if } y \in S \text{ and } y \geq x \text{ then } y = x\};$$

the *weakly Pareto optimal subset of S*, denoted $W(S)$, which is just the boundary of S; and the *individually rational subset of S with respect to d*, denoted

$$S_d := \{x \in S \mid x \geq d\}.$$

We are now sufficiently equipped to define our first series of properties for a solution f.

Individual Rationality (IR): $f(S, d) \geq d$ for every game (S, d).

Pareto Optimality (PO): $f(S, d) \in P(S)$ for every game (S, d).

Weak Pareto Optimality (WPO): $f(S, d) \in W(S)$ for every game (S, d).

Independence of Non-Individually Rational Outcomes (INIR):
$f(S, d) = f(\mathrm{com}(S_d), d)$ for every game (S, d).

The first three of these properties need no further discussion. All main solutions discussed in this chapter are individually rational, and, apart from the Egalitarian solution of Sect. 7 which is only weakly Pareto optimal, they are all Pareto optimal. Therefore, it will be convenient to use the expression *standard solution* for a Pareto optimal, individually rational solution. The last property, INIR, requires the solution outcome of a game to depend only on the individually rational subset.

Remark 1 Although IR is implied by the combination of INIR and PO, as is easy to prove, we shall nevertheless talk about standard solutions with the INIR property.

In order to define further properties for a solution f, we need some additional notation. For a non-empty subset T of $\mathbb{R}^2$, let $\mathrm{conv}(T)$ denote the *convex hull of T*, i.e., the smallest convex set containing T, and let $\mathrm{comv}(T)$ $(= \mathrm{com}(\mathrm{conv}(T)) = \mathrm{conv}(\mathrm{com}(T)))$ denote the *convex comprehensive hull of T*.

Split-the-difference (Spl): For all $x, y \in \mathbb{R}^2$ with $x_1 > y_1$ and $y_2 > x_2$ we have $f(\mathrm{comv}(\{x, y\}), (y_1, x_2)) = \frac{1}{2}(x + y)$.

Weak Split-the-difference (WSpl): For all $x, y \in \mathbb{R}^2$ with $x_1 - y_1 = y_2 - x_2 > 0$ we have $f(\mathrm{comv}(\{x, y\}), (y_1, x_2)) = \frac{1}{2}(x + y)$.

The Split-the-difference property exhibits symmetry as well as independence of the particular utility presentations chosen; the latter makes sense especially if the utility functions are of the von Neumann-Morgenstern type. The second property WSpl is strictly weaker: for instance, the Egalitarian solution (see Sect. 7) satisfies WSpl but not Spl, whereas all other main solutions to be discussed in this chapter satisfy Spl.

The next property requires a status quo set to contain the straight (half)line through the status quo point and the solution point.

Linearity (Lin): For every game (S, d) and every interior point e of S on the straight line $\{\alpha d + (1 - \alpha) f(S, d) \mid \alpha \in \mathbb{R}\}$ through d and $f(S, d)$, we have $f(S, e) = f(S, d)$.

An interpretation of the Linearity property is as follows. If, for the set of feasible outcomes S, the status quo point d gives rise to the outcome $f(S, d) = x$, then every other interior point e of S which preserves the ration of the "gains" over the status quo outcome, i.e., satisfies $(x_2 - d_2)/(x_1 - d_1) = (x_2 - e_2)/(x_1 - e_1)$, should also give x as the solution outcome, i.e., $f(S, e) = x$. Of course, this is just a slight reformulation of the mathematical linearity condition, but it has an apparent economic interpretation. We shall also consider the following weaker version of Linearity.

Restricted Linearity (RLin): For every game (S, d) with $S = \mathrm{com}(S_d)$, we have $\mathrm{int}(S) \cap \{\alpha d + (1 - \alpha) f(S, d) \mid \alpha \geq 1\} \subseteq D(S, f, f(S, d))$.

Restricted Linearity is strictly weaker than Linearity, for instance, the Kalai-Smorodinsky solution (see Sect. 6) satisfies RLin but not Lin. For further discussion on this condition, see Sect. 6.

In order to introduce the next property, suppose that we have a game (S, d) and a point $e \in S$, $e \leq d$, such that $f(S, d) = f(S, e)$. One may imagine negotiations starting from e and going through d on the way to agreement. It may be that this "negotiation path" is independent of what comes "after" d, i.e., of S_d. Such a kind of "path independence" is required in the following property, albeit in a weaker form. For a game (S, d), we introduce the set $T(S_d) := \mathrm{comv}(\{(d_1, g_2), (g_1, d_2)\})$, where g is the global utopia point of $\mathrm{com}(S_d)$ (the "T" is from "Triangular").

Independence of Strongly Individually Rational Outcomes (ISIR): For every game (S, d) with $S = \mathrm{com}(S_d)$ and every $e \in S$ with $e \leq d$ we have: if $f(T(S_d), e) = f(T(S_d), d)$, then $f(S, e) = f(S, d)$.

For the next property, let (S, d) and (S, e) be games with $d_1 > e_1$ and $d_2 < e_2$. Then d may be considered an improvement for player 1 and a deterioration for player 2 when compared with e, and one could expect of a solution f that $f(S, d)$ be unequal to $f(S, e)$. In order to phrase this as a property, call, for a game (S, d) and a point $x \in S$, the status quo set $D(S, f, x)$ *discriminating* if $e > e'$ or $e' > e$ for any two distinct points e, e' of $D(S, f, x)$. Further, call a game (S, d) *rectangular* if $S = \mathrm{com}(\{x\})$ for some $x > d$.

Discrimination (Disc): For every non-rectangular game (S, d) and every $x \in S$ the status quo set $D(S, f, x)$ is discriminating.

We have to exclude rectangular games in this definition, since otherwise no standard solution would have the Discrimination property. Of the main solutions studied in this chapter, only the Nash solution does not have the Discrimination property.

A discriminating status quo set that is a curve in the plane, will be the graph of a strictly monotonically increasing function. The next and final property that we need requires this function to be differentiable.

Differentiability (Diff): For every $(S, d) \in \mathcal{B}$ with $D(S, f, f(S, d))$ discriminating, there exists a number $\beta < d_1$, and a differentiable function on the interval $(\beta, f_1(S, d))$ such that $\{x \geq d \mid x \in \text{int}(S), f(S, x) = f(S, d)\}$ is the graph of that function on $[d_1, f_1(S, d))$.

The Differentiability property requires the proportion of infinitesimally small utility gains with respect to a status quo point to be equal to the proportion of infinitesimally small utility losses, under the assumption that the solution outcome remains unaltered. Of course, just as was the case with the interpretation we gave of the Linearity property, this interpretation is, in essence, the mathematical definition of differentiability, which can be said to have some economic content here. Diff will be used in the characterization of the Continuous Raiffa solution in Sect. 8.

4 The Nash Solution

The *Nash solution* $N : \mathcal{B} \to \mathbb{R}^2$ assigns to every $(S, d) \in \mathcal{B}$ the point of S_d where the product $(x_1 - d_1)(x_2 - d_2)$ is maximized. This solution was introduced and characterized in the seminal article of Nash (1950). The main property used in that characterization is the *Independence of Irrelevant Alternatives* property (IIA): if (S, d) and (T, d) are games with $S \subseteq T$ and $f(T, d) \in S$, then $f(S, d) = f(T, d)$. There has been much discussion on IIA in the literature (e.g., Kalai & Smorodinsky, 1975; Luce & Raiffa, 1957), and other characterizations of Nash's solution have been given (for an overview see Peters, 1992). IIA-dislikers may like the now following characterization of the Nash solution, which does not use the IIA property.

Theorem 1 *The Nash solution is the unique standard solution with the properties INIR, Spl, and Lin.*

Proof IR, PO, and INIR of the Nash solution N are straightforward from its definition. The properties Lin and Spl follow from the following geometric characterization of N:

For every game (S, d), the point z in $P(S)$ is the Nash solution point if and only if there is a supporting line of S at z with slope equal to the negative of the slope of the straight line through d and z. (∗)

For a proof of (∗), see, e.g., Lemma IX.1.4 in Owen (1995) or Lemma 2.2 in Peter (1992).

Now let $f : \mathcal{B} \to \mathbb{R}^2$ be a standard solution satisfying INIR, Spl, and Lin. Let $(S, d) \in \mathcal{B}$, let $z = N(S, d)$ (observe that $z > d$), let ℓ be the supporting line of S at z as in (∗), and let $p, q \in W(S)$ with $d_1 \leq p_1 < z_1$ and $d_2 \leq q_2 < z_2$ and such that the straight line ℓ' through p and q is parallel to ℓ. Let $T \subseteq \mathbb{R}^2$ consist of all

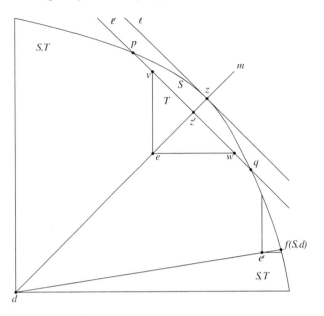

Fig. 1 Illustrating the proof of Theorem 1

points of S except those strictly above ℓ'. We first prove that $N(T, d) = f(T, d)$ (see Fig. 1).

In view of $(*)$, $z' = N(T, d)$ is the point of intersection of ℓ' and the straight line m through d and z. Note that z' lies strictly in between p and q. Choose e on m with $d \le e < z'$, $p_1 \le e_1$, and $q_2 \le e_2$. Let $v, w \in \ell'$ with $v_1 = e_1$ and $w_2 = e_2$. Since the slope of ℓ' is equal to the negative of the slope of m, we have $z' = \frac{1}{2}(v + w)$, so by Spl: $f(\text{comv}(\{v, w\}), e) = z'$. So by INIR: $f(T, e) = z'$ which implies, by Lin: $f(T, d) = z'$. Hence, $f(T, d) = N(T, d)$.

Finally, we prove that $N(S, d) = f(S, d)$. Suppose not, then by PO: $f_1(S, d) > N_1(S, d)$ or $f_2(S, d) > N_2(S, d)$. Say $f_1(S, d) > N_1(S, d)$; we derive a contradiction. Let p and q be as above with, additionally, $q \in P(S)$ such that $q_2 > f_2(S, d)$. Let e' be a point on the straight line through d and $f(S, d)$ with $d \le e' \le f(S, d)$ and $q_1 \le e'_1 < f_1(S, d)$. By Lin: $f(S, e') = f(S, d)$. So by INIR: $f(T, e') = f(S, d)$. Hence by Lin: $f(T, d) = f(S, d)$, which implies (by the first part of the proof) $f(S, d) = N(T, d) = z'$, a contradiction since $f_1(S, d) > z'_1$. $\quad\square$

Note that Remark 1 applies in this theorem: we could omit IR and obtain a stronger theorem, since IR is implied by the combination of PO and INIR. Note also that we cannot dispense with the PO property in Theorem 1: the solution that assigns $N(S, d)$ to every non-rectangular game (S, d) and (x_1, d_2) to every rectangular game $(\text{com}(\{x\}), d)$, satisfies every property in the theorem except PO.

The Nash solution satisfies all other properties introduced in Sect. 3 except ISIR and Disc. These statements follow elementarily, or with the aid of $(*)$ in the proof of Theorem 1. In particular, if for some game (S, d) the Pareto optimal surface $P(S)$

is not smooth in some point $\bar{x}$, then the status quo set $D(S, N, \bar{x})$ is not a straight (half)line but a cone, as follows from $(*)$. Thus, N does not satisfy Disc.

5 The Kalai–Rosenthal Solution

The *Kalai–Rosenthal solution* $KR : \mathcal{B} \rightarrow \mathbb{R}^2$ assigns to every game (S, d) the point of $P(S)$ on the straight line through d and the global utopia point $g(S)$ of S (see Sect. 3). The solution KR was introduced in Kalai and Rosenthal (1978), and characterized in Peters and Tijs (1985) with the aid of a property called *global individual monotonicity* in which, not surprisingly, the global utopia point plays an important role. This may be seen as a drawback since the global utopia point can depend on non-individually rational outcomes. The following characterization of the solution KR, in which the ISIR property is used, may be less liable to such criticism: in this respect, it is of special interest to note already that the Kalai–Smorodinsky solution – to be considered in Sect. 6, and the Continuous Raiffa solution of Sect. 8, satisfy ISIR as well as INIR.

Theorem 2 *The Kalai–Rosenthal solution is the unique standard solution with the properties ISIR, Spl, Lin, and Disc.*

Proof IR, PO, ISIR, Spl, Lin, and Disc of KR follow straightforwardly from its definition. Now let $f : \mathcal{B} \rightarrow \mathbb{R}^2$ be a solution satisfying these six properties. We will prove that $f = KR$ by an argument based on contradiction. Suppose that $f(S, d) \neq KR(S, d)$ for some $(S, d) \in \mathcal{B}$. Take $\alpha \geq 1$ so large that for $e := \alpha d + (1 - \alpha)KR(S, d)$ we have $S = \text{com}(S_e)$. Then $KR(S, e) = KR(S, d)$ and, by Lin of f and $f(S, d) \neq KR(S, d) = KR(S, e)$, we have $f(S, e) \neq KR(S, e)$. For notational convenience we suppose from now on, without loss of generality, that

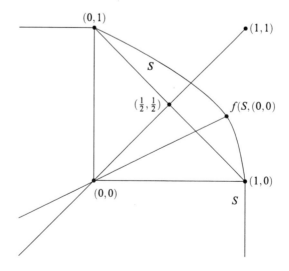

Fig. 2 Illustrating the proof of Theorem 2

$e = (0, 0)$, $g(S) = (1, 1)$, $f_1(S, e) > f_2(S, e)$ (See Fig. 2). Then, in view of Disc of f, we have:

$$D(S, f, f(S, (0, 0))) \text{ is discriminating.} \tag{4}$$

By Spl, $f(\text{comv}(\{(1, 0), (0, 1)\}), (0, 0)) = (\frac{1}{2}, \frac{1}{2})$, so by Lin, $f(\text{comv}(\{(1, 0), (0, 1)\}), (\beta, \beta)) = (\frac{1}{2}, \frac{1}{2})$ for every $\beta \le 0$. From this, we conclude by ISIR that $f(S, (\beta, \beta)) = f(S, (0, 0))$ for every $\beta \le 0$. Since, by Lin of f, also $f(S, x) = f(S, (0, 0))$ for every $x \le (0, 0)$ with x on the straight line through $(0, 0)$ and $f(S, (0, 0))$, we conclude that (4) is violated.   □

The Kalai–Rosenthal solution satisfies all properties introduced in Sect. 3 except, typically, INIR.

6 The Kalai–Smorodinsky Solution

The *Kalai–Smorodinsky solution* $KS : \mathcal{B} \to \mathbb{R}^2$ assigns to every game (S, d) the point of $P(S)$ on the straight line through d and the so-called *utopia point* $h(S, d) := g(\text{com}(S_d))$ of (S, d). So, in contrast with the Kalai–Rosenthal solution, this solution depends only on the individually rational subset of S, for a game (S, d). In other words, KS satisfies INIR. It was introduced by Raiffa (1953) and characterized by Kalai and Smorodinsky (1975), who proposed it as an alternative for the Nash solution. They used a monotonicity property, usually referred to as *individual monotonicity*.

Note that KS is a standard solution which satisfies Spl, Disc, and ISIR (and of course WPO and WSpl). Further, it does not satisfy Lin but it does have the Restricted Linearity property Rlin. Recall that in RLin attention is restricted to games (S, d) with $S = \text{com}(S_d)$ (which is equivalent to $h(S, d) = g(S)$) and that its conclusion applies only to points x on the straight line through d and $f(S, d)$ which lie "below" d and for which, consequently, $h(S, x)$ is constant, namely $h(S, d)$, for a standard solution f.

The following example shows that KS does not have the differentiability property.

Example 1 Let $S = \text{comv}(\{(1, \frac{1}{2}), (0, 1)\})$ and $d = (0, 0)$. Then $KS(S, d) = (\frac{2}{3}, \frac{2}{3})$, and the status quo set $D(S, KS, (\frac{2}{3}, \frac{2}{3}))$ is the graph of the function j defined by:

$$j(t) := \begin{cases} t & \text{for } -\infty < t \le 0 \\ 2t - \frac{3}{2}t^2 & \text{for } 0 \le t \le \frac{1}{3} \\ \frac{1}{2}t + \frac{1}{3} & \text{for } \frac{1}{2} \le t < \frac{2}{3}. \end{cases}$$

Note that j is not differentiable, so KS does not satisfy Diff.

Another example exhibits a standard solution satisfying INIR, Spl, RLin, and ISIR, but not Disc, and which is not the Kalai–Smorodinsky solution.

Example 2 For a non-rectangular game (S, d), let $\max(S, d)$ be the maximal (with respect to $\geq$) point of $\{x \in S_d \mid \text{com}(S_x) = \text{com}(S_d)\}$, and otherwise let $\max(S, d) = d$. We define the solution $f : B \to \mathbb{R}^2$ by $f(S, d) := KS(S, \max(S, d))$. It is an easy exercise (left to the reader) to show that this is a standard solution with the four properties mentioned above and not Disc.

We conclude from this example that the four properties INIR, Spl, RLin, and ISIR do not determine a unique standard solution. Adding Disc, however, we obtain a characterization of KS.

Theorem 3 *The Kalai–Smorodinsky solution is the unique standard solution with the properties INIR, Spl, RLin, ISIR, and Disc.*

Proof We leave it to the reader to verify that KS is a standard solution which has the five mentioned properties. Let now $f : B \to \mathbb{R}^2$ be a standard solution which has these five properties, and let $(S, d) \in B$. We want to prove:

$$f(S, d) = KS(S, d). \tag{5}$$

In view of INIR of f and KS we may suppose that $S = \text{com}(S_d)$. For notational convenience we assume (without loss of generality) $d = (0, 0)$ and $h(S, (0, 0)) = (1, 1)$. In view of Spl and Rlin, we have $f(\text{comv}(\{(1, 0), (0, 1)\}), (\alpha, \alpha)) = (\frac{1}{2}, \frac{1}{2})$ for every $\alpha \leq 0$, so by ISIR of f we have $f(S, (\alpha, \alpha)) = f(S, (0, 0))$ for every $\alpha \leq 0$. Since, in view of Disc, the status quo set of S with respect to f and $f(S, d)$ is discriminating, we conclude with Rlin that $f(S, (0, 0)) = KS(S, (0, 0))$, thus that (5) holds. $\square$

7 The Egalitarian Solution

The *Egalitarian solution* $E : B \to \mathbb{R}^2$ assigns to every game (S, d) the point $z \in W(S)$ such that $z_1 - d_1 = z_2 - d_2$. Both players receive the same surplus utility above status quo, so the Egalitarian solution implies a utility comparison between the players. The Egalitarian solution has been characterized in several ways, e.g. Kalai (1977) and Peters (1992). We present another characterization below.

Note that E satisfies IR, WPO but not PO, Wspl but not Spl, INIR, ISIR, Lin (and RLin), Disc, and Diff. So E is not a standard solution, and only splits the difference in *symmetric* triangular games. A characterization is given in the following theorem.

Theorem 4 *The egalitarian solution is the unique solution with the properties IR, WPO, WSpl, INIR, ISIR, Lin, and Disc.*

Proof (See Fig. 3.) We have already noticed that E has the properties listed in the theorem. Now let f be a solution with these properties, and let $T = \text{comv}(\{x, y\})$ where $x, y \in \mathbb{R}^2$ such that $x_1 < y_1$ and $x_2 > y_2$. We first prove

$$f(T, (x_1, y_2)) = E(T, (x_1, y_2)). \tag{6}$$

Fig. 3 Illustrating the proof
of Theorem 4

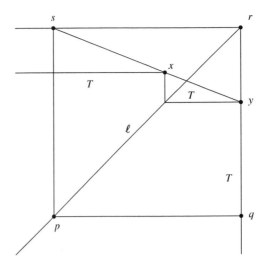

If $y_1 - x_1 = x_2 - y_2$, then (6) follows from WSpl. Suppose, without loss of generality, that $y_1 - x_1 > x_2 - y_2$. Then let $r \in \mathbb{R}^2$ be defined by $r = (y_1, y_2 + y_1 - x_1)$, let s be the point on the straight line through x and y with second coordinate r_2, and let $p, q \in \mathbb{R}^2$ with $p_1 = s_1$, $q_1 = r_1$, $p_2 = q_2 < r_2$ such that p, q, r, and s are the vertices of a square. Let ℓ be the straight line through p and r. By WSpl and Lin, we have $f(\text{comv}(\{q, s\}), z) = \frac{1}{2}(q + s)$ for all z on ℓ with $z \le p$. By WPO and IR, $f(\text{comv}(\{y, s\}), p) \in \text{conv}(\{q, y\}) \cup \text{conv}(\{y, s\})$. Let m denote the straight line through p and $f(\text{comv}(\{y, s\}), p)$. By Lin, we have $f(\text{comv}(\{y, s\}), z) = f(\text{comv}(\{y, s\}), p)$ for all z on m with $z \le p$. By ISIR, also $f(\text{comv}(\{y, s\}), z) = f(\text{comv}(\{y, s\}), p)$ for all z on ℓ with $z \le p$. So by Disc, ℓ and m must coincide. Consequently, $f(\text{comv}(\{y, s\}), p) = E(\text{comv}(\{y, s\}), p)$, since the slope of ℓ is equal to 1. Hence by Lin, $f(\text{comv}(\{y, s\}), (x_1, y_2)) = E(\text{comv}(\{y, s\}), (x_1, y_2))$. Now (6) follows by INIR.

Next, let (S, d) be an arbitrary game. Then, with the aid of (6) applied to the triangular game $(T(S_d), d)$ (see Sect. 3), the proof of $f(S, d) = E(S, d)$ is analogous to the proof of Theorem 3.   □

8 The Continuous Raiffa Solution

This section is devoted to a characterization of a solution originally proposed by Raiffa (1953). For a game (S, d), let us start in the point d and go into the direction of the utopia point $h(S, d)$. Having travelled an infinitesimally small distance Δd, we change our route into the direction of the new utopia point $h(S, d + \Delta d)$. In this way we travel to some point on the Pareto optimal frontier of S, which will be the solution outcome. The solution just described is the *Continuous Raiffa solution*: it is based on the idea underlying the (Raiffa–)Kalai–Smorodinsky solution combined with a continuous adjustment of the utopia point. As Raiffa saw it, this solution has also a Nash-like feature: the curve described above will intersect the Pareto optimal subset of S with a slope equal to the negative of the slope of a supporting line of the set of feasible outcomes at the point of intersection, i.e., the solution point. The reader should compare this with condition (∗) in the proof of Theorem 1.

We shall now formally describe the continuous Raiffa solution. For a game (S, d) in B, let the *upper Pareto function* $u : (-\infty, g_1(S)) \to \mathbb{R}$ be defined by $u(\alpha) := \max\{\beta \in \mathbb{R} \mid (\alpha, \beta) \in S\}$ for every $\alpha \in (-\infty, g_1(S))$ and let the *lower Pareto function* $l : (-\infty, g_2(S)) \to \mathbb{R}$ be defined by $l(\beta) := \max\{\alpha \in \mathbb{R} \mid (\alpha, \beta) \in S\}$ for every $\beta \in (-\infty, g_2(S))$. Let further the function $r_S : \mathrm{int}(S) \to \mathbb{R}$ be defined by

$$r_S(x) := (u(x_1) - x_2)(l(x_2) - x_1)^{-1} \text{ for every } x \in \mathrm{int}(S). \qquad (7)$$

The function r_S assigns to every interior point x of S the slope of the straight line through x and the utopia point $h(S, x)$. We consider the following problem:

Find a solution R of the first order ordinary differential equation $dx_2/dx_1 = r_S(x)$ $(x \in \mathrm{int}(S))$, defined on an interval (γ, δ) containing d_1, with $R(d_1) = d_2$ and with the point $(\delta, \lim_{x_1 \to \delta} R(x_1)) \in W(S)$.   (∗∗)

A solution R of problem (∗∗) is a differentiable strictly monotonically increasing function describing the curve in the first paragraph of this section, and the point $(\delta, \lim_{x_1 \to \delta} R(x_1))$ is the continuous Raiffa solution outcome of the game. We have:

Lemma 1 *Problem* (∗∗) *has a unique solution.*

Proof Let $a_1 = (a_1, a_2)$ be a point in the interior of S with $a > d$. Let $V(a)$ denote the rectangle with vertices (a_1, a_2), $(a_1, 2d_2 - a_2)$, $(2d_1 - a_1, a_2)$, $(2d_1 - a_1, 2d_2 - a_2)$ (see Fig. 4). Note that r_S is continuous on $V(a)$. We show that r_S satisfies a Lipschitz condition (with respect to x_2) on $V(a)$. To this end, let $2d_1 - a_1 \le x_1 \le a_1$, and let (x_1, x_2) and $(x_1, \bar{x}_2)$ in $V(a)$, say with $\bar{x}_2 \ge x_2$. It is easy to show, with the aid of the convexity of S, that $r_S(x_1, \bar{x}_2) \le r_S(x_1, x_2)$. Hence:

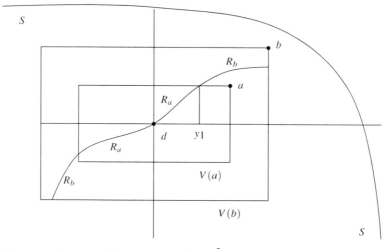

Fig. 4 Illustrating the proof of Lemma 1; here, $b := a^2$

$$|r_S(x_1, \bar{x}_2) - r_S(x_1, x_2)| = r_S(x_1, x_2) - r_S(x_1, \bar{x}_2)$$
$$= (u(x_1) - x_2)(l(x_2) - x_1)^{-1} - (u(x_1) - \bar{x}_2)$$
$$(l(\bar{x}_2) - x_1)^{-1}$$
$$= (\bar{x}_2 - x_2)(l(x_2) - x_1)^{-1}$$
$$\leq (\bar{x}_2 - x_2)(l(a_2) - a_1)^{-1}.$$

This shows that r_S satisfies a Lipschitz condition with Lipschitz constant $(l(a_2) - a_1)^{-1}$. So, by a standard theorem (e.g., Theorem 2.3 or Theorem 3.1 in Chap. 1 of Coddington and Levinson (1984)) there exists a unique solution R_a of the equation $dx_2/dx_1 = r_S(x)$ ($x \in V(a)$) with $R_a(d_1) = d_2$, and with either

(i) $R_a(y_1) = a_2$ for some $d_1 < y_1 < a_1$, or
(ii) $R_a(a_1)$ exists (and $d_2 < R_a(a_1) \leq a_2$).

Let $a^1 := a$. The next step is to choose a point a^2 in the interior of S with $a^2 > (y_1, R_{a^1}(y_1))$ if (i) above holds, and $a^2 > (a^1_1, R_{a^1}(a^1_1))$ if (ii) holds, and then repeat the whole argument for the rectangle $V(a^2)$, which is defined similar to $V(a^1)$. We then obtain a unique solution R_{a^2} of the equation $dx_2/dx_1 = r_S(x)$ ($x \in V(a^2)$) with $R_{a^2}(d_1) = d_2$, which (by uniqueness) coincides with R_{a^1} on the common part of their domains. By choosing, next, points $a^3, a^4, \ldots$ similarly as a^2, and such that the sequence $a^1, a^2, a^3, a^4, \ldots$ approaches $W(S)$, we obtain the desired result, with $R := R_{a^1}$ on the domain of R_{a^1}, $R := R_{a^2}$ on the domain of R_{a^2}, and so on.   □

In view of Lemma 1, the Continuous Raiffa solution, from now on denoted $CR : \mathcal{B} \rightarrow \mathbb{R}^2$, is well defined. Also, the graph of the unique solution R of (∗∗) is a subset of the status quo set of S with respect to CR and $CR(S, d)$. But in fact, it can be shown (see Livne, 1989b) that (except for rectangular games) the unique solutions of (∗∗) for different status quo points either coincide completely, or result in different limit points on the boundary. This implies that the Continuous Raiffa solution satisfies Disc.

Also, CR is individually rational (since R in (∗∗) is monotonically increasing) and Pareto optimal (since the part of the graph of R which is in S_d, is a subset of conv($\{d\} \cup P(S)$), as follows from (7). So CR is a standard solution. Further, it follows in a more or less straightforward manner from the definition of CR that it satisfies ISIR, INIR, Spl, and Diff.

We now show that all these properties together characterize CR.

Theorem 5 *The Continuous Raiffa solution is the unique standard solution with the properties ISIR, INIR, Spl, Disc, and Diff.*

Proof We have already observed that CR has all mentioned properties. Now let $f : \mathcal{B} \rightarrow \mathbb{R}^2$ be a standard solution satisfying ISIR, INIR, Spl, Disc, and Diff. Let (S, d) be a non-rectangular game (see Fig. 5). By Diff, there is a differentiable function $g : (\alpha, f_1(S, d)) \rightarrow \mathbb{R}$ for some $\alpha < d_1$ such that $\{x \geq d \mid x \in \text{int}(S), f(S, x) =$

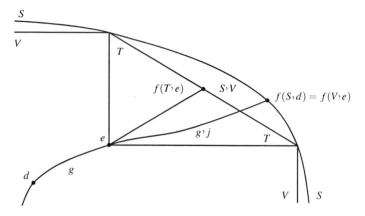

Fig. 5 Illustrating the proof of Theorem 5

$f(S, d)\}$ is the graph of that function on the interval $[d_1, f_1(S, d))$. Let $d_1 \leq \beta < f_1(S, d)$. In order to prove that $CR(S, d) = f(S, d)$ we have to prove:

$$g'(\beta) = (u(\beta) - g(\beta))(l(g(\beta)) - \beta)^{-1}. \tag{8}$$

Denote $e := (\beta, g(\beta))$, and $V := \text{com}(S_e)$. By INIR we have $f(V, e) = f(S, d)$, and by Disc: $D(V, f, f(V, e))$ is discriminating. So by Diff, there is a differentiable function $j : (\gamma, f_1(S, d)) \to \mathbb{R}$ for some $\gamma < e_1$ such that $\{x \geq e \mid x \in \text{int}(V), f(V, x) = f(S, d)\}$ is the graph of that function on $[e_1, f_1(S, d))$. By INIR, the graphs of g and j coincide on $[e_1, f_1(S, d))$. So in order to prove (8), it is sufficient to show:

$$j'(e_1) = (u(e_1) - j(e_1))(l(j(e_1)) - e_1)^{-1}. \tag{9}$$

Now consider the game (T, e) where $T := \text{comv}(\{(e_1, u(e_1)), (l(e_2), e_2)\})$. By Disc, $D(T, f, f(T, e))$ is discriminating. By ISIR we have: $\{x \in D(T, f, f(T, e)) \mid \gamma < x_1 \leq e_1\}$ is equal to the graph of j on $(\gamma, e_1]$. By INIR and Spl, we have $\{x \in D(T, f, f(T, e)) \mid e_1 \leq x_1 < f_1(T, e)\}$ is equal to $\{\alpha e + (1 - \alpha)(\frac{1}{2}(e_1, u(e_1)) + \frac{1}{2}(l(e_2), e_2)) \mid 0 < \alpha \leq 1\}$. By Diff applied to $D(T, f, f(T, e))$, we conclude that (9) holds. □

9 Overview, Comparison and Independence of the Properties

All solutions occurring in this chapter have been characterized by different subsets of one family of properties, and none of the properties is the "privilege" of one particular solution. Thus, rather than emphasizing the differences between the solutions, our results show the relationships between them.

Table 1 supports these statements. In this table also the so-called *Super-Additive Solution PM* proposed in Perles and Maschler (1981) is included, in order to

Table 1 Overview of properties and solutions. A "+" means that a particular solution has a particular property, a "−" means that the solution does not have the property. Characterizing (sets of) properties are indicated by ∗. The numbers between parentheses refer to the examples showing independence, see the text.

Properties	N	KR	KS	E	CR	PM
IR	$+^*$	$+^*$	$+^*$	$+^*$	$+^*$	$+$
PO	$+^*$	$+^*$	$+^*$	$-$	$+^*$	$+$
WPO	$+$	$+$	$+$	$+^*$	$+$	$+$
Spl	$+^*$	$+^*$	$+^*$	$-$	$+^*$	$+$
WSpl	$+$	$+$	$+$	$+^*$	$+$	$+$
INIR	$+^*$ (1)	$-$	$+^*$ (1)	$+^*$ (1)	$+^*$ (1)	$+$
ISIR	$-$	$+^*$ (3)	$+^*$ (5)	$+^*$ (8)	$+^*$ (10)	$+$
Lin	$+^*$ (2)	$+^*$ (2)	$-$	$+^*$ (2)	$-$	$-$
RLin	$+$	$+$	$+^*$ (6)	$+$	$-$	$+$
Disc	$-$	$+^*$ (4)	$+^*$ (7)	$+^*$ (9)	$+^*$ (11)	$-^a$
Diff	$+$	$+$	$-$	$+$	$+^*$ (2)	$+^a$

[a] For the PM solution, no status quo set is ever discriminating and therefore it trivially satisfies Diff. However, the individually rational part of a status quo set may have non-smooth points.

illustrate that the properties used in this chapter are not tailor made for particular solutions. The table shows which solutions satisfy which properties, and which properties are sufficient to characterize a particular solution. Proofs, as far as not contained in the foregoing sections, are left to the reader.

We conclude this section by reflecting on the independence of the properties used in the five characterizations. We have seen already (Remark 1) that IR is implied by the combination of PO and INIR: this fact may be used in the characterizations of the solutions N, KS, and KR. Although further relaxations may be possible, we shall pay no further attention to the properties (W)PO and IR. Omitting (W)Spl may lead to characterizations of nonsymmetric solutions: also this point will not be further elaborated.

We shall now consider the remaining properties in a systematic way. Corresponding to each number in Table 1 we shall give an example of a solution different from the one being characterized (column) and having all the properties (starred, in the column) except for the property with that particular number.

(1) KR

(2) KS

(3) Take $f : \mathcal{B} \to \mathbb{R}^2$ defined by $f(S,d) = N(S,d)$ if $P(S)$ is smooth in $N(S,d)$, $f(S,d) = KR(S,d)$ otherwise.

(4) For $(S,d) \in \mathcal{B}$, let $\bar{p}(S)$ and $\underline{p}(S)$ denote the left and right endpoints, respectively, of $P(S)$, and let $m(S) := KS(S, (\bar{p}_1(S), \underline{p}_2(S)))$. We define a solution $f : \mathcal{B} \to \mathbb{R}^2$ by defining its status quo sets, as follows:

$$D(S,f,x) := \begin{cases} \{s \in \text{int}(S) \mid s_2 = x_2\} & \text{if } x \in P(S) \text{ with } x_2 > m_2(S) \\ \{s \in \text{int}(S) \mid s_1 = x_1\} & \text{if } x \in P(S) \text{ with } x_2 < m_2(S) \\ \{s \in \text{int}(S) \mid s \le x\} & \text{if } x = m(S) \\ \emptyset & \text{otherwise.} \end{cases}$$

(5) Take $f : \mathcal{B} \rightarrow \mathbb{R}^2$ defined by $f(S, d) = N(S, d)$ if $P(S)$ is smooth in $N(S, d)$, $f(S, d) = KS(S, d)$ otherwise.

(6) CR

(7) See Example 2.

(8) Take $f : \mathcal{B} \rightarrow \mathbb{R}^2$ defined by $f(S, d) = N(S, d)$ if $P(S)$ is smooth in $N(S, d)$, $f(S, d) = E(S, d)$ otherwise.

(9) Let, for $(S, d) \in \mathcal{B}$, $\max(S, d)$ be the point defined in Example 2, and let $f(S, d) := E(S, \max(S, d))$.

(10) N

(11) Let, for $(S, d) \in \mathcal{B}$, $\max(S, d)$ be the point defined in Example 2, and let $f(S, d) := CR(S, \max(S, d))$.

10 Overview of Related Literature

In this section we briefly reference the main literature on the topic of this chapter. We apologize beforehand for not being complete.

Modified and extended versions of some of the results of Peters (1986), notably on the Nash solution and the continuous Raiffa solution, were published in Peters and van Damme (1991). In particular, these authors replace the Linearity property by a weaker condition called *Disagreement Point Convexity* and use this in a characterization of the n-person Nash bargaining solution.

For more results on and alternative characterizations of the Continuous Raiffa solution see the work of Livne (1989a, 1989b) and Furth (1990). These authors provide proofs of the fact that CR is discriminating. See also Livne (1986) for an early reference on changing status quo points.

Another natural condition is *disagreement point monotonicity*: if the status quo point changes in favor of one of the players, then the solution outcome should also change favor of that player. Most well-known solutions have this property, see Thomson (1987). Chun and Thomson (1990a, 1990b) obtain, among other results, a characterization of the n-person Nash bargaining solution using a modified version of disagreement point convexity.

Calvo and Gutiérrez (1994) use status quo sets to extend the Perles–Maschler solution (Perles and Maschler, 1981) to games with more than two players.

Calvo and Peters (2000) characterize the two-person equal area bargaining solution by properties of its status quo set.

Recently, Anbarci and Sun (2009) use properties of the status quo set to derive, among other things, a characterization of a discrete version of the Raiffa solution.

Finally, we mention that properties of the status quo sets (in particular, convexity) already played a role in the literature on arbitration games (see, e.g., Tijs & Jansen, 1982).

Acknowledgments Special thanks go to Dave Furth for his stimulating remarks on Peters (1986), which forms the basis for this chapter.

References

Anbarci, N., & Sun, C. (2009). *Interim outcomes and bargaining solutions*. Working Paper, Deakin University, Australia.

Calvo, E., & Gutiérrez, E. (1994). Extension of the Perles–Maschler solution to N-person bargaining games. *International Journal of Game Theory, 23*, 325–346.

Coddington, E. A., & Levinson, N. (1984). *Theory of ordinal differential equations*. Malabar, FL: Robert E. Krieger Publishing Company, Inc.

Calvo, E., & Peters, H. (2000). Dynamics and axiomatics of the equal area solution. *International Journal of Game Theory, 29*, 81–92.

Chun, Y., & Thomson, W. (1990a). Bargaining problems with uncertain disagreement points. *Econometrica, 58*, 951–959.

Chun, Y., & Thomson, W. (1990b). Nash solution and uncertain disagreement points. *Games and Economic Behavior, 2*, 213–223.

Furth, D. (1990). Solving bargaining games by differential equations. *Mathematics of Operations Research, 15*, 724–735.

Kalai, E. (1977). Proportional solutions to bargaining situations: Interpersonal utility comparisons. *Econometrica, 45*, 1623–1630.

Kalai, E., & Rosenthal, R. W. (1978). Arbitration of two-party disputes under ignorance. *International Journal of Game Theory, 7*, 65–72.

Kalai, E., & Smorodinsky, M. (1975). Other solutions to Nash's bargaining problem. *Econometrica, 43*, 513–518.

Livne, Z. (1986). The bargaining problem: Axioms concerning changes in the conflict point. *Economics Letters, 21*, 131–134.

Livne, Z. (1989a). Axiomatic characterizations of the Raiffa and the Kalai–Smorodinsky solutions to the bargaining problem. *Operations Research, 37*, 972–980.

Livne, Z. (1989b). On the status quo sets induced by the Raiffa solution to the two-person bargaining problem. *Mathematics of Operations Research, 14*, 688–692.

Luce, R. D., & Raiffa, H. (1957). *Games and decisions*. New York: John Wiley and Sons.

Nash, J. F. (1950). The bargaining problem. *Econometrica, 18*, 155–162.

Owen, G. (1995). *Game theory*. New York: Academic Press.

Perles, M. A., & Maschler, M. (1981). The super-additive solution for the Nash bargaining game. *International Journal of Game Theory, 10*, 163–193.

Peters, H. (1986). *Characterizations of bargaining solutions by properties of their status quo sets*. Research Memorandum RM-86-012, University of Limburg, Maastricht.

Peters, H. (1992). *Axiomatic bargaining game theory*. Dordrecht: Kluwer.

Peters, H., & van Damme, E. (1991). Charaterizing the Nash and Raiffa bargaining solutions by properties of their status quo sets. *Mathematics of Operations Research, 16*, 447–461.

Peters, H., & Tijs, S. (1985). Characterization of all individually monotonic bargaining solutions. *International Journal of Game Theory, 14*, 219–228.

Raiffa, H. (1953). Arbitration schemes for generalized two-person games. *Annals of Mathematics Studies, 28*, 361–387.

Thomson, W. (1987).Monotonicity of bargaining solutions with respect to the disagreement point. *Journal of Economic Theory, 42*, 50–58.

Tijs, S., & Jansen, M. (1982). On the existence of values for arbitration games. *International Journal of Game Theory, 11*, 87–104.

Monotonicity Properties of Interval Solutions and the Dutta–Ray Solution for Convex Interval Games

Elena Yanovskaya, Rodica Branzei, and Stef Tijs

1 Introduction

Cooperative interval games are introduced and studied in Alparslan Gök, Miquel, and Tijs (2009) and Alparslan Gök, Branzei, and Tijs (2008, 2009), where the interval core plays a central role. Such games model situations with cooperation with incomplete information of agents and of their coalitions about the payoffs they can obtain for sure.

There are many real-life situations in which people or businesses are uncertain about their coalitional payoffs. Situations with uncertain payoffs in which the agents cannot await the realizations of their coalition payoffs cannot be modeled according to classical game theory. Several models that are useful to handle uncertain payoffs exist in the game theory literature. We refer here to chance-constrained games (Charnes & Granot, 2007), cooperative games with stochastic payoffs (Suijs, Borm, de Waegenaere, & Tijs, 1999), cooperative games with random payoffs (Timmer, Borm, & Tijs, 2005). In all these models stochastics plays an important role.

This paper deals with a model of cooperative games where only bounds for payoffs of coalitions are known with certainty. Such games are called cooperative interval games. Formally, a *cooperative interval game* in coalitional form (Alparslan Gök et al., 2009) is an ordered pair $\langle N, w \rangle$ where $N = \{1, 2, \ldots, n\}$ is the set of players, and $w : 2^N \rightarrow I(\mathbb{R})$ is the characteristic function such that $w(\emptyset) = [0, 0]$, where $I(\mathbb{R})$ is the set of all nonempty, compact intervals in $\mathbb{R}$. For each $S \in 2^N$, the worth set (or worth interval) $w(S)$ of the coalition S in the interval game $\langle N, w \rangle$ is of the form $[\underline{w}(S), \overline{w}(S)]$. We denote by IG_N the family of all interval games with player set N. Note that if all the worth intervals are degenerate intervals, i.e. $\underline{w}(S) = \overline{w}(S)$ for each $S \in 2^N$, then the interval game $\langle N, w \rangle$ corresponds in a natural way to

E. Yanovskaya (✉)
St. Petersburg Institute for Economics and Mathematics, Russian Academy of Sciences, 191187 St. Petersburg, Russia
e-mail: eyanov@emi.nw.ru

A. Van Deemen, A. Rusinowska (eds.), *Collective Decision Making,*
Theory and Decision Library C 43, DOI 10.1007/978-3-642-02865-6_16,
© Springer-Verlag Berlin Heidelberg 2010

the classical cooperative game $\langle N, v \rangle$ where $v(S) = \underline{w}(S)$ for all $S \in 2^N$. Some classical TU-games associated with an interval game $w \in IG_N$ will play a key role, namely the *border* games $\langle N, \underline{w} \rangle$, $\langle N, \overline{w} \rangle$ and the *length* game $\langle N, |w| \rangle$, where $|w|(S) = \overline{w}(S) - \underline{w}(S)$ for each $S \in 2^N$. Note that $\overline{w} = \underline{w} + |w|$. An interval solution concept $\mathcal{F}$ on IG_N is a map assigning to each interval game $\langle N, w \rangle \in IG_N$ a set of n-dimensional vectors whose components belong to $I(\mathbb{R})$. We denote by $I(\mathbb{R})^N$ the set of all such interval payoff vectors. Cooperative interval games are very suitable to describe real-life situations in which people or firms that consider cooperation have to sign a contract when they cannot pin down the attainable coalition payoffs, knowing with certainty only their lower and upper bounds. The contract should specify how the players' payoff shares will be obtained when the uncertainty of the worth of the grand coalition is resolved at an ex post stage. In the following we briefly explain how interval solutions for cooperative interval games are useful to support decision making regarding cooperation and related binding contracts. A vector interval allocation obtained by an agreed upon solution concept offers at the ex ante stage an estimation of what individual players may receive, between two bounds, when the uncertainty on the reward of the grand coalition is resolved in the ex post stage. We notice that the agreement on a particular interval allocation $(I_1, I_2, \ldots, I_n)$ based on an interval solution concept merely says that the payoff x_i that player i will receive in the interim or ex post stage is in the interval I_i. This is a very weak contract to settle cooperation within the grand coalition. Therefore, writing down in the contract the procedure to be used to transform an interval allocation into a classical payoff vector when the uncertainty on $w(N)$ is resolved at the ex post stage, is compulsory. Such procedures are described in Branzei, Tijs, and Alparslan Gök (2008).

The first step in the study of interval game solutions is to extend classical theory of cooperative game solutions to interval games. For example, we can apply some single-valued solution concept to both border games, and in the case when the solution of the upper game weakly dominates that of the lower game, the corresponding interval vector could be admitted as the interval solution, *generated* by a classical cooperative game solution. Just in this manner the interval Shapley value for convex interval games was defined in Alparslan Gök et al., 2009. The same approach can be applied to the extension of set-valued solutions as well (Alparslan Gök et al., 2008, 2009).

Naturally, the problem of existence of such interval solution arises. In fact if for some interval game $\langle N, w \rangle$ the characteristic function values of the lower and upper games on the grand coalition coincide, i.e., $\underline{w}(N) = \overline{w}(N)$, then for any single-valued classical solution φ the (vector) inequality $\varphi(N, \underline{w}) \leq \varphi(N, \overline{w})$ is impossible, and this approach cannot be applied to the extension of the solution φ to the interval game $\langle N, w \rangle$.

It is clear that the possibility of the extension of a classical cooperative game solution to interval games depends both on the class of interval games into consideration and on monotonicity properties of the classical cooperative game solution itself. Thus, in the paper by Alparslan Gök et al., 2009 the class of convex interval games was introduced. It turned out that the most known cooperative game solutions such as the core, the Shapley value, and the Weber set are extendable to the class of convex interval games (though, as for the classical case, they exist on larger classes of interval games).

This paper examines different monotonicity properties of classical cooperative game solutions on the class of convex games and with the help of these properties verifies the existence or not existence of the corresponding interval game solutions.

A special attention is devoted to the extension of the (constrained egalitarian) Dutta–Ray solution (Dutta, 1990; Dutta & Ray, 1989) to the interval setting. It is shown that this solution exists on the class of convex interval games, belongs to the interval core, and has the same monotonicity properties as the classical Dutta–Ray solution. The last one has two nice axiomatic characterizations on the class of convex TU games both with the consistency axioms: the first uses the Davis–Maschler definition of the reduced games, and the second uses the Hart–Mas-Colell definition. It turns out that the interval Dutta–Ray solution has only one characterization with the help of consistency in the sense of Hart–Mas-Colell definition (HMC-consistency), because the Davis–Maschler reduced game of a convex interval game may not belong to the class of convex interval games.

The outline of the paper is as follows. In Sect. 2 we recall basic definitions, notation and results on (convex) interval games. In Sect. 3 we recall the known monotonicity properties of TU game solutions and connect them with the existence of the corresponding generated interval solutions and the inheritance by them of the monotonicity properties. In Sect. 4 we prove that the interval Dutta–Ray solution of a convex interval game belongs to the interval core of the game. The Lorenz domination on the product vector set is determined and it is shown that the interval Dutta–Ray solution Lorenz dominates each other interval core element. Section 5 provides an axiomatic characterization of the Dutta–Ray solution for convex interval games. We conclude in Sect. 6 with remarks about alternative ways to axiomatically characterize the (Dutta–Ray) constrained egalitarian interval solution on the class of convex interval games.

2 Definitions and Notation

An *interval game* is a triple $\langle N, (\underline{w}, \overline{w}) \rangle$ where N is a finite set of players, $\underline{w}, \overline{w} : 2^N \to \mathbb{R}$ are a *lower* and a *upper* characteristic functions, respectively, such that for each coalition $S \subset N$, $\underline{w}(S) \leq \overline{w}(S)$. The TU games $\langle N, \underline{w} \rangle$, $\langle N, \overline{w} \rangle$ are called the *lower* and the *upper* games of the interval game $\langle N, (\underline{w}, \overline{w}) \rangle$, respectively.

Let G_N be an arbitrary class of TU games with the player set N. Further we denote by IG_N the class of interval games with the player set N such that for any $\langle N, (\underline{w}, \overline{w}) \rangle \in IG_N$ both the lower and upper games $\langle N, \underline{w} \rangle$, $\langle N, \overline{w} \rangle$ belong to the class G_N.

Denote by $X(N, \underline{w})$, $X(N, \overline{w})$ the sets of feasible payoff vectors of the lower and upper games, and by $Y(N, \underline{w})$, $Y(N, \overline{w})$ the sets of *efficient* payoff vectors, respectively:

$$X(N, \underline{w}) = \{x \in \mathbb{R}^N \mid \sum_{i \in N} x_i \leq \underline{w}(N)\},$$
$$X(N, \overline{w}) = \{x \in \mathbb{R}^N \mid \sum_{i \in N} x_i \leq \overline{w}(N)\},$$

$$Y(N, \underline{w}) = \{x \in X(N, \underline{w}) \mid \sum_{i \in N} x_i = \underline{w}(N)\},$$
$$Y(N, \overline{w}) = \{x \in X(N, \overline{w}) \mid \sum_{i \in N} x_i = \overline{w}(N)\}.$$

Definition 1 A *single-valued solution (value)* ϕ for a class IG_N of interval games is a mapping assigning to each interval game $\langle N, (\underline{w}, \overline{w}) \rangle \in IG_N$ a pair of vectors $\phi(N, (\underline{w}, \overline{w})) = (x, y) \in \mathbb{R}^N \times \mathbb{R}^N$ such that $x \in X(N, \underline{w})$, $y \in X(N, \overline{w})$ and $x \leq y$.

Definition 2 An interval value ϕ on a class of interval games IG_N is *generated by a TU game value* φ if

$$\phi(N, (\underline{w}, \overline{w})) = (\varphi(N, \underline{w}), \varphi(N, \overline{w})). \tag{1}$$

Equality (1) implies that the inequality

$$\varphi(N, \underline{w}) \leq \varphi(N, \overline{w}) \tag{2}$$

should hold, and, hence, not all TU game values can be extended to the generated interval values, or some value can be extended only for some special classes of TU classical and interval games.

In the sequel we consider only interval values generated by some known TU classical game values.

Consider the class G_N^c of convex TU games with a finite set of players N. Define the class IG_N^c of *convex interval games* with the set of players N by the following way:

$$\langle N, (\underline{w}, \overline{w}) \rangle \in IG_N^c \iff \langle N, \overline{w} \rangle, \langle N, \underline{w} \rangle, \langle N, \overline{w} - \underline{w} \rangle \in G_N^c \text{ and } \underline{w}(S) \leq \overline{w}(S)$$
$$\text{for all } S \subset N.$$

Given a vector $x \in \mathbb{R}^N$ and a coalition $S \subset N$, by x_S we denote the projection of the vector x on the subspace $\mathbb{R}^S$, and by $x(S)$ the sum $x(S) = \sum_{i \in S} x_i$.

An interval $[a_1, a_2]$ *dominates* an interval $[b_1, b_2]$, $[a_1, a_2] \succcurlyeq [b_1, b_2]$, if $a_1 \geq b_1, a_2 \geq b_2$. An interval vector $\mathbf{a} = ([a_1, a_1'], \ldots, [a_n, a_n'])$ *dominates* an interval vector $\mathbf{b} = ([b_1, b_1'], \ldots, [b_n, b_n'])$, $\mathbf{a} \succcurlyeq \mathbf{b}$, if $[a_i, a_i'] \succcurlyeq [b_i, b_i']$ for $i = 1, \ldots, n$.

In the next section we study which TU game values for convex games can be extended to the generated interval values and which ones can not.

By $C(N, v)$ we denote the core of $\langle N, v \rangle$, and by $\mathcal{C}(N, w)$ the *interval core* of the interval game $\langle N, (\underline{w}, \overline{w}) \rangle$, $w = (\underline{w}, \overline{w})$:

$$\mathcal{C}(N, w) = \{(x, y) \in \mathbb{R}^N \times \mathbb{R}^N \mid x \in C(N, \underline{w}), y \in C(N, \overline{w}), x \leq y\}.$$

We notice that this definition is different from the usual one, which regards the interval core as a set of $|N|$-dimensional vectors in $I(\mathbb{R})^N$, but it is equivalent in its consequences.

3 Monotonicity Properties of TU Game Values and of the Corresponding Generated Interval Values

3.1 Existence of Interval Values Generated by TU Game Values

In this section we consider the interval values on the class of convex interval games IG_N^c.

Given a TU value φ for the class G_N^c, the existence of the generated by it interval value ϕ on IG_N^c, i.e. the fulfilment of inequality (2) is equivalent to the following monotonicity property of φ:

Convex monotonicity (CvM). If $\langle N, v \rangle$, $\langle N, v' \rangle$, $\langle N, v' - v \rangle \in G_N^c$, and $v'(S) \geq v(S)$ for all $S \subset N$, then $\varphi(N, v') \geq \varphi(N, v)$.

Let us compare this property with other known monotonicity properties of TU game solutions[1]:

Aggregate monotonicity (AM). If $v'(N) > v(N)$ and $v'(S) = v(S)$ for all $S \subsetneq N$, then $\varphi(N, v') \geq \varphi(N, v)$.

Contribution monotonicity (CM). For each $i \in N$ inequalities $v'(S \cup \{i\}) - v'(S) \geq v(S \cup \{i\}) - v(S)$ for all $S \not\ni i$ imply $\varphi_i(N, v') \geq \varphi_i(N, v)$.

Weak contribution monotonicity (WCM) (Hokari & van Gellekom, 2002). If for all $i \in N$ and all coalitions $S \not\ni i$ the inequalities $v'(S \cup \{i\}) - v'(S) \geq v(S \cup \{i\}) - v(S)$ hold, then $\varphi(N, v') \geq \varphi(N, v)$.

Note that all these properties were defined for games with the same sets of players. It is clear that

$$\text{CM} \implies \text{WCM} \implies \text{AM}. \tag{3}$$

Let us check where convex monotonicity is placed in relations (3).

Proposition 1 *On the class of convex games* G_N^c

$$\text{WCM} \implies \text{CvM} \implies \text{AM}.$$

Proof Let $\langle N, v \rangle$, $\langle N, v' \rangle$, $\langle N, v' - v \rangle$ be convex games such that $v'(S) \geq v(S)$ for all $S \subset N$. Then for all $i \in N$ and $S \not\ni i$

$$v'(S \cup \{i\}) - v'(S) \geq v(S \cup \{i\}) - v(S). \tag{4}$$

---

[1] The definitions of the properties are given for arbitrary classes of TU games, so they are not indicated.

If a value φ on G_N^c satisfies weak contribution monotonicity, then $\varphi(N, v') \geq \varphi(N, v)$, and φ satisfies convex monotonicity.

Let now φ' be any value on the class G_N^c that satisfies convex monotonicity. Then for games $\langle N, v \rangle$, $\langle N, v' \rangle$ inequalities (4) hold, inclusively for those such that $v(S) = v'(S)$ for all $S \subsetneqq N$, $v'(N) > v(N)$, implying $\varphi(N, v') \geq \varphi(N, v)$.

□

Relations (3) and Proposition 1 permit to check for what TU game values for convex games the generated interval values exist or not.

It is well-known that the Shapley value satisfies contribution monotonicity. Therefore, there exists the interval Shapley value on the class of convex interval games (Alparslan Gök et al., 2009).

On the other hand, it is known that the prenucleolus and the τ-value on the class of convex games do not satisfy aggregate monotonicity (Hokari, 2000; Hokari & van Gellekom, 2002). Therefore, the interval prenucleolus and the interval τ-value do not exist on the class IG_N^c.

The (constrained) egalitarian solution for TU games was defined by Dutta and Ray (1989) as the unique Lorenz maximal allocation in the Lorenz core. We call it the *Dutta–Ray solution (DR)*. This solution can be empty, its existence was proved in the same paper for the class of convex games. For each convex game $\langle N, v \rangle$ the Dutta–Ray solution is the unique allocation in the core which Lorenz dominates every other core allocation. This solution was characterized on the class of convex games by Dutta (1990) in two ways, both using consistency properties: he proved that the DR solution is the unique solution satisfying constrained egalitarianism (CE) for two-person games and consistency either in the definition due to Davis and Maschler (1965), or in the definition due to Hart and Mas-Colell (1987).

The Dutta–Ray solution on the class of convex TU games possesses many attractive properties. In particular, Hokari and van Gellekom (2002) proved that the DR solution over the class of convex games satisfies *weak contribution monotonicity*, hence, by Proposition 1 it satisfies convex monotonicity providing the existence of the generated Dutta–Ray interval solution on the class of convex interval games.

The properties and a characterization of the interval Dutta–Ray solution will be the main subject of the next sections.

The last monotonicity property compares players' payoffs with respect to solution vectors in the initial game and its subgames:

Population monotonicity. If $\langle N, v \rangle$ is a convex game and $N' \subset N$, then $\varphi_i(N, v) \geq \varphi_i(N', v)$ for all $i \in N'$, where $\langle N', v \rangle$ is the subgame of $\langle N, v \rangle$.

This property assures the existence of population monotonic allocation schemes (Sprumont, 1990). Recall that for a game $v \in G_N$, which is totally balanced, a scheme $a = (a_{iS})_{i \in S, S \in 2^N \setminus \{\emptyset\}}$ of real numbers is a population monotonic allocation scheme of v if

(i) $\sum_{i \in S} a_{iS} = v(S)$ for all $S \in 2^N \setminus \{\emptyset\}$,
(ii) $a_{iS} \leq a_{iT}$ for all $S, T \in 2^N \setminus \{\emptyset\}$ with $S \subset T$ and for each $i \in S$.

We notice that convexity of v is a sufficient condition for the existence of population monotonic allocation schemes.

3.2 Inheritance of Monotonicity Properties by Interval Values

It is not difficult to extend the above defined monotonicity properties (except for convex monotonicity) to interval values. For interval values we demand that the properties hold both for the lower and upper games. Let ϕ be an interval value for the class IG_N^C of interval convex games. The following definitions are the extensions to interval convex games of the given above monotonicity properties of TU game values.

Aggregate monotonicity. If $\langle N, (\underline{w}, \overline{w}) \rangle$ and $\langle N, (\underline{w}', \overline{w}') \rangle$ are interval convex games such that $\underline{w}(S) = \underline{w}'(S)$, $\overline{w}(S) = \overline{w}'(S)$ for all $S \subsetneq N$, and $\underline{w}'(N) > \underline{w}(N)$, $\overline{w}'(N) > \overline{w}(N)$, then $\phi(N, (\underline{w}', \overline{w}')) \succcurlyeq \phi(N, (\underline{w}, \overline{w}))$.

Contribution monotonicity. For interval convex games $\langle N, (\underline{w}, \overline{w}) \rangle$ and $\langle N, (\underline{w}', \overline{w}') \rangle$ and for each $i \in N$ inequalities $\underline{w}'(S \cup \{i\}) - \underline{w}'(S) \geq \underline{w}(S \cup \{i\}) - \underline{w}(S)$, $\overline{w}'(S \cup \{i\}) - \overline{w}'(S) \geq \overline{w}(S \cup \{i\}) - \overline{w}(S)$ for all $S \not\ni i$ imply $\phi_i(N, (\underline{w}', \overline{w}')) \succcurlyeq \phi_i(N, (\underline{w}, \overline{w}))$.

Weak contribution monotonicity. If for interval convex games $\langle N, (\underline{w}, \overline{w}) \rangle$ and $\langle N, (\underline{w}', \overline{w}') \rangle$, for all $i \in N$, and all coalitions $S \not\ni i$ the inequalities $\underline{w}'(S \cup \{i\}) - \underline{w}'(S) \geq \underline{w}(S \cup \{i\}) - \underline{w}(S)$, $\overline{w}'(S \cup \{i\}) - \overline{w}'(S) \geq \overline{w}(S \cup \{i\}) - \overline{w}(S)$ hold, then $\phi(N, (\underline{w}', \overline{w}')) \succcurlyeq \phi(N, (\underline{w}, \overline{w}))$.

Population monotonicity. If $\langle N, (\underline{w}, \overline{w}) \rangle$ is an interval convex game and $N' \subset N$, then $\phi_i(N, (\underline{w}, \overline{w})) \succcurlyeq \phi_i(N', (\underline{w}, \overline{w}))$ for all $i \in N'$, where $\langle N', (\underline{w}, \overline{w}) \rangle$ is the subgame of $\langle N, (\underline{w}, \overline{w}) \rangle$.

From the definitions it follows that all these properties are inherited by interval values generated by TU game values: if a value φ on the class of TU convex games G_N^C satisfies one of the monotonicity properties, then the generated interval value ϕ on the class IG_N^C satisfies the same property in the interval setting.

In particular, since the Shapley value and the Dutta–Ray solution on the class of convex games are population monotonic, we obtain that the interval Shapley value and the interval Dutta–Ray solution are population monotonic on the class of convex interval games as well.

This last monotonicity property provides the existence of population monotonic interval allocation schemes (Alparslan Gök et al., 2009). Recall that for a game $w \in IG_N$ a scheme $A = (A_{iS})_{i \in S, S \in 2^N \setminus \{\emptyset\}}$ with $A_{iS} \in I(\mathbb{R})^N$ is a population monotonic interval allocation scheme of w if

(i) $\sum_{i \in S} A_{iS} = w(S)$ for all $S \in 2^N \setminus \{\emptyset\}$,
(ii) $A_{iS} \preccurlyeq A_{iT}$ for all $S, T \in 2^N \setminus \{\emptyset\}$ with $S \subset T$ and for each $i \in S$.

We notice that convexity of w is a sufficient condition for the existence of population monotonic interval allocation schemes.

4 The Interval Dutta–Ray Solution on the Class of Convex Interval Games

4.1 Properties of the Interval Dutta–Ray Solution

The solution CE of *constrained egalitarianism* on the class of two-person superadditive games is defined for each game $\langle \{i, j\}, v \rangle$ as follows:

$$
\mathrm{CE}_i(\{i, j\}, v) = \begin{cases} \frac{v(\{i, j\})}{2} & \text{if } \frac{v(\{i, j\})}{2} \geq \max\{v(\{i\}), v(\{j\})\}, \\ v(\{i\}), & \text{if } v(\{j\}) \leq \frac{v(\{i, j\})}{2} < v(\{i\}), \\ v(\{i, j\}) - v(\{j\}), & \text{if } v(\{i\}) \leq \frac{v(\{i, j\})}{2} < v(\{j\}). \end{cases} \tag{5}
$$

Definition (5) shows that the CE solution assigns to each two-person superadditive game the payoff vector in the core nearest to the diagonal, i.e. to the equal share efficient payoff vector. This solution vector Lorenz dominates every other vector from the core: $\mathrm{CE}(\{i, j\}, v) \succ_{\mathrm{Lor}} x$ for all $x \in C(\{i, j\}, v) \setminus \{\mathrm{CE}(\{i, j\}, v)\}$. Recall the definition of Lorenz domination between vectors $x, y \in \mathbb{R}^n_+$ such that $\sum_{i=1}^n x_i = \sum_{i=1}^n y_i = I$. Denote by $\hat{x} = (\hat{x}_1, \ldots, \hat{x}_n)$ the vector obtained by rearranging its coordinates in a non-decreasing order, that is, $\hat{x}_1 \leq \hat{x}_2 \leq \ldots \leq \hat{x}_n$. Then x *Lorenz dominates* y, $x \succ_{\mathrm{Lor}} y$ whenever $\sum_{i=1}^p \hat{x}_i \geq \sum_{i=1}^p \hat{y}_i$ for all $p \in \{1, \ldots, n-1\}$, with at least one strict inequality.

The *Dutta-Ray solution* extends the CE solution to all convex TU games: it assigns to each convex game $\langle N, v \rangle \in G^c_N$ the vector $\mathrm{DR}(N, v) \in C(N, v)$ which Lorenz dominates every other vector from the core:

$$
\mathrm{DR}(N, v) \succ_{\mathrm{Lor}} x \text{ for all } x \in C(N, v) \setminus \{\mathrm{DR}(N, v)\}. \tag{6}
$$

Proposition 1 permits to define the interval Dutta–Ray solution for interval convex games as a mapping assigning to each convex interval game $\langle N, (\underline{w}, \overline{w}) \rangle$ the pair of vectors $(\mathrm{DR}(N, \underline{w}), \mathrm{DR}(N, \overline{w}))$. This definition can be done in the form of the Lorenz domination as for convex TU games. For this, first we should extend the Lorenz domination to sets of ordered pairs of vectors $(x, y) \in \mathbb{R}^N \times \mathbb{R}^N$ such that $x \leq y$.

Let $A = \{(x, y) \mid x \in \mathbb{R}^N, y \in \mathbb{R}^N, x \leq y\}$ be a set of pairs of vectors, and let $(x, y), (x', y') \in A$. We say that (x, y) *Lorenz dominates* (x', y') if the *Lorenz curve* $L(x, y)$ Pareto dominates the Lorenz curve $L(x', y')$. Note that in a weakly increasing ordering of the vector (x, y) defining the Lorenz curve $L(x, y)$, it may happen that $x_i > y_j$ for some components $i > j$.

Proposition 2 *For any convex interval game* $\langle N, w \rangle = \langle N, (\underline{w}, \overline{w}) \rangle \in IG_N^c$ *the interval Dutta–Ray solution* $(DR(N, \underline{w}), DR(N, \overline{w}))$ *belongs to the interval core* $\mathcal{C}(N, w)$ *and Lorenz dominates every other pair of vectors* $(x, y) \in \mathcal{C}(N, w)$.

Proof Since $DR(N, \underline{w}) \in C(N, \underline{w}), DR(N, \overline{w}) \in C(N, \overline{w})$ and $DR(N, \underline{w}) \leq DR(N, \overline{w})$, we have $(DR(N, \underline{w}), DR(N, \overline{w})) \in \mathcal{C}(N, w)$.

By the definition of the DR solution on the class G_N^c,

$$DR(N, \underline{w}) = x^* \succ_{\text{Lor}} x, \quad DR(N, \overline{w}) = y^* \succ_{\text{Lor}} y \text{ for all } x \in C(N, \underline{w}) \setminus \{x^*\},$$
$$y \in C(N, \overline{w}) \setminus \{y^*\}.$$

Then, by separability of the Lorenz domination,

$$(x^*, y) \succ_{\text{Lor}} (x, y) \text{ for any } y \in \mathbb{R}^N \text{ and all } x \in C(N, \underline{w}) \setminus \{x^*\},$$
$$(x, y^*) \succ_{\text{Lor}} (x, y) \text{ for any } x \in \mathbb{R}^N \text{ and all } y \in C(N, \overline{w}) \setminus \{y^*\}. \tag{7}$$

It is clear that relations (7) imply the demanded result.   □

The DR solution on the class G_N^c is covariant with respect to identical affine transformations of players' utilities. It means that for any game $\langle N, v \rangle \in G_N^c$, any positive number $\alpha \in \mathbb{R}_+$, and arbitrary vector $\boldsymbol{b} = (b, b \ldots, b) \in \mathbb{R}^N$ with equal components, it holds

$$DR(N, \alpha v + \boldsymbol{b}) = \alpha DR(N, v) + \boldsymbol{b}, \tag{8}$$

where for all $S \subset N, (\alpha v + \boldsymbol{b})(S) = \alpha v(S) + b \cdot |S|$.

It turns out that this property can be extended to the interval DR solution even in a stronger manner:

Proposition 3 *For any finite N the interval DR solution on the class IG_N^c is covariant with respect to identical affine transformations of players' utilities, which may be different for lower and upper games: for arbitrary $\langle N, (\underline{w}, \overline{w}) \rangle \in IG_N^c$, numbers $\alpha, \alpha' \in \mathbb{R}_+$ such that $\alpha \leq \alpha'$, and vectors $\boldsymbol{a} = (a, \ldots, a), \boldsymbol{b} = (b, \ldots, b) \in \mathbb{R}^N$ with equal components such that $a \leq b$, it holds*

$$DR(N, \alpha(\underline{w} + \boldsymbol{a}, \overline{w} + \boldsymbol{b}) = \Big(\alpha DR(N, \underline{w}) + \boldsymbol{a}, \alpha DR(N, \overline{w}) + \boldsymbol{b} \Big).$$

Moreover, if the upper game is positive, i.e. $\overline{w}(S) \geq 0$ for all $S \subset N$, then

$$DR(N, (\alpha \underline{w} + \boldsymbol{a}, \alpha' \overline{w} + \boldsymbol{b}) = \Big(\alpha DR(N, \underline{w}) + \boldsymbol{a}, \alpha' DR(N, \overline{w}) + \boldsymbol{b} \Big).$$

Proof First, notice that the pair $\langle N, \alpha \underline{w} + \boldsymbol{a} \rangle, \langle N, \alpha \overline{w} + \boldsymbol{b} \rangle$ defines the convex interval game $\langle N, (\alpha \underline{w} + \boldsymbol{a}, \alpha \overline{w} + \boldsymbol{b}) \rangle$.

Let now $\alpha' > \alpha > 0, \overline{w}(S) \geq 0$ for all $S \subset N$. Then both border games $\langle N, \alpha \underline{w} + \boldsymbol{a} \rangle, \langle N, \alpha' \overline{w} + \boldsymbol{b} \rangle$ are convex and $\alpha \underline{w}(S) + a \cdot |S| \leq \alpha' \cdot \overline{w}(S) + b \cdot |S|$ for all $S \subset N$. The length game $\langle N, \alpha' \overline{w} - \alpha \underline{w} + \boldsymbol{b} - \boldsymbol{a} \rangle$ is also convex because for each S,

$$\alpha'\overline{w}(S) - \alpha\underline{w}(S) + (b-a)|S| = (\alpha' - \alpha)\overline{w}(S) + \alpha(\overline{w}(S) - \underline{w}(S)) + (b-a)|S|,$$

and the sum of convex games is also convex.

Now equalities (8) establish the result. $\qquad\qquad\qquad\qquad\qquad\qquad\qquad\square$

Similar to the classical TU game theory, given an interval game $\langle N, (\underline{w}, \overline{w})\rangle$, $\alpha' \geq \alpha > 0$, $\boldsymbol{a} = (a, \dots, a)$, $\boldsymbol{b} = (b, \dots, b)$ with $a \leq b$, we call the game $\langle N, (\alpha\underline{w} + \boldsymbol{a}, \alpha\overline{w} + \boldsymbol{b})\rangle$ *strategically equivalent* to the game $\langle N, (\underline{w}, \overline{w})\rangle$.

If the upper game $\langle N, \overline{w}\rangle$ is positive, then $\langle N, (\alpha\underline{w} + \boldsymbol{a}, \alpha'\overline{w} + \boldsymbol{b})\rangle$ is called *strategically equivalent* to the game $\langle N, (\underline{w}, \overline{w})\rangle$.

Recall Dutta's algorithm (Dutta, 1990) for the calculation of the DR solution for convex TU games. Let for a convex TU game $\langle N, v\rangle$, $x = \mathrm{DR}(N, v)$, and let the players be ordered with respect to their decreasing solution payoffs:

$$x = (\underbrace{a_1, \dots, a_1}_{T_1}, \underbrace{a_2, \dots, a_2}_{T_2}, \dots \underbrace{a_k \dots, a_k}_{T_k}). \tag{9}$$

The numbers $a_1 > a_2 > \dots, > a_k$ are found subsequently:

$$
\begin{aligned}
a_1 &= \max_{S \subset N} \frac{v(S)}{|S|} = \frac{v(T_1)}{|T_1|}, \\
&\vdots \quad \vdots \\
a_j &= \max_{S \subset N \setminus \cup_{i=1}^{j-1} T_i} \frac{v^j(S)}{|S|} = \frac{v^j(T_j)}{|T_j|}, \; j = 2, \dots, k,
\end{aligned}
\tag{10}
$$

where

$$v^j(S) = v(\bigcup_{i=1}^{j-1} T_i \cup S) - v(\bigcup_{i=1}^{j-1} T_i) \text{ for all } S \subset N \setminus \bigcup_{i=1}^{j-1} T_i.$$

It is clear that for finding the interval DR solution we should apply the algorithm for the lower and upper games $\langle N, \underline{w}\rangle$, $\langle N, \overline{w}\rangle$ separately. Then, in the general case, the corresponding partitions of the player set N may be different for the lower and upper games. However, it is clear that if the lower and upper games are strategically equivalent, then the partitions of N in coalitions whose players have equal shares corresponding to the DR solutions $\mathrm{DR}(N, \underline{w})$, $\mathrm{DR}(N, \overline{w})$ are the same. The analogous result holds for the interval DR solution:

Proposition 4 *Let two convex interval games* $\langle N, (\underline{w}, \overline{w})\rangle$, $\langle N, (\underline{w}', \overline{w}')\rangle$ *be strategically equivalent, and let* $DR(N, (\underline{w}, \overline{w})) = (x, y)$ *where*

$$x = \mathrm{DR}(N, \underline{w}) = (\underbrace{x_1, \dots, x_1}_{T_1}, \underbrace{x_2, \dots, x_2}_{T_2}, \dots \underbrace{x_k \dots, x_k}_{T_k}),$$

$$y = \mathrm{DR}(N, \overline{w}) = (\underbrace{y_1, \dots, y_1}_{Q_1}, \underbrace{y_2, \dots, y_2}_{Q_2} \dots \underbrace{y_r \dots, y_r}_{Q_r}),$$

and $x_1 > \ldots > x_k$, $y_1 > \ldots > y_r$. *Then* $DR(N, (\underline{w}', \overline{w}')) = (x', y')$, *where*

$$x' = (\underbrace{x'_1, \ldots, x'_1}_{T_1}, \underbrace{x'_2, \ldots, x'_2}_{T_2}, \ldots \underbrace{x'_k \ldots, x'_k}_{T_k}),$$

$$y' = (\underbrace{y'_1, \ldots, y'_1}_{Q_1}, \underbrace{y'_2, \ldots, y'_2}_{Q_2} \ldots \underbrace{y'_r \ldots, y'_r}_{Q_r}),$$

and $x'_1 > \ldots > x'_k$, $y'_1 > \ldots > y'_r$. *Moreover,* $x' = \alpha x + b$, $y' = \alpha' y + b'$ *for some* $\alpha' \geq \alpha > 0$, $b = (b, \ldots, b)$, $b' = (b', \ldots, b')$, $b' \geq b$.

Proof From the definition of strategically equivalent interval games it follows that $\underline{w}' = \alpha \underline{w} + b$, $\overline{w}' = \alpha' \overline{w} + b'$, where $b' \geq b$, $\alpha' \geq \alpha > 0$, and $\alpha' > \alpha$ only if $\overline{w}(S), \overline{w}'(S) \geq 0$ for all $S \subset N$. Then formulas (9) and (10) give the result.   □

Monotonicity properties of the interval Dutta–Ray solution have been already discussed in the previous section. Now we are going to define and to show consistency properties of the interval Dutta–Ray solution.

5 Consistency of the Dutta–Ray Solution on the Class of Convex Interval Games and Its Axiomatic Characterization

Consistency properties of a solution connect the solution vectors of TU games with different sets of players. More exactly, a TU game solution σ is *consistent*, if, given a TU game $\langle N, v \rangle$ and a solution vector $x \in \sigma(N, v)$, for any coalition $S \subset N$ the vector $x_{N \setminus S}$ belongs to the solution $\sigma(N \setminus S, v^x)$ ($\sigma(N \setminus S, v^\sigma)$) of the *reduced game*, obtained from $\langle N, v \rangle$ after leaving the coalitions S. The characteristic function of the reduced game is defined in different ways depending on the methods of aggregating the values $v(T \cup Q)$ for $T \subset N \setminus S$, $Q \subset S$ and x_S or on the solution σ itself into a unique characteristic function value $v^x_{N \setminus S}(T)$ ($v^\sigma_{N \setminus S}$) of the reduced game.

Thus, to consider consistency properties of a solution, we should put into consideration the classes of games with different sets of players. Let $\mathcal{N}$ be an arbitrary *universal* set of players. Denote by $G_{\mathcal{N}} = \bigcup_{N \subset \mathcal{N}} G_N$, $IG_{\mathcal{N}} = \bigcup_{N \subset \mathcal{N}} IG_N$ the classes of all TU classical and interval games whose finite sets of players are contained in the universal set $\mathcal{N}$, and characteristic functions are defined by the classes $G_N, IG_N, N \subset \mathcal{N}$, respectively.

Dutta (1990) showed that the DR solution on the class of convex TU games $G^c_{\mathcal{N}}$ with an arbitrary set $\mathcal{N}$ is consistent in the definition of Davis–Maschler (max consistency) (Davis & Maschler, 1965) and of Hart–Mas-Colell (self consistency) (Hart & Mas-Colell, 1987). We extend the definitions of consistency of TU game solutions to the generated by them interval solutions by demanding consistency of the corresponding TU game solutions for both border games. Since the Dutta–Ray solution is single-valued both for TU classical and interval convex games, we give the definitions of interval consistency in the definitions of Davis–Maschler and of Hart–Mas-Colell only for single-valued solutions.

A single-valued solution ϕ on a class $IG_{\mathcal{N}}$ of interval games generated by a TU game solution φ on a class $G_{\mathcal{N}}^c$ is *DM-consistent* or satisfies the *reduced game property in the sense of Davis–Maschler* if for any game $\langle N, (\underline{w}, \overline{w}) \rangle \in IG_{\mathcal{N}}$ and a coalition $S \subset N$,

$$(\varphi(N, \underline{w}), \varphi(N, \overline{w}))_S = (\varphi(S, \underline{w}^x), \varphi(S, \overline{w}^y)), \tag{11}$$

where $x = \varphi(N, \underline{w})$, $y = \varphi(N, \overline{w})$, $\langle S, (\underline{w}^x, \overline{w}^y) \rangle \in IG_S$ and the characteristic functions of the upper and lower reduced games are defined as follows:

$$\underline{w}^x(T) = \begin{cases} \underline{w}(N) - x(N \setminus S), & \text{if } T = S, \\ \max\limits_{Q \subset N \setminus S} \left(\underline{w}(T \cup Q) - x(Q) \right) & \text{for other } T \subset S, \end{cases} \tag{12}$$

$$\overline{w}^y(T) = \begin{cases} \overline{w}(N) - y(N \setminus S), & \text{if } T = S, \\ \max\limits_{Q \subset N \setminus S} \left(\overline{w}(T \cup Q) - y(Q) \right) & \text{for other } T \subset S. \end{cases} \tag{13}$$

Moreover, the reduced interval games $\langle S, (\underline{w}^x, \overline{w}^y) \rangle$ should belong to the class $IG_{\mathcal{N}}^c$ for all $S \subset N$.

In definitions (12) and (13) the characteristic functions of the reduced on S interval game depend on the solution payoffs x_i of players $i \in N \setminus S$ leaving the game. Hart and Mas-Colell (1987) proposed another approach to the definition of reduced games, where they depend on the solutions of subgames of the initial game.

A solution ϕ on the class $IG_{\mathcal{N}}^c$ of interval games, generated by a TU game solution φ, is *HMC-consistent* or satisfies the *reduced game property in the sense of Hart–Mas-Colell* if for any game $\langle N, (\underline{w}, \overline{w}) \rangle \in IG_{\mathcal{N}}$, and every coalition $S \subset N$, it holds

$$(\varphi(N, \underline{w}), \varphi(N, \overline{w}))_S = (\varphi(S, \underline{w}^\varphi), \varphi(S, \overline{w}^\varphi)), \tag{14}$$

where the reduced games $\langle S, \underline{w}^\varphi \rangle$, $\langle S, \overline{w}^\varphi \rangle \in IG_{\mathcal{N}}^c$ are defined as follows:

$$\underline{w}^\varphi(T) = \begin{cases} \underline{w}(N) - \sum_{i \in N \setminus S} \varphi_i(N, \underline{w}), & \text{if } T = S, \\ \underline{w}(T \cup (N \setminus S)) - \sum_{j \in N \setminus S} \underline{\varphi}_j(T \cup (N \setminus S), \underline{w}), & \text{for } T \subsetneq S, \end{cases}$$

where $\langle T \cup (N \setminus S), \underline{w} \rangle$, are the subgames of the lower game $\langle N, \underline{w} \rangle$.

The reduced game of the upper game are defined analogously.

An interval solution φ is *bilateral DM-consistent* (*bilateral HMC-consistent*) if equality (11) ((14)) only holds for two-person coalitions S, i.e. $|S| = 2$.

Since the given above definitions of consistency are applied separately to lower and upper games, it may seem that the results about consistency of TU games solutions can be directly extended to interval games. However, convex interval games demand convexity not only of lower and upper games, but also convexity of the length game. Just this property can be violated by the classical reduced games that does not permit to extend consistency of the DR solution to the interval setting.

Proposition 5 *The Dutta–Ray solution over the class $IG^c_\mathcal{N}$ with $|\mathcal{N}| \geq 4$ does not satisfy bilateral DM-consistency.*

Proof We give an example of three-person convex interval game whose Davis–Maschler reduced interval games with respect to the DR solution do not belong to the class $IG^c_\mathcal{N}$.

Example 1 Let $N = \{1, 2, 3\}$. Consider the following interval game $\langle N, (\underline{w}, \overline{w}) \rangle$:

$$\overline{w}(S) = \begin{cases} 3, & \text{if } S = \{1, 2\}, \\ 5, & \text{if } S = \{1, 2, 3\}, \\ 0 & \text{for other } S, \end{cases}$$

$$\underline{w}(S) = \begin{cases} 3, & \text{if } S = \{1, 2\}, \\ 4, & \text{if } S = \{1, 2, 3\}, \\ 0 & \text{for other } S. \end{cases}$$

Then

$$(\overline{w} - \underline{w})(S) = \begin{cases} 1 & \text{for } S = \{1, 2, 3\}, \\ 0 & \text{for other } S, \end{cases},$$

$\overline{w}(S) \geq \underline{w}(S)$ for all $S \subset N$, and all games $\langle N, \underline{w} \rangle, \langle N, \overline{w} \rangle, \langle N, \overline{w} - \underline{w} \rangle$ are convex. We have

$$\mathrm{DR}(N, \underline{w}) = \left(\frac{3}{2}, \frac{3}{2}, 1 \right) = x, \quad \mathrm{DR}(N, \overline{w}) = \left(\frac{5}{3}, \frac{5}{3}, \frac{5}{3} \right) = y.$$

Consider the reduced games $\langle \{2, 3\}, \overline{w}^y \rangle, \langle \{2, 3\}, \underline{w}^x \rangle$ of the games $\langle N, \overline{w} \rangle, \langle N, \underline{w} \rangle$ on the player set $\{2, 3\}$ and with respect to the payoff vectors y and x, respectively. Then

$$\overline{w}^y(2) = \max\{0, 3 - \tfrac{5}{3}\} = \tfrac{4}{3},$$
$$\underline{w}^x(2) = \max\{0, 3 - \tfrac{3}{2}\} = \tfrac{3}{2},$$

and we obtain $\overline{w}^y(\{2\}) < \underline{w}^x(\{2\})$ that means the reduced interval game $\langle \{2, 3\}, (\overline{w}^y, \underline{w}^x) \rangle \notin IG^c_\mathcal{N}$. $\qquad\square$

Let us consider HMC-consistency of the interval DR solution. To begin with we should return to the DR solution on the class of convex TU games $G^c_\mathcal{N}$. Dutta (1990) showed that the DR solution on the class of convex TU games $G^c_\mathcal{N}$ is both DM-consistent and HMC-consistent. However, he did proved that the Hart–Mas-Colell reduced games of a convex TU game with respect to the DR solution are convex only for two-person reduced games. The follows example shows this fact.

Example 2 $N = \{1, 2, 3, 4\}$, $v(\{i\}) = 0$ for all $i \in N$, $v(N) = 6 + 3\varepsilon$,
$v(\{1, 2\}) = 4$, $v(\{1, 3\}) = 1/2$, $v(\{i, j\}) = 1$ for other $(i, j) \neq (1, 3)$,
$v(\{1, 2, 3\}) = 5 + 2\varepsilon$, $v(\{1, 2, 4\}) = 5 + \varepsilon$, $v(\{1, 3, 4\}) = v(\{2, 3, 4\}) = 2$.

Then for sufficiently small positive ε this game $\langle N, v \rangle$ is convex, and $\text{DR}(N, v) = (2, 2, 1 + 2\varepsilon, 1 + \varepsilon)$.

Consider the Hart–Mas-Colell reduced game $\langle N \setminus \{1\}, v^{\text{DR}} \rangle$ on the set $\{2, 3, 4\}$ with respect to the DR solution. Then
$v^{\text{DR}}(\{2\}) = 2$, $v^{\text{DR}}(\{3\}) = 1/4$, $v^{\text{DR}}(\{4\}) = 1/2$,
$v^{\text{DR}}(\{2, 3\}) = 3 + 2\varepsilon$, $v^{\text{DR}}(\{2, 4\}) = 3 + \varepsilon$, $v^{\text{DR}}(\{3, 4\}) = 4/3$, $v^{\text{DR}}(\{2, 3, 4\}) =$
$\qquad 4 + 3\varepsilon$,
and for $\varepsilon < 1/12$, it holds

$$v^{\text{DR}}(\{2, 3\}) + v^{\text{DR}}(v\{3, 4\}) = 4\frac{1}{3} + 2\varepsilon > 4\frac{1}{4} + 3\varepsilon = v^{\text{DR}}(\{2, 3, 4\}) + v^{\text{DR}}(\{3\}),$$

implying that the reduced game $\langle \{2, 3, 4\}, v^{\text{DE}} \rangle$ is not convex.

$\square$

However, it is possible to establish bilateral HMC-consistency of the interval DR solution:

Proposition 6 *The interval DR solution is bilateral HMC-consistent on the class $IG_{\mathcal{N}}$ for all $\mathcal{N}$, $|\mathcal{N}| \geq 3$.*

Proof Let $\langle N, (\underline{w}, \overline{w}) \rangle \in IG_{\mathcal{N}}^c$ be an arbitrary game, $y = \text{DR}(N, \overline{w})$, $x = \text{DR}(N, \underline{w})$, $i, j \in N$. Consider the reduced game $\langle \{i, j\}, (\underline{w}^{\text{DR}}, \overline{w}^{\text{DR}}) \rangle$ on the set $\{i, j\}$ with respect to the interval DR solution. Then by the definition of HMC-consistency and population monotonicity of the classical DR solution:

$$\begin{aligned}
\overline{w}^{\text{DR}}(\{i\}) &= \text{DR}_i(N \setminus \{j\}, \overline{w}) \leq y_i, \\
\overline{w}^{\text{DR}}(\{j\}) &= \text{DR}_j(N \setminus \{i\}, \overline{w}) \leq y_j, \\
\overline{w}^{\text{DR}}(\{i, j\}) &= y_i + y_j.
\end{aligned} \tag{15}$$

From (15) it follows that the reduced game is superadditive and, hence, convex. Similarly, it is proved that the reduced game $\langle \{i, j\}, \underline{w}^{\text{DR}} \rangle$ and the length game $\langle \{i, j\}, (\overline{w}^{\text{DR}} - \underline{w}^{\text{DR}}) \rangle$ are both superadditive.

Let us show that $\underline{w}^{\text{DR}} \leq \overline{w}^{\text{DR}}$. By Proposition 1 providing the existence of the interval DR solution, we have

$$\underline{w}^{\text{DR}}(\{i\}) = \text{DR}_i(N \setminus \{j\}, \underline{w}) \leq \text{DR}_i(N \setminus \{j\}, \overline{w}) = \overline{w}^{\text{DR}}(\{i\}).$$

The same equalities and inequality hold when we interchange i with j. At last,

$$\underline{w}^{\text{DR}}(\{i, j\}) = x_i + x_j \leq y_i + y_j = \overline{w}^{\text{DR}}(\{i, j\}).$$

Thus, the reduced game on the two-player set $\{i, j\}$ belongs to the class $IG_{\mathcal{N}}^c$. Bilateral HMC-consistency of the classical DR solution on the class of convex TU games implies the equalities $(x_i, x_j) = \mathrm{DR}(\{i, j\}, \underline{w}^{\mathrm{DR}})$, $(y_i, y_j) = \mathrm{DR}(\{i, j\}, \overline{w}^{\mathrm{DR}})$ proving the proposition. □

It turns out that bilateral HMC-consistency of the interval DR solution together with its coincidence with the CE solution on two-person convex interval games are sufficient for the characterization of the interval DR solution on the class IG^c_N. To establish this result, first, let us prove an auxiliary one.

Lemma 1 *If a single-valued solution φ on the class G^c_N of convex TU games is bilateral HMC-consistent and coincides with the solution of constrained egalitarianism on the class of two-person superadditive games, then it is efficient and belongs to the core.*

Proof First, let us show efficiency of φ. Let $\langle N, v \rangle \in \mathcal{G}^c_N$ be an arbitrary game and let $y = \varphi(N, v)$. By efficiency of the solution of constrained egalitarianism, bilateral consistency of φ, and the definition of the Hart–Mas-Colell reduced games for any $i, j \in N$, we have

$$y_i + y_j = v^\varphi(\{i, j\}) = v(N) - \sum_{k \in N \setminus \{i,j\}} \varphi_k(N, v) = v(N) - \sum_{k \neq i,j} y_k, \qquad (16)$$

where $\langle \{i, j\}, v^\varphi \rangle$ is the Hart–Mas-Colell reduced game on the player set $\{i, j\}$ with respect to the solution φ. From (16) it follows $\sum_{i \in N} y_i = v(N)$.

The next claim is to prove that $y \in C(N, \overline{w})$. We will prove the claim by induction on the number of players.

For two-person games we have $CE = \varphi$ and, hence, $\varphi(\{i, j\}, v) \in C(\{i, j\}, v)$. Assume that the claim is valid for all convex TU games whose number of players is less than $|N|$.

By bilateral HMC-consistency of φ, for every $i, j \in N$,

$$y_i \geq v^\varphi_{\{i,j\}}(\{i\}) = \varphi_i(N \setminus \{j\}, v). \qquad (17)$$

By the inductive hypothesis equality (17) implies $y(S) \geq v(S)$ for all S, $|S| \leq n-1$. For $S = N$ efficiency of φ gives $y(N) = v(N)$ and we obtain $y \in C(N, v)$. □

Now we are ready to obtain an axiomatic characterization of the interval DR solution on the class of convex interval games.

Theorem 1 *For any universal set $\mathcal{N}$ the Dutta–Ray solution is the unique solution on the class IG^c_N satisfying constrained egalitarianism for two-person games and bilateral HMC-consistency.*

Proof In view of Proposition 3 only the uniqueness should be proved. Let φ be an arbitrary solution on the class IG^c_N satisfying the properties given in the Theorem, and for an arbitrary interval game $\langle N, (\underline{w}, \overline{w}) \rangle \in IG^c_N$ let $y = \varphi(N, \overline{w})$, $x = \varphi(N, \underline{w})$.

Let us prove the equalities $y = \mathrm{DR}(N, \overline{w})$, $x = \mathrm{DR}(N, \underline{w})$. It suffices to prove only one equality, the second one is proved analogously. Note that by Lemma 1, $y \in C(N, \overline{w})$.

Consider the following cases:

1^0. $y_i = y_j = \frac{\overline{w}(N)}{|N|}$ for all $i, j \in N$. Since $y \in C(N, \overline{w})$, this vector Lorenz dominates every other vector from the core, that yields $y = \mathrm{DR}(N, \overline{w})$.

2^0. There are $i, j \in N$ such that $y_i > y_j$. Represent y in the form

$$y = (\underbrace{y_1, \ldots, y_1}_{Q_1}, \underbrace{y_2, \ldots, y_2}_{Q_2}, \ldots \underbrace{y_l \ldots, y_l}_{Q_l}), \quad \text{where } y_1 > y_2 > \ldots > y_l,$$

and

$$\mathrm{DR}(N, \overline{w}) = z = (\underbrace{z_1, \ldots, z_1}_{T_1}, \underbrace{z_2, \ldots, z_2}_{T_2}, \ldots \underbrace{z_m \ldots, z_m}_{T_m}), \quad \text{where } z_1 > z_2 \ldots > z_m.$$

Then by bilateral HMC-consistency of $\overline{\varphi}$ and the definition of constrained egalitarianism, for each $i \in N \setminus Q_l$ and $j \in Q_l$,

$$y_i = \overline{w}^\varphi_{\{i, j\}}(\{i\}) = \overline{\varphi}_i(N \setminus \{j\}, \overline{w}), \tag{18}$$

where $\langle \{i, j\}, \overline{w}^\varphi_{\{i,j\}} \rangle$ is the Hart–Mas-Colell reduced game on the player set $\{i, j\}$.

By the inductive hypothesis equality (18) implies

$$y_i = \mathrm{DR}_i(N \setminus \{j\}, \overline{w}) \text{ for each } i \in N \setminus Q_l, j \in Q_l. \tag{19}$$

Let us show that $T_1 \cap Q_l = \emptyset$. In fact, equality (19) and the population monotonicity of the DR solution imply $y_i \leq z_1$ for all $i \in N \setminus Q_1$, and $y_j < y_i$ for such i and $j \in Q_l$. Therefore, if $T_1 \cap Q_l \neq \emptyset$, then $y(T_1) = \sum_{i \in T_1} y_i < z_1 |T_1| = \overline{w}(T_1)$, that would contradict the membership of $y = \varphi(N, \overline{w})$ to the core.

Thus, we have obtained the equalities

$$y_i = \overline{\varphi}_i(N \setminus \{j\}, \overline{w}) = \mathrm{DR}_i(N \setminus \{j\}, \overline{w}) = \mathrm{DR}_i(N, \overline{w}) = z_1 \text{for all } i \in T_1, j \in Q_l.$$

Consider the following possibilities:

2^0a. $T_1 \cup Q_l = N$. If $m = 2$, then $y = z$, and the proof is complete.

If $m > 2$, then $Q_l = T_2 \cup \ldots \cup T_m$, and for $i \in T_k$, $j \in T_l$, $k < l$, $k, l = 2, \ldots, m$, we have $\mathrm{DR}_i(N, \overline{w}) = z_k > z_l = \mathrm{DR}_j(N, \overline{w})$. Let $k \in \{2, \ldots, m\}$ be a number such that

$$z_r > y_l \text{ for } r < k$$
$$z_r \leq y_l \text{ for } r \geq k.$$

Such a k does exist because $y(Q_l) = z(Q_l)$ and $y_j = y_l$ for all $j \in Q_l$. Denote $Z_k = \bigcup_{t=1}^k T_t$. Then by the definition of the interval DR solution and by the equalities $y_j = z_j$ for $j \in T_1$,

$$\overline{w}(R_k) = z(R_k) = z_1 |T_1| + \sum_{t=2}^k z_t |T_t| > y(T_1) + y_l \sum_{t=2}^k |T_t|,$$

that again would contradict the membership of y to the core $C(N, \overline{w})$, Thus, the case $T_1 \cap Q_l = \emptyset, m > 2$ is impossible and we return to the case $m = 2$.

2^0b. $T_1 \cup Q_l \subsetneq N$. Repeat the procedure for the set T_2. First, let us show that $T_2 \cap Q_l = \emptyset$. As in the proof of the previous case, equality (19) and population monotonicity of the interval DR solution imply $y_i \leq z_1$ for all $i \in N \setminus Q_1$, and $y_j < y_i$ for such i and $j \in Q_l$. Therefore, if $T_2 \cap Q_l \neq \emptyset$, then $y(T_2) = \sum_{i \in T_2} y_i < z_2|T_2|$, and this inequality together with the proven equality $y(T_1) = z(T_1)$ yield

$$y(T_1 \cup T_2) < z(T_1 \cup T_2) = \sum_{i \in T_1 \cup T_2} \mathrm{DR}_i(N, \overline{w}) = \overline{w}(T_1 \cup T_2),$$

that would contradict the membership of y to the core $C(N, \overline{w})$.

Hence, $T_2 \cap Q_l = \emptyset$, implying that for any $i \in T_2, j \in Q_l$,

$$y_i = \overline{\varphi}(N \setminus \{j\}, \overline{w}) = \mathrm{DR}_i(N \setminus \{j\}, \overline{w}) = \mathrm{DR}_i(N, \overline{w}) = z_2,$$

and we obtain the equality $z_{T_2} = y_{T_2}$. If $m = 3$, then the process finished and $z = y$. If $m > 3$, then we again repeat the procedure, and in the $(m - 1)$-th step we obtain $y = z$, that completes the proof.   □

6 Concluding Remarks and Perspectives

Our main contribution in this paper regards the constrained egalitarian solution for convex interval games, which we refer to as the Dutta–Ray solution. We have introduced this solution, studied its basic properties, and provided an axiomatic characterization which is a special generalization of the characterization of the constrained egalitarian solution for classical convex games by Dutta (1990), using the constrained egalitarianism for two-person games and consistency in the sense of Hart and Mas-Colell (1987). A central role for our findings has been played by special monotonicity properties of the constrained egalitarian solution for classical convex games. Alternative axiomatic characterizations of the interval Dutta–Ray solution for convex interval games may be obtained by extending to the interval setting the characterizations of the constrained egalitarian solution for classical convex games by Klijn, Slikker, and Zarzuelo (2000).

Acknowledgments Stef Tijs and Elena Yanovskaya acknowledge the financial support from the Dutch Science Foundation and the Russian Foundation for Basic Research (the joint project NWO 047-017-017/ RFBR 05-01-89005). Financial support from the Government of Spain and FEDER under project MTM2008-0678-C02-01 is gratefully acknowledged by the second and the third authors.

References

Alparslan Gök, S. Z., Branzei, R., & Tijs, S. (2008). Cores and stable sets for interval-valued games. Preprint no. 113, Institute of Applied Mathematics, METU and Tilburg University, Center for Economic Research. The Netherlands, CentER, DP 63, Tilburg.

Alparslan Gök, S. Z., Branzei, R., & Tijs, S. (2009). Convex interval games. *Journal of Applied Mathematics and Decision Sciences, 2009*, 14pp, Article ID 342089, DOI: 0.1115/2009/342089.

Alparslan Gök, S. Z., Miquel, S., & Tijs, S. (2009). Cooperation under interval uncertainty. *Mathematical Methods of Operations Research, 69*(1), 99–109.

Branzei, R., Tijs, S., & Alparslan Gök, S. Z. (2008). How to handle interval solutions for cooperative interval games. Preprint no.110, Institute of Applied Mathematics, METU.

Charnes, A., & Granot, D. (2007). *Prior solutions: Extensions of convex nucleolus solutions to chance-constrained games* (pp. 323–332). Proceedings of the Computer Science and Statistics 7th Symposium at Iowa State University.

Davis, M., & Maschler, M. (1965). The kernel of a cooperative game. *Naval Research Logistic Quarterly, 12*, 223–259.

Dutta, B. (1990). The egalitarian solution and the reduced game properties in convex games. *International Journal of Game Theory, 19*, 153–159.

Dutta, B., & Ray, D. (1989). A concept of egalitarianism under participation constraints. *Econometrica, 57*, 615–630.

Hart, S., & Mas-Colell, A. (1987). Potential, value, and consistency. *Econometrica, 57*, 589–614.

Hokari, T. (2000). The nucleolus is not aggregate monotonic on the domain of convex games. *International Journal of Game Theory, 29*, 133–137.

Hokari, T., & van Gellekom, A. (2002). Population monotonicity and consistency in convex games: Some logical relations. *International Journal of Game Theory, 31*, 593–607.

Klijn, F., Slikker, M., & Zarzuelo, J. (2000). The egalitarian solution for convex games: Some characterizations. *Mathematical Social Sciences, 40*, 111–121.

Sprumont, Y. (1990). Population monotonic allocation schemes for cooperative games with transferable utility. *Games and Economic Behavior, 2*, 378–394.

Suijs, J., Borm, P., de Waegenaere, A., & Tijs, S. (1999). Cooperative games with stochastic payoffs. *European Journal of Operational Research, 133*, 193–205.

Timmer, J., Borm, P., & Tijs, S. (2005). Convexity in stochastic cooperative situations. *International Game Theory Review, 7*, 25–42.

Breinigsville, PA USA
21 October 2010
247767BV00007B/168/P